T0364934

Hyundai i10
Owners Workshop Manual

Euan Doig

(6414 - 224)

Models covered

Hatchback with 1.2 litre (1248cc) petrol engine

Does NOT cover 1.0 or 1.1 litre petrol engines, 1.1 litre diesel engine or LPG models, 'Grand i10' or 'Electric'
Does NOT cover new Hyundai i10 range introduced January 2014

ABCDE
FGHIJ
KLMNO
PQRST

ISBN **978 1 78521 414 1**

British Library Cataloguing in Publication Data
A catalogue record for this book is available from the British Library.

Printed in Malaysia

Haynes Publishing
Sparkford, Yeovil, Somerset BA22 7JJ, England

Haynes North America, Inc
859 Lawrence Drive, Newbury Park, California 91320, USA

Printed using NORBRITE BOOK 48.8gsm (CODE: 40N6533) from NORPAC; procurement system certified under Sustainable Forestry Initiative standard. Paper produced is certified to the SFI Certified Fiber Sourcing Standard (CERT - 0094271)

Contents

LIVING WITH YOUR HYUNDAI i10

Roadside repairs

Weekly checks

Lubricants and fluids

Tyre pressures

MAINTENANCE

Routine maintenance and servicing

Contents

The Hyundai i10 range covered by this manual was introduced in January 2008, in 5-door hatchback form, with a choice of petrol engines. The engine covered is the popular 1.2-litre (16-valve) unit, with multi-point fuel injection, and the latest emission control systems, which was introduced in July 2008. The engine is of a well-proven design and has been used extensively in a range of Hyundai vehicles.

Fully independent front suspension is fitted, with semi-independent torsion beam suspension used at the rear. Electrically operated power steering is standard equipment on all models. A five-speed manual transmission is fitted.

In September 2010, the facelifted i10 was introduced, with new lights, bumpers, and a revised interior. This continued until the model was replaced in January 2014.

The i10 is very well equipped for a small car. Standard and optional equipment includes multi-airbags, trip computer, electric front and rear windows, ABS, central locking, air conditioning, DAB radio and heated front seats.

For the home mechanic, the i10 is a straightforwards car to maintain, and most of the items requiring frequent attention are easily accessible.

Your Hyundai i10 manual

The aim of this manual is to help you get the best value from your vehicle. It can do so in several ways. It can help you decide what work must be done (even should you choose to get it done by a garage). It will also provide information on routine maintenance and servicing, and give a logical course of action and diagnosis when random faults occur. However, it is hoped that you will use the manual by tackling the work yourself. On simpler jobs it may even be quicker than booking the car into a garage and going there twice, to leave and collect it. Perhaps most important, a lot of money can be saved by avoiding the costs a garage must charge to cover its labour and overheads.

The manual has drawings and descriptions to show the function of the various components so that their layout can be understood. Tasks are described and photographed in a clear step-by-step sequence. The illustrations are numbered by the Section number and paragraph number to which they relate – if there is more than one illustration per paragraph, the sequence is denoted alphabetically.

References to the "left" or "right" of the vehicle are in the sense of a person in the driver's seat, facing forwards.

Acknowledgements

Thanks are due to Draper Tools, who provided some of the workshop tools, and to all those people at Sparkford who helped in the production of this manual.

This manual is not a direct reproduction of the vehicle manufacturer's data, and its publication should not be taken as implying any technical approval by the vehicle manufacturers or importers.

We take great pride in the accuracy of information given in this manual, but vehicle manufacturers make alterations and design changes during the production run of a particular vehicle of which they do not inform us. No liability can be accepted by the authors or publishers for loss, damage or injury caused by any errors in, or omissions from, the information given.

Project vehicles

The main vehicle used in the preparation of this manual, and which appears in many of the photographic sequences, was a 1.2 L DOHC 16-valve petrol engine with manual transmission.

Hyundai i10

Working on your car can be dangerous. This page shows just some of the potential risks and hazards, with the aim of creating a safety-conscious attitude.

General hazards

Scalding

• Don't remove the radiator or expansion tank cap while the engine is hot.
• Engine oil, transmission fluid or power steering fluid may also be dangerously hot if the engine has recently been running.

Burning

• Beware of burns from the exhaust system and from any part of the engine. Brake discs and drums can also be extremely hot immediately after use.

Crushing

• When working under or near a raised vehicle, always supplement the jack with axle stands, or use drive-on ramps. *Never venture under a car which is only supported by a jack*.

• Take care if loosening or tightening high-torque nuts when the vehicle is on stands. Initial loosening and final tightening should be done with the wheels on the ground.

Fire

• Fuel is highly flammable; fuel vapour is explosive.
• Don't let fuel spill onto a hot engine.
• Do not smoke or allow naked lights (including pilot lights) anywhere near a vehicle being worked on. Also beware of creating sparks (electrically or by use of tools).
• Fuel vapour is heavier than air, so don't work on the fuel system with the vehicle over an inspection pit.
• Another cause of fire is an electrical overload or short-circuit. Take care when repairing or modifying the vehicle wiring.
• Keep a fire extinguisher handy, of a type suitable for use on fuel and electrical fires.

Electric shock

• Ignition HT and Xenon headlight voltages can be dangerous, especially to people with heart problems or a pacemaker. Don't work on or near these systems with the engine running or the ignition switched on.

• Mains voltage is also dangerous. Make sure that any mains-operated equipment is correctly earthed. Mains power points should be protected by a residual current device (RCD) circuit breaker.

Fume or gas intoxication

• Exhaust fumes are poisonous; they can contain carbon monoxide, which is rapidly fatal if inhaled. Never run the engine in a confined space such as a garage with the doors shut.
• Fuel vapour is also poisonous, as are the vapours from some cleaning solvents and paint thinners.

Poisonous or irritant substances

• Avoid skin contact with battery acid and with any fuel, fluid or lubricant, especially antifreeze, brake hydraulic fluid and Diesel fuel. Don't syphon them by mouth. If such a substance is swallowed or gets into the eyes, seek medical advice.
• Prolonged contact with used engine oil can cause skin cancer. Wear gloves or use a barrier cream if necessary. Change out of oil-soaked clothes and do not keep oily rags in your pocket.
• Air conditioning refrigerant forms a poisonous gas if exposed to a naked flame (including a cigarette). It can also cause skin burns on contact.

Asbestos

• Asbestos dust can cause cancer if inhaled or swallowed. Asbestos may be found in gaskets and in brake and clutch linings. When dealing with such components it is safest to assume that they contain asbestos.

Special hazards

Hydrofluoric acid

• This extremely corrosive acid is formed when certain types of synthetic rubber, found in some O-rings, oil seals, fuel hoses etc, are exposed to temperatures above 4000C. The rubber changes into a charred or sticky substance containing the acid. *Once formed, the acid remains dangerous for years. If it gets onto the skin, it may be necessary to amputate the limb concerned.*
• When dealing with a vehicle which has suffered a fire, or with components salvaged from such a vehicle, wear protective gloves and discard them after use.

The battery

• Batteries contain sulphuric acid, which attacks clothing, eyes and skin. Take care when topping-up or carrying the battery.
• The hydrogen gas given off by the battery is highly explosive. Never cause a spark or allow a naked light nearby. Be careful when connecting and disconnecting battery chargers or jump leads.

Air bags

• Air bags can cause injury if they go off accidentally. Take care when removing the steering wheel and trim panels. Special storage instructions may apply.

Diesel injection equipment

• Diesel injection pumps supply fuel at very high pressure. Take care when working on the fuel injectors and fuel pipes.

⚠ *Warning: Never expose the hands, face or any other part of the body to injector spray; the fuel can penetrate the skin with potentially fatal results.*

Remember...

DO

• Do use eye protection when using power tools, and when working under the vehicle.

• Do wear gloves or use barrier cream to protect your hands when necessary.

• Do get someone to check periodically that all is well when working alone on the vehicle.

• Do keep loose clothing and long hair well out of the way of moving mechanical parts.

• Do remove rings, wristwatch etc, before working on the vehicle – especially the electrical system.

• Do ensure that any lifting or jacking equipment has a safe working load rating adequate for the job.

DON'T

• Don't attempt to lift a heavy component which may be beyond your capability – get assistance.

• Don't rush to finish a job, or take unverified short cuts.

• Don't use ill-fitting tools which may slip and cause injury.

• Don't leave tools or parts lying around where someone can trip over them. Mop up oil and fuel spills at once.

• Don't allow children or pets to play in or near a vehicle being worked on.

The following pages are intended to help in dealing with common roadside emergencies and breakdowns. You will find more detailed fault finding information at the back of the manual, and repair information in the main chapters.

If your car won't start and the starter motor doesn't turn

- ☐ If it's a model with automatic transmission, make sure the selector is in 'P' or 'N'.
- ☐ Open the bonnet, and make sure the battery terminals are clean and tight.
- ☐ Switch on the headlights and try to start the engine. If the headlights go very dim when you're trying to start, the battery is probably flat. Get out of trouble by jump starting using a friend's car.

If your car won't start even though the starter motor turns as normal

- ☐ Is there fuel in the tank?
- ☐ Is there moisture on electrical connections under the bonnet? Switch off the ignition, then wipe off any obvious dampness with a dry cloth. Spray a water-dispersant aerosol product (WD-40 or equivalent) on ignition and fuel system electrical connectors like those shown in the photos.

A Check the condition and security of the battery connections

B Check the security of the fuel injection system components wiring plugs

C Check the ignition coil HT connections

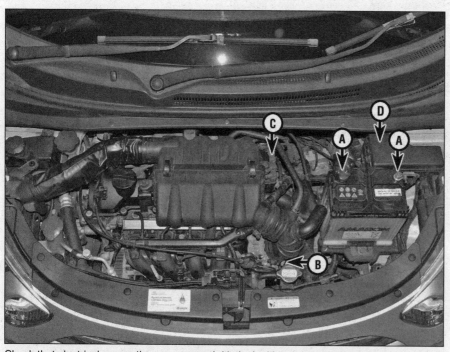

D Check the engine compartment fuses

Check that electrical connections are secure (with the ignition switched off) and spray them with a water-dispersant spray such as WD-40 if you suspect a problem due to damp

Jump starting

 Jump starting will get you out of trouble, but you must correct whatever made the battery go flat in the first place. There are three possibilities:

1 *The battery has been drained by repeated attempts to start, or by leaving the lights on.*

2 *The charging system is not working properly (alternator drivebelt slack or broken, alternator wiring fault or alternator itself faulty).*

3 *The battery itself is at fault (electrolyte low, or battery worn out).*

When jump-starting a car using a booster battery, observe the following precautions:

Caution: Remove the key in case the central locking engages when the jump leads are connected.

✓ Before connecting the booster battery, make sure that the ignition is switched off.
✓ Ensure that all electrical equipment (lights, heater, wipers, etc) is switched off.
✓ Take note of any special precautions printed on the battery case.
✓ Make sure that the booster battery is the same voltage as the discharged one in the vehicle.

✓ If the battery is being jump-started from the battery in another vehicle, the two vehicles MUST NOT TOUCH each other.
✓ Make sure that the transmission is in neutral (or PARK, in the case of automatic transmission)

 Budget jump leads can be a false economy, as they often do not pass enough current to start large capacity or diesel engines. They can also get hot.

1 Connect one end of the red jump lead to the positive (+) terminal of the flat battery

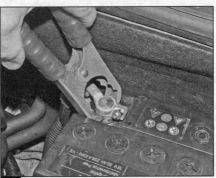

2 Connect the other end of the red lead to the positive (+) terminal of the booster battery.

3 Connect one end of the black jump lead to the negative (-) terminal of the booster battery

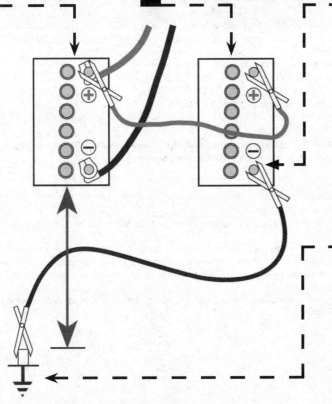

4 Connect the other end of the black jump lead to the negative (-) terminal of the flat battery

5 Make sure that the jump leads will not come into contact with the fan, drive-belts or other moving parts of the engine.

6 Start the engine using the booster battery and run it at idle speed. Switch on the lights, rear window demister and heater blower motor, then disconnect the jump leads in the reverse order of connection. Turn off the lights etc.

Wheel changing

Warning: Do not change a wheel in a situation where you risk being hit by another vehicle. On busy roads, try to stop in a lay-by or a gateway. Be wary of passing traffic while changing the wheel – it is easy to become distracted by the job in hand.

Preparation

☐ When a puncture occurs, stop as soon as it is safe to do so.

☐ Park on firm level ground, if possible, and well out of the way of other traffic. If jacking on a slope is unavoidable, chock the wheel diagonally opposite the one to be removed on the downhill side, using the chock provided in the toolkit.

☐ Use hazard warning lights if necessary.

☐ If the ground is soft, use a flat piece of wood to spread the load under the jack.

1 The tool kit and spare wheel are located under the luggage compartment floor panel. Lift the panel, unscrew the plastic nut, then lift out the toolkit holder and spare wheel.

2 Where locking wheel bolts are fitted, use the adaptor supplied with the vehicle.

3 Using the wheel brace supplied, slacken the wheel bolts.

4 Position the jack head beneath the jacking point (indicated by a notch each side) under the sill closest to the punctured wheel. Engage the jack head with the sill flange, then smoothly raise the vehicle undo the tyre is clear of the road surface.

5 Unscrew the wheel bolts, and remove the wheel.

6 Fit the spare wheel, and screw-in the bolts. Lightly tighten the bolts with the wheelbrace, then lower the vehicle to the ground. Securely tighten the wheel bolts. Note that the wheel bolts should be slackened and retightened to the specified torque at the earliest possible opportunity.

Caution: If a temporary 'space-saver' spare wheel is fitted, do not exceed 50 mph (80 kmh), and take particular care when cornering.

Finally

☐ Remove the wheel chocks.

☐ Stow the punctured wheel and tools back in the luggage compartment, and secure them in position.

☐ Check the tyre pressure on the tyre just fitted. If it is low, or if you don't have a pressure gauge with you, drive slowly to the next garage and inflate the tyre to the correct pressure. In the case of the narrow 'space-saver' spare wheel this pressure is much higher than for a normal tyre.

☐ Have the punctured wheel repaired as soon as possible, or another puncture will leave you stranded.

Identifying leaks

The smell of a fluid leaking from the car may provide a clue to what's leaking. Some fluids are distinctly coloured. It may help to clean the car carefully and to park it over some clean paper overnight as an aid to locating the source of the leak. Remember that some leaks may only occur while the engine is running.

Puddles on the garage floor or drive, or obvious wetness under the bonnet or underneath the car, suggest a leak that needs investigating. I can sometimes be difficult to decide where the leak is coming from, especially if the engine bay is very dirty already. Leaking oil of fluid can also be blown rearwards by the passage of air under the car, giving a false impression of where the problem lies.

⚠ **Warning: Most automotive oils and fluids are poisonous, Wash them off skin, and change out of contaminated clothing without delay.**

Sump oil
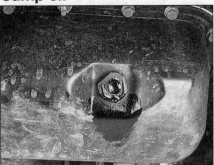
Engine oil may leak from the drain plug...

Oil from filter
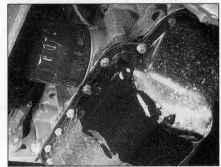
...or from the base of the oil filter.

Antifreeze

Leaking antifreeze often leaves a crystalline deposit like this.

Brake fluid

A leak occurring at a wheel is almost certainly brake fluid.

Gearbox oil

Gearbox oil can leak from the seals at the inboard end of the driveshafts

Towing

Remove the cap from the front bumper

☐ When all else fails, you may find yourself having to get a tow home – or of course you may be helping somebody else. Long-distance recovery should only be done by a garage or breakdown service. For shorter distances, DIY towing using another car is easy enough, but observe the following points:
☐ Use a proper tow-rope – they are not expensive. The vehicle being towed must display an ON TOW sign in its rear window.
☐ Always turn the ignition to the 'on' position when the vehicle is being towed, so that the steering lock is released, and that the direction indicator and brake lights will work.
☐ The front towing eye socket is located in the front bumper. Press in the top of the cap in the front bumper, at the same time pulling out the bottom edge of the cap. Retrieve the towing hook from the tool kit beneath the boot floor and screw it clockwise into the socket in the front bumper.
☐ The rear towing eye hook is located beneath the rear bumper.
☐ Before being towed, release the handbrake and make sure the transmission is in neutral.
☐ Note that greater-than-usual pedal pressure will be required to operate the brakes, since the vacuum servo unit is only operational with the engine running, and no power assistance will be available for the steering.
☐ The driver of the car being towed must keep the tow-rope taut at all times to avoid snatching.
☐ Only drive at moderate speeds, and keep the distance towed to a minimum. Drive smoothly, and allow plenty of time for slowing down at junctions.

Introduction

There are some very simple checks which need only take a few minutes to carry out, but which could save you a lot of inconvenience and expense.

☐ These *Weekly checks* require no great skill or special tools, and the small amount of time they take to perform could prove to be very well spent, for example:

☐ Keeping an eye on tyre condition and pressures, will not only help to stop them wearing out prematurely, but could also save your life.

☐ Many breakdowns are caused by electrical problems. Battery-related faults are particularly common, and a quick check on a regular basis will often prevent the majority of these.

☐ If your car develops a brake fluid leak, the first time you might know about it is when your brakes don't work properly. Checking the level regularly will give advance warning of this kind of problem.

☐ If the oil or coolant levels run low, the cost of repairing any engine damage will be far greater than fixing the leak, for example.

Underbonnet check points

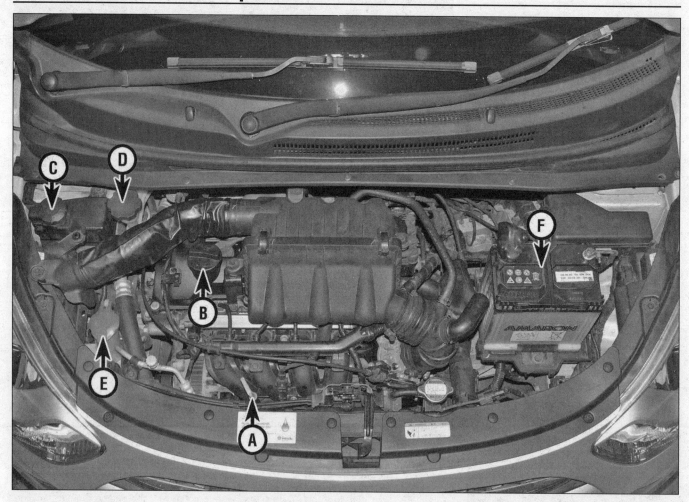

A *Engine oil level dipstick*
B *Engine oil filler cap*
C *Coolant expansion tank*
D *Brake fluid reservoir*
E *Screen/headlight washer fluid reservoir*
F *Battery*

Engine oil level

Before you start
✔ Make sure that your car is on level ground
✔ Check the oil level before the car is driven, or at least 5 minutes after the engine has been switched off.

The correct oil
Modern engines place great demands on their oil. It is very important that the correct oil for your car is used (see *Lubricants and fluids*).

 HAYNES HiNT *If the oil is checked immediately after driving the vehicle, some of the oil will remain in the upper engine components, resulting in an inaccurate reading on the dipstick!*

Car care
● If you have to add oil frequently, you should check whether you have any oil leaks. Place some clean paper under the car overnight, and check for stains in the morning. If there are no leaks, the engine may be burning oil (see *Fault finding*).
● Always maintain the level between the upper and lower dipstick marks. If the level is too low severe engine damage may occur. Oil seal failure may result if the engine is overfilled by adding too much oil.

1 Withdraw the dipstick. Using a clean rag or paper towel, wipe all the oil from the dipstick. Insert the clean dipstick into the tube as far as it will go, then withdraw it again..

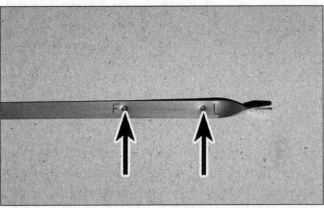

2 Note the oil level on the end of the dipstick, which should be between the upper mark and the lower mark.

3 Oil is added through the filler cap on top of the engine. Rotate the cap through a quarter-turn anti-clockwise and withdraw it. Top-up the level.

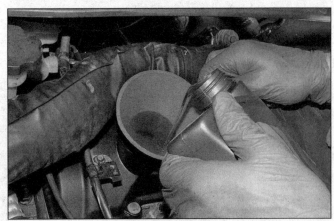

4 A funnel may help to reduce spillage. Add the oil slowly, checking the level on the dipstick often. Do not overfill.

Coolant level

Warning: DO NOT attempt to remove the expansion tank pressure cap when the engine is hot, as there is a very great risk of scalding. Do not leave open containers of coolant about, as it is poisonous.

Car care

● With a sealed-type cooling system, adding coolant should not be necessary on a regular basis. If frequent topping-up is required, it is likely there is a leak. Check the radiator, all hoses and joint faces for signs of staining or wetness, and rectify as necessary.

● It is important that antifreeze is used in the cooling system all year round, not just during the winter months. Don't top-up with water alone, as the antifreeze will become too diluted.

● The coolant level varies with the temperature of the engine. When the engine is cold, the coolant level should be level with the mark on the side of the reservoir. When the engine is hot, the level will rise approximately 15 mm.

18 If topping-up is necessary, wait until the engine is cold, then slowly unscrew the expansion tank filler cap anti-clockwise, to release any pressure in the system, and remove it.

19 Add a mixture of water and antifreeze through the expansion tank filler neck, until the coolant is level with the 'F' mark on the side of the expansion tank. Refit the cap, turning it clockwise as far as it will go until it is secure.

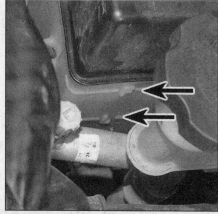
1 The full 'F' and low 'L' coolant levels are marked on the side of the coolant expansion tank

Brake (and clutch) fluid level

Warning: Brake fluid can harm your eyes and damage painted surfaces, so use extreme caution when handling and pouring it.
Caution: Do not use fluid that has been standing open for some time, as it absorbs moisture from the air, which can cause a dangerous loss of braking effectiveness.

Note: *The fluid level in the reservoir will drop slightly as the brake pads wear down, but the fluid level must never be allowed to drop below the "MIN" mark.*

Safety first!

● If the reservoir requires repeated topping-up this is an indication of a fluid leak somewhere in the system, which should be investigated immediately.

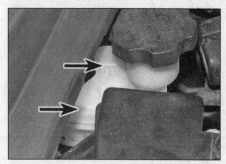
1 The brake fluid reservoir is mounted on the right-hand side of the bulkhead. The MAX and MIN level marks are indicated on the side of the reservoir and the fluid level should be maintained between these marks at all times.

2 On manual transmission models, the clutch master cylinder is supplied with fluid from the brake master cylinder reservoir. If topping-up is necessary, wipe the area around the filler cap with a clean rag before removing the cap. It's a good idea to inspect the reservoir. The fluid should be changed if dirt is visible.

3 Carefully add fluid, avoiding spilling it on surrounding paintwork. Use only the specified hydraulic fluid; mixing different types of fluid can cause damage to the system and/or a loss of braking effectiveness. After filling to the correct level, refit the cap securely. Wipe off any spilt fluid.

Battery

Caution: Before carrying out any work on the vehicle battery, read the precautions given in "Safety first" at the start of this manual.

✔ Make sure that the battery tray is in good condition, and that the clamp is tight. Corrosion on the tray, retaining clamp and the battery itself can be removed with a solution of water and baking soda. Thoroughly rinse all cleaned areas with water. Any metal parts damaged by corrosion should be covered with a zinc-based primer, then painted.

✔ Periodically (approximately every three months), check the charge condition of the battery as described in Chapter 5A.

✔ If the battery is flat, and you need to jump start your vehicle, see *Jump starting*.

✔ The battery is located at the front-left-hand side of the engine compartment. The exterior of the battery should be inspected periodically for damage such as a cracked case or cover.

> **HAYNES HiNT** *Battery corrosion can be kept to a minimum by applying a layer of petroleum jelly to the clamps and terminals after they are reconnected.*

1 Check the tightness of the battery cable clamps to ensure good electrical connections. You should not be able to move them. Also check each cable for cracks and frayed conductors.

2 If corrosion (white, fluffy deposits) is evident, remove the cables from the battery terminals, clean them with a small wire brush, then refit them. Automotive stores sell a tool for cleaning the battery post ...

3 ... as well as the battery cable clamps

Electrical systems

✔ Check all external lights and the horn. Refer to the appropriate Sections of Chapter 12 for details if any of the circuits are found to be inoperative.

✔ Visually check all accessible wiring connectors, harnesses and retaining clips for security, and for signs of chafing or damage.

> **HAYNES HiNT** *If you need to check your brake lights and indicators unaided, back up to a wall or garage door and operate the lights. The reflected light should show if they are working properly.*

1 If a single indicator light, brake light or headlight has failed, it is likely that a bulb has blown and will need to be replaced. Refer to Chapter 12 Section 6 for details. If both brake lights have failed, it is possible that the stop-light switch operated by the brake pedal has failed. Refer to Section for details.

2 If more than one indicator light or headlight has failed, it is likely that either a fuse has blown or that there is a fault in the circuit (see Chapter 12). The main fusebox is located on the right-hand side of the facia, other fuseboxes are described in Chapter 12 Section 3.

3 To replace a blown fuse, pull it out directly from the fusebox. A plastic tool to remove fuses is attached to the underside of the fusebox lid in the engine compartment. Fit a new fuse of the same rating, available from car accessory shops. It is important that you find the reason that the fuse blew (see "Electrical fault finding" Chapter 12 Section 2).

Wiper blades

Front wiper blade   **Rear wiper blade**

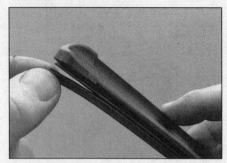

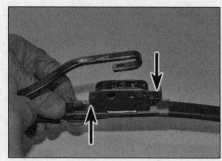

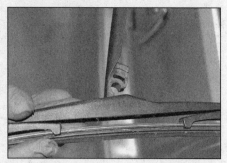

1 Check the condition of the wiper blades. If they are cracked or show any signs of deterioration, or if the glass swept area is smeared, renew them. For maximum clarity of vision, wiper blades should be renewed annually, as a matter of course.

1 Lift the wiper arms away from the windscreen, then fold down the front cover, press the tab at the rear, and slide the blade from the arm.

2 Pull the blade away from the screen, and pull the blade from the arm

Screen washer fluid level

● Screenwash additives not only keep the windscreen clean during foul weather, they also prevent the washer system freezing in cold weather – which is when you are likely to need it most. Don't top up using plain water as the screenwash will become too diluted, and will freeze during cold weather.

 Warning: On no account use coolant antifreeze in the washer system – this could discolour or damage paintwork.

1 The reservoir for the windscreen and rear window washer systems is located in the front right-hand corner of the engine compartment. If topping up is necessary, open the cap.

2 When topping-up the reservoir a screenwash additive should be added in the quantities recommended on the container.

Tyre condition and pressure

It is very important that tyres are in good condition, and at the correct pressure – having a tyre failure at any speed is highly dangerous. Tyre wear is influenced by driving style – harsh braking and acceleration, or fast cornering, will all produce more rapid tyre wear. As a general rule, the front tyres wear out faster the the rears. Interchanging the tyres from front to rear ("rotating" the tyres) may result in more even wear. However, if this is completely effective, you may have the expense of replacing all four tyres at once!

Remove any nails or stones embedded in the tread before they penetrate the tyre to cause deflation. If removal of a nail does reveal that the tyre has been punctured, refit the nail so that its point of penetration is marked. Then immediately change the wheel, and have the tyre repaired by a tyre dealer.

Regularly check the tyres for damage in the form of cuts or bulges, especially in the side walls. Periodically remove the wheels, and clean any dirt or mud from the inside and outside surfaces. Examine the wheel rims for signs of rusting, corrosion or other damage. Light alloy wheels are easily damaged by "kerbing" whilst parking; steel wheels may also become dented or buckled. A new wheel is very often the only way to overcome severe damage.

New tyres should be balanced when they are fitted, but it may become necessary to re-balance them as they ear, or if the balance weights fitted to the wheel rim should fall off. Unbalanced tyres will wear more quickly, as will the steering and suspension components. Wheel imbalance is normally signified by vibration, particularly at t certain speed (typically around 50 mph). If this vibration is felt only through the steering wheel, then it is likely that just the front wheels need balancing. If, however, the vibration is felt through the whole car, the rear wheels could be out of balance. Wheel balancing should be carried out by a tyre dealer or garage.

1 Tread Depth - visual check
The original tyres have tread wear safety bands (B), which will appear when the tread depth reaches approximately 1.6 mm. The band positions are indicated by a triangular mark on the tyre sidewall (A).

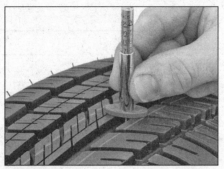

2 Tread Depth - manual check
Alternatively, tread wear can be monitored with a simple, inexpensive device known as a tread depth indicator gauge.

3 Tyre Pressure Check
Check the tyre pressures regularly with the tyres cold. Do not adjust the tyre pressures immediately after the vehicle has been used, or an inaccurate setting will result.

Tyre tread wear patterns

Shoulder Wear

Underinflation (wear on both sides)
Under-inflation will cause overheating of the tyre, because the tyre will flex too much, and the tread will not sit correctly on the road surface. This will cause a loss of grip and excessive wear, not to mention the danger of sudden tyre failure due to heat build-up.
Check and adjust pressures
Incorrect wheel camber (wear on one side)
Repair or renew suspension parts
Hard cornering
Reduce speed!

Centre Wear

Overinflation
Over-inflation will cause rapid wear of the centre part of the tyre tread, coupled with reduced grip, harsher ride, and the danger of shock damage occurring in the tyre casing.
Check and adjust pressures

If you sometimes have to inflate your car's tyres to the higher pressures specified for maximum load or sustained high speed, don't forget to reduce the pressures to normal afterwards.

Uneven Wear

Front tyres may wear unevenly as a result of wheel misalignment. Most tyre dealers and garages can check and adjust the wheel alignment (or "tracking") for a modest charge.
Incorrect camber or castor
Repair or renew suspension parts
Malfunctioning suspension
Repair or renew suspension parts
Unbalanced wheel
Balance tyres
Incorrect toe setting
Adjust front wheel alignment
Note: *The feathered edge of the tread which typifies toe wear is best checked by feel.*

Lubricants and fluids

Engine oil . . . . 5W/20 meeting Hyundai specification API Service SL or above, ACEA A3 or above. Castrol Edge 5W20

Coolant . . . . Ethylene glycol base coolant for aluminium radiator

Manual gearbox . . . . API Service GL-4 SAE 75W/85. Tutela Car Technyx

Automatic transmission . . . . DIAMOND ATF SP-III, SK ATF SP-III

Brake/clutch fluid . . . . FMVSS116 DOT-3 or DOT-4

Check with dealer for latest specifications.

Tyre pressures

All models	Front	Rear
155/70 R13:		
Medium load	2.3 bar (33 psi)	2.3 bar (33 psi)
Full load	2.5 bar (35 psi)	2.5 bar (35 psi)
165/60 R14:		
Medium load	2.3 bar (33 psi)	2.3 bar (33 psi)
Full load	2.5 bar (35 psi)	2.5 bar (35 psi)
175/50 R15:		
Medium load	2.3 bar (33 psi)	2.3 bar (33 psi)
Full load	2.5 bar (35 psi)	2.5 bar (35 psi)
175/60 R14:		
Medium load	2.3 bar (33 psi)	2.3 bar (33 psi)
Full load	2.5 bar (35 psi)	2.5 bar (35 psi)
T105/70 D14		
Medium load	4.2 bar (60 psi)	4.2 bar (60 psi)
Full load	4.2 bar (60 psi)	4.2 bar (60 psi)

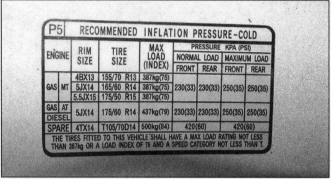

The tyre pressure are displayed on a stick affixed to the drivers or passengers door pillar

Chapter 1
Routine maintenance and servicing

Contents

Degrees of difficulty

| Easy, suitable for novice with little experience | 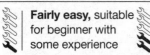 | Fairly easy, suitable for beginner with some experience | | Fairly difficult, suitable for competent DIY mechanic | | Difficult, suitable for experienced DIY mechanic | | Very difficult, suitable for expert DIY or professional | |

Servicing specifications

Lubricants and fluids . . . . Refer to ''*Weekly checks*''

Capacities
Engine oil (with filter): . . . . 3.6 litres
Cooling system . . . . 4.2 litres
Fuel tank . . . . 35 litres
Manual transmission . . . . 1.9 litres
Automatic transmission . . . . 6.1 litres

Cooling system
Protection at mixture of 50% anti-freeze and 50% water . . . . -40°C

Engine
Valve clearances (cold):
   Intake . . . . 1.3 mm
   Exhaust . . . . 1.75 mm

Ignition system
Ignition timing . . . . Refer to Chapter 5B Section 4
Spark plugs: . . . . Champion RER8YC or NGK 4288

Braking system
Brake pad friction material minimum thickness (front and rear) . . . . 1.5 mm
Brake shoe friction material minimum thickness . . . . 2.0 mm

Torque wrench settings

	Nm	lbf ft
Engine oil drain plug:	39	29
Manual transmission		
Drain plug	68	50
Filler plug	68	50
Roadwheel bolts	100	73
Spark plugs	18	13

1 Maintenance schedule

The maintenance intervals in this manual are provided with the assumption that you, not the dealer, will be carrying out the work. These are the minimum maintenance intervals recommended by us for vehicles driven daily. If you wish to keep your vehicle in peak condition at all times, you may wish to perform some of these procedures more often. We encourage frequent maintenance, because it enhances the efficiency, performance and resale value of your vehicle.

When the vehicle is new, it should be serviced by a factory-authorised dealer service department, in order to preserve the factory warranty.

Every 250 miles or weekly
☐ Refer to *'Weekly checks'*

Every 6000 miles or 6 months, whichever occurs first
☐ Renew the engine oil and filter (Section 4).

Note: *Frequent oil and filter changes are good for the engine. We recommend changing the oil at the mileage specified here, or at least twice a year if the mileage covered is less.*

Every 12 000 miles or 12 months, whichever occurs first
In addition to the item listed in the previous service, carry out the following:
☐ Check the auxiliary drivebelt (Section 5).
☐ Hose and fluid leak check (Section 6).
☐ Check the brake pads for wear (Section 7).
☐ Check the condition of the driveshaft gaiters (Section 8).
☐ Check the steering and suspension components for condition and security (Section 9).
☐ Check the underbody and sealant for damage (Section 10).
☐ Check the condition of the exhaust system and its mountings (Section 11).
☐ Check and if necessary adjust the handbrake (Section 12).
☐ Lubricate all hinges and locks (Section 13).
☐ Road test (Section 14).

Every 24 months or 22 500 miles, whichever occurs first
☐ Renew the spark plugs (Section 15).
☐ Renew the air filter element (Section 21).
☐ Check the condition of the spark plug HT leads (Section 16).
☐ Check the engine management system (Section 17).
☐ Renew the pollen filter (Section 18).
☐ Check the anti-freeze concentration (Section 19).

Every 2 years, regardless of mileage
☐ Renew the brake fluid (Section 20).

Every 36 000 miles or 3 years – whichever occurs first
☐ Check and if necessary top-up the manual transmission oil level (Section 22).

Every 48 000 miles or 4 years – whichever occurs first
☐ Check the operation of the evaporative loss system (Section 23).
☐ Check the condition and operation of the crankcase emission control system (Section 24).

Note: *Although the normal interval for timing belt renewal is 72 000 miles (120 000 km), it is strongly recommended that the belt is renewed at 48 000 miles on vehicles which are subjected to intensive use, ie, mainly short journeys or a lot of stop-start driving. The actual belt renewal interval is therefore very much up to the individual owner, but bear in mind that severe engine damage will result if the belt breaks.*

Every 10 years, regardless of mileage
☐ Renew the coolant (Section 25).

Front underbody view

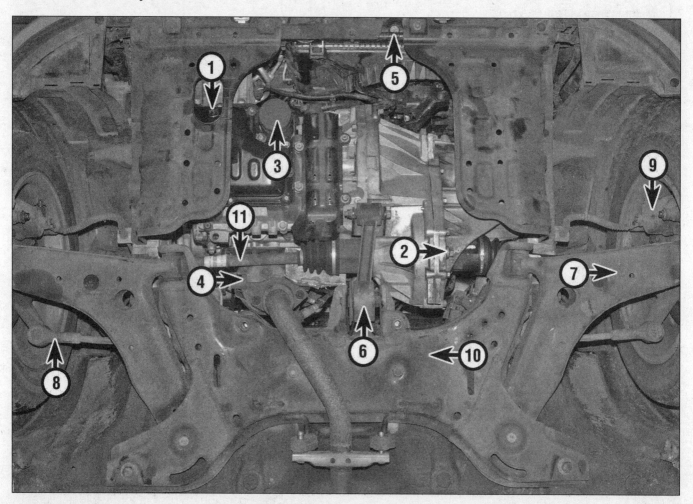

1 Engine oil drain plug
2 Transmission drain plug
3 Engine oil filter
4 Catalytic converter

5 Coolant drain plug
6 Rear engine mounting rod
7 Suspension lower arm
8 Steering track rod end

9 Brake caliper
10 Subframe
11 Driveshaft

Rear underbody view

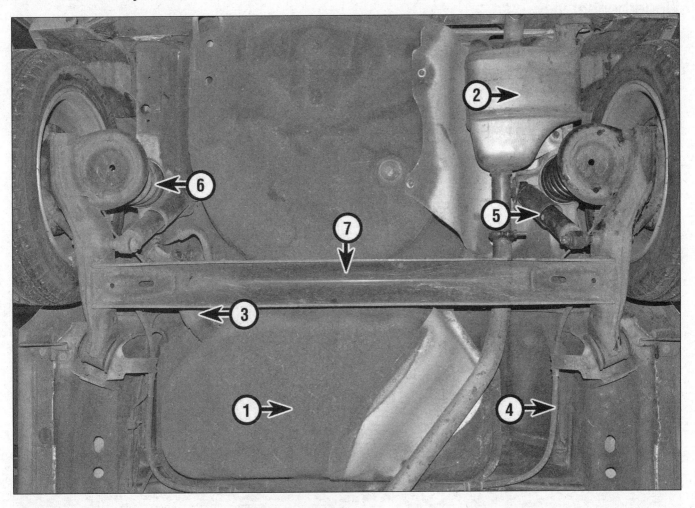

1 Fuel tank
2 Exhaust silencer
3 Fuel filler pipe

4 Handbrake cable
5 Shock absorber

6 Coil spring
7 Rear axle

Underbonnet view

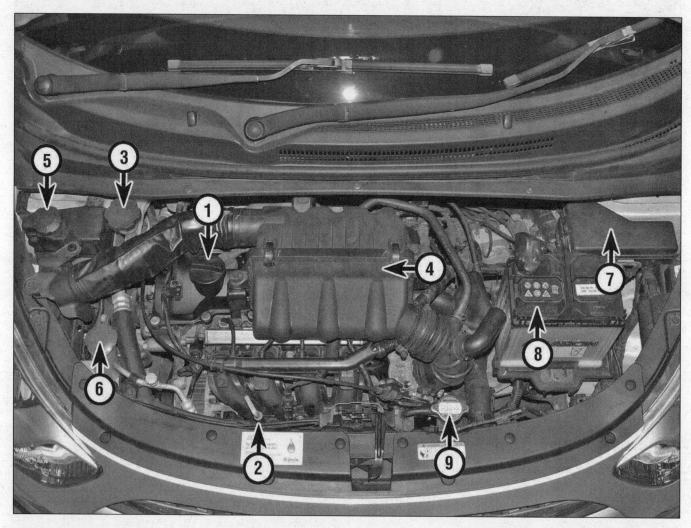

1 Engine oil filler cap
2 Engine oil level dipstick
3 Brake/clutch fluid reservoir

4 Air filter cover
5 Coolant expansion tank cap
6 Screenwash fluid reservoir cap

7 Engine compartment fusebox
8 Battery
9 Radiator cap

2 Introduction

1 This Chapter is designed to help the home mechanic maintain his/her vehicle for safety, economy, long life and peak performance.

2 The Chapter contains a maintenance schedule, followed by Sections dealing specifically with each task in the schedule. Visual checks, adjustments, component renewal and other helpful items are included. Refer to the accompanying illustrations of the engine compartment and the underside of the vehicle for the locations of the various components.

3 Servicing your vehicle in accordance with the above recommendations and the following Sections will provide a planned maintenance programme, which should result in a long and reliable service life. This is a comprehensive plan, so maintaining some items, but not others at the specified service intervals, will not produce the same results.

4 As you service your vehicle, you will discover that many of the procedures can – and should – be grouped together, because of the particular procedure being performed, or because of the proximity of two otherwise-unrelated components to one another. For example, if the vehicle is raised for any reason, the exhaust can be inspected at the same time as the suspension and steering components.

5 The first step in this maintenance programme is to prepare yourself before the actual work begins. Read through all the Sections relevant to the work to be carried out, then make a list and gather all the parts and tools required. If a problem is encountered, seek advice from a parts specialist, or a dealer service department.

3 Regular maintenance

1 If, from the time the vehicle is new, the routine maintenance schedule is followed closely, and frequent checks are made of fluid levels and high-wear items, as suggested

throughout this manual, the engine will be kept in relatively good running condition, and the need for additional work will be minimised.

2 It is possible that there will be times when the engine is running poorly due to the lack of regular maintenance. This is even more likely if a used vehicle, which has not received regular and frequent maintenance checks, is purchased. In such cases, additional work may need to be carried out, outside of the regular maintenance intervals.

3 If engine wear is suspected, a compression test (refer to Chapter 2A Section 2) will provide valuable information regarding the overall performance of the main internal components. Such a test can be used as a basis to decide on the extent of the work to be carried out. If, for example, a compression test indicates serious internal engine wear, conventional maintenance as described in this Chapter will not greatly improve the performance of the engine, and may prove a waste of time and money, unless extensive overhaul work is carried out first.

4 The following series of operations are those most often required to improve the performance of a generally poor-running engine:

Primary operations

a) Clean, inspect and test the battery (see Weekly checks).

b) Check all the engine-related fluids (refer to Weekly checks).

c) Check the condition and tension of the auxiliary drivebelt (Section 5).

d) Check the condition of all hoses, and check for fluid leaks (Section 6).

e) Renew the spark plugs (Section 15).

f) Inspect the HT leads (Section 16).

g) Check the condition of the air filter, and renew if necessary (Section 21).

5 If the above operations do not prove fully effective, carry out the following secondary operations:

Secondary operations

6 All items listed under Primary operations, plus the following:

a) Check the charging system (Chapter 5A Section 5).

b) Check the ignition system (Chapter 5B Section 2).

c) Check the fuel system (Chapter 4A Section 9).

4 Engine oil and filter renewal

1 Frequent oil and filter changes are the most important preventative maintenance which can be undertaken by the DIY owner. As engine oil ages, it becomes diluted and contaminated, which leads to premature engine wear.

2 Before starting this procedure, gather all the necessary tools and materials. Also make sure that you have plenty of clean rags and newspapers handy to mop-up any spills. Ideally, the engine oil should be warm, as it will drain better, and any impurities suspended in the oil will be removed with it. Take care, however, not to touch the exhaust or any other hot parts of the engine when working under the vehicle. To avoid any possibility of scalding, and to protect yourself from possible skin irritants and other harmful contaminants in used engine oils, it is advisable to wear gloves when carrying out this work. Access to the underside of the vehicle will be greatly improved if it can be raised on a lift, driven onto ramps, or jacked up and supported on axle stands as described in 'Vehicle jacking and support'. Whichever method is chosen, make sure that the vehicle remains level, or if it is at an angle, that the drain plug is at the lowest point.

3 Slacken the drain plug about half a turn (see illustration). Position the draining container under the drain plug, then remove the plug completely (see Haynes Hint).

4 Allow some time for the old oil to drain, noting that it may be necessary to reposition the container as the oil flow slows to a trickle.

5 After all the oil has drained, wipe off the drain plug with a clean rag, then clean the area around the drain plug opening and refit the plug using a new seal (see illustration). Tighten the plug to the specified torque.

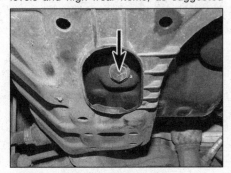

4.3 Sump drain plug

Keep the drain plug pressed into the sump while unscrewing it by hand the last couple of turns. As the plug releases, move it away sharply so the stream of oil issuing from the sump runs into the container, not up your sleeve.

4.5 Renew the sump plug sealing washer

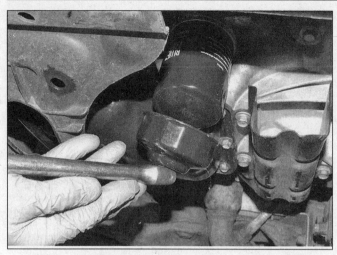

4.7 Use an oil filter removal tool to initially slacken the filter

4.9 Apply a light coating of engine oil to the filter sealing ring

6 Move the container into position under the oil filter, which is located on the front engine.

7 Using an oil filter removal tool (68/14) if necessary, slacken the filter initially, then unscrew it by hand the rest of the way **(see illustration)**. Empty the oil in the old filter into the container.

8 Use a clean rag to remove all oil, dirt and sludge from the filter sealing area on the engine. Check the old filter to make sure that the rubber sealing ring has not stuck to the engine. If it has, carefully remove it.

9 Apply a light coating of clean engine oil to the sealing ring on the new filter, then screw it into position on the engine **(see illustration)**. Tighten the filter firmly by hand only – do not use any tools.

10 Remove the old oil and all tools from under the car then lower it to the ground (if applicable).

11 Withdraw the dipstick, and remove the oil filler cap from the cylinder head cover. Fill the engine, using the correct grade and type of oil (see Lubricants and fluids 0 Section 5). An oil can spout or funnel may help to reduce spillage. Pour in half the specified quantity of oil first, then wait a few minutes for the oil to run to the sump. Continue adding oil a small quantity at a time until the level is up to the MAX mark on the dipstick. Refit the filler cap.

12 Start the engine and run it for a few minutes; check for leaks around the oil filter seal and the sump drain plug. Note that there may be a delay of a few seconds before the oil pressure warning light goes out when the engine is first started, as the oil circulates through the engine oil galleries and the new oil filter before the pressure builds-up.

13 Switch off the engine, and wait a few minutes for the oil to settle in the sump once more. With the new oil circulated and the filter completely full, recheck the level on the dipstick, and add more oil as necessary.

14 Dispose of the used engine oil and filter safely, referring to General repair procedures in the Reference Chapter. Do not discard the old filter with domestic household waste. The facility for waste oil disposal provided by many local council refuse tips generally has a filter receptacle alongside.

5 Auxiliary drivebelt check and renewal

Check

1 Slacken the right-hand front roadwheel bolts, raise the front of the vehicle, and support it securely on axle stands, as described in 'Vehicle jacking and support'. Remove the roadwheel.

2 Undo the fasteners and remove the lower/front section of the wheelarch liner **(see illustration)**.

3 Using a socket on the crankshaft pulley bolt, rotate the crankshaft so that the full length of the drivebelt can be examined. Look for cracks, splitting and fraying on the surface of the belt; check also for signs of glazing (shiny patches) and separation of the belt plies. If damage or wear is visible, the belt should be renewed.

4 If the condition of the belt is satisfactory, where applicable check the drivebelt tension as described below.

Renewal

Note: *Not the direction in which the drivebelt runs. If it is to be reused, mark it with an arrow in the correct direction.*

5 Insert SST 09252-03100 or a similarly flat-edged tool between the belt and the crankshaft pulley, then rotate the pulley clockwise to derail the belt from place **(see illustrations)**.

6 Remove the drivebelt from the crankshaft pulley.

7 When renewing a drivebelt, ensure that the correct type is used.

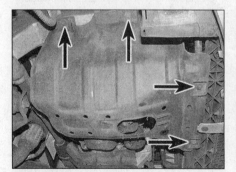

5.2 Undo the fasteners and remove the liner

5.5a Insert a tool between the belt and crankshaft pulley ...

5.5b ... then rotate the pulley to derail the belt

8 Fit the belt around the alternator, coolant pump and compressor (where applicable) pulleys, then locate the belt into the grooves under the crankshaft pulley, and rotate the crankshaft clockwise feeding the belt around the pulley, ensuring it locates correctly.
9 Refit the wheel arch liner panel and roadwheel, then lower the car to the ground.

6 Hose and fluid leak check

1 Visually inspect the engine joint faces, gaskets and seals for any signs of water or oil leaks. Pay particular attention to the areas around the camshaft cover, cylinder head, oil filter and sump joint faces. Bear in mind that, over a period of time, some very slight seepage from these areas is to be expected – what you are really looking for is any indication of a serious leak. Should a leak be found, renew the offending gasket or oil seal by referring to the appropriate Chapters in this manual.
2 Also check the security and condition of all the engine-related pipes and hoses. Ensure that all cable-ties or securing clips are in place and in good condition. Clips that are broken or missing can lead to chafing of the hoses, pipes or wiring, which could cause more serious problems in the future.
3 Carefully check the radiator hoses and heater hoses along their entire length. Renew any hose which is cracked, swollen or deteriorated. Cracks will show up better if the hose is squeezed. Pay close attention to the hose clips that secure the hoses to the cooling system components. Hose clips can pinch and puncture hoses, resulting in cooling system leaks.
4 Inspect all the cooling system components (hoses, joint faces, etc) for leaks. A leak in the cooling system will usually show up as white- or antifreeze-coloured deposits on the area adjoining the leak (see **Haynes Hint**). Where any problems of this nature are found on system components, renew the component or

A leak in the cooling system will usually show up as white-or antifreeze coloured deposits on the area adjoining the leak.

gasket with reference to Chapter 3.
5 With the vehicle raised, inspect the fuel tank and filler neck for punctures, cracks and other damage. The connection between the filler neck and tank is especially critical. Sometimes a rubber filler neck or connecting hose will leak due to loose retaining clamps or deteriorated rubber.
6 Carefully check all rubber hoses and metal fuel lines leading away from the petrol tank. Check for loose connections, deteriorated hoses, crimped lines, and other damage. Pay particular attention to the vent pipes and hoses, which often loop up around the filler neck and can become blocked or crimped. Follow the lines to the front of the vehicle, carefully inspecting them all the way. Renew damaged sections as necessary.
7 Closely inspect the metal brake pipes, which run along the vehicle underbody. If they show signs of excessive corrosion or damage they must be renewed.
8 From within the engine compartment, check the security of all fuel hose attachments and pipe unions, and inspect the fuel hoses and vacuum hoses for kinks, chafing and deterioration.

7 Brake pad check

1 Brake discs are fitted to the front of all models.
2 Raise the front of the vehicle and support it securely on axle stands as described in *'Vehicle jacking and support'*. Remove the roadwheels.
3 Using a steel rule, measure the thickness of the friction material of the brake pads on both front brakes. This must not be less than 1.5 mm. Check the thickness of the pad friction material through the hole on the caliper **(see illustration)**.
4 For a comprehensive check, the brake pads should be removed and cleaned. The operation of the caliper can then also be checked, and the condition of the brake disc itself can be fully examined on both sides. Refer to Chapter 9 for further information.
5 If any pad's friction material is worn to the specified thickness or less, all four pads on the front axle must be renewed as a set. Refer to Chapter 9 Section 4.
6 On completion refit the roadwheels and lower the car to the ground.

8 Driveshaft gaiter check

1 With the car raised and securely supported on stands (see *'Vehicle jacking and support'*), turn the steering onto full lock, then slowly rotate the roadwheel. Inspect the condition of the outer constant velocity (CV) joint rubber gaiters, squeezing the gaiters to open out the folds. Check for signs of cracking, splits or deterioration of the rubber, which may allow the grease to escape, and lead to water and grit entry into the joint. Also check the security and condition of the retaining clips. Repeat these checks on the inner CV joints **(see illustration)**. If any damage or deterioration

7.3 Check the thickness of the pad friction material through the hole in the caliper

8.1 Check the condition of the driveshaft gaiter

is found, the gaiters should be renewed (see Chapter 8 Section 4).

2 At the same time, check the general condition of the CV joints themselves by first holding the driveshaft and attempting to rotate the wheel. Repeat this check by holding the inner joint and attempting to rotate the driveshaft. Any appreciable movement indicates wear in the joints, wear in the driveshaft splines, or a loose driveshaft retaining nut.

9 Steering and suspension check

Front suspension and steering

1 Raise the front of the vehicle and support it securely on axle stands, as described in *'Vehicle jacking and support'*.

2 Inspect the balljoint dust covers and the steering rack and pinion gaiters for splits, chafing or deterioration. Any wear of these will cause loss of lubricant, together with dirt and water entry, resulting in rapid deterioration of the balljoints or steering gear.

3 Grasp the roadwheel at the 12 o'clock and 6 o'clock positions, and try to rock it **(see illustration)**. Very slight free play may be felt, but if the movement is appreciable, further investigation is necessary to determine the source. Continue rocking the wheel while an assistant depresses the footbrake. If the movement is now eliminated or significantly reduced, it is likely that the hub bearings are at fault. If the free play is still evident with the footbrake depressed, then there is wear in the suspension joints or mountings.

4 Now grasp the wheel at the 9 o'clock and 3 o'clock positions, and try to rock it as before. Any movement felt now may again be caused by wear in the hub bearings or the steering

track rod balljoints. If the inner or outer balljoint is worn, the visual movement will be obvious.

5 Using a large screwdriver or flat bar, check for wear in the suspension mounting bushes by levering between the relevant suspension component and its attachment point. Some movement is to be expected as the mountings are made of rubber, but excessive wear should be obvious. Also check the condition of any visible rubber bushes, looking for splits, cracks or contamination of the rubber.

6 With the car standing on its wheels, have an assistant turn the steering wheel back-and-forth about an eighth of a turn each way. There should be very little, if any, lost movement between the steering wheel and roadwheels. If this is not the case, closely observe the joints and mountings previously described, but in addition check the steering column universal joints for wear, and the rack and pinion steering gear itself.

Strut/shock absorber check

7 Check for any signs of fluid leakage around the suspension strut/shock absorber body, or from the rubber gaiter around the piston rod. Should any fluid be noticed, the suspension strut/shock absorber is defective internally, and should be renewed.

Note: *Suspension struts/shock absorbers should always be renewed in pairs on the same axle.*

8 The efficiency of the suspension strut/shock absorber may be checked by bouncing the vehicle at each corner. Generally speaking, the body will return to its normal position and stop after being depressed. If it rises and returns on a rebound, the suspension strut/shock absorber is probably suspect. Examine also the suspension strut/shock absorber upper and lower mountings for any signs of wear.

10 Underbody sealant check

1 Jack up the front and rear of the car and support it securely on axle stands, as described in *'Vehicle jacking and support'*. Alternatively position the car over an inspection pit.

2 Check the underbody, wheel housings and side sills for rust and/or damage to the underbody sealant. If evident, repair as necessary.

11 Exhaust system check

1 With the engine cold (at least an hour after the vehicle has been driven), check the complete exhaust system from the engine to the end of the tailpipe. The exhaust system is most easily checked with the car raised on a hoist, or suitably supported on axle stands, as described in *'Vehicle jacking and support'*, so that the exhaust components are readily visible and accessible.

2 Check the exhaust pipes and connections for evidence of leaks, severe corrosion and damage. Make sure that all brackets and mountings are in good condition, and that all relevant nuts and bolts are tight **(see illustration)**. Leakage at any of the joints or in other parts of the system will usually show up as a black sooty stain in the vicinity of the leak.

3 Rattles and other noises can often be traced to the exhaust system, especially the brackets and mountings. Try to move the pipes and silencers. If the components are able to come into contact with the body or suspension parts, secure the system with new mountings. Otherwise separate the joints (if possible) and twist the pipes as necessary to provide additional clearance.

9.3 Rock a roadwheel to check for wear in the steering/ suspension components

11.2 Check the condition of the exhaust rubber mountings

15.3 Disconnect the HT leads by pulling up the rubber caps

15.5 Remove the spark plugs using a deep socket and extension bar

12 Handbrake check and adjustment

1 Apply the handbrake by pulling it through a maximum of 7 clicks of the ratchet mechanism and check that this locks the rear wheels, holding the vehicle stationary on an incline. In this position, there should be sufficient reserve travel in the handbrake lever to allow for brake shoe/pad wear and cable stretching. If not, the handbrake mechanism should be adjusted as described in Chapter 9 Section 13.

13 Hinge and lock lubrication

1 Lubricate the hinges of the bonnet, doors and tailgate with a light general-purpose oil. Similarly, lubricate all latches, locks and lock strikers. At the same time, check the security and operation of all the locks.
2 Lightly lubricate the bonnet release mechanism with a suitable grease.

14 Road test

Instruments and electrical equipment

1 Check the operation of all instruments and electrical equipment.
2 Make sure that all instruments read correctly, and switch on all electrical equipment in turn, to check that it functions properly.

Steering and suspension

3 Check for any abnormalities in the steering, suspension, handling or road feel.

4 Drive the vehicle, and check that there are no unusual vibrations or noises.
5 Check that the steering feels positive, with no excessive sloppiness, or roughness, and check for any suspension noises when cornering and driving over bumps.

Drivetrain

6 Check the performance of the engine, clutch, transmission and driveshafts.
7 Listen for any unusual noises from the engine, clutch and gearbox/transmission.
8 Make sure that the engine runs smoothly when idling, and that there is no hesitation when accelerating.
9 Check that the clutch action is smooth and progressive, that the drive is taken up smoothly, and that the pedal travel is not excessive. Also listen for any noises when the clutch pedal is depressed.
10 Check that all gears can be engaged smoothly without noise, and that the gear lever action is smooth and not abnormally vague or notchy.
11 Listen for a metallic clicking sound from the front of the vehicle, as the vehicle is driven slowly in a circle with the steering on full lock. Carry out this check in both directions. If a clicking noise is heard, this indicates wear in a driveshaft joint, in which case renew the joint if necessary.

Braking system

12 Make sure that the vehicle does not pull to one side when braking, and that the wheels do not lock when braking hard.
13 Check that there is no vibration through the steering when braking.
14 Check that the handbrake operates correctly without excessive movement of the lever, and that it holds the vehicle stationary on a slope.
15 Test the operation of the brake servo unit as follows. With the engine off, depress the footbrake four or five times to exhaust the vacuum. Hold the brake pedal depressed,

then start the engine. As the engine starts, there should be a noticeable give in the brake pedal as vacuum builds-up. Allow the engine to run for at least two minutes, and then switch it off. If the brake pedal is depressed now, it should be possible to detect a hiss from the servo as the pedal is depressed. After about four or five applications, no further hissing should be heard, and the pedal should feel considerably harder.

15 Spark plug renewal

1 The correct functioning of the spark plugs is vital for the correct running and efficiency of the engine. It is essential that the plugs fitted are appropriate for the engine (a suitable type is specified at the beginning of this Chapter). If this type is used and the engine is in good condition, the spark plugs should not need attention between scheduled replacement intervals. Spark plug cleaning is rarely necessary, and should not be attempted unless specialised equipment is available, as damage can easily be caused to the firing ends.
2 Remove the air cleaner assembly as described in Chapter 4A Section 2.
3 Pulling up the rubber HT caps, disconnect the HT leads from the top of each spark plug (see illustration). Note that the leads are different lengths, and numbered 1 to 4 to correspond with their respective cylinder. No.1 is at the timing chain end (drivers side) of the engine.
4 It is advisable to remove the dirt from the spark plug recesses using a clean brush, vacuum cleaner or compressed air before removing the plugs, to prevent dirt dropping into the cylinders.
5 Unscrew the plugs using a spark plug spanner, suitable box spanner or a deep socket and extension bar (see illustration).

Keep the socket aligned with the spark plug – if it is forcibly moved to one side, the ceramic insulator may be broken off. As each plug is removed, examine it as follows.

6 Examination of the spark plugs will give a good indication of the condition of the engine. If the insulator nose of the spark plug is clean and white, with no deposits, this is indicative of a weak mixture or too hot a plug (a hot plug transfers heat away from the electrode slowly, a cold plug transfers heat away quickly).

7 If the tip and insulator nose are covered with hard black-looking deposits, this indicates that the mixture is too rich. If the plug is black and oily, then it is likely that the engine is fairly worn, as well as the mixture being too rich.

8 If the insulator nose is covered with light tan to greyish-brown deposits, then the mixture is correct and it is likely that the engine is in good condition.

9 Note that the electrode gap on the recommended spark plugs is pre-set, and requires no adjustment.

10 Carefully locate the new plug into the threaded hole in the cylinder head, and finger-tighten them only (see **Haynes Hint**).

11 Remove the rubber hose (if used), and tighten the plug to the specified torque using the spark plug socket and a torque wrench. Refit the remaining spark plugs in the same manner.

12 The remainder of refitting is a reversal of removal.

16 HT lead check

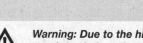

Warning: Due to the high voltages produced by the electronic ignition system, extreme care *must be taken when working on the system with the ignition switched on. Persons with surgically-implanted cardiac pacemaker devices should keep well clear of the ignition circuits, components and test equipment.*

1 The spark plug (HT) leads should be checked whenever new spark plugs are fitted.

2 Remove the air cleaner assembly as described in Chapter 4A Section 2.

3 Pull the leads from the plugs by gripping the end fitting, not the lead, otherwise the lead connection may be fractured.

4 Check inside the end fitting for signs of corrosion, which will look like a white crusty powder. Push the end fitting back onto the spark plug, ensuring that it is a tight fit on the plug. If not, remove the lead again and use pliers to carefully crimp the metal connector inside the end fitting until it fits securely on the end of the spark plug.

5 Using a clean rag, wipe the entire length of the lead to remove any built-up dirt and grease. Once the lead is clean, check for burns, cracks and other damage. Do not bend the lead excessively, nor pull the lead lengthways – the conductor inside might break.

6 Disconnect the other end of the lead from the ignition coil. Again, pull only on the end fitting. Check for corrosion and a tight fit in the same manner as the spark plug end. Refit the lead securely on completion.

7 Check the remaining leads one at a time, in the same way.

8 If new spark plug (HT) leads are required, purchase a set for your specific car and engine.

9 Refit the air cleaner assembly on completion of the checks.

10 Even with the ignition system in first-class condition, some engines may still occasionally experience poor starting attributable to damp ignition components. To disperse moisture, a water-dispersant aerosol should be liberally applied.

17 Engine management system check

1 This check is part of the manufacturer's maintenance schedule, and involves testing the engine management system using special dedicated test equipment. Such testing will allow the test equipment to read any fault codes stored in the electronic control unit memory.

2 Unless a fault is suspected, this test is not essential, although it should be noted that it is recommended by the manufacturers.

3 If access to suitable test equipment is not possible, make a thorough check of all ignition, fuel and emission control system components, hoses, and wiring, for security and obvious signs of damage. Further details of the fuel system, emission control system and ignition system can be found in the relevant parts of Chapter 4A, 4B and Chapter 5B.

18 Pollen filter renewal

1 Remove the glovebox as described in Chapter 11 Section 26.

2 Carefully squeeze together the tabs at each end and remove the pollen filter cover (**see illustration**).

It is very often difficult to insert spark plugs into their holes without cross-threading them. To avoid this possibility, fit a short length of 8 mm internal diameter rubber hose over the end of the spark plug. The flexible hose acts as a universal joint to help align the plug with the plug hole. Should the plug begin to cross-thread, the hose will slip on the spark plug, preventing thread damage to the cylinder head.

18.2 Squeeze the tabs at each end of the pollen filter housing

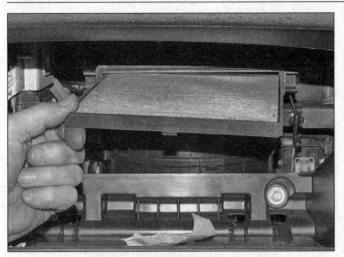

18.3 Slide the pollen filter from the housing

18.4 The arrows on the filter must point downwards

3 Withdraw the filter from its housing **(see illustration)**.

4 Wipe clean the housing, then fit the new filter, noting the arrows on the filter element must point downwards in the direction of the airflow **(see illustration)**.

5 Refit the centre console panel and glovebox.

19 Antifreeze concentration check

1 The cooling system should be filled with the recommended antifreeze and corrosion protection fluid. Over a period of time, the concentration of fluid may be reduced due to topping-up (this can be avoided by topping-up with the correct antifreeze mixture) or fluid loss. If loss of coolant has been evident, it is important to make the necessary repair before adding fresh fluid. The exact mixture of antifreeze-to-water which you should use depends on the relative weather conditions. The mixture should contain at least 40% anti-freeze, but not more than 70%. Consult the mixture ratio chart on the antifreeze container before adding coolant. Use antifreeze which meets the car manufacturer's specifications.

2 With the engine cold, carefully remove the cap from the expansion tank. If the engine is not completely cold, place a cloth rag over the cap before removing it, and remove it slowly to allow any pressure to escape.

3 Antifreeze checkers are available from car accessory shops. Draw some coolant from the expansion tank and observe how many plastic balls are floating in the checker. Usually, 2 or 3 balls must be floating for the correct concentration of antifreeze, but follow the manufacturer's instructions.

4 If the concentration is incorrect, it will be necessary to either withdraw some coolant and add antifreeze, or alternatively drain

the old coolant and add fresh coolant of the correct concentration.

20 Brake fluid renewal

> ⚠️ *Warning: Brake hydraulic fluid can harm your eyes and damage painted surfaces, so use extreme caution when handling and pouring it. Do not use fluid that has been standing open for some time, as it absorbs moisture from the air. Excess moisture can cause a dangerous loss of braking effectiveness.*

1 The procedure is similar to that for the bleeding of the hydraulic system as described in Chapter 9 Section 2, except that the brake fluid reservoir should be emptied by syphoning, using a clean poultry baster or similar before starting, and allowance should be made for the old fluid to be expelled when bleeding a section of the circuit.

2 Working as described in Chapter 9 Section 2, open the first bleed screw in the sequence, and pump the brake pedal gently until nearly all the old fluid has been emptied from the master cylinder reservoir.

3 Top-up to the MAX level with new fluid, and continue pumping until only the new fluid remains in the reservoir, and new fluid can be seen emerging from the bleed screw. Tighten the screw, and top the reservoir level up to the MAX level line.

4 Work through all the remaining bleed screws in the sequence until new fluid can be seen at all of them. Be careful to keep the master cylinder reservoir topped-up to above the MIN level at all times, or air may enter the system and greatly increase the length of the task.

5 When the operation is complete, check that all bleed screws are securely tightened, and that their dust caps are refitted. Wash off all traces of spilt fluid, and recheck the master cylinder reservoir fluid level.

6 Check the operation of the brakes before taking the car on the road.

21 Air filter element renewal

1 Undo the retaining clips **(see illustration)**.

2 Pull forward the front of the filter cover and manoeuvre the filter from place **(see illustration)**.

21.1 Undo the filter cover clips

21.2 Manoeuvre the filter from place

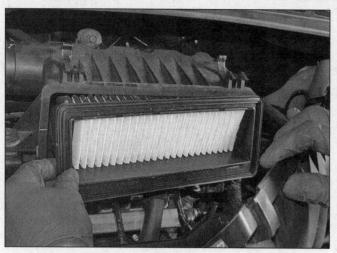

21.4 Locate the new filter element in the housing

22.2 Transmission filler/level plug

3 Remove any debris that may have collected inside the air cleaner and wipe the inner surfaces clean.

4 Fit a new filter element in position, ensuring the edges are securely seated **(see illustration)**.

5 Refit the cover and tighten the retaining clips securely.

22 Manual transmission oil level check

1 Park the car on a level surface, if possible over an inspection pit or on a ramp as the filler/level plug is best reached from under the engine compartment. The oil level must be checked before the car is driven, or at least 5 minutes after the engine has been switched off. If the oil is checked immediately after driving the car, some of the oil will remain distributed around the transmission components, resulting in an inaccurate level reading.

2 Wipe clean the area around the filler/level plug, which is situated on the front of the transmission **(see illustration)**. Using an Allen key, unscrew the plug and clean it.

3 The oil level should reach the lower edge of the filler/level hole. A certain amount of oil will have gathered behind the filler/level plug, and will trickle out when it is removed; this does not necessarily indicate that the level is correct. To ensure that a true level is established, wait until the initial trickle has stopped, then add oil as necessary until a trickle of new oil can be seen emerging. The level will be correct when the flow ceases; use only good-quality oil of the specified type. Make sure that the vehicle is completely level when checking the level and do not overfill.

4 When the level is correct refit and tighten the plug and wipe away any spilt oil.

23 Evaporative loss system check

1 Refer to Chapter 4B Section 1 and check that all wiring and hoses are correctly connected to the evaporative loss system components.

24 Emission control system check

1 Refer to Chapter 4B. A full check of the emissions control systems must be made by a Hyundai dealer.

25 Coolant renewal

⚠️ **Warning: Wait until the engine is cold before starting this procedure. Do not allow anti-freeze to come into contact with your skin, or with the painted surfaces of the vehicle. Rinse off spills immediately with plenty of water. Never leave antifreeze lying around in an open container, or in a puddle in the driveway or on the garage floor. Children and pets are attracted by its sweet smell, but antifreeze can be fatal in ingested.**

Coolant system draining

1 Raise the front of the vehicle and support it securely on axle stands as described in 'Vehicle jacking and support'.

2 With the engine completely cold, cover the radiator cap with a wad of rag, and slowly turn the cap anti-clockwise to relieve the pressure in the cooling system (a hissing sound will normally be heard). Wait until any

pressure remaining in the system is released, then continue to turn the cap until it can be removed.

3 Place a suitable container beneath the radiator, then gently undo the drain tap, allowing the coolant to drain **(see illustration)**.

4 When the coolant has finished draining, close the drain tap and remove the container.

Cooling system flushing

5 If coolant renewal has been neglected, or if the antifreeze mixture has become diluted, then in time, the cooling system may gradually lose efficiency, as the coolant passages become restricted due to rust, scale deposits, and other sediment. The cooling system efficiency can be restored by flushing the system clean.

6 The radiator should be flushed independently of the engine, to avoid contamination.

Radiator flushing

7 To flush the radiator disconnect the top and bottom hoses and any other relevant hoses from the radiator, with reference to Chapter 3.

8 Insert a garden hose into the radiator top inlet. Direct a flow of clean water through the radiator, and continue flushing until clean

25.3 Undo the drain tap

water emerges from the radiator bottom outlet.

9 If after a reasonable period, the water still does not run clear, the radiator can be flushed with a good proprietary cooling system cleaning agent. It is important that their manufacturer's instructions are followed carefully. If the contamination is particularly bad, insert the hose in the radiator bottom outlet, and reverse-flush the radiator.

Engine flushing

10 To flush the engine, remove the thermostat housing as described in Chapter 3 Section 4.

11 With the top and bottom hoses disconnected from the radiator, insert a garden hose into the radiator bottom hose. Direct a clean flow of water through the engine, and continue flushing until clean water emerges from the thermostat housing opening in the cylinder head.

12 On completion of flushing, refit the thermostat housing and reconnect the hoses with reference to Chapter 3 Section 4.

Cooling system filling

13 Before attempting to fill the cooling system, make sure that all hoses and clips are in good condition, and that the clips are tight.

Note that an antifreeze mixture must be used all year round, to prevent corrosion of the engine components (see below).

14 If the coolant is being renewed, place a funnel into the radiator filler neck and fill with pre-mixed anti-freeze. Periodically squeeze the radiator top and bottom hoses to help expel any trapped air in the system.

15 Top-up the coolant level to the bottom of the radiator fill neck and refit the cap.

16 Remove the expansion tank filler cap, and slowly pour coolant into the expansion tank to prevent airlocks from forming. Fill to Full level and replace the expansion tank cap.

17 Start the engine and run it at idling speed for two to three minutes. Allow the engine to continue running until the electric cooling fan operates, but during this time periodically increase the engine speed gradually to 2000 to 3000 rpm.

18 Stop the engine and allow it to cool down completely.

19 Check for leaks, particularly around disturbed components. Check the coolant level in the expansion tank, and top-up if necessary. Note that the system must be cold before an accurate level is indicated in the expansion tank.

Anti-freeze mixture

20 The antifreeze should always be renewed at the specified intervals. This is necessary not only to maintain the antifreeze properties, but also to prevent corrosion which would otherwise occur as the corrosion inhibitors become progressively less effective.

21 Always use a monoethylene-glycol based antifreeze of the specified type (see Lubricants and fluids). The quantity of antifreeze and levels of protection are indicated in the Specifications.

22 Before adding antifreeze, the cooling system should be completely drained, preferably flushed, and all hoses checked for condition and security.

23 After filling with antifreeze, a label should be attached to the expansion tank, stating the type and concentration of antifreeze used, and the date installed. Any subsequent topping-up should be made with the same type and concentration of antifreeze.

24 Do not use engine antifreeze in the windscreen/tailgate washer system, as it will cause damage to the vehicle paintwork. A screenwash additive should be added to the washer system in the quantities stated on the bottle.

Chapter 2 Part A
1.2L engine in-car repair procedures

Contents

Degrees of difficulty

Easy, suitable for novice with little experience

Fairly easy, suitable for beginner with some experience

Fairly difficult, suitable for competent DIY mechanic

Difficult, suitable for experienced DIY mechanic

Very difficult, suitable for expert DIY or professional

Specifications

General

Engine type:

1.2 L	4-cylinder in-line petrol double overhead camshaft (DOHC) 16v variable valve timing
Engine code	G4LA
Bore	71.0 mm
Stroke...	78.8 mm
Capacity...	1248 cc
Firing order..	1-3-4-2
No. 1 cylinder location	Timing (right-hand) end of the engine
Direction of crankshaft rotation	Clockwise (seen from the right-hand side of the vehicle)
Compression ratio	10.5 : 1
Output:	
Maximum power..	64 kW @ 6000 rpm
Maximum torque	119 Nm @ 4000 rpm

Lubrication system

Minimum system pressure:	
At idle speed..	0.76 bar
Pump outer rotor-to-housing clearance.......................	0.180 to 0.258mm
Rotor axial clearance	0.040 to 0.090mm

Torque wrench settings

	Nm	lbf ft
Camshaft housing-to-cylinder head bolts	8	6
Front camshaft housing bolt caps	12	9
Camshaft housing bolt caps	19	14
Connecting rod bolts:	13	10
Crankshaft pulley bolt	60	44
Cylinder head bolts: *		
Stage 1	15	11
Stage 2	Angle-tighten a further 90°	
Stage 3	Angle-tighten a further 120°	
Cylinder head cover bolts	8	7
Engine/transmission mountings:		
Engine mounting bracket and body fixing bolt.	56	42
Engine mounting bracket and engine support bracket fixing bolt . . .	56	42
Engine mounting bracket and engine support bracket fixing nut . . .	56	42
Transaxle mounting bracket and body fixing bolt	56	42
Transaxle mounting insulator and transaxle support bracket fixing bolt. .	56	42
Rear mounting rod-to-subframe:	56	42
Rear mounting rod-to-transmission bracket	56	42
Rear roll stopper bracket and rear roll stopper support bracket bolt. .	56	42
Flywheel bolts: *	74	54
Lower crankcase/Main bearing cap bolts:		
Stage 1	20	14
Stage 2	Angle-tighten a further 90°	
Oil pump cover screws.	7	5
Oil pump bolts	11	8
Oil pressure warning switch	10	7
Oil screen bolt	11	8
Sump drain plug.	39	29
Sump bolts:	11	8
Timing belt tensioner nut	11	8
Timing chain cover bolts		
M6 bolts	10	7
M8 bolts	21	14
M10 bolts	48	36

*Do not re-use

---

1 General information

How to use this Chapter

1 This Part of Chapter 2 is devoted to in-car repair procedures for the 1.2-litre Double OverHead Camshaft (DOHC) 16v petrol engine. Part B covers the removal of the engine/transmission as a unit, and describes the engine dismantling and overhaul procedures.

2 In Part A, the assumption is made that the engine is installed in the car, with all ancillaries connected. If the engine has been removed for overhaul, the preliminary dismantling information which precedes each operation may be ignored.

3 Note that while it may be possible physically to overhaul items such as the piston/connecting rod assemblies with the engine in the vehicle, such tasks are not usually carried out as separate operations and usually require the execution of several additional procedures (not to mention the cleaning of components and of oilways). For this reason, all such tasks are classed as major overhaul procedures and are described in Chapter 2B.

Engine description

4 The engine covered in this Part of Chapter 2 is a water-cooled, double overhead camshaft (DOHC), in-line four-cylinder unit, with cast-aluminium cylinder block and aluminium-alloy cylinder head. The engine is mounted transversely at the front of the car, with the transmission bolted to the left-hand end.

5 The intake and exhaust camshafts act directly onto their respective valves/followers. The valve followers incorporate hydraulic compensation elements, which maintain the correct clearance at all times, and are 'maintenance free'. A timing chain, driven by the crankshaft sprocket, rotates the camshafts. In earlier models, a variable valve timing unit (VVT) varies the position of the intake camshaft in relation to the crankshaft. Later models have a dual VVT system, and alter the positions of both camshafts. This variable valve timing results in increased output/driveability, and reduced exhaust emissions. The operation of the VVT unit is actuated by engine oil pressure, controlled by an electrically operated solenoid valve(s), itself controlled by the engine management ECU. The cylinder head houses the inlet and exhaust valves, which are closed by coil springs, and run in guides pressed into the cylinder head.

6 The cylinder head contains integral oilways which supply and lubricate the followers (hydraulic tappets).

7 The crankshaft is supported by five main bearings, and endfloat is controlled by a thrust bearing fitted to the upper section of the second main bearing.

8 Engine coolant is circulated by a pump, driven by the auxiliary drivebelt. For details of the cooling system, refer to Chapter 3.

9 Lubricant is circulated under pressure by a pump, driven from the front of the crankshaft. Oil is drawn from the sump through a strainer, and then forced through an externally-mounted, renewable screw-on filter. From there, it is distributed to the cylinder head,

where it lubricates the camshaft journals and tappets, and also to the crankcase, where it lubricates the main bearings, connecting rod big and small-ends, gudgeon pins and cylinder bores.

Repair operations possible with the engine in the car

10 The following operations can be carried out with the engine in the car:
a) Compression pressure – testing
b) Camshaft housing – removal and refitting.
c) Timing chain covers – removal and refitting
d) Timing chain – removal, refitting and adjustment
e) Camshafts and followers – removal, inspection and refitting.
f) Cylinder head – removal and refitting.
g) Cylinder head and pistons* – decarbonising.
h) Sump – removal and refitting.
i) Oil pump – removal and refitting.
j) Crankshaft oil seals – renewal.
k) Engine mountings – inspection and renewal.
l) Flywheel – inspection and renewal.

Note: *Although it is possible to remove these components with the engine in place, for reasons of access and cleanliness it is recommended that the engine be removed.

2 Compression test – description and interpretation

1 When engine performance is down, or if misfiring occurs which cannot be attributed to the ignition or fuel systems, a compression test can provide diagnostic clues as to the engine's condition. If the test is performed regularly, it can give warning of trouble before any other symptoms become apparent.
2 The engine must be fully warmed-up to normal operating temperature, the battery must be fully charged, and all the spark plugs must be removed (see Chapter 1 Section 15). The aid of an assistant will also be required.
3 Disable the ignition by disconnecting the ignition coil wiring plug as described in Chapter 5B Section 3.

4 Fit a compression tester to the No 1 cylinder spark plug hole – the type of tester which screws into the plug thread is to be preferred.
5 Make sure the battery is fully charged so you can obtain an engine speed of 250 rpm or more. Crank the engine on the starter motor with the accelerator pedal fully depressed; after one or two revolutions, the compression pressure should build-up to a maximum figure, and then stabilise. Record the highest reading obtained.
6 Repeat the test on the remaining cylinders, recording the pressure in each.
7 All cylinders should produce very similar pressures; a difference of more than 2 bars between any two cylinders indicates a fault. Note that the compression should build-up quickly in a healthy engine; low compression on the first stroke, followed by gradually increasing pressure on successive strokes, indicates worn piston rings. A low compression reading on the first stroke, which does not build-up during successive strokes, indicates leaking valves or a blown head gasket (a cracked head could also be the cause). Deposits on the undersides of the valve heads can also cause low compression.
8 Hyundai specifies that a healthy engine should have pressure of at least 14.7 bar, with 16.6 bar being ideal. Refer to a Hyundai dealer or other specialist if in doubt as to whether a particular pressure reading is acceptable.
9 If the pressure in any cylinder is low, carry out the following test to isolate the cause. Introduce a teaspoonful of clean oil into that cylinder through its spark plug hole, and repeat the test.
10 If the addition of oil temporarily improves the compression pressure, this indicates that bore or piston wear is responsible for the pressure loss. No improvement suggests that leaking or burnt valves, or a blown head gasket, may be to blame.
11 A low reading from two adjacent cylinders is almost certainly due to the head gasket having blown between them; the presence of coolant in the engine oil will confirm this.
12 If the compression reading is unusually high, the combustion chambers are probably coated with carbon deposits. If this is the

case, the cylinder head should be removed and decarbonised.
13 On completion of the test, refit the spark plugs and reconnect the ignition coil wiring plug.

3 Engine assembly/valve timing settings – general information and usage

Caution: Do not attempt to rotate the engine while the camshafts are locked in position. If the engine is to be left in this state for a long period of time, it is a good idea to place suitable warning notices inside the car, and in the engine compartment. This will reduce the possibility of the engine being accidentally cranked on the starter motor, which is likely to cause damage with the locking tools in place.

1 To accurately set the valve timing for all operations requiring removal and refitting of the timing chain, there are timing marks on the camshaft sprockets which align with the top surface of the cylinder head. If the timing chain is to be re-used, make appropriate marks on the sprockets and chain to aid refitment.
2 Remove the spark plugs as described in Chapter 1 Section 15.
3 Remove the cylinder head cover as described in Section 9.
4 Turn the crankshaft clockwise until the notch on the circumference of the crankshaft pulley aligns with the cast 'T' mark on the timing chain cover (see illustration).
5 The No.1 piston is on the compression stroke when the two marks on the camshafts' sprockets align with each other and the upper surface of the cylinder head (see illustration). If the marks are not aligned, rotate the crankshaft a further 360° clockwise.
6 If the timing chain is to be re-used, with the engine set correctly at TDC on No. 1 cylinder, use paint (or similar) to mark the position of the chain in relation to the camshaft and crankshaft sprockets (see illustration).

3.4 Align the notch in crankshaft pulley with 'T' mark on timing chain cover

3.5 Align the marks on the camshafts with the top edge of the cylinder head

3.6 Mark the position of the chain and camshaft sprockets

4.4 Alternator upper mounting bracket bolts

4.5 Remove the coolant pump pulley

11 Carefully apply sealant to the timing chain cover (**see illustration**), and refit the cover within 5 minutes. After that, the sealant will have hardened too much.

12 Tighten all bolts to the required torque setting.

13 The remainder of refitting is a reversal of removal.

5 Timing chain – general information, removal and refitting

4.9 Gradually prise away the timing chain cover

4 Timing chain cover – removal and refitting

Removal

1 Remove the right-hand engine mounting assembly as described in Section 13.

2 Slacken the coolant pump pulley bolts, then remove the auxiliary drivebelt as described in Chapter 1 Section 5.

3 Remove the alternator as described in Chapter. 5A Section 6

4 Undo the 2 bolts and remove the alternator upper mounting bracket and lifting eye (**see illustration**).

5 Fully unscrew the retaining bolts and remove the coolant pump pulley (**see illustration**).

6 Remove the cylinder head cover as described in Section 9.

7 Remove the crankshaft pulley as described in Section 7.

8 Remove the coolant pump as described in Chapter 3 Section 7.

9 Undo the retaining bolts, then carefully and gradually prise the timing chain cover from place (**see illustration**). There are specified points around the edge to be used for prising off the cover.

Caution: Take care when prising the cover from place. Do not lever between the sealing surfaces as they are easily damaged.

Refitting

10 Before refitting the timing chain cover, make sure all residue of old gaskets and sealants are removed from the required surfaces.

General information

1 The primary function of the timing chain is to drive the camshafts. Should the chain slip or break in service, the valve timing will be disturbed and piston-to-valve contact will occur, resulting in serious engine damage.

Removal

2 Set the engine as described in Section 3.

3 Remove the air filter assembly as described in Chapter 4A Section 2.

4 Remove the timing chain cover as described in Section 4.

5 Remove the spark plugs as described in Chapter 1 Section 15.

6 Undo the 2 bolts and remove the timing chain upper guide (**see illustration**).

7 Undo the 2 bolts and remove the timing chain crank guide (**see illustration**).

8 Compress the tensioner arm, then insert a 1.5 mm pin to lock the tensioner in place (**see illustration**).

9 Undo the 2 bolts and remove the tensioner assembly.

10 If the timing chain is to be re-used, make alignment marks between the chain, camshaft sprockets, and crankshaft sprocket.

11 Taking care not to disturb the positions

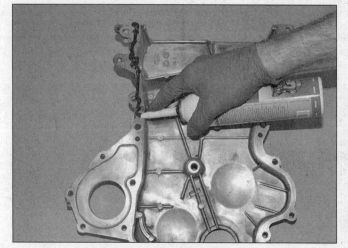

4.11 Apply the sealant around the inside of the holes on the timing chain cover

5.6 Timing chain upper guide bolts

5.7 Remove the timing chain crank guide

5.8 Use a pin to lock the tensioner in place

of the camshafts or crankshaft, remove the timing chain **(see illustration)**.

12 Check the timing chain carefully for any signs of uneven wear. Renew it if there is the slightest doubt about its condition. If the engine is undergoing an overhaul, renew the chain as a matter of course, regardless of its apparent condition. The cost of a new chain is nothing compared with the cost of repairs should it break in service. If signs of oil contamination are found, trace the source of the oil leak and rectify it. Wash down the engine timing chain area and all related components to remove all traces of oil.

Refitting

13 Thoroughly clean the timing chain sprockets. Check that the tensioner pulley rotates freely and smoothly. If necessary, renew it as described in Section 6.

14 Ensure the camshafts and crankshaft are set as described in Section 3.

15 Refit the timing chain lower guide, and tighten the retaining bolts to the specified torque.

16 Install the timing chain. We recommend fitting the chain around the sprockets in the following order: crankshaft sprocket, oil pump sprocket, timing chain guide, intake camshaft sprocket, exhaust camshaft sprocket. The timing mark of each sprocket should be matched with timing mark (coloured link) of the timing chain.

17 Tightening all bolts to the specified torque, install the timing chain tensioner and remove the locking pin.

18 Install the timing chain crank guide, ensuring that the central mark below the flat surface is facing outwards **(see illustration)**, then the timing chain upper guide, tightening all bolts to the specified torque.

19 Turn the crankshaft clockwise for 2 revolutions and check that the timing marks still line up.

Note: *Always turn the crankshaft clockwise. Turning the crankshaft counter-clockwise before building up oil pressure in the hydraulic timing chain tensioner could result in the chain disengaging from the sprocket teeth.*

20 The remainder of refitting is a reversal of removal.

6 Timing chain tensioner and sprockets – removal, inspection and refitting

Timing chain tensioner

Removal

1 Remove the timing chain as described in Section 5.

2 Remove the timing chain tensioner as described in Section 5.

Inspection

3 Wipe the tensioner clean but do not use solvents that may contaminate the bearings. Spin the tensioner pulley on its hub by hand. Stiff movement or excessive freeplay is an indication of severe wear; the tensioner is not a serviceable component, and should be renewed.

Refitting

4 Slide the tensioner pulley onto the mounting stud, and fit the retaining nut, tightening it to the specified torque.

5.11 Remove the timing chain

5.18 Ensure that chain crank guide central mark (arrowed) faces outwards

6.10 Install the crankshaft sprocket with the indentation facing outwards

7.2 Prevent the pulley from rotating, then slacken the bolt

5 Refit the timing chain as described in Section 5.

Crankshaft sprocket

Removal

6 Remove the timing chain as described in Section 5.

7 Slide off the crankshaft sprocket.

Inspection

8 Check the sprocket teeth for damage. If damaged, replace the sprocket.

9 Wipe clean the sprocket and crankshaft mating surfaces.

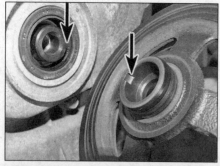

7.4 Align the keyway with the key

Refitting

10 Slide the sprocket into place on the end of the crankshaft, aligning the key with with keyway, and ensuring that the small indentation on the surface faces outwards from the engine **(see illustration)**.

11 Refit the timing chain as described in Section 5.

7 Crankshaft pulley – removal and refitting

Removal

1 Remove the auxiliary drivebelt as described in Chapter 1 Section 5.

2 In order to prevent crankshaft rotation as the pulley bolt is slackened, Hyundai use special tool No. 09231-2B100, which locates across the starter motor aperture, and engages with the flywheel ring-gear teeth once the starter motor has been removed **(see illustration)**. In the absence of this tool, a crankshaft pulley holding tool will prevent the pulley from moving as the bolt is undone.

3 Remove the bolt and withdraw the pulley.

Refitting

4 Refitting is a reversal of removal. Align

the keyway in the pulley with the key in the crankshaft, then refit the pulley, and tighten the bolt to the specified torque **(see illustration)**. Prevent the crankshaft from rotating using the method employed on removal.

8 Oil seals – renewal

Crankshaft oil seals

Right-hand side oil seal

1 The seal is located on the right-hand end of the crankshaft. Remove the crankshaft pulley as described in Section 7.

2 Carefully drill a small hole in the side of the oil seal **(see illustration)**.

3 Screw a self-tapping screw into the hole, then pull out the oil seal using a pair of long-nosed pliers **(see illustration)**.

4 Clean the seating in the housing and the surface of the crankshaft. To prevent damage to the new oil seal as it is being fitted, lubricate the seal and an oil seal-fitting sleeve.

5 Lubricate the oil seal lip with clean engine oil then offer it up to the timing chain cover. Ensure that the sealing lip is facing inwards **(see illustration)**.

8.2 Drill a small hole in the oil seal

8.3 Insert a screw, then pull the seal out with pliers

8.5 Locate the new oil seal on the timing chain cover with the sealing lips facing inwards

8.6 Using a suitable drift, drive the oil seal into the casing

8.9a Drill a hole in the oil seal ...

8.9b ... the screw in a self-tapping screw ...

8.9c ... and use grip to remove

8.11a Locate the seal and guide sleeve over the end of the crankshaft ...

8.11b ... then drive the seal squarely into place until the outer edge is flush with the cylinder block/sump

6 Using a suitable drift, drive the oil seal squarely into the casing **(see illustration)**. Remove the fitting sleeve.

7 Refit the crankshaft pulley as described in Section 7.

Left-hand side oil seal

Note: *The seal is located on the left-hand end of the crankshaft*

8 Remove the flywheel as described in Section 12.

9 Drill a small hole in the oil seal, then screw in a self-tapping screw **(see illustrations)**.

10 Clean the cylinder block mating face, and the seal contact face on the crankshaft.

11 Lubricate the lip of the new seal, then fit the seal over a guide sleeve (often supplied with the new seal). Position the sleeve over the end of the crankshaft, then drive the seal squarely into place **(see illustrations)**.

12 Refit the flywheel as described in Section 12.

9 Cylinder head cover – removal and refitting

Removal

1 Remove the air filter as described in Chapter 4A Section 2.

2 Disconnect the spark plug leads, noting which lead goes to which cylinder **(see illustration)**.

Caution: When removing the spark plug lead, pull on the spark plug boot and not the cable because you could damage it.

3 Slide back the sleeve, release the clamp and disconnect the front breather hose **(see illustration)**.

4 Disconnect the rear breather hose.

5 Disconnect the coolant temperature sensor, then undo the 3 bolts and move the accelerator cable and wiring loom to the side.

9.2 Pull the spark plug HT caps upwards from place

9.3 Disconnect the front breather hose

9.6 Depress the clip and disconnect the camshaft position sensor wiring plug

9.7 Air filter mounting bracket bolt

6 Disconnect the camshaft position sensor wiring plug **(see illustration)**.

7 Undo the bolt and remove the air filter mounting bracket **(see illustration)**.

8 Undo the retaining bolts and remove the cylinder head cover **(see illustration)**.

9 Examine the condition of the head cover rubber seal, and renew if necessary.

Refitting

10 Where necessary, fit a new seal to the cylinder head cover **(see illustration)**.

11 Refit the cylinder head cover, then gradually and evenly, tighten the retaining bolts to the specified torque.

12 The remainder of refitting is a reversal of removal.

10 Camshafts and followers
– removal, inspection and refitting

Removal

1 Remove the timing chain as described in Section 5.

2 Gradually and evenly, undo the retaining bolts and lift the bearing caps from place **(see illustrations)**. The caps are clearly marked for each intake and exhaust camshaft.

3 Carefully lift the camshafts from position.

Note: *Mark one of the camshafts and the cylinder head so you know which one goes where.*

4 Remove the rockers and cam followers from their locations in the cylinder head and place them in an oil-tight compartmented box labelled 1 to 8 (intake) and 1 to 8 (exhaust)

9.8 Undo the bolts and remove the cover

9.10 Ensure the seal locates correctly in the cover groove

10.2a Undo the retaining bolts and remove the caps

10.2b The bearing caps are marked for identification

10.4a Lift the rockers and cam followers from place ...

10.4b ... and store them in order

10.8 Carefully lay the camshafts in place

(see illustrations). Alternatively, place them into individual storage jars or containers suitably marked. Fill the box or the jars with clean engine oil until each cam follower is just submerged.

Inspection

5 Examine the camshaft bearing surfaces and cam lobes for signs of wear ridges and scoring. If you see any signs of wear or damage, take the camshaft to an automotive machine shop.

6 Examine the cam follower bearing surfaces which contact the camshaft lobes for wear ridges and scoring. Renew any follower on which these conditions are apparent. If a follower bearing surface is badly scored, also examine the corresponding lobe on the camshaft for wear, as it is likely that both will be worn. Renew worn components as necessary.

Refitting

Note: *Thoroughly clean all parts to be reused.*
7 Re-install the cam followers and rocker arms into their original locations.

8 Lubricate the camshaft bearing locations and the rocker arms with clean engine oil, then carefully lay the camshafts into their original locations in the cylinder head **(see illustration)**. Ensure the timing marks on the camshaft sprockets align with the upper surface of the cylinder head, as described in Section 3.

9 Lubricate the camshaft bearing surfaces, then refit the bearing caps to their original

locations. Ensure the arrows on the caps point to the outside of the engine **(see illustration)**. Insert the retaining bolts, then gradually and evenly, tighten the bolts to their specified torque setting.

Caution: It's essential that the bolts are tightened gradually and evenly. If the camshafts are tensioner unevenly, they may fracture!

10 Thereafter, refitting is a reversal of removal.

11 Cylinder head –
removal and refitting

Removal

1 Disconnect the battery negative lead as described in Chapter 5A Section 4.

2 Remove the timing chain as described in Section 5.

3 Remove the throttle body as described in Chapter 4A Section 10.

4 Remove the intake manifold as described in Section 4A Section 11.

5 Remove the exhaust manifold as described in Chapter 4A Section 12.

6 Drain the engine coolant as described in Chapter 1 Section 25.

7 Remove the rockers and camshaft followers as described in Section 10.

8 Undo the retaining bolt and remove the camshaft position sensor from the left-hand end of the cylinder head **(see illustration)**.

9 Disconnect the heater pipe from the cylinder head.

10 Working gradually from the centre outwards, undo and remove the cylinder head bolts, loosening each half a turn at a time. Discard the bolts, because they should not be re-used.

11 Lift the cylinder head off the cylinder block and place on wooden blocks on a bench. If it is stuck tight insert pieces of wood into the exhaust ports, and use them as levers to rock the head off the block. On no account drive levers into the gasket joint, or attempt to tap the head sideways, as it is located on positioning dowels. Remove the cylinder head gasket and discard.

12 Refer to Chapter 2B Section 6 for cylinder head dismantling and inspection procedures.

Preparation for refitting

13 The mating faces of the cylinder head and cylinder block must be perfectly clean before refitting the head. Use a hard plastic or wooden scraper to remove all traces of gasket and carbon; also clean the piston crowns. Take particular care when cleaning the piston crowns as the soft aluminium alloy is easily damaged. Make sure that the carbon is not allowed to enter the oil and water passages – this is particularly important for the lubrication system, because carbon could block the oil supply to the engine's components. Using adhesive tape and paper, seal the water, oil and bolt holes in the cylinder block. To prevent carbon entering the gap between the pistons and bores, smear a little grease in the gap. After cleaning each piston, use a small brush to remove all traces of grease and carbon from the gap, then wipe away the remainder with a clean rag. Clean all the pistons in the same way.

14 Check the mating surfaces of the cylinder block and the cylinder head for nicks, deep scratches and other damage. If slight, they may be removed carefully with a file, but if excessive, machining may be the only alternative to renewal. If warpage of the cylinder head gasket surface is suspected, use a straight-edge to check it for distortion as described in Chapter 2B Section 7.

15 Do not re-use the cylinder head bolts.

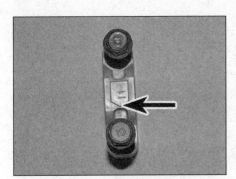

10.9 The arrows on the bearing caps must point to the outside of the engine

11.8 Camshaft position sensor retaining bolt

11.16a Apply sealant to the top edge at the front ...

11.16b ... and rear of the cylinder block surface

11.17a Locate the new gasket over the dowels ...

11.17b ... then apply a thin smear of sealant to the same areas at the front ...

11.17c ... and the rear

11.18 Lower the cylinder head over the dowels

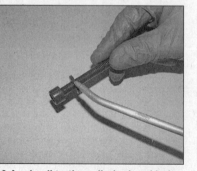

11.19 Apply oil to the cylinder head bolt washers

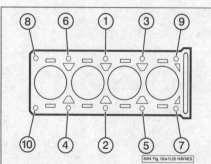

11.20 Cylinder head bolt tightening sequence

Refitting

16 Apply suitable sealant (Hyundai TB1217/LT5900 or equivalent) to the cylinder block top surface as shown **(see illustrations)**.

17 Place the gasket on the cylinder block, taking care that it is the right way up and the right way round, and apply some sealant in the same area **(see illustrations)**.

18 Lower the cylinder head onto the block so that it locates on the positioning dowels **(see illustration)**.

19 Apply a small drop of oil to the cylinder head bolt washers **(see illustration)**.

20 Lower the new cylinder head bolts carefully into their positions. Don't drop the bolts into place – the threads may be damaged. Working in the sequence shown, tighten the bolts and washers to the specified torque **(see illustration)**.

Note: *Special tool SST (09221-4A000) or a 12-bladed Torx socket is needed to fit the new cylinder head bolts.*

21 The remainder of refitting is a reversal of removal, noting the following points:
a) *Tighten all fasteners to their specified torque.*
b) *Refill the cooling system as described in Chapter 1 Section 25.*
c) *Reconnect the battery negative lead as described in Chapter 5A Section 4.*

12 Flywheel/driveplate –
removal, inspection and refitting

Removal

1 Remove the clutch assembly as described in Chapter 6 Section 3.

2 The flywheel/driveplate must now be held stationary while the 6 bolts are loosened. To prevent the flywheel/driveplate from rotating, using a suitable tool (Hyundai tool No. 09231-2B100 or equivalent) to lock the flywheel/driveplate in place **(see illustration)**.

3 Undo the mounting bolts and remove the flywheel. Discard the bolts – new ones must be fitted.

12.2 Lock the flywheel with a suitable tool

12.8 Align the pin with the corresponding hole

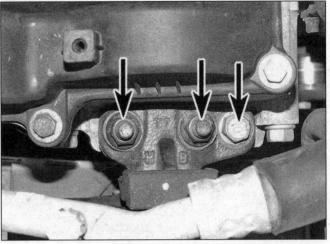

13.6 Mounting-to-support bracket bolt/nuts

Inspection

4 If the flywheel's clutch mating surface is deeply scored, cracked or otherwise damaged, the flywheel must be renewed. However, it may be possible to have it surface-ground; seek the advice of a Hyundai dealer or engine reconditioning specialist.

5 If the ring gear is badly worn or has missing teeth, the flywheel/driveplate must be renewed.

Refitting

6 Clean the mating surfaces of the flywheel/driveplate and crankshaft. Remove any remaining locking compound from the threads of the crankshaft holes, using the correct-size tap, if available.

7 If the new retaining bolts are not supplied with their threads already precoated, apply a suitable thread-locking compound to the threads of each bolt.

8 Offer up the flywheel/driveplate to the crankshaft, aligning the pin in the crankshaft with the corresponding hole in the flywheel/driveplate, and fit the new retaining bolts **(see illustration)**.

9 Lock the flywheel/driveplate using the special tool, and tighten the retaining bolts to the specified torque.

10 Refit the clutch as described in Chapter 6 Section 3.

13 Engine mountings – inspection and renewal

Inspection

1 Firmly apply the handbrake, then jack up the front of the car and support it securely on axle stands as described in 'Vehicle jacking and support'.

2 Check the mounting rubbers to see if they are cracked, hardened or separated from the

metal at any point; renew the mounting if any such damage or deterioration is evident.

3 Check that all the mounting's fasteners are securely tightened; use a torque wrench to check if possible.

4 Using a large screwdriver or a crowbar, check for wear in the mounting by carefully levering against it to check for free play. Where this is not possible enlist the aid of an assistant to move the engine/transmission back-and-forth, or from side-to-side, while you watch the mounting. While some free play is to be expected, even from new components, excessive wear should be obvious. If excessive free play is found, check first that the fasteners are correctly secured, then renew any worn components as described below.

Renewal

Right-hand mounting

5 Place a trolley jack beneath the right-hand side of the engine, with a block of wood on the jack head. Raise the jack until it is supporting the weight of the engine.

6 Undo the bolts securing the mounting to the vehicle body, and the bolt/nuts securing the mounting to the support bracket **(see illustration)**. Remove the mounting.

7 Refitting is a reversal of removal, tightening the retaining bolts to the specified torque.

Left-hand mounting

8 Remove the battery and battery tray as described in Chapter 5A Section 4.

9 Place a trolley jack beneath the transmission, with a block of wood on the jack head. Raise the jack until it is supporting the weight of the engine/transmission.

10 Undo the retaining bolts securing the mounting to the vehicle body and support bracket, and remove the mounting **(see illustration)**.

11 Refitting is a reversal of removal, tightening the retaining bolts to their specified torque.

Rear mounting

12 Raise the front of the vehicle and support it securely on axle stands, as described in 'Vehicle jacking and support'.

13 Undo the bolts and manoeuvre the rear mounting link rod from place **(see illustration)**.

Note: Mark the rear mounting link rod direction for proper installation.

14 Refitting is a reversal of removal, tightening the retaining bolts to their specified torque.

13.10 Support bracket-to-mounting bolts

13.13 Undo the bolts and remove the rear mounting link rod

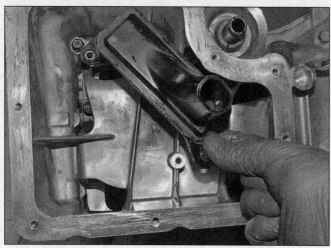

14.4 Remove the oil pick-up tube

15.3 Oil pump retaining bolts

14 Sump – removal and refitting

Removal

1 Firmly apply the handbrake, then jack up the front of the car and support it securely on axle stands as described in 'Vehicle jacking and support'.

2 Drain the engine oil as described in Chapter 1 Section 4.

3 Undo the bolts and remove the sump, using Hyundai special tool SST(09215-3C000) or a similarly flat-edged tool.

● Insert the tool between the ladder frame and the sump by tapping it with a plastic hammer.

● Be careful not to damage the contact surfaces of the ladder frame and sump.

4 If required, undo the bolts and remove the oil pick-up tube **(see illustration)**. Renew the O-ring seal.

5 Thoroughly clean the sump and the cylinder block mating surfaces ensuring that all traces of old sealant are removed.

Refitting

6 Remove all traces of old gasket sealant from all facing surfaces using a gasket scraper.

7 Before offering up the sump, apply a 3-4 mm bead of liquid sealant (Hyundai TB1217H or LT5900H or equivalent).

Note: *The sump must be assembled within 5 minutes of the sealant being applied or it will become too hard to form a proper seal.*

8 Gradually and evenly tighten the sump retaining bolts to the specified torque.

9 Refill the engine with oil as described in Chapter 1 Section 4.

15 Oil pump – removal, inspection and refitting

Removal

1 Drain the engine oil and remove the oil filter as described in Chapter 1 Section 4.

2 Remove the timing chain as described in Section 5.

3 Undo the oil pump retaining bolts and remove the oil pump from the engine block **(see illustration)**.

Inspection

4 Inspect the pump rotors, pump casing and cover for any signs of wear or damage. If satisfactory, refit the rotors to the pump casing ensuring that the circular indentation faces outwards **(see illustration)**.

5 If the pump is unworn, lubricate the rotors with clean engine oil then place the cover plate in position. Apply thread locking compound to the retaining screws and tighten the screws securely.

Refitting

6 Ensure that the oil pump and cylinder block mating faces are clean.

7 Locate the pump on the cylinder block, insert the retaining bolts and tighten them progressively to the specified torque.

8 The remainder of refitting is a reversal of removal.

16 Engine oil pressure warning light switch – removal and refitting

1 Raise the front of the vehicle and support it securely on axle stands as described in 'Vehicle jacking and support'.

2 Disconnect the wiring plug from the switch, then unscrew it from the housing **(see illustration)**. Be prepared for oil spillage.

3 Screw the new switch into the housing and tighten it to the specified torque.

4 Reconnect the wiring plug and lower the vehicle to the ground. Check the engine oil level as described in 'Weekly checks'.

15.4 Refit the pump rotor with the circular indentation marks facing outwards

16.2 The oil pressure warning switch is located on the front face of the cylinder block

Chapter 2 Part B
General engine removal and overhaul procedures

Contents

Degrees of difficulty

Easy, suitable for novice with little experience | **Fairly easy,** suitable for beginner with some experience | **Fairly difficult,** suitable for competent DIY mechanic | **Difficult,** suitable for experienced DIY mechanic | **Very difficult,** suitable for expert DIY or professional

Specifications

Cylinder head
Maximum gasket face distortion . . . . 0.05 mm

Valves
Valve stem diameter:
  Intake . . . . 5.465 to 5.480 mm
  Exhaust. . . . . 5.448 to 5.460 mm
Valve clearance: . . . . Hydraulic adjustment

Crankshaft
Endfloat: . . . . 0.07 to 0.25 mm

Pistons
Ring end gap:
  1st compression ring . . . . 0.13 to 0.25 mm
  2nd compression ring. . . . . 0.30 to 0.45 mm
  Oil control ring . . . . 0.1 to 0.4 mm

1 General information

1 Included in this Part of Chapter 2 are details of removing the engine from the car and general overhaul procedures for the cylinder head, cylinder block/crankcase and all other engine internal components.

2 The information given ranges from advice concerning preparation for an overhaul and the purchase of parts, to detailed step-by-step procedures covering removal, inspection, renovation and refitting of engine internal components.

2 Engine overhaul – general information

1 It is not always easy to determine when, or if, an engine should be completely overhauled, as a number of factors must be considered.

2 High mileage is not necessarily an indication that an overhaul is needed, while low mileage does not preclude the need for an overhaul. Frequency of servicing is probably the most important consideration. An engine which has had regular and frequent oil and filter changes, as well as other required maintenance, should give many thousands of miles of reliable service. Conversely, a neglected engine may require an overhaul very early in its life.

3 Excessive oil consumption is an indication that piston rings, valve seals and/or valve guides are in need of attention. Make sure that oil leaks are not responsible before deciding that the rings and/or guides are worn. Perform a compression test, as described in Part A or B of this Chapter (as applicable), to determine the likely cause of the problem.

4 Check the oil pressure with a gauge fitted in place of the oil pressure switch, and compare it with that specified in Part A or B. If it is extremely low, the main and big-end bearings, and/or the oil pump, are probably worn out.

5 Loss of power, rough running, knocking or metallic engine noises, excessive valve gear noise, and high fuel consumption may also point to the need for an overhaul, especially if they are all present at the same time. If a complete service does not remedy the situation, major mechanical work is the only solution.

6 A full engine overhaul involves restoring all internal parts to the specification of a new engine. During a complete overhaul, the pistons and the piston rings are renewed, and the cylinder bores are reconditioned. New main and big-end bearings are generally fitted; if necessary, the crankshaft may be reground, to compensate for wear in the journals. The valves are also serviced as well, since they are usually in less-than-perfect condition at this point. Always pay careful attention to the condition of the oil pump when overhauling the engine, and renew it if there is any doubt as to its serviceability. The end result should be an as-new engine that will give many trouble-free miles.

Note: *Critical cooling system components such as the hoses, thermostat and coolant pump should be renewed when an engine is overhauled. The radiator should be checked carefully, to ensure that it is not clogged or leaking. Also, it is a good idea to renew the oil pump whenever the engine is overhauled.*

7 Before beginning the engine overhaul, read through the entire procedure, to familiarise yourself with the scope and requirements of the job. Overhauling an engine is not difficult if you follow carefully all of the instructions, have the necessary tools and equipment, and pay close attention to all specifications. It can, however, be time-consuming. Plan on the car being off the road for a minimum of two weeks, especially if parts must be taken to an engineering works for repair or reconditioning. Check on the availability of parts and make sure that any necessary special tools and equipment are obtained in advance. Most work can be done with typical hand tools, although a number of precision measuring tools are required for inspecting parts to determine if they must be renewed. Often the engineering works will handle the inspection of parts and offer advice concerning reconditioning and renewal.

Note: *Always wait until the engine has been completely dismantled, and until all components (especially the cylinder block/crankcase and the crankshaft) have been inspected, before deciding what service and repair operations must be performed by an engineering works. The condition of these components will be the major factor to consider when determining whether to overhaul the original engine, or to buy a reconditioned unit. Do not, therefore, purchase parts or have overhaul work done on other components until they have been thoroughly inspected. As a general rule, time is the primary cost of an overhaul, so it does not pay to fit worn or sub-standard parts.*

8 As a final note, to ensure maximum life and minimum trouble from a reconditioned engine, everything must be assembled with care, in a spotlessly-clean environment.

3 Engine removal – methods and precautions

1 If you have decided that the engine must be removed for overhaul or major repair work, several preliminary steps should be taken.

2 Locating a suitable place to work is extremely important. Adequate workspace, along with storage space for the car, will be needed. If a workshop or garage is not available, at the very least, a flat, level, clean work surface is required.

3 Cleaning the engine compartment and engine/transmission before beginning the removal procedure will help keep tools clean and organised.

4 An engine hoist will also be necessary. Make sure the equipment is rated in excess of the weight of the engine (and transmission if both are being removed). Safety is of primary importance, considering the potential hazards involved in lifting the engine out of the car.

5 If this is the first time you have removed an engine, an assistant should ideally be available. Advice and aid from someone more experienced would also be helpful. There are many instances when one person cannot simultaneously perform all of the operations required when lifting the engine out of the vehicle.

6 Plan the operation ahead of time. Before starting work, arrange for the hire of or obtain all of the tools and equipment you will need. Some of the equipment necessary to perform engine removal and installation safely and with relative ease (in addition to an engine hoist) is as follows: a heavy duty trolley jack, complete sets of spanners and sockets (see Tools and working facilities 13 Section 6), wooden blocks, and plenty of rags and cleaning solvent for mopping-up spilled oil, coolant and fuel. If the hoist must be hired, make sure that you arrange for it in advance, and perform all of the operations possible without it beforehand. This will save you money and time.

7 Plan for the car to be out of use for quite a while. An engineering works will be required to perform some of the work, which the do-it-yourselfer cannot accomplish without special equipment. These places often have a busy schedule, so it would be a good idea to consult them before removing the engine, in order to accurately estimate the amount of time required to rebuild or repair components that may need work.

8 During the engine/transmission removal procedure, it is advisable to make notes of the locations of all brackets, cable ties, earthing points, etc, as well as how the wiring harnesses, hoses and electrical connections are attached and routed around the engine and engine compartment. An effective way of doing this is to take a series of photographs of the various components before they are disconnected or removed; the resulting photographs will prove invaluable when the engine/transmission is refitted.

9 Always be extremely careful when removing and refitting the engine. Serious injury can result from careless actions. Plan ahead and take your time, and a job of this nature, although major, can be accomplished successfully.

10 The engine and transmission assembly is removed downwards from the engine compartment on all models described in this manual.

4.7a Bulkhead panel retaining bolts (left-hand side bolts arrowed)

4.7b Press through the connector and grommet

4 Engine and transmission – removal, separation and refitting

Removal

Note: *On models with air conditioning, have the refrigerant circuit evacuated by a Hyundai dealer or suitably equipped repairer. The system will need to be recharged upon completion.*

1 Remove the battery and battery tray as described in Chapter 5A Section 4.

2 Slacken the front roadwheel bolts, raise the front of the vehicle and support it securely on axle stands as described in *'Vehicle jacking and support'*. Remove both front roadwheels.

3 Drain the coolant system as described in Chapter 1 Section 25.

4 Drain the gearbox oil as described in Chapter 7A Section 2.

5 Remove the air filter as described in Chapter 1 Section 21.

6 Remove the wiper motor assembly as described in Chapter 12 Section 15.

7 Undo the retaining bolts and lift out the bulkhead panel, pressing the connector and

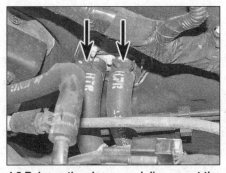

4.8 Release the clamps and disconnect the heating system hoses

rubber grommet through as you do so **(see illustrations)**.

8 Disconnect the heating system hoses from the bulkhead **(see illustration)**.

Note: *One of the hoses is marked 'inlet', and is attached to the passenger side connector.*

9 Remove the cooling fan as described in Chapter 3 Section 5.

10 Disconnect all the individual wiring connectors and harness clips from the various components on the engine and transmission

4.11 Fuel injector wiring loom mounting bolts

to enable the main engine wiring harness to be removed. Make notes or attach labels to each connector to aid reconnection.

11 Undo the mounting bolts and remove the loom from the fuel injectors **(see illustration)**.

12 Disconnect the wiring loom from the fusebox **(see illustration)**.

13 Undo bolt and disconnect wiring loom from battery positive lead.

14 Undo bolt and disconnect earth strap **(see illustration)**.

4.12 Undo the nut and remove the wiring loom from the fusebox

4.14 Unbolt the earth strap from the left-hand chassis member

4.17 Disconnect the servo pipe

4.24 Attach a hoist to the lifting eyes

15 Remove the accelerator cable as described in Chapter 4A Section 4.

16 Disconnect the fuel hose as described in Chapter 4A Section 6.

17 Disconnect the servo vacuum pipe **(see illustration)**.

18 Disconnect the gearchange/selector cables from the transmission as described in Chapter 7A Section 3 or Chapter 7B Section 4.

19 Remove both driveshafts as described in Chapter 8 Section 2.

20 Remove the rear engine mount link rod as described in Chapter 2A Section 13.

Note: *Mark the rear mounting link rod direction for proper installation.*

21 Remove the exhaust front section as described in Chapter 4A Section 13.

22 On models with air-conditioning, remove the compressor as described in Chapter 3 Section 10.

23 Using a floor jack, support the engine and transmission assembly.

Note: *Place a wooden or rubber block between the jack and sump, to avoid the possibility of damage.*

24 Attach a hoist to the engine lifting eyes **(see illustration)**.

25 Undo the engine mounts as described in Chapter 2A Section 13.

26 Make a final check to ensure that all necessary hoses, wiring etc have been disconnected.

Note: *Make a final check to ensure that all necessary hoses, wiring etc have been disconnected.*

27 Carefully lower the engine and gearbox from place, taking care not to damage any other components or bodywork.

Separation

28 Rest the engine/transmission assembly on a firm, flat surface, and use wooden blocks as wedges to keep the unit steady.

29 On manual transmission models, remove the clutch cable bracket **(see illustration)**.

30 Disconnect the reversing light switch wiring plug and the vehicle speed sensor wiring plug.

31 Undo the retaining bolt and remove the crankshaft position sensor from place **(see illustration)**.

32 Remove the gearshift cable bracket.

33 Remove the gearbox upper mounting bolts.

34 Disconnect the alternator wiring loom, then undo the retaining bolt for the bracket and remove from place.

35 Ensure that both engine and transmission are individually supported, then remove the remaining bolts securing the transmission bellhousing to the engine. Note the correct fitted positions of each bolt to aid refitting.

36 Withdraw the transmission from the engine, ensuring that the weight of the transmission is not allowed to hang on the input shaft while it is engaged with the clutch friction plate.

37 If they are loose, remove the locating dowels from the engine or transmission.

4.29 Remove the clutch cable bracket

4.31 Crankshaft position sensor retaining bolt

Connection

38 If the engine and transmission have not been separated, proceed to Refitting.

39 Ensure the transmission input shaft splines are clean and free from any debris.

40 Ensure that the locating dowels are correctly positioned in the engine or transmission, and that the release bearing is correctly engaged with the fork.

41 Carefully offer the transmission to the engine, until the locating dowels are engaged. Ensure that the weight of the transmission is not allowed to hang on the input shaft as it is engaged with the clutch friction plate.

42 Refit the the engine-to-transmission bolts, and tighten them to the specified torque.

43 Refit and reconnect the wiring harness to the components on the engine/transmission assembly, making sure it is correctly routed.

Refitting

44 Refitting is a reversal of removal, taking care to tighten all bolts to their specified torque, noting the following points:

Refill the gearbox oil as described in Chapter 7A Section 2 or Chapter 7B.

Refill the coolant system as described in Chapter 1 Section 25.

45 Where applicable, have the refrigerant circuit recharged by a Hyundai dealer or suitably equipped repairer.

5 Engine overhaul – dismantling sequence

1 It is preferable to dismantle and work on the engine with it mounted on a portable engine stand. These stands can generally be hired from a tool hire shop. Before the engine is mounted on a stand, the flywheel/driveplate should be removed, so that the stand bolts can be tightened into the end of the cylinder block.

2 If a stand is not available, it is possible to dismantle the engine with it blocked up on a sturdy workbench, or on the floor. Be extra careful not to tip or drop the engine when working without a stand.

3 If a reconditioned engine is to be obtained, or if the original engine is to be overhauled, the external components in the following list must be removed first. These components can then be transferred to the reconditioned engine, or refitted to the existing engine after overhaul.

a) Alternator (including mounting brackets, where fitted) (Chapter 5A Section 6).
b) Engine mounting brackets.
c) The ignition system and HT components including all sensors, etc. (Chapter 5B).
d) The fuel injection system components (Chapter 4A).
e) Intake manifold (Chapter 4A Section 11).
f) All remaining electrical switches, actuators, sensors and the engine wiring harness.
g) Engine oil level dipstick.
h) Oil filter (Chapter 1 Section 4).
i) Cooling system components (Chapter 3).
j) Flywheel (Chapter 2A Section 12).

Note: When removing the external components from the engine, pay close attention to details that may be helpful or important during refitting. Note the fitted position of gaskets, seals, spacers, pins, washers, bolts, and other small components.

4 If a 'short' engine is to be obtained (cylinder block, crankshaft, pistons and connecting rods all assembled), then the cylinder head, sump, oil pump, timing chain, sprockets and tensioner will have to be removed also.

5 If a complete overhaul of the existing engine is being undertaken, the engine can be dismantled, in the order given below.

a) Flywheel.
b) Timing chain, sprockets and tensioner.
c) Intake manifold.
d) Cylinder head.
e) Sump.
f) Oil pump.
g) Pistons/connecting rods.
h) Crankshaft.

6 Cylinder head – dismantling

Note: New and reconditioned cylinder heads are available from the manufacturer, and from engine reconditioning specialists. Some specialist tools are required for dismantling and inspection, and new components may not be readily available. It may therefore be more practical and economical to obtain a reconditioned head, rather than overhaul the original head.

1 During dismantling, it is essential that each valve is stored together with its collets, retainer, spring, and spring seat. The valves should also be kept in their correct sequence, unless they are so badly worn that they are to be renewed. If they are going to be kept and used again, place each valve assembly in a labelled polythene bag or similar small container **(see illustration)**. Number the bags or containers 1 to 8, or 1 to 8 inlet, and 1 to 8 exhaust, as applicable. Note that No 1 valve is at the timing belt end of the engine.

2 Remove the cylinder head as described in Chapter 2A Section 11.

3 Remove the rockers and followers as described in Chapter 2A Section 10.

4 Starting with valve No 1, compress the valve spring using a suitable spring compression tool, and extract the split collets from the top of the valve stem.

5 Remove the spring retainer, valve spring and the valve.

6 Using a suitable tool, remove the valve stem seal **(see illustration)**.

7 Remove all the remaining valves in the same way.

6.1 Keep groups of components together in labelled bags or boxes

6.6 Pull the seal from the valve guide

7 Cylinder head and valves – cleaning and inspection

1 Thorough cleaning of the cylinder head and valve components, followed by a detailed inspection, will enable you to decide how much valve service work must be carried out during the engine overhaul. **Note:** *If the engine has been severely overheated, it is best to assume that the cylinder head is warped – check carefully for signs of this.*

Cleaning

2 Scrape away all traces of old gasket material from the cylinder head.
3 Scrape away the carbon from the combustion chambers and ports, then wash the cylinder head thoroughly with paraffin or a suitable solvent.
4 Scrape off any heavy carbon deposits that may have formed on the valves, then use a power-operated wire brush to remove deposits from the valve heads and stems.

Inspection

Note: *Be sure to perform all the following inspection procedures before concluding that the services of a machine shop or engine overhaul specialist are required. Make a list of all items that require attention.*

Cylinder head

5 Inspect the head very carefully for cracks, evidence of coolant leakage, and other damage. If cracks are found, a new cylinder head should be obtained.
6 Use a straight-edge and feeler blade to check that the cylinder head gasket surface is not distorted **(see illustration)**. If it is, it may be possible to have it machined, provided that the cylinder head is not reduced to less than the specified height.
7 Examine the valve seats in each of the combustion chambers. If they are severely pitted, cracked, or burned, they will need to be renewed or recut by an engine overhaul specialist. If they are only slightly pitted, this can be removed by grinding-in the valve heads and seats with fine valve-grinding compound, as described later in this Section.

8 Check the valve guides for wear by inserting the relevant valve, and checking for side-to-side motion of the valve. A very small amount of movement is acceptable. If the movement seems excessive, remove the valve. Measure the valve stem diameter (see later in this Section), and renew the valve if it is worn. If the valve stem is not worn, the wear must be in the valve guide, and the guide must be renewed. The renewal of new valve guides should be entrusted to a Hyundai dealer or engine overhaul specialist, who will have the necessary tools available.
9 If renewing the valve guides, the valve seats should be recut or reground only after the guides have been fitted.
10 Examine the camshaft bearing surfaces in the cylinder head and the bearing caps for signs of wear or damage. If the bearings are excessively worn, consult a Hyundai dealer, or an engine overhaul specialist for further advice.

Valves

11 Examine the head of each valve for pitting, burning, cracks, and general wear. Check the valve stem for scoring and wear ridges. Rotate the valve, and check for any obvious indication that it is bent. Look for pits or excessive wear on the tip of each valve stem. Renew any valve that shows any such signs of wear or damage.
12 If the valve appears satisfactory at this stage, measure the valve stem diameter at several points using a micrometer. Any significant difference in the readings obtained indicates wear of the valve stem. Should any of these conditions be apparent, the valve(s) must be renewed.
13 If the valves are in satisfactory condition, they should be ground (lapped) into their respective seats, to ensure a smooth, gas-tight seal. If the seat is only lightly pitted, or if it has been recut, fine grinding compound should be used to produce the required finish. Coarse valve-grinding compound should not be used, unless a seat is badly burned or deeply pitted. If this is the case, the cylinder head and valves should be inspected, to decide whether seat recutting, or even the renewal of the valve or seat insert (where possible) is required.

14 Valve grinding is carried out as follows. Place the cylinder head upside-down on a bench.
15 Smear a trace of (the appropriate grade of) valve-grinding compound on the seat face, and press a suction grinding tool onto the valve head **(see illustration)**. With a semi-rotary action, grind the valve head to its seat, lifting the valve occasionally to redistribute the grinding compound. A light spring placed under the valve head will greatly ease this operation.
16 If coarse grinding compound is being used, work only until a dull, matt even surface is produced on both the valve seat and the valve, then wipe off the used compound, and repeat the process with fine compound. When a smooth unbroken ring of light grey matt finish is produced on both the valve and seat, the grinding operation is complete. Do not grind-in the valves any further than absolutely necessary, or the seat will be prematurely sunk into the cylinder head.
17 When all the valves have been ground-in, carefully wash off all traces of grinding compound using paraffin or a suitable solvent, before reassembling the cylinder head.

Valve components

18 Examine the valve springs for signs of damage and discoloration. Compare the length of the valve springs with that of a new component, where possible, and if necessary renew the springs.
19 Stand each spring on a flat surface, and check it for squareness. If any of the springs are damaged, distorted or have lost their tension, obtain a complete new set of springs. It is normal to renew the valve springs as a matter of course if a major overhaul is being carried out.
20 Renew the valve stem oil seals regardless of their apparent condition.

8 Cylinder head – reassembly

Reassembly

1 Lubricate the stems of the valves, and insert the valves into their original locations **(see illustration)**. If new valves are being

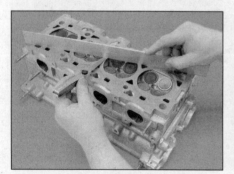

7.6 Check for distortion using a straight-edge

7.15 Grinding-in a valve

8.1 Insert the valves into their original locations

8.2 Press the seal into place using a suitable socket

8.3a Refit the seat ...

8.3b ... spring ...

8.3c ... and cap

fitted, insert them into the locations to which they have been ground.

2 Working on the first valve, dip the new valve stem seal in fresh engine oil. New seals are normally supplied with protective sleeves, which should be fitted to the tops of the valve stems to prevent the collet grooves from damaging the oil seals. If no sleeves

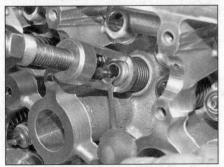

8.4 Locate the split collets

are supplied, wind a little thin tape round the top of the valve stems to protect the seals. Carefully locate the seal over the valve and onto the guide. Take care not to damage the seal as it is passed over the valve stem. Use a suitable socket or tube to press the seal firmly onto the guide **(see illustration)**. Remove the sleeve from the valve stem.

3 Refit the seat, then locate the valve spring on top of it, then refit the spring cap **(see illustrations)**.

4 Fit the compressor tool, then compress the valve spring and locate the split collets in the recess in the valve stem **(see illustration)**. Release the compressor, then repeat the procedure on the remaining valves.

5 With all the valves installed, support the cylinder head on blocks of wood and, using a hammer and interposed block of wood, tap the end of each valve stem to settle the components.

6 Refit the cylinder head as described in Chapter 2A Section 11.

9 Piston/connecting rod assembly – removal

Removal

1 Remove the flywheel as described in Chapter 2A Section 12.

2 Remove the timing chain as described in Chapter 2A Section 5.

3 Remove the cylinder head as described in Section 6.

4 Turn the engine upside down and remove the sump as described in Chapter 2A Section 14. Be prepared for fluid spillage.

5 Remove the ladder frame using special tool SST 09215-3C000 or a similarly flat-bladed tool by inserting its blade between the ladder frame and the cylinder block.

6 If there is a pronounced wear ridge at the top of any bore, it may be necessary to remove it with a scraper or ridge reamer, to avoid piston damage during removal. Such a ridge indicates excess bore wear.

7 Check to see if the big-end caps and connecting rods are numbered. If no numbers are visible, use quick-drying paint, or similar, to mark each connecting rod and big-end cap with its respective cylinder number on the flat machined surface provided. Note that No 1 cylinder is at the timing chain end of the engine.

8 Turn the crankshaft to bring pistons 1 and 4 to BDC (bottom dead centre).

9 Unscrew the bolts from No 1 piston big-end bearing cap, and remove the big-end cap and bearing shell. If the bearing shells are to be re-used, tape the cap and the shell together.

10 Using a hammer handle, push the piston up through the bore, and remove it from the top of the cylinder block. Recover the bearing shell, and tape it to the connecting rod for safe-keeping.

11 Loosely refit the big-end cap to the connecting rod, and secure with the bolts – this will help to keep the components in their correct order.

12 Remove No. 4 assembly in the same way.

13 Turn the crankshaft 180° to bring pistons 2 and 3 to BDC (bottom dead centre), and remove them in the same way.

10 Crankshaft – removal

1 Remove the sump, oil pump/pick-up tube, and flywheel/driveplate as described in Chapter 2A Section 14 or Chapter 2A Section 12.

2 Remove the pistons and connecting rods, as described in Section 9. If no work is to be done on the pistons and connecting rods there is no need to remove the cylinder head, or to push the pistons out of the cylinder bores. The pistons should just be pushed far enough up the bores that they are positioned clear of the crankshaft journals.

3 Remove the ladder frame.

4 Check the crankshaft endfloat as described in Section 13, then proceed as follows.

5 Examine the crankshaft bearing surfaces for signs of wear ridges and scoring. If you see any signs of wear or damage, take the crankshaft to an automotive machine shop. Renew the bearings at the same time.

6 Lift the crankshaft out of the engine, taking care not to damage any of the journals.

11 Cylinder block/crankcase – cleaning and inspection

Cleaning

1 Remove all external components, brackets and electrical switches/sensors from the block. Note the position of any mounting brackets before removal by taking reference pictures. For complete cleaning, the core

plugs should ideally be removed. Drill a small hole in the plugs, and then insert a self-tapping screw into the hole. Pull out the plugs by pulling on the screw with a pair of grips, or by using a slide hammer.

2 Where applicable, undo the retaining bolts and remove the piston oil jet spray tubes from inside the cylinder block.

3 Remove all traces of gasket/sealant from the cylinder block, and from the lower crankcase, taking care not to damage the gasket/sealing surfaces.

4 Remove all oil gallery plugs (where fitted). The plugs are usually very tight – they may have to be drilled out, and the holes retapped. Use new plugs when the engine is reassembled.

5 If the castings are extremely dirty, they should be steam-cleaned.

6 After the castings have been steam-cleaned, clean all oil holes and oil galleries one more time. Flush all internal passages with warm water until the water runs clear. Dry thoroughly, and apply a light film of oil to all mating surfaces, to prevent rusting. Also oil the cylinder bores. If you have access to compressed air, use it to speed up the drying process, and to blow out all the oil holes and galleries.

 Warning: Wear eye protection when using compressed air.

7 If the castings are not very dirty, you can do an adequate cleaning job with hot (as hot as you can stand!), soapy water and a stiff brush. Take plenty of time, and do a thorough job. Regardless of the cleaning method used, be sure to clean all oil holes and galleries very thoroughly, and to dry all components well. Protect the cylinder bores as described above, to prevent rusting.

8 All threaded holes must be clean, to ensure accurate torque readings during reassembly. To clean the threads, run the correct-size tap into each of the holes to remove rust, corrosion, thread sealant or sludge, and to restore damaged threads **(see illustration)**. If possible, use compressed air to clear the holes of debris produced by this operation.

9 Ensure that all threaded holes in the cylinder block are dry.

10 After coating the mating surfaces of the new core plugs with suitable sealant, fit them to the cylinder block. Make sure that they

11.8 Clean the cylinder block threads using a correct-sized tap

are driven in straight and seated correctly, or leakage could result.

11 Where applicable, fit the new oil gallery plugs.

12 If the engine is not going to be reassembled right away, cover it with a large plastic bag to keep it clean; protect all mating surfaces and the cylinder bores as described above, to prevent rusting.

Inspection

13 Visually check the castings for cracks and corrosion. Look for stripped threads in the threaded holes. If there has been any history of internal water leakage, it may be worthwhile having an engine reconditioning specialist check the cylinder block with special equipment. If defects are found, have them repaired if possible, or renew the assembly.

14 Check each cylinder bore for scuffing and scoring. Check for signs of a wear ridge at the top of the cylinder, indicating that the bore is excessively worn.

15 Accurate measuring of the cylinder bores requires specialised equipment and experience. We recommend having the bores measured by an engine reconditioning specialist who will also be able to supply appropriate pistons should a rebore be necessary.

16 If the cylinder bores and pistons are in reasonably good condition, and not worn beyond the specified limits, and if the piston-to-bore clearances can be maintained, then it will only be necessary to renew the piston rings. If this is the case, the cylinder bores must be honed to allow the new piston rings to bed-in correctly and provide the best possible seal. An engine reconditioning specialist will carry out this work at moderate cost.

17 If the engine is not going to be reassembled right away, cover it with a large plastic bag to keep it clean and prevent rusting. If the engine is ready for reassembly Apply suitable sealant to the new oil gallery plugs, and insert them into the holes in the block. Tighten the plugs securely

18 Where applicable, refit the piston oil jet spray tubes to the cylinder block, and securely tighten the retaining bolts. Bend over the tabs to lock the bolts.

19 Refit all the external components and electrical switches/sensors removed prior to cleaning.

12 Piston/connecting rod assembly – cleaning and inspection

1 Before the inspection process can begin, the piston/connecting rod assemblies must be cleaned, and the original piston rings removed from the pistons.

Note: *Always use new piston rings when the engine is reassembled.*

2 Carefully expand the old rings over the top of the pistons. The use of two or three old feeler blades will be helpful in preventing the rings dropping into empty grooves. Be careful not to scratch the piston with the ends of the ring. The rings are brittle, and will snap if they are spread too far. They are also very sharp – protect your hands and fingers.

3 Scrape away all traces of carbon from the top of the piston. A hand-held wire brush (or a piece of fine emery cloth) can be used, once the majority of the deposits have been scraped away.

4 Remove the carbon from the ring grooves in the piston, using an old ring. Break the ring in half to do this (be careful not to cut your fingers – piston rings are sharp). Be careful to remove only the carbon deposits – do not remove any metal, and do not nick or scratch the sides of the ring grooves.

5 Once the deposits have been removed, clean the piston/connecting rod assembly with paraffin or a suitable solvent, and dry thoroughly. Make sure that the oil return holes in the ring grooves are clear.

6 If the pistons and cylinder bores are not damaged or worn excessively, and if the cylinder block does not need to be rebored, the original pistons can be refitted. Normal piston wear shows up as even vertical wear on the piston thrust surfaces, and slight looseness of the top ring in its groove. New piston rings, however, should always be used when the engine is reassembled.

7 Carefully inspect each piston for cracks around the skirt, around the gudgeon pin holes, and at the piston ring lands (between the ring grooves).

8 Look for scoring and scuffing on the piston skirt, holes in the piston crown, and burned areas at the edge of the crown. If the skirt is scored or scuffed, the engine may have been suffering from overheating, and/or abnormal combustion which caused excessively high operating temperatures. The cooling and lubrication systems should be checked thoroughly. Scorch marks on the sides of the pistons show that blow-by has occurred. A hole in the piston crown, or burned areas at the edge of the piston crown, indicates that abnormal combustion has been occurring. If any of the above problems exist, the causes must be investigated and corrected, or the damage will occur again.

9 Corrosion of the piston, in the form of pitting, indicates that coolant has been leaking into the combustion chamber and/or the crankcase. Again, the cause must be corrected, or the problem may persist in the rebuilt engine.

10 Examine each connecting rod carefully for signs of damage, such as cracks around the big-end and small-end bearings. Check that the rod is not bent or distorted. Damage is highly unlikely, unless the engine has been seized or badly overheated. Detailed checking of the connecting rod assembly can only be carried out by an engine reconditioning specialist with the necessary equipment.

11 On all engines, the gudgeon pins are an interference fit in the connecting rod small-end bearing. Therefore, piston and/or connecting rod renewal should be entrusted to an engine reconditioning specialist who will have the necessary tooling to remove and install the gudgeon pins.

12 It is highly recommended that the big-end cap bolts are renewed as a complete set prior to refitting.

13 Crankshaft – inspection

Checking endfloat

1 If the crankshaft endfloat is to be checked, this must be done when the crankshaft is still installed in the cylinder block/crankcase, but is free to move.

2 Check the endfloat using a dial gauge in contact with the end of the crankshaft. Push the crankshaft fully one way, and then zero the gauge. Push the crankshaft fully the other way, and check the endfloat. The result can be compared with the figures given in the Specifications, and will give an indication as to whether new thrustwashers are required **(see illustration)**.

3 If a dial gauge is not available, feeler blades can be used. First push the crankshaft fully towards the flywheel end of the engine, then use feeler blades to measure the gap between the crankpin web and the main bearing thrustwasher.

Inspection

4 Clean the crankshaft using paraffin or a suitable solvent, and dry it, preferably with compressed air if available. Be sure to clean the oil holes with a pipe cleaner or similar probe, to ensure that they are not obstructed.

5 Check the main and big-end bearing journals for uneven wear, scoring, pitting and cracking.

6 Big-end bearing wear is accompanied by distinct metallic knocking when the engine is running (particularly noticeable when the engine is pulling from low speed) and some loss of oil pressure.

7 Main bearing wear is accompanied by severe engine vibration and rumble – getting progressively worse as engine speed increases – and again by loss of oil pressure.

8 Check the bearing journal for roughness by running a finger lightly over the bearing

13.2 Using a dial gauge to check the crankshaft endfloat

surface. Any roughness (which will be accompanied by obvious bearing wear) indicates that the crankshaft requires regrinding (where possible) or renewal.

9 If the crankshaft has been reground, check for burrs around the crankshaft oil holes (the holes are usually chamfered, so burrs should not be a problem unless regrinding has been carried out carelessly). Remove any burrs with a fine file or scraper, and thoroughly clean the oil holes.

10 Have the crankshaft inspected and measured by a Hyundai dealer or engine reconditioning specialist. They will be able to advise of any reconditioning work needed, and supply the appropriate replacement bearings etc.

14 Main and big-end bearings – inspection

Inspection

1 Even though the main and big-end bearings should be renewed during the engine overhaul, the old bearings should be retained for close examination, as they may reveal valuable information about the condition of the engine. Main and big-end bearings are available in standard sizes and a range of undersizes to suit reground crankshafts. The engine reconditioner will select the correct bearing shells for a standard or machined crankshaft.

2 Bearing failure can occur due to lack of lubrication, the presence of dirt or other foreign particles, overloading the engine, or corrosion. Regardless of the cause of bearing failure, the cause must be corrected (where applicable) before the engine is reassembled, to prevent it from happening again **(see illustration)**.

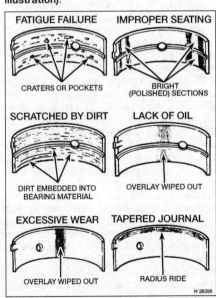

14.2 Typical bearing failures

3 When examining the bearing shells, remove them from the cylinder block/crankcase, the main bearing caps, the connecting rods and the connecting rod big-end caps. Lay them out on a clean surface in the same general position as their location in the engine. This will enable you to match any bearing problems with the corresponding crankshaft journal. Do not touch any shell's bearing surface with your fingers while checking it.

4 Dirt and other foreign matter gets into the engine in a variety of ways. It may be left in the engine during assembly, or it may pass through filters or the crankcase ventilation system. It may get into the oil, and from there into the bearings. Metal chips from machining operations and normal engine wear are often present. Abrasives are sometimes left in engine components after reconditioning, especially when parts are not thoroughly cleaned using the proper cleaning methods. Whatever the source, these foreign objects often end up embedded in the soft bearing material, and are easily recognised. Large particles will not embed in the bearing, and will score or gouge the bearing and journal. The best prevention for this cause of bearing failure is to clean all parts thoroughly, and keep everything spotlessly-clean during engine assembly. Frequent and regular engine oil and filter changes are also recommended.

5 Lack of lubrication (or lubrication breakdown) has a number of interrelated causes. Excessive heat (which thins the oil), overloading (which squeezes the oil from the bearing face) and oil leakage (from excessive bearing clearances, worn oil pump or high engine speeds) all contribute to lubrication breakdown. Blocked oil passages, which can be the result of misaligned oil holes in a bearing shell, will also oil-starve a bearing, and destroy it. When lack of lubrication is the cause of bearing failure, the bearing material is wiped or extruded from the steel backing of the bearing. Temperatures may increase to the point where the steel backing turns blue from overheating

6 Driving habits can have a definite effect on bearing life. Full-throttle, low-speed operation (labouring the engine) puts very high loads on bearings, tending to squeeze out the oil film. These loads cause the bearings to flex, which produces fine cracks in the bearing face (fatigue failure). Eventually, the bearing material will loosen in pieces, and tear away from the steel backing.

7 Short-distance driving leads to corrosion of bearings, because insufficient engine heat is produced to drive off the condensed water and corrosive gases. These products collect in the engine oil, forming acid and sludge. As the oil is carried to the engine bearings, the acid attacks and corrodes the bearing material.

8 Incorrect bearing installation during engine assembly will lead to bearing failure as well. Tight-fitting bearings leave insufficient bearing running clearance, and will result in oil starvation. Dirt or foreign particles trapped behind a bearing shell result in high spots on the bearing, which lead to failure.

9 Do not touch any shell's bearing surface with your fingers during reassembly; there is a risk of scratching the delicate surface, or of depositing particles of dirt on it.

10 As mentioned at the beginning of this Section, the bearing shells should be renewed as a matter of course during engine overhaul; to do otherwise is false economy.

15 Engine overhaul – reassembly sequence

1 Before reassembly begins, ensure that all new parts have been obtained, and that all necessary tools are available. Read through the entire procedure to familiarise yourself with the work involved, and to ensure that all items necessary for reassembly of the engine are at hand. In addition to all normal tools and materials, thread-locking compound will be needed. A suitable tube of sealant will also be required for the joint faces that are fitted without gaskets. It is recommended that Hyundai's own products are used, which are specially formulated for this purpose.

2 In order to save time and avoid problems, engine reassembly can be carried out in the following order:
a) Crankshaft.
b) Piston/connecting rod assemblies.
c) Oil pump.
d) Sump.
e) Flywheel.
f) Cylinder head.
g) Coolant pump.
h) Timing chain tensioner, sprockets and timing chain.
i) Engine external components.

3 At this stage, all engine components should be absolutely clean and dry, with all faults repaired. The components should be laid out on a completely clean work surface.

16 Piston rings – refitting

1 Before fitting new piston rings, the ring end gaps must be checked as follows.

2 Lay out the piston/connecting rod assemblies and the new piston ring sets, so that the ring sets will be matched with the same piston and cylinder during the end gap measurement and subsequent engine reassembly.

3 Insert the top ring into the first cylinder, and push it down the bore using the top of the piston. This will ensure that the ring remains square with the cylinder walls. Position the ring near the bottom of the cylinder bore, at

16.4 Measure the end gap with feeler blades

the lower limit of ring travel. Note that the top and second compression rings are different. The second ring is easily identified by the step on its lower surface, and by the fact that its outer face is tapered.

4 Measure the end gap using feeler blades **(see illustration)**.

5 Repeat the procedure with the ring at the top of the cylinder bore, at the upper limit of its travel and compare the measurements with the figures given in the Specifications.

6 If the gap is too small (unlikely if reputable parts are used), it must be enlarged, or the ring ends may contact each other during engine operation, causing serious damage. Ideally, new piston rings providing the correct end gap should be fitted. As a last resort, the end gap can be increased by filing the ring ends very carefully with a fine file. Mount the file in a vice equipped with soft jaws, slip the ring over the file with the ends contacting the file face, and slowly move the ring to remove material from the ends. Take care, as piston rings are sharp, and are easily broken.

7 With new piston rings, it is unlikely that the end gap will be too large. If the gaps are too large, check that you have the correct rings for the engine and for the cylinder bore size.

8 Repeat the checking procedure for each ring in the first cylinder, and then for the rings in the remaining cylinders. Remember to keep rings, pistons and cylinders matched up.

9 Once the ring end gaps have been checked and if necessary corrected, the rings can be fitted to the pistons.

Note: *Always follow any instructions supplied with the new piston ring sets – different manufacturers may specify different procedures. Do not mix up the top and second compression rings, as they have different cross-sections.*

10 Fit the piston rings using the same technique as for removal. Fit the bottom (oil control) ring first, and work up. Ensure that the second compression ring is fitted the correct way up, with its identification mark (either a dot of paint or the word TOP stamped on the ring surface) at the top.

11 Position the rings so that the end gaps are 180° apart and are offset from the gudgeon pin centreline.

17 Crankshaft – bearing selection and refitting

Bearing selection

1 Main bearings for the engines described in this Chapter are available in standard sizes and a range of undersizes to suit reground crankshafts. Refer to your Hyundai dealer or engine reconditioning specialist for details.

Refitting

Note: *Upper bearings have an oil groove of oil holes; lower bearings do not.*
2 Clean the backs of the bearing shells, and the bearing locations in both the cylinder block and the bearing ladder or lower crankcase.
3 Align the bearing tab with the groove of the cylinder block, push in the 5 upper bearings.
4 Install the 2 thrust washers either side of the No.3 journal position of the cylinder block with the oil grooves facing outward.
5 Install the crankshaft lower main bearing. Align the bearing tab with the groove of the crankshaft lower bearing and crankshaft main bearing cap.
6 Install the main bearing cap.
Note: *Always use new main bearing cap bolts, and if any of the bearing cap bolts is broken or deformed, replace it.*
7 Lower the crankshaft into position.
8 Apply a light coat of engine oil on the threads and under the bearing cap bolts. Install and uniformly tighten the 10 bearing cap bolts to the specified torque, in several passes, from the centre outwards **(see illustration)**.
9 Check that the crankshaft turns smoothly.
10 Check the crankshaft end float once more.

18 Piston/connecting rod assembly – bearing selection and refitting

Bearing selection

1 Big-end bearings for the engines described in this Chapter are available in standard sizes and a range of undersizes to suit reground crankshafts. Refer to your Hyundai dealer or engine reconditioning specialist for details.

Refitting

2 Clean the backs of the bearing shells, and the bearing locations in the connecting rods, bearing caps and ladders.

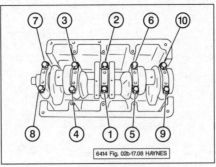

17.8 Main bearing cap bolts tightening sequence

3 Press the bearing shells into their locations, ensuring that the tab on each shell engages in the notch in the connecting rod and cap. Take care not to touch any shell's bearing surface with your fingers.
4 Note that the following procedure assumes that the crankshaft and main bearing caps/lower crankcase are in place.
5 Lubricate the cylinder bores, the pistons, and piston rings, then lay out each piston/connecting rod assembly in its respective position.
6 Start with assembly No 1. Position the piston ring gaps as described in Section 16, then clamp them in position with a piston ring compressor **(see illustration)**.
7 Insert the piston/connecting rod assembly into the top of cylinder No 1, ensuring that the arrow on the piston crown is pointing towards the timing chain end of the engine.
8 Using a block of wood or hammer handle against the piston crown, tap the assembly into the cylinder until the piston crown is flush with the top of the cylinder.
9 Ensure that the bearing shell is still correctly installed. Liberally lubricate the crankpin and both bearing shells. Taking care not to mark the cylinder bores, tap the piston/connecting rod assembly down the bore and onto the crankpin.
10 Refit the big-end bearing cap, tightening its retaining bolts finger-tight at first. Note that the faces with the identification marks must match (which means that the bearing shell locating tabs abut each other).
11 Tighten the bearing cap retaining bolts evenly and progressively to the Stage 1 torque setting, then angle-tighten them to the specified Stage 2 angle using an angle-measuring gauge.
12 Once the bearing cap retaining bolts have been correctly tightened, rotate the crankshaft. Check that it turns freely; some

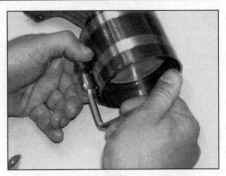

18.6 Use a piston ring compressor

stiffness is to be expected if new components have been fitted, but there should be no signs of binding or tight spots.
13 Refit the remaining piston/connecting rod assemblies in the same way.
14 Continue with the engine reassembly in the sequence given in Section 15.

19 Engine – initial start-up after overhaul

1 With the engine refitted in the car, double-check the engine oil and coolant levels. Make a final check that everything has been reconnected, and that there are no tools or rags left in the engine compartment.
2 Start the engine, noting that this may take a little longer than usual, due to the fuel system components having been disturbed. Make sure that the oil pressure warning light goes out then allow the engine to idle.
3 While the engine is idling, check for fuel, water and oil leaks. Don't be alarmed if there are some odd smells and smoke from parts getting hot and burning off oil deposits.
4 Assuming all is well, keep the engine idling until hot water is felt circulating through the top hose, then switch off the engine.
5 After a few minutes, recheck the oil and coolant levels as described in *'Weekly checks'*, and top-up as necessary.
6 Note that there is no need to retighten the cylinder head bolts once the engine has first run after reassembly.
7 If new pistons, rings or crankshaft bearings have been fitted, the engine must be treated as new, and run-in for the first 500 miles (800 km). Do not operate the engine at full-throttle, or allow it to labour at low engine speeds in any gear. It is recommended that the oil and filter be changed at the end of this period.

Chapter 3
Cooling, heating and ventilation systems

Contents

Degrees of difficulty

| Easy, suitable for novice with little experience | Fairly easy, suitable for beginner with some experience | Fairly difficult, suitable for competent DIY mechanic | Difficult, suitable for experienced DIY mechanic | Very difficult, suitable for expert DIY or professional |

Specifications

System
Type . . . . Pressurised, pump-assisted with front mounted radiator and ECM controlled cooling fan

Thermostat
Type . . . . Wax
Operating temperatures
  Starts to open... 83.5 to 86.5° C
  Fully open.. 95° C

Expansion tank
Cap pressure . . . . 0.95 bar

Air conditioning system
Refrigerant R134a
Refrigerant charge quantity . . . . 450 ± 25g
Refrigerant oil ND-Oil8

Torque wrench settings	Nm	lbf ft
Compressor mounting bolts.	27	20
Coolant pump.	10	8
Coolant pump pulley	10	8
Thermostat housing bolts.	10	8

1 General information and precautions

General information

1 The engine cooling system is of pressurised type, comprising of a coolant pump driven by the auxiliary drivebelt, a crossflow radiator, a coolant expansion tank, an electric cooling fan, a thermostat, heater matrix, and all associated hoses and switches.

2 The system functions as follows: the coolant pump circulates cold water around the cylinder block and head passages, and through the intake manifold, heater matrix and throttle body to the thermostat housing.

3 When the engine is cold, the thermostat remains closed and prevents coolant from circulating through the radiator. When the coolant reaches a predetermined temperature, the thermostat opens, and the coolant passed through the top hose to the radiator. As the coolant circulates through the radiator, it is cooled by the in-rush of air when the car is in forward motion. the airflow is supplemented by the action of the electric cooling fan, when necessary.

4 When the engine is at normal operating temperature, the coolant expands, and some if it is displaced in to the expansion tank. Coolant collects in the tank, and is returned to the radiator when the system cools.

5 The electric cooling fan is mounted at the rear of the radiator and controlled by the engine management electronic control unit, in conjunction with the engine coolant temperature sensor.

Precautions

⚠️ *Warning: Do not attempt to remove the pressure cap, or disturb any part of the cooling system, while the engine is hot, because there is a high risk of scalding. If the pressure cap must be removed before the engine and radiator have fully cooled (even though this is not recommended), the pressure in the cooling system must*

first be relieved. Cover the cap with a thick layer of cloth, to avoid scalding, and slowly unscrew the pressure cap until a hissing sound is heard (be prepared to refit the cap quickly if bubbling noises are heard and hot coolant starts to come out). When the hissing stops, indicating that the pressure has reduced, slowly unscrew the pressure cap until it can be removed; if more hissing sounds are heard, wait until they have stopped before unscrewing the cap completely. At all times, keep your face well away from the pressure cap opening, and protect your hands.

⚠️ *Warning: Do not allow antifreeze to come into contact with your skin, or with the painted surfaces of the vehicle. Rinse off spills immediately with plenty of water. Never leave antifreeze lying around in an open container, or in a puddle in the driveway or on the garage floor. Children and pets are attracted by its sweet smell, but antifreeze can be fatal if ingested.*

⚠️ *Warning: The cooling fan could cut in even if the engine is not running (if the ignition is on). Be careful to keep your hands, hair, and any loose clothing well clear when working in the engine compartments.*

2 Cooling system hoses – disconnection and renewal

⚠️ *Warning: Never work on the cooling system when it is hot. Release any pressure from the system by loosening the expansion tank cap, having first covered it with a cloth to avoid any possibility of scalding.*

1 The number, routing and pattern of hoses will vary according to model, but the same basic procedure applies. Before commencing work, make sure that the new hoses are to hand, along with new hose clips if needed. It is good practice to renew the hose clips at the same time as the hoses.

2 Drain the cooling system as described in Chapter 1 Section 25, saving the coolant if it is fit for re-use. Squirt a little penetrating oil onto the hose clips if they are corroded.

3 Release the hose clips from the hose concerned. Three types of clip are used; worm-drive, spring, and crimped. The worm-drive clip is released by turning its screw anti-clockwise. The spring clip is released by squeezing its tags together with pliers, at the same time working the clip away from the hose stub. The crimped clips are not re-usable, and are best cut off with snips or side-cutters **(see illustration)**.

4 Unclip any wires, cables or other hoses, which may be attached to the hose being removed. Make notes for reference when reassembling, if necessary.

5 Release the hose from its stubs with a twisting motion. Be careful not to damage the stubs on delicate components such as the radiator, or thermostat housings. If the hose is stuck fast, the best course is often to cut it off using a sharp knife, but again be careful not to damage the stubs.

6 Before fitting the new hose, smear the stubs with washing-up liquid or a suitable rubber lubricant to aid fitting. Do not use oil or grease, which may attack the rubber.

7 Fit the hose clips over the ends of the hose, and then fit the hose over its stubs. Work the hose into position. When satisfied, locate and tighten the hose clips.

8 Refill the cooling system as described in Chapter 1 Section 25. Run the engine, and check that there are no leaks.

9 Recheck the tightness of the hose clips on any new hoses after a few hundred miles.

10 Top-up the coolant level if necessary, as described in 'Weekly checks'.

3 Radiator – removal, inspection and refitting

Note: *If leakage is the reason for removing the radiator, bear in mind that minor leaks can often be cured using proprietary radiator sealing compound, with the radiator in situ.*

Removal

1 Raise the front of the vehicle and support it securely on axle stands, as described in 'Vehicle jacking and support'.

2 Disconnect the battery negative lead as described in Chapter 5A Section 4.

3 Drain the coolant as described in Chapter 1 Section 25.

4 Release the clamp and disconnect the upper radiator hose **(see illustration)**.

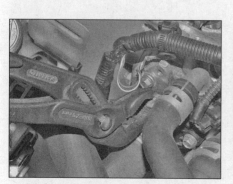

2.3 Compress the tabs to release the spring-type clamps

3.4 Disconnect the upper radiator hose

3.5 Remove the lower hose

3.7 Undo the bolts and remove radiator mounting brackets (bottom right bracket bolts arrowed)

3.8 Upper mounting bolt (right-hand side arrowed)

3.9 Lower the radiator from the vehicle

5 Release the clamp and disconnect the lower radiator hose **(see illustration)**.

6 Remove the the radiator fan as described in Section 5.

7 Undo the 8 bolts and remove the radiator mounting brackets **(see illustration)**.

8 Undo 2 upper bolts holding the radiator to the air conditioning condenser **(see illustration)**.

9 Lower the radiator from the mounting pegs on the bottom of the condenser and gently lower the radiator from the vehicle **(see illustration)**.

Inspection

10 If the radiator was removed because of clogging (causing overheating) then try reverse flushing using a garden hose or, in severe cases, use a radiator cleanser strictly in accordance with the manufacturer's instructions.

11 If necessary, a radiator specialist can perform a flow test on the radiator, to establish whether an internal blockage exists.

12 A leaking radiator must be referred to a specialist for permanent repair. Do not attempt to weld or solder a leaking radiator, as damage to the plastic components may result.

13 Inspect the radiator rubber mounting grommets, and renew them if necessary.

Refitting

14 Refitting is a reversal of removal, bearing in mind the following points:

a) *On completion, refill the cooling system as described in Chapter 1 Section 25.*

b) *Tighten all connections to the specified torque.*

---

4 Thermostat –
removal, testing and refitting

Note: *The thermostat housing is bolted to the front right-hand end of the engine.*

Removal

1 Drain the cooling system as described in Chapter 1 Section 25 so its level is below that of the thermostat.

2 Disconnect the battery negative lead as described in Chapter 5A Section 4.

3 Remove the auxiliary drive belt as described in Chapter 1 Section 5.

4 Undo the 4 bolts and manoeuvre the air conditioning compressor slightly out of the way. There's no need to disconnect the refrigerant pipes.

5 Release the clamps and disconnect the coolant hoses from the thermostat housing, then undo the 2 bolts and remove the thermostat housing **(see illustration)**.

6 Gently remove the thermostat from place.

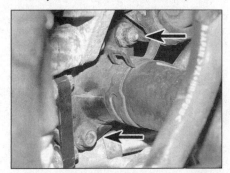

4.5 Remove the hose, then undo the bolts and remove the thermostat housing

4.11 Ensure the locating tab is positioned correctly

Testing

7 A rough test of the thermostat may be made by submerging it in a container full of water. Heat the water to bring it to the boil and observe the movement of the valve shaft.

8 The thermostat valve must be fully open by the time the water boils. If not, renew the complete thermostat/housing assembly.

9 If a thermometer is available, the precise opening temperature of the thermostat may be determined; compare with the figures given in the Specifications. The opening temperature is also marked on the thermostat housing.

10 Note that a thermostat which fails to close completely as the water cools must also be renewed.

Refitting

11 Fit the new thermostat, ensuring that the locating tab on the thermostat gasket is positioned correctly in the housing **(see illustration)**.

12 Tighten the thermostat bolts to the specified torque.

13 Reconnect the coolant hoses to the thermostat housing, and secure them with the clamps where applicable.

14 Manoeuvre the air conditioning compressor back into place and tighten the bolts.

15 Refit the auxiliary drivebelt as described in Chapter 1 Section 5.

16 Reconnect the battery negative lead as described in Chapter 5A Section 4.

17 Refill the cooling system as described in Chapter 1 Section 25.

5 Electric cooling fan assembly – testing, removal and refitting

Testing

1 Detailed fault diagnosis should be carried out by a Hyundai dealer or suitably equipped repairer using dedicated test equipment, but basic diagnosis can be carried out as follows.

2 If the fan does not appear to work, run the engine until normal operating temperature is reached, then allow it to idle. The fan should cut in within a few minutes (before the warning light illuminates, or the temperature gauge needle enters the red section). If not, switch off the engine and disconnect the cooling fan motor wiring connector.

3 The motor can be tested by disconnecting it from the wiring loom, and connecting a 12 volt supply directly to it. The motor should operate – if not, the motor, or the motor wiring, is faulty.

4 If the motor operates when tested as described, the fault is likely to be in one of the cooling fan relays, the relay fuse, or the engine wiring harness. If these components are satisfactory any further fault diagnosis should be referred to a suitably equipped Hyundai dealer or repairer – do not attempt to test the engine management electronic control unit.

Removal

5 Disconnect the battery negative lead as described in Chapter 5A Section 4.

6 Undo the mounting bolts, disconnect the wiring plug and move the bonnet catch to one side **(see illustration)**.

7 Disconnect the expansion tank hose, and the fan motor wiring plug, then undo the 2 screws securing the fan assembly to the radiator **(see illustrations)**.

8 Undo the front mounting bolt from the rear engine mounting and pull the bottom of the engine backwards **(see illustration)**. Use a cable tie or rope to hold it in place.

9 Lift the cooling fan off its bottom mounting lugs and lower from place **(see illustration)**.

Refitting

10 Refitting is a reversal of removal.

5.6 Undo the 4 mounting bolts (right side arrowed) and move the bonnet catch out of the way

5.7a Detach the expansion tank hose …

5.7b … disconnect the wiring plug …

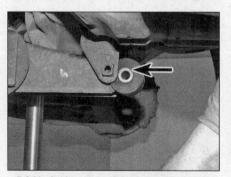

5.7c … and undo the fan's mounting bolts (left side arrowed)

5.8 Undo the rear engine mounting bolt, and pull the engine rearwards slightly

5.9 Lift the cooling fan off its mounting lugs

6.1 Engine coolant temperature sensor

7.4 Undo the bolts and remove the water pump pulley

6 Engine coolant temperature sensor (ECT) – testing, removal and refitting

Testing

1 The engine coolant temperature sensor is fitted into the thermostat housing at the left-hand end of the cylinder head (see illustration).
2 The unit contains a thermistor – an electronic component whose electrical resistance decreases at a predetermined rate as its temperature rises.
3 The engine management ECU supplies the sensor with a set voltage and then, by measuring the current flowing in the sensor circuit, it determines the engine temperature. This information is then used, in conjunction with other inputs, to control the engine management system and associated components. The sensor signal is also used to operate the temperature gauge and/or warning light on the instrument panel.
4 If the sensor circuit should fail to provide plausible information, the ECU back-up facility will override the sensor signal. In this event, the ECU assumes a predetermined setting which will allow the engine management system to operate, albeit at reduced efficiency. When this occurs, the engine warning light on the instrument panel will illuminate, and the advice of a Fiat dealer or repairer should be sought. The sensor itself can be tested by removing it, and checking the resistances at various temperatures using an ohmmeter (heat the sensor in a container of water, and monitor the temperature with a thermometer). The resistance values are given in the Specifications.

Removal

5 Disconnect the battery negative lead as described in Chapter 5A Section 4.
6 Disconnect the wiring plug from the coolant temperature sensor, located on the thermostat housing at the left-hand end of the cylinder head.
7 Partially drain the cooling system to just below the level of the sensor (see Chapter 1 Section 25). Alternatively, have ready a suitable bung to plug the aperture in the housing when the sensor is removed.
8 Carefully unscrew the sensor and recover the sealing ring. If the system has not been drained, plug the sensor aperture to prevent further coolant loss.

Refitting

9 Check the condition of the sealing ring and renew it if necessary.

10 Refitting is a reversal of removal, tightening the sensor to the specified torque. Refill (or top-up) the cooling system as described in Chapter 1 Section 25 or 'Weekly checks'.
11 On completion, start the engine and run it until it reaches normal operating temperature. Continue to run the engine until the cooling fan cuts in and out correctly.

7 Coolant pump – removal, inspection and refitting

Removal

1 Drain the cooling system as described in Chapter 1 Section 25.
2 Disconnect the battery negative lead as described in Chapter 5A Section 4.
3 Remove the auxiliary drivebelt as described in Chapter. 1 Section 5
4 Slacken the 4 bolts and remove the pulley from the front of the water pump (see illustration).
5 Unscrew the retaining bolts and withdraw the coolant pump (see illustration). If the pump is stuck, tap it gently using a soft-faced mallet – do not lever between the pump and cylinder block mating faces.

Inspection

6 Check the pump body and impeller for signs of excessive corrosion or evidence of coolant leakage. Turn the impeller, and check for stiffness due to corrosion, or roughness due to excessive end play. If any of these conditions are apparent, the pump must be renewed as a complete assembly.

Refitting

7 Renew the pump O-ring seal (see illustration).
8 Place the pump in position in the cylinder block, then refit and tighten the bolts to the specified torque.
9 The remainder of refitting is a reversal of removal.

7.5 Undo the 3 bolts and remove the coolant pump

7.7 Replace the water pump O-ring seal

8.1 Prise up the trim around the gearlever

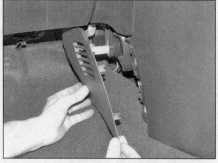

8.2a Remove the left-hand side cover …

8.2b … then the right-hand side cover

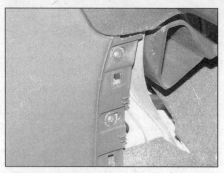

8.3 Undo 2 screws on each side of lower panel (right side shown)

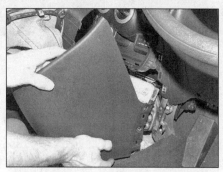

8.4 Pull lower panel rearwards to release

8.5 Undo the mounting screws (arrowed) then prise the panel rearwards

8 Heating and ventilation system components – removal and refitting

Heater control panel

Removal

1 Using a flat-bladed trim removal tool, gently price up the gear lever surround trim (see illustration).

2 Gently prise rearwards the left- and right-hand side facia side covers (see illustrations).

3 Undo the 2 mounting screws on each side of the lower facia panel (see illustration).

4 Pull the lower facia panel rearwards to release from place (see illustration).

5 Undo the 2 mounting screws then use a trim removal tool to prise the heater panel rearwards (see illustration).

6 Disconnect all the wiring plugs (see illustration).

7 Release the clips and remove the heater control cables (see illustration).

Refitting

8 Refitting is a reversal of removal.

9 Check that all the cables operate to the full extent of their travel when reassembled.

Heater blower motor

Removal

10 Disconnect the battery negative lead as described in Chapter 5A Section 4.

11 Remove the glovebox as described in Chapter 11 Section 26.

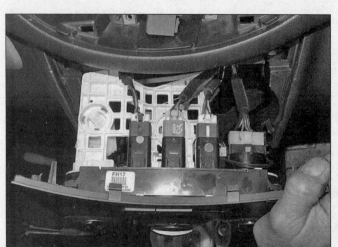

8.6 Disconnect all wiring plugs

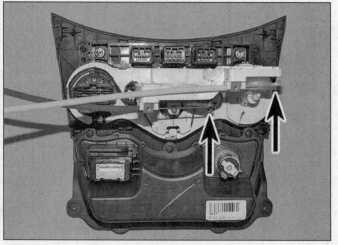

8.7 Remove the heater control cables (panel removed for clarity)

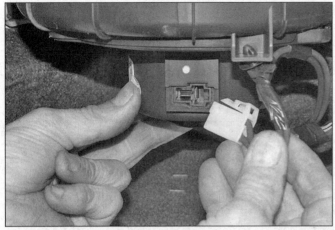

8.12 Disconnect the wiring plug

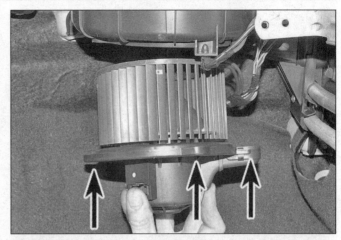

8.13 Undo the screws and lower the blower from the facia

12 Disconnect the wiring plug from the blower motor **(see illustration)**.
13 Undo the 3 mounting screws and lower the blower unit from place **(see illustration)**.

Refitting

14 Refitting is a reversal of removal.

Heater blower motor resistor

Removal

15 Remove the blower motor as described previously in this Section.
16 Disconnect the wiring plug on the blower motor resistor then undo the 2 screws and remove from place **(see illustration)**.

Refitting

17 Refitting is a reversal of removal.

Heater matrix

Caution: This is an extremely complex and involved procedure that requires removal of the entire dashboard and supporting framework, plus the removal of the entire heating system. It should be undertaken only by someone who is experienced and confident in their abilities.

8.16 Disconnect the blower motor resistor plug then undo 2 mounting screws

Removal

18 Drain the cooling system as described in Chapter 1 Section 25.
19 Remove the complete facia as described in Chapter 11 Section 26.
20 Remove the steering column as described in Chapter 10 Section 13.
21 Remove the gearchange lever assembly as described in Chapter 7A Section 4.
22 Undo the gear lever mounting framework

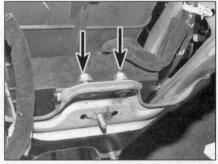

8.23 Undo the bolts and detach the Body Control Module

and gearshift cable mounting frame as described in Chapter 7A Section 3.
23 Undo the 2 bolts and detach the Body Control Module **(see illustration)**.
24 Undo the 2 bolts and lower the fusebox from place **(see illustration)**.
25 Undo the 2 bolts and remove the fixing bracket from the base of the central framework **(see illustration)**.
26 Undo the 16 bolts, release all clips, fixings

8.24 Lower the fusebox out of the way

8.25 Remove the fixing bracket from the bottom of the crossbeam central framework

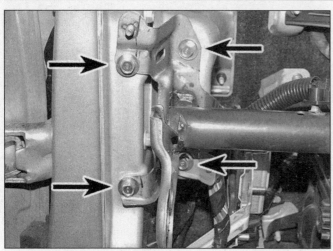

8.26a Undo the 4 bolts at each end of the crossbeam ...

8.26b ... the 8 bolts at the bottom of the central framework (one side shown) ...

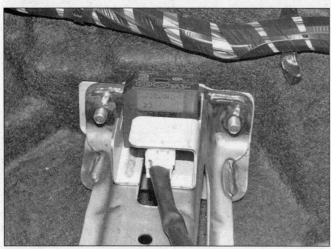

8.26c ... and the 2 bolts on the bulkhead (access them from the engine compartment)

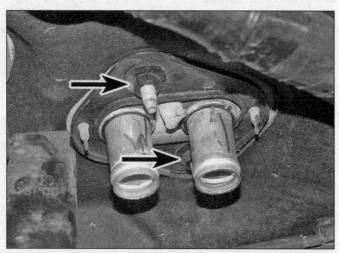

8.27 Undo 2 nuts and remove the bulkhead grommet

and 4 earth connections as they become available, then remove the facia crossbeam (see illustrations).

27 Working in the engine compartment, undo the 2 nuts and remove the heater pipes' bulkhead grommet (see illustration).

28 Undo the bolt and remove the cover for the air conditioning refrigerant connector at the engine compartment bulkhead (see illustration).

29 Undo the 2 bolts and disconnect the air conditioning refrigerant pipes at the engine compartment bulkhead (see illustration). Note: *Block the pipe openings to prevent contamination.*

30 Disconnect the 4 wiring plugs on the blower motor housing and heater housing (see illustration).

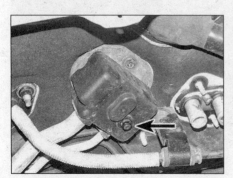

8.28 Unscrew the bolt and remove the cover

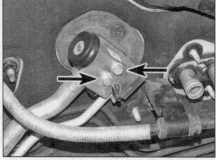

8.29 Unscrew the bolts and separate the air conditioning pipes from the bulkhead

8.30 Disconnect the 4 wiring plugs

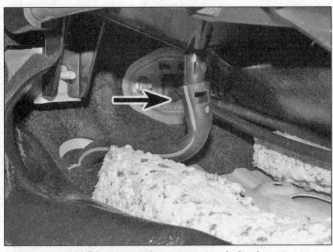

8.31 Disconnect the evaporator drain pipe

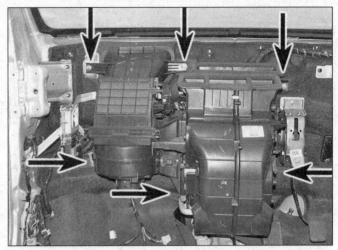

8.32 Undo the nuts and remove the heater and blower from place

8.33a Undo the 2 screws on the front of the assembly ...

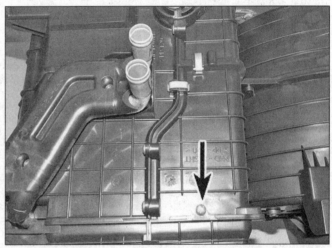

8.33b ... followed by the screw on the rear

31 Disconnect the evaporator drain pipe (see illustration).
32 Undo the mounting nuts and manoeuvre the heater assembly from place (see illustration).
33 The heater matrix assembly must now be separated from the blower motor housing. To do this, undo the two screws on the front of the assembly, then undo the screw on the back of the assembly (see illustrations).
34 Undo the 2 mounting screws for the shroud on the heater pipes (see illustration).

35 Once the shroud is removed, the heater matrix can be slid out from place (see illustration).

Refitting

36 Refitting is a reversal of removal.

9 Air conditioning system – general information and precautions

1 An air conditioning system is fitted as standard equipment on some models. In conjunction with the heater, the system enables any reasonable air temperature to be achieved inside the car, it also reduces the humidity of the incoming air, aiding demisting even when cooling is not required.
2 The refrigeration circuit of the air conditioning system functions in a similar way to a domestic refrigerator. A compressor, belt-driven from the crankshaft pulley,

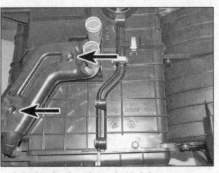

8.34 Undo the shroud retaining screws

8.35 Slide the matrix from the housing

9.4 Air conditioning service ports

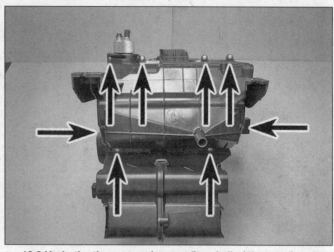

10.2 Undo the the screws (arrowed) and clip (obscured) and remove lower cover

draws refrigerant in its gaseous state from an evaporator. The refrigerant heats up as a result of being compressed, but is then passed through a condenser (mounted in front of the engine radiator) where it loses heat and enters its liquid state. After dehydration, the refrigerant is passed through an evaporator (mounted alongside the heater/ventilation unit) where it is allowed to expand and reverts to being gas. This change of state has the effect of absorbing heat from the air passing over the evaporator fins, reducing its temperature. This cool air is mixed with warm air from the heater unit to achieve the desired cabin temperature. The refrigerant is directed back to the compressor and the cycle is then repeated.

3 Various subsidiary controls and sensors protect the system against excessive temperature and pressures. Additionally, engine idle speed is increased when the system is in use to compensate for the additional load imposed by the compressor. Electronic sensors detect the rotational speed differential between the engine and the compressor – if this becomes too great (due to a malfunctioning compressor), the compressor clutch is disengaged, to preserve the drivebelt.

4 The air conditioning refrigerant service ports are located in the front-right and rear-left corners of the engine compartment (see illustration).

Note: The air conditioning electronic control system can only be tested using dedicated equipment. For this reason, it is recommended that problems with the operation of the air conditioning system are referred to a Hyundai dealer or suitably equipped repairer for diagnosis.

⚠ Warning: The refrigeration circuit contains pressurised liquid refrigerant. The refrigerant is potentially dangerous, and should only be handled by qualified persons. Refrigerant that is allowed to come into contact with the skin will cause severe frostbite. It is not itself poisonous, but in the presence of a naked flame (including inhalation through a lighted cigarette), it forms a poisonous gas. Uncontrolled discharging of the refrigerant is dangerous and is also extremely damaging to the environment. For these reasons, disconnection of any part of the system without specialised knowledge and equipment is not recommended.

Caution: Do not allow refrigerant lines to be exposed to temperatures in excess of 110°C, for example during welding or paint-drying operations.

Caution: Do not operate the air conditioning system if it is known to be short of refrigerant, or component damage may result.

10 Air conditioning system components – removal and refitting

⚠ Warning: Refer to the previous Section before proceeding. Before carrying out any of the procedures detailed below, the air conditioning system MUST be professionally discharged by a garage or air conditioning specialist.

Note: The car may be driven once the system has been discharged, but the air conditioning system should NOT be switched on, as this will cause damage to the compressor. The safest option is to have the system discharged where the car is to be worked on, and not move the car until the system has been recharged. With air conditioning becoming an increasingly common fitment, mobile air conditioning specialists are becoming more widespread.

Evaporator

Removal

1 Remove the heater matrix as described earlier in this Section 8.

2 Undo the 8 screws and release the joining clip and remove the heater's lower cover (see illustration).

3 Gently slide the evaporator core from place (see illustration).

4 Disconnect the evaporator wiring plug (see illustration).

Refitting

5 Refitting is a reversal of removal, noting the following point:
● Have the refrigerant circuit recharged and leak tested by a Hyundai dealer or suitably equipped specialist.

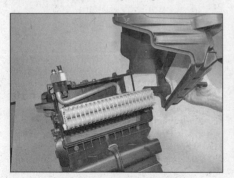

10.3 Slide out the evaporator

10.4 Disconnect the evaporator plug

10.11 Undo the 2 nuts and disconnect the air conditioning pipes from the condenser

10.12 Release the clips and displace the side cover

Condenser

Removal

6 Have the air conditioning refrigerant circuit evacuated by a Hyundai dealer or suitably equipped repairer.

7 Disconnect the battery negative lead as described in Chapter 5A Section 4.

8 Raise the front of the vehicle and support it securely on axle stands as described in 'Vehicle jacking and support'.

9 Remove the front bumper as described in Chapter 11 Section 6.

10 Remove the horn as described in Chapter 12 Section 12.

11 Remove 2 nuts, and then disconnect the refrigerant pipes from the condenser. Plug or cap the lines immediately after disconnecting them to avoid moisture and dust contamination **(see illustration)**.

12 Release the top and bottom clips to displace the condenser side cover **(see illustration)**.

13 Undo the bolt securing the crash sensor behind the left-hand end of the crash bar **(see illustration)**.

14 Undo 3 bolts securing left-hand end of crash bar. Pull forward and place a wedge behind to hold it in place **(see illustrations)**.

15 Remove the 2 top fixing bolts, and then lift up the condenser to disengage the feet and slide it towards the right-hand side of the car **(see illustrations)**.

Refitting

16 Refitting is a reversal of removal, noting the following points:

a) Renew the pipe O-ring seals, and smear a little refrigerant oil on the seals prior

10.13 Undo the bolts and remove the crash sensor

10.14a Undo the 3 bolts securing the left end of the crash bar, pull it forward ...

10.14b ... then place a wedge behind the crash bar end to hold it in place

10.15a Remove the top left fixing bolt ...

10.15b ... and the top right fixing bolt ...

10.15c ... then slide the condenser to the right-hand side and manoeuvre it forward from place

10.20 Plug the air conditioning ports to avoid contamination

10.21 Disconnect the plug then undo the securing bolts (compressor removed from vehicle for clarity)

to reassembly. Be sure to use the right O-rings for R-134a to avoid leakage.
b) Have the refrigerant circuit recharged by a Hyundai dealer or suitably equipped repairer.

Compressor

Removal

17 Have the air conditioning refrigerant circuit evacuated by a Hyundai dealer or suitably equipped repairer.
18 Disconnect the battery negative lead as described in Chapter 5A Section 4.
19 Remove the auxiliary drivebelt as described in Chapter 1 Section 5.
20 Remove the bolts, then disconnect the refrigerant pipes from the compressor **(see illustration)**.
Note: *Plug or cap the pipes immediately after disconnecting them to avoid moisture and dust contamination.*
21 Disconnect the compressor clutch wiring

plug, and then remove 4 mounting bolts and the compressor **(see illustration)**.

Refitting

22 Manoeuvre the compressor into position, insert the mounting bolts and tighten them to the specified torque, starting with the bolt at the top left and working anti-clockwise thereafter.
23 The remainder of refitting is a reversal of removal, noting the following points:
a) *If you're installing a new compressor, drain all the refrigerant oil from the removed compressor, and measure its volume, Subtract the volume of drained oil from 120cc (4.20 oz.) the result is the amount of oil you should drain from the new compressor (through the suction fitting).*
b) *Replace the O-rings with new ones, and apply a thin coat of refrigerant oil before installing them. Be sure to use the right O-rings for R-134a to avoid leakage.*

c) *Have the refrigerant circuit recharged by a Hyundai dealer or suitably equipped repairer.*

Pressure sensor

24 Have the air conditioning refrigerant circuit evacuated by a Hyundai dealer or suitably equipped repairer.
25 Disconnect the battery negative lead as described in Chapter 5A Section 4.
26 The sensor is located in the refrigerant pipe at the top rear edge of the engine. Disconnect the wiring plug and unscrew the sensor from the pipe. Plug the openings to prevent contamination.
Caution: Take care not to bend or damage the pipes.
27 Refit the sensor and tighten it to the specified torque.
28 Reconnect the wiring plug.
29 Have the refrigerant circuit recharged by a Hyundai dealer or suitably equipped repairer.

Chapter 4 Part A
Fuel and exhaust systems

Contents

Degrees of difficulty

Easy, suitable for novice with little experience	**Fairly easy,** suitable for beginner with some experience	**Fairly difficult,** suitable for competent DIY mechanic
Difficult, suitable for experienced DIY mechanic	**Very difficult,** suitable for expert DIY or professional	

Specifications

System type

All engines	Bosch ME 7.6.3 multi-point sequential fuel injection/ignition
Fuel pressure at idle speed (all models).	3.7 bar
Fuel pump type	Electric, immersed in the fuel tank
Fuel pump delivery rate	110 litres/hour minimum
Crankshaft position sensor resistance @ 20°C	950 to 1350 ohms
Injector electrical resistance:	13.8 to 15.2 ohms
Minimum octane rating.	95 RON unleaded

Torque wrench settings

	Nm	lbf ft
Camshaft position sensor	11	8
Crankshaft position sensor	11	8
ECU retaining nuts	11	8
Exhaust manifold-to-cylinder head:	32	24
Exhaust bracket	45	33
Intake manifold.	23	17

1 General information and precautions

General information

1 The fuel supply system consists of a fuel tank (which is mounted under the centre of the car, with an electric fuel pump immersed in it) and fuel feed line. The fuel pump supplies fuel to the fuel rail, which acts as a reservoir for the four fuel injectors which inject fuel into the inlet tracts.

2 The fuel injection and ignition functions are combined into a single engine management system. The systems fitted are manufactured by Bosch. The only significant differences being in the software contained in the system Electronic Control Unit (ECU), and certain specific component variations according to engine type. Each system incorporates a closed-loop catalytic converter and an evaporative emission control system, and complies with the latest emission control standards. Refer to Chapter 5B for information on the ignition side of each system; the fuel side of the system operates as follows.

3 The fuel pump supplies fuel from the tank to the fuel rail (mounted directly above the fuel injectors) by means of a 'returnless' system. With this arrangement, the fuel filter and fuel pressure regulator are an integral part of the fuel pump assembly located in the fuel tank. The regulator maintains a constant fuel pressure in the supply line to the fuel rail and allows excess fuel to recirculate in the fuel tank, by means of a bypass channel, if the regulated fuel pressure is exceeded. As the fuel filter is an integral part of the pump assembly, fuel filter renewal is no longer necessary as part of the maintenance and servicing schedule.

4 The fuel injectors are electromagnetic pintle valves which spray atomised fuel into the intake ports under the control of the ECU. There are four injectors, one per cylinder, mounted in the inlet manifold close to the cylinder head. Each injector is mounted at an angle that allows it to spray fuel directly onto the back of the inlet valve(s). The ECU controls the volume of fuel injected by varying the length of time for which each injector is held open. The fuel injection systems are of the sequential type, whereby each injector operates individually in cylinder sequence.

5 The electrical control system consists of the ECU, along with the following sensors:

a) *Throttle position sensor – informs the ECU of the throttle valve position and rate-of-change.*

b) *Engine coolant temperature sensor – informs the ECU of the engine temperature (Chapter 3 Section 6).*

c) *Intake air temperature/pressure sensor – informs the ECU of intake air temperature and load on the engine (expressed in terms of inlet manifold vacuum).*

d) *Ambient air pressure sensor – informs the ECU of the ambient air pressure, to allow for fueling corrections in relation to altitude.*

e) *Lambda sensors – inform the ECU of the oxygen content of the exhaust gases (explained in greater detail in Part B of this Chapter).*

f) *Crankshaft position sensor – informs the ECU of engine speed and crankshaft angular position.*

g) *Knock sensor – informs the ECU of pre-ignition (detonation) within the cylinders (refer to Chapter 5B Section 5).*

h) *Camshaft position sensor – informs the ECU of the camshaft position.*

6 Signals from each of the sensors are compared by the ECU and, based on this information, the ECU selects the response appropriate to those values, and controls the fuel injectors (varying the pulse width – the length of time the injectors are held open – to provide a richer or weaker air/fuel mixture, as appropriate). The air/fuel mixture is constantly varied by the ECU, to provide the best settings for cranking, starting (with either a hot or cold engine) and engine warm-up, idle, cruising and acceleration.

7 The ECU also has full control over the engine idle speed, via the motorised throttle body. The ECU also carries out 'fine tuning' of the idle speed by varying the ignition timing to increase or reduce the torque of the engine as it is idling. This helps to stabilise the idle speed when electrical or mechanical loads (such as headlights, air conditioning, etc) are switched on and off.

8 The ECU also varies the camshaft timing via an electrically operated solenoid valve, which controls the flow of pressurised engine oil to the phase transformer integral with the camshaft sprocket. The ECU adjusts the timing of the camshafts during various engine load conditions to improve driveabilty, engine output, and to reduce emissions. On early engines, only the position of the intake camshaft is varied, whilst on later engines, the positions of both camshafts are varied.

9 The exhaust and evaporative loss emission control systems are described in more detail in Chapter 4B.

10 If there is any abnormality in any of the readings obtained from the main engine sensors, the ECU enters its 'back-up' mode. If this happens, the erroneous sensor signal is overridden, and the ECU assumes a preprogrammed 'back-up' value, which will allow the engine to continue running, albeit at reduced efficiency. If the ECU enters this mode, the warning lamp on the instrument panel will be illuminated, and the relevant fault code will be stored in the ECU memory.

11 If the warning light illuminates, the vehicle should be taken to a Hyundai dealer or suitably equipped repairer at the earliest opportunity. Once there, a complete test of the engine management system can be carried out, using a special electronic diagnostic test unit which is plugged into the system's diagnostic connector **(see illustration)**.

Precautions

 Warning: Many of the procedures in this Chapter require the removal of fuel lines and connections, which may result in some fuel spillage. Before carrying out any operation on the fuel system, refer to the precautions given in 'Safety first!' at the beginning of this manual, and follow them implicitly. Petrol is a highly dangerous and volatile liquid, and the precautions necessary when handling it cannot be overstressed. Note that residual pressure will remain in the fuel lines long after the vehicle was last used. When disconnecting any fuel line, first depressurise the fuel system as described in Section 5.

2 Air cleaner assembly – removal and refitting

Removal

1 Undo the bolt and disconnect the cold air intake hose fitting from the inner wing **(see illustration)**.

1.11 The diagnostic connector is located under the driver's side of the facia

2.1 Air intake hose fitting retaining bolt

2.2 Disconnect the air outlet hose

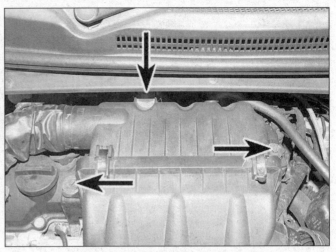

2.3 Air cleaner assembly retaining bolts

2 Slacken the clamp and disconnect the air outlet hose **(see illustration)**.
3 Undo the retaining bolts and manoeuvre the air cleaner assembly from place **(see illustration)**.

Refitting

4 Refitting is a reversal of removal.

3	Accelerator cable –
	removal and refitting

Removal

1 Working at the front of the engine, remove the lower bolt, slacken the upper, and pivot down the throttle quadrant cover **(see illustration)**.

2 Disengage the cable end fitting from the quadrant, then slide out the clip and pull the outer cable from the bracket **(see illustration)**.
3 Note their fitted positions, then release the accelerator cable from any bracket/clips in the engine compartment.
4 Remove the driver's-side lower facia panel as described in Chapter 11 Section 26.
5 Working under the dashboard, detach the end of the accelerator cable from the top of the pedal assembly **(see illustration)**.
6 Press the tabs and push the accelerator cable sleeve forwards through the bulkhead.
7 Manoeuvre the accelerator cable from place.
Note: *It is worth tying a piece of string/wire to the end of the cable when you remove it from place. Then tie the string to the new accelerator cable and use the string to pull it back into place.*

Refitting

8 Refitting is a reversal of removal, noting the tip about attaching string to the new cable.

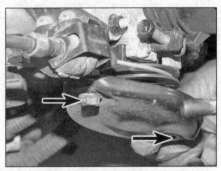

3.1 Slacken the upper bolt, and undo the lower bolt

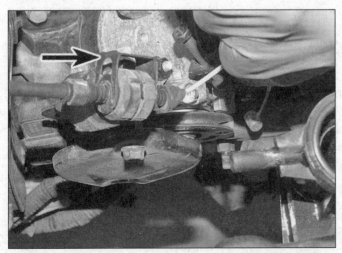

3.2 Slide out the clip and pull the outer cable from the bracket

3.5 Detach the cable from the pedal arm

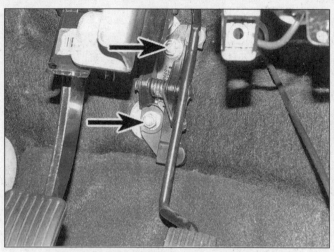

4.3 Undo the mounting nuts and remove the pedal

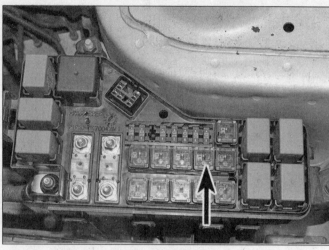

5.3 The fuel pump relay is located in the engine compartment fuse/relay box

4 Accelerator pedal – removal and refitting

Removal

1 Remove the driver's side lower facia panel as described in Chapter 11 Section 26.
2 Detach the accelerator cable from the pedal as described in Section 3.
3 Undo the 2 mounting nuts and remove the accelerator pedal from place **(see illustration)**.

Refittng

4 Refitting is a reversal of removal.

5 Fuel system – depressurisation

Note: *Refer to the warning given in Section 1 before proceeding.*
Warning: The following procedure will merely relieve the pressure in the fuel system – remember that fuel will still be present in the system components and take precautions accordingly before disconnecting any of them.
1 The fuel system referred to in this Section is defined as the tank-mounted fuel pump, the fuel rail, the fuel injectors, and the metal pipes and flexible hoses of the fuel lines between these components. All these contain fuel which will be under pressure while the engine is running and/or while the ignition is switched on. The pressure will remain for some time after the ignition has been switched off, and must be relieved before any of these components are disturbed for servicing work.
2 Disconnect the battery negative lead as described in Chapter 5A Section 4.

3 Remove the fuel pump relay **(see illustration)**.
4 Reconnect the battery negative (-) terminal as described in Section 5A Section 4 and start the engine, allowing it to run until it stops of its own accord.
5 Disconnect the battery (-) terminal, and then reinstall the fuel pump relay.
6 Reconnect the battery (-) terminal.
7 Delete the Diagnostic Trouble Code (DTC) related the fuel pump relay with a diagnostic tester.

6 Fuel pipes and fittings – general information and disconnection

1 Depressurise the fuel system (see Section 5) and disconnect the cable from the negative battery terminal (see Chapter 5A Section 4) before proceeding.
2 The fuel supply pipe connects the fuel pump in the fuel tank to the fuel rail on the engine.
3 Whenever you're working under the vehicle, be sure to inspect all fuel and evaporative emission pipes for leaks, kinks, dents and other damage. Always replace a damaged fuel pipe immediately.
4 If you find signs of dirt in the pipes during disassembly, disconnect all pipes and blow them out with compressed air. Inspect the fuel strainer on the fuel pump pick-up unit for damage and deterioration.

Steel tubing

5 It is critical that the fuel pipes be replaced with pipes of equivalent type and specification.
6 Some steel fuel pipes have threaded fittings. When loosening these fittings, hold the stationary fitting with a spanner while turning the union nut.

Plastic tubing

> ⚠️ **Warning: When removing or installing plastic fuel tubing, be careful not to bend or twist it too much, which can damage it. Also, plastic fuel tubing is NOT heat resistant, so keep it away from excessive heat.**

7 When replacing fuel system plastic tubing, use only original equipment replacement plastic tubing.

Flexible hoses

8 When replacing fuel system flexible hoses, use original equipment replacements, or hose to the same specification.
9 Don't route fuel hoses (or metal pipes) within 100 mm of the exhaust system or within 280 mm of the catalytic converter. Make sure that no rubber hoses are installed directly against the vehicle, particularly in places where there is any vibration. If allowed to touch some vibrating part of the vehicle, a hose can easily become chafed and it might start leaking. A good rule of thumb is to maintain a minimum of 8.0 mm clearance around a hose (or metal pipe) to prevent contact with the vehicle underbody.

Disconnecting fuel pipe fittings

10 Typical fuel pipe fittings:

6.10a Two-tab type fitting; depress both tabs with your fingers, then pull the fuel pipe and the fitting apart

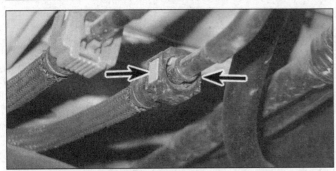

6.10b On this type of fitting, depress the two buttons on opposite sides of the fitting, then pull it off the fuel pipe

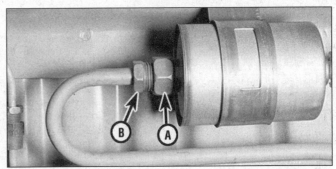

6.10c Threaded fuel pipe fitting; hold the stationary portion of the pipe or component (A) while loosening the union nut (B) with a flare-nut spanner

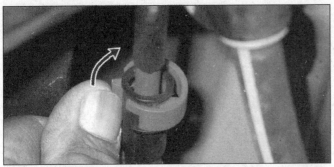

6.10d Plastic collar-type fitting; rotate the outer part of the fitting

6.10e Metal collar quick-connect fitting; pull the end of the retainer off the fuel pipe and disengage the other end from the female side of the fitting ...

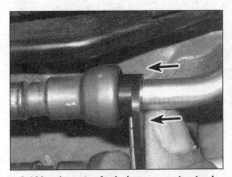

6.10f ... insert a fuel pipe separator tool into the female side of the fitting, push it into the fitting and pull the fuel pipe off the pipe

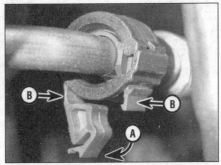

6.10g Some fittings are secured by lock tabs. Release the lock tab (A) and rotate it to the fully-opened position, squeeze the two smaller lock tabs (B) ...

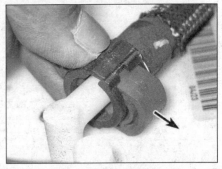

6.10h ... then push the retainer out and pull the fuel pipe off the pipe

6.10i Spring-lock coupling; remove the safety cover, install a coupling release tool and close the tool around the coupling ...

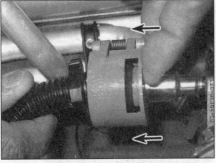

6.10j ... push the tool into the fitting, then pull the two pipes apart

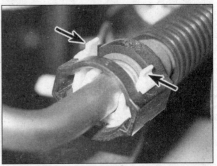

6.10k Hairpin clip type fitting: push the legs of the retainer clip together, then push the clip down all the way until it stops and pull the fuel pipe off the pipe

7 Fuel pump and fuel level sensor unit – removal and refitting

Note: *Refer to the warning given in Section 1 before proceeding.*

Removal

1 Disconnect the battery negative lead as described in Chapter 5A Section 4.

2 Depressurise the fuel system as described in Section 5.

3 Remove the rear seat cushion as described in Chapter 11 Section 21.

4 Prise up and lift the cover from the aperture in the floor panel **(see illustration)**.

5 Disconnect the wiring plug from the top of the fuel pump.

6 Disconnect the fuel feed tube quick-connector and vapour hose **(see illustration)**.

Note: *Plug all hoses and opening to prevent contamination.*

7 Brush away the worst of the dust and dirt to minimise the chance of contamination.

Note: *Mark the top of the fuel pump assembly to assist with orientation when reassembling.*

8 Undo the ring of retaining nuts, then carefully lift out the fuel pump assembly **(see illustrations)**.

Caution: Take care not to spill the excess fuel as it drains.

9 If required, the sender unit can be checked using a digital multimeter measuring resistance across the socket terminals. Measure the resistance at zero deflection and full deflection of the float **(see illustration)**.

Float full deflection (full tank)	8 ohms (approx)
Float zero deflection (empty tank)	198 ohms (approx)

7.4 Prise up the cover from the floor panel

10 If the result varies significantly from these, the unit may be defective.

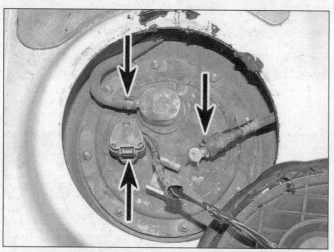

7.6 Disconnect the wiring plug and the hoses

7.8a Undo the 8 retaining nuts ...

7.8b ... and lift out the pump/sender assembly

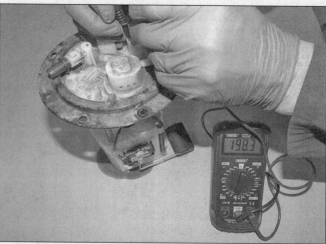

7.9 Use a multimeter to measure the resistance of the sender

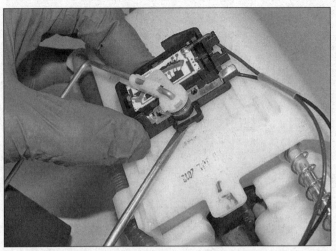

7.11 Release the clip and slide the sender unit upwards

7.12 Renew the rubber seal

11 To remove the sender unit, release the clip and slide it up from place **(see illustration)**. Disconnect the wiring as the unit is withdrawn.

Refitting

12 Refitting is a reversal of removal, making sure to use a new seal **(see illustration)**. Prior to refitting the access cover, reconnect the battery, start the engine and check the fuel pipe for signs of leakage.

8 Fuel tank – removal and refitting

Note: *Refer to the warning given in Section 1 before proceeding.*

Removal

1 Before removing the fuel tank, all fuel must be drained from the tank. Since a fuel tank drain plug is not provided, it is therefore preferable to carry out the removal operation when the tank is nearly empty. Before proceeding, disconnect the battery negative terminal (Chapter 5A Section 4), and syphon or hand-pump the remaining fuel from the tank.

2 Working as described in Section 7, disconnect the fuel pump wiring plug and the fuel supply line from the top of the pump.

3 Raise the rear of the vehicle and support it securely on axle stands as described in *'Vehicle jacking and support'*. Support the fuel tank with a jack.

4 Working underneath the vehicle, remove the exhaust system as described in Section 13.

5 Disconnect the fuel filler hose, the leveling hose and the vapour hose from the tank.

6 Disconnect the canister vapour hose at the side of fuel tank.

7 Remove the fuel tank mounting 2 bolts and 2 nuts and then remove the fuel tank **(see illustration)**.

8 If the tank is contaminated with sediment or water, remove the fuel pump/fuel level sensor unit as described in Section 7, and swill the tank out with clean fuel. The tank is injection-moulded from a synthetic material – if seriously damaged, it should be renewed. However, in certain cases, it may be possible to have small leaks or minor damage repaired. Seek the advice of a specialist before attempting to repair the fuel tank.

Refitting

9 Refitting is a reversal of removal, ensuring that all pipes and hoses are correctly routed and securely connected.

9 Fuel injection system – testing and adjustment

Testing

1 If a fault appears in the fuel injection/engine management system, first ensure that all the system wiring connectors are securely connected and free of corrosion. Ensure that the fault is not due to poor maintenance; ie, check that the air cleaner filter element is clean, the spark plugs are in good condition

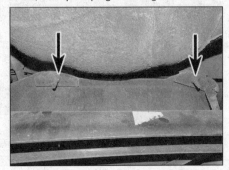

8.7 Fuel tank rear mounting nuts

and correctly gapped, the valve clearances are correctly adjusted (where applicable), the cylinder compression pressures are correct, and that the engine breather hoses are clear and undamaged, referring to the relevant Parts of Chapter and Chapter 2A for further information.

2 If these checks fail to reveal the cause of the problem, the vehicle should be taken to a Hyundai dealer or suitably equipped garage for testing. A diagnostic socket is located below the driver's side of the facia in which a fault code reader or other suitable test equipment can be connected. By using the code reader or test equipment, the engine management ECU (and the various other vehicle system ECUs) can be interrogated, and any stored fault codes can be retrieved. This will allow the fault to be quickly and simply traced, alleviating the need to test all the system components individually, which is a time-consuming operation that carries a risk of damaging the ECU.

Adjustment

3 Experienced home mechanics with a considerable amount of skill and equipment (including a tachometer and an accurately calibrated exhaust gas analyser) may be able to check the exhaust CO level and the idle speed. However, if these are found to be outside the specified tolerance, the car must be taken to a suitably equipped garage for further testing. Neither the mixture adjustment (exhaust gas CO level) nor the idle speed are adjustable, and should either be incorrect, a fault may be present in the engine management system.

4 Note that the engine management ECU has a 'self-learning' capability. If a component has been renewed, allow at least 15 minutes of driving time for the ECU to adapt to the characteristics of the new component.

10.9 Throttle body retaining bolts/nuts

10.10 Fit a new seal

10 Fuel injection components – removal and refitting

Note: *Refer to the warning given in Section 1 before proceeding.*

1 Before attempting any of the following procedures, disconnect the battery negative lead as described in Chapter 5A Section 4.

Throttle body

2 Drain the cooling system to below the level of the throttle body.

3 Remove the air cleaner assembly as described in Section 2.

4 Slacken the clamp and disconnect the inlet hose from the throttle body.

5 Undo the clips and disconnect the 2 coolant pipes from the throttle body.

6 Disconnect the throttle position sensor and idle speed actuator wiring plugs.

7 Disconnect the vacuum hose from the throttle body.

8 Disconnect the accelerator cable as described in Section 3.

9 Undo the retaining bolts/nuts and manoeuvre the throttle body from place **(see illustration)**.

10 Renew the throttle body seal **(see illustration)**.

11 Refitting is a reversal of removal.

Fuel rail and injectors

Removal

12 Remove the air cleaner assembly as described in Section 2.

13 Depressurise the fuel system as described in Section 5.

14 Disconnect the fuel supply pipe **(see illustration)**.

15 Disconnect the wiring connectors at the fuel injectors. Release the injector wiring harness from the retaining clips on the fuel

10.14 Undo the nuts and and disconnect the fuel supply pipe

rail and move the harness to one side **(see illustration)**.

16 Unscrew the two bolts securing the fuel rail assembly to the cylinder head, then carefully pull the injectors from the cylinder head, along with the fuel rail **(see illustration)**.

17 The injectors can be removed individually

10.15 Depress the clips and disconnect the injector wiring plugs

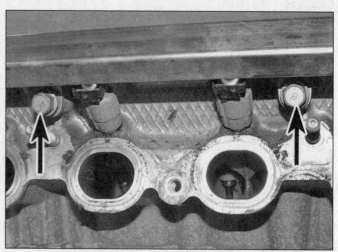

10.16 Fuel rail retaining bolts (manifold removed for clarity)

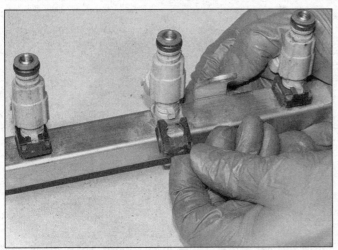

10.17a Prise open the clip and slide out

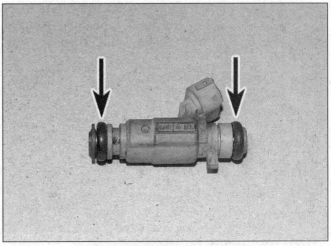

10.17b Renew the O-ring seals

from the fuel rail by prising open the relevant metal clip and easing the injector out of the rail. Remove the injector O-ring seals **(see illustrations)**.

18 Check the electrical resistance of the injector using a multimeter and compare it with the Specifications.

Note: *If a faulty injector is suspected, before condemning the injector it is worth trying the effect of one of the proprietary injector-cleaning treatments.*

Refitting

19 Refitting is a reversal of the removal procedure, bearing in mind the following points:

a) *Renew the injector O-ring seals, and smear them with a little petroleum jelly before assembling. Take care when fitting the injectors to the fuel rail and do not press them in further than required to fit the retaining clip otherwise the O-ring seal may be damaged.*

b) *Ensure that the injector retaining clips are securely seated.*

c) *On completion check the fuel rail and injectors for fuel leaks.*

Coolant temperature sensor

20 Refer to Chapter 3 Section 6.

Oxygen sensor

21 Refer to Chapter 4B Section 2.

Crankshaft position sensor

Removal

22 The crankshaft position sensor is located on the underside of the transmission bellhousing **(see illustration)**.

23 Disconnect the sensor wiring plug, undo the retaining bolt and remove the sensor.

Refitting

24 Refitting is a reversal of removal, tightening the retaining bolt to the specified torque.

Knock sensor

25 Refer to Chapter 5B Section 5.

10.22 Crankshaft position sensor

Camshaft position sensor(s)

Removal

26 Two camshaft position sensors may be fitted. One is located at the left-hand end of the cylinder head cover, and one at the left-hand end of the cylinder head **(see illustrations)**.

10.26a Camshaft position sensor on the cylinder head cover ...

10.26b ... and on the end of the cylinder head

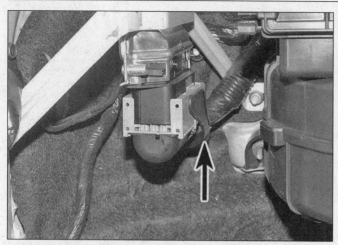

10.30 Fold open the locking catch to disconnect the wiring plug

10.34 The MAP sensor is fitted to the left-hand end of the intake manifold

27 Disconnect the wiring plug, undo the retaining bolt and withdraw the sensor from position.

Refitting

28 Refitting is a reversal of removal.

Electronic control unit (ECU)

Removal

29 Remove the glovebox as described in Chapter 11 Section 26.
30 Disconnect the ECU wiring plug **(see illustration)**.
31 Undo the nut and detach the earth connection from the ECU.
32 Undo the 4 retaining nuts and withdraw the ECU.

Refitting

33 Refitting is a reversal of removal. If a new ECU has been fitted, carry out the following 'self-learning' procedure:
a) *Turn on the ignition (don't start the engine or press the accelerator pedal), and wait at least 30 seconds. Engine temperature must be between 5 and 100°C.*

b) *On models with climate control, turn on the climate control system, and set the blower speed to position 2 for at least 15 seconds.*
c) *On models with cruise control, activate the system fro a few seconds by turning the switch on the control lever to ON.*

Manifold Absolute Pressure sensor (MAP)

34 The MAP is located on the front of the intake manifold **(see illustration)**.
35 Disconnect the wiring plug, undo the retaining screw and withdraw the sensor. Renew the O-ring seal if necessary.
36 Refitting is a reversal of removal.

11 Intake manifold – removal and refitting

Removal

1 Disconnect the battery negative lead as described in Chapter 5A Section 4.

2 Remove the air cleaner assembly as described in Section 2.
3 Disconnect the accelerator cable as described in Section 3.
4 Disconnect the knock sensor wiring plug.
5 Disconnect the wiring plugs from the ISA (Idle Speed Actuator), TPS (Throttle Position Sensor), MAP (Manifold Absolute Pressure) Sensor, and the ECT (Engine Coolant Temperature) sensor as described in Section 10.
6 Remove the throttle body as described in Section 10.
7 Remove the dipstick and knock sensor wiring brackets **(see illustration)**.
8 Undo the bolts and remove the intake manifold assembly. Renew the manifold seals **(see illustration)**.

Refitting

9 Refitting is a reverse of the removal procedure, ensuring that the manifold and cylinder head mating surfaces are clean

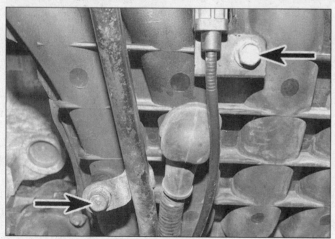

11.7 Remove dipstick and knock sensor wiring brackets

11.8 Renew the manifold seals

12.4 The oxygen sensor wiring plugs are located at the left-hand end of the engine

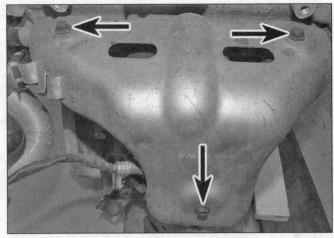

12.6 Heat shield retaining bolts

and dry. Refit the manifold and tighten the fasteners to their specified torque.

12 Exhaust manifold – removal and refitting

Removal

1 Raise the front of the vehicle and support it securely on axle stands, as described in 'Vehicle jacking and support'.
2 Disconnect the battery negative lead as described in Chapter 5A Section 4.
3 Remove the air cleaner as described in Section 2.
4 Disconnect the oxygen sensors wiring plugs (see illustration).
5 Remove the front pipe of the exhaust system as described in Section 13.
6 Undo the retaining bolts and remove the exhaust manifold heat shield (see illustration).

7 Undo the retaining nuts and remove the heat shield for the driveshaft.
8 Undo the bolts to remove the exhaust manifold bracket assembly.
9 Undo the 5 nuts and remove the exhaust manifold from place (see illustration).

Refitting

10 Refitting is a reversal of the removal procedure but use a new manifold gasket, and new front pipe flange gasket (see illustration). Tighten all fasteners to the specified torque where given.

13 Exhaust system – general information and component renewal

General information

1 A three-piece exhaust system is fitted comprising a front pipe, intermediate silencer

and rear silencer. The front pipe is connected to the exhaust manifold downpipe by means of a flange joint, and contains a flexible section to cater for engine movement. A catalytic converter is fitted to all models, and is an integral part of the exhaust manifold.
2 The system is suspended throughout its entire length by rubber mountings.
3 The intermediate and rear silencers can be individually renewed by unbolting the original system at the clamped joints.

Component renewal

Exhaust manifold and catalytic converter

4 Refer to Section 12.

Intermediate and rear silencers

5 Raise the front and rear of the vehicle, and support it securely on axle stands, as described in 'Vehicle jacking and support'.
6 Unscrew the nuts and disconnect the front

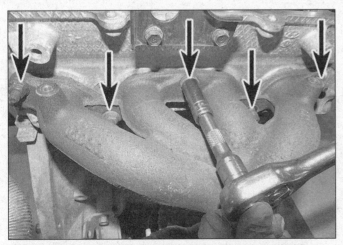

12.9 Undo the nuts and remove the exhaust manifold

12.10 Renew the cylinder head-to-exhaust manifold gasket

13.6 Front pipe flange nuts

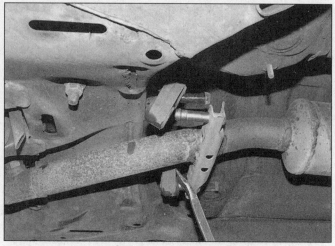

13.7 Release the rubber mounting

pipe flange from the manifold downpipe **(see illustration)**. Recover the gasket.

7 Undo the bolt securing the rear exhaust system mounting bracket to the underbody and release the front rubber mounting **(see illustration)**. Lower the system and suitably support it.

8 Remove the section you want to replace. Locate the new section in place in the clamping sleeve.

9 Reconnect the front pipe flange to the manifold downpipe using a new gasket, and tighten the nuts securely.

10 Align the exhaust system sections so that there is adequate clearance between the system and vehicle underbody, then securely tighten the clamping sleeve nut.

11 On completion, lower the vehicle to the ground.

Chapter 4 Part B
Emission control systems

Contents

Degrees of difficulty

Easy, suitable for novice with little experience	Fairly easy, suitable for beginner with some experience	Fairly difficult, suitable for competent DIY mechanic	Difficult, suitable for experienced DIY mechanic	Very difficult, suitable for expert DIY or professional

Specifications

Torque wrench setting	Nm	lbf ft
Oxygen sensors	44	32

1 General information

1 All models use unleaded petrol and are controlled by engine management systems that are 'tuned' to give the best compromise between driveability, fuel consumption and exhaust emission production. In addition, a number of systems are fitted that help to minimise other harmful emissions: a crankcase emission-control system that reduces the release of pollutants from the crankcase, an evaporative loss emission control system to reduce the release of hydrocarbons from the fuel tank, and a catalytic converter to reduce exhaust gaspollutants.

Crankcase emission control

2 To reduce the emission of unburned hydrocarbons from the crankcase into the atmosphere, the engine is sealed and the blow-by gases and oil vapour are drawn from inside the crankcase, into the inlet tract to be burned by the engine during normal combustion.   Under conditions of high manifold depression (idling, deceleration) the gases will by sucked positively out of the crankcase. Under conditions of low manifold depression (acceleration, full-throttle running) the gases are forced out of the crankcase by the (relatively) higher crankcase pressure; if the engine is worn, the raised crankcase pressure (due to increased blow-by) will cause

some of the flow to return under all manifold conditions.

Exhaust emission control

3 To minimise the amount of pollutants which escape into the atmosphere, a catalytic converter is fitted integrally into the exhaust manifold. The fuel system is of the closed-loop type, in which two lambda (or oxygen) sensors in the exhaust system provide the engine management system ECU with constant feedback, enabling the ECU to adjust the air/fuel mixture to optimise combustion. One lambda sensor is fitted 'upstream' of the catalytic converter, and the second sensor is fitted 'downstream' of the converter. The ECU compares the voltage signals from the two sensors to obtain the optimum inlet air/fuel ratio.

4 The lambda sensors have a heating element built-in that is controlled by the ECU to quickly bring the sensor's tip to its optimum operating temperature. The sensor's tip is sensitive to oxygen and provides a voltage signal to the ECU that varies according on the amount of oxygen in the exhaust gas. If the inlet air/fuel mixture is too rich, the exhaust gases are low in oxygen so the sensor sends a low-voltage signal, the voltage rising as the mixture weakens and the amount of oxygen rises in the exhaust gases. Peak conversion efficiency of all major pollutants occurs if the inlet air/fuel mixture is maintained at the chemically-correct ratio for the complete combustion of petrol of 14.7 parts (by weight) of air to 1 part

of fuel (the stoichiometric ratio). The sensor output voltage alters in a large step at this point, the ECU using the signal change as a reference point and correcting the inlet air/fuel mixture accordingly by altering the fuel injector pulse width.

Evaporative emission control

5 To minimise the escape of unburned hydrocarbons into the atmosphere, an evaporative loss emission control system is fitted. The fuel tank filler cap is sealed and a charcoal canister is mounted by it to collect the petrol vapours released from the fuel contained in the fuel tank. It stores them until they can be drawn from the canister (under the control of the engine management system ECU) via the evaporative emission control solenoid (purge) valve into the inlet tract, where they are then burned by the engine during normal combustion.

2 Engine emission control systems – component renewal

Crankcase emission control

1 The crankcase emission control system consists of a hose from the camshaft cover/camshaft housing to the air cleaner (or inlet duct).

2 The system requires no attention other than to check at regular intervals that the hose is free of blockages and undamaged.

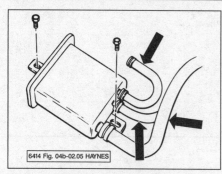

2.5 Disconnect the hoses

Evaporative emission control (EVAP)

3 The evaporative loss emission control system consists of the control solenoid, the activated charcoal filter canister and connecting fuel vapour hoses.

Charcoal canister

4 Remove the fuel tank as described in Section 4A Section 8.
5 Disconnect the vapour hoses **(see illustration)**.
6 Unscrew 2 bolts and remove the canister assembly from the fuel tank.
7 Refitting is a reversal of removal.

Exhaust emission control

Catalytic converter renewal

8 The catalytic converter is an integral part of the exhaust manifold. Refer to Chapter 4A Section 12 for exhaust manifold removal and refitting procedures.

Oxygen (lambda) sensors renewal

Caution: The oxygen sensors are delicate

and will not work if dropped or knocked, if their power supply is disrupted, or if any cleaning materials are used on them.
9 The two sensors are threaded into the exhaust manifold – one 'upstream' and one 'downstream' of the catalytic converter.
10 Disconnect the battery negative lead as described in Chapter 5A Section 4.
11 Trace the wiring from the sensor(s), and disconnect the wiring plug(s) located at the left-hand end of the engne.
12 Unscrew the sensor, taking care to avoid damaging the sensor probe as it is removed **(see illustrations)**.
Note: *As a flying lead remains connected to the sensor after it has been disconnected, if the correct spanner is not available, a slotted socket will be required to remove the sensor.*
13 Apply a little anti-seize grease to the sensor threads – avoid contaminating the probe tip.
14 Refit the sensor, tightening it to the specified torque. Reconnect the wiring connector.
15 Reconnect the battery as described in Chapter 5A Section 4.

3 Catalytic converter – general information and precautions

1 The catalytic converter is a reliable and simple device which needs no maintenance in itself, but there are some facts of which an owner should be aware if the converter is to function properly for its full service life.
a) DO NOT use leaded petrol or LRP in a car equipped with a catalytic converter

– the lead will coat the precious metals, reducing their converting efficiency and will eventually destroy the converter.
b) Always keep the ignition and fuel systems well-maintained in accordance with the manufacturer's schedule.
c) If the engine develops a misfire, do not drive the car at all (or at least as little as possible) until the fault is cured.
d) DO NOT push- or tow-start the car – this will soak the catalytic converter in unburned fuel, causing it to overheat when the engine does start.
e) DO NOT switch off the ignition at high engine speeds.
f) DO NOT use fuel or engine oil additives – these may contain substances harmful to the catalytic converter.
g) DO NOT continue to use the car if the engine burns oil to the extent of leaving a visible trail of blue smoke.
h) Remember that the catalytic converter operates at very high temperatures. DO NOT, therefore, park the car in dry undergrowth, over long grass or piles of dead leaves after a long run.
i) Remember that the catalytic converter is FRAGILE – do not strike it with tools during servicing work.
j) In some cases a sulphurous smell (like that of rotten eggs) may be noticed from the exhaust. This is common to many catalytic converter-equipped cars and once the car has covered a fewthousand miles the problem should disappear.
k) The catalytic converter, used on a well-maintained and well-driven car, should last for between 50-000 and100-000 miles – if the converter is no longer effective it must be renewed.

2.12a The upstream sensor is fitted into the side of the exhaust manifold

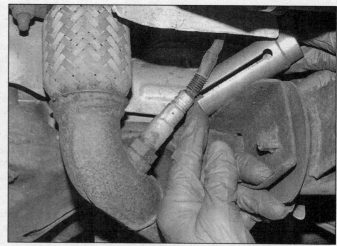

2.12b The downstream sensor is fitted into the front exhaust pipe – note the slotted socket

Chapter 5 Part A
Starting and Charging systems

Contents

Degrees of difficulty

Easy, suitable for novice with little experience	Fairly easy, suitable for beginner with some experience	Fairly difficult, suitable for competent DIY mechanic	Difficult, suitable for experienced DIY mechanic	Very difficult, suitable for expert DIY or professional

Specifications

System type .... 12-volt, negative earth

Alternator 70A
Starter motor: .... 0.9 kW
Battery: 32-20DL
Battery charge condition:
  Poor .... 12.5 volts
  Normal .... 12.6 volts
  Good .... 12.7 volts

Torque wrench settings	Nm	lbf ft
Alternator:		
Upper bolt	35	26
Lower bolts	23	18
Starter motor bolts	48	35

1 General information and precautions

General information

1 The engine electrical system consists mainly of the charging and starting systems. Because of their engine-related functions, these components are covered separately from the body electrical devices such as the lights, instruments, etc (which are covered in Chapter 12). Information on the ignition system is covered in Part B of this Chapter.

2 The electrical system is of 12-volt negative earth type.

3 The battery fitted as original equipment is of maintenance-free (sealed for life) type and is charged by the alternator, which is belt-driven from the crankshaft pulley. If a non-original battery is fitted it may be of standard or low maintenance type.

4 The starter motor is of the pre-engaged type incorporating an integral solenoid. On starting, the solenoid moves the drive pinion into engagement with the flywheel ring gear before the starter motor is energised. Once the engine has started, a one-way clutch prevents the motor armature being driven by the engine until the pinion disengages from the flywheel.

Precautions

5 Further details of the various systems are given in the relevant Sections of this Chapter. While some repair procedures are given, the usual course of action is to renew the component concerned. The owner whose interest extends beyond mere component renewal should obtain a copy of the Automotive Electrical & Electronic Systems Manual, available from the publishers of this manual.

6 It is necessary to take extra care when working on the electrical system to avoid damage to semi-conductor devices (diodes and transistors), and to avoid the risk of personal injury. In addition to the precautions given in *Safety first!* at the beginning of this manual, observe the following when working on the system:

● Always remove rings, watches, etc before working on the electrical system. Even with the battery disconnected, capacitive discharge could occur if a component's live terminal is earthed through a metal object. This could cause a shock or nasty burn.

● Do not reverse the battery connections. Components such as the alternator, electronic control units, or any other components having semi-conductor circuitry could be irreparably damaged

● If the engine is being started using jump leads and a slave battery, connect the batteries positive-to-positive and negative-to-negative (see Jump starting 0 Section

4). This also applies when connecting a battery charger but in this case both of the battery terminals should first be disconnected.

● Never disconnect the battery terminals, the alternator, any electrical wiring or any test instruments when the engine is running.

● Do not allow the engine to turn the alternator when the alternator is not connected.

● Never test for alternator output by flashing the output lead to earth.

● Never use an ohmmeter of the type incorporating a hand-cranked generator for circuit or continuity testing.

● Always ensure that the battery negative lead is disconnected when working on the electrical system.

● Before using electric-arc welding equipment on the car, disconnect the battery, alternator and components such as the fuel injection/ignition electronic control unit to protect them from the risk of damage.

2 Electrical fault finding – general information

1 Refer to Chapter 12 Section 2.

3 Battery – testing and charging

Testing

1 Topping-up and testing of the electrolyte in each cell is not possible. The condition of the battery can therefore only be tested using a voltmeter.

2 Connect the voltmeter across the battery and compare the result with those given in the Specifications under "charge condition". The test is only accurate if the battery has not been subjected to any kind of charge for the previous six hours. If this is not the case, switch on the headlights for 30 seconds, then wait four to five minutes before testing the battery after switching off the headlights. All other electrical circuits must be switched off,

so check that the doors and tailgate are fully shut when making the test.

3 If the voltage reading is less than 12.2 volts, then the battery is discharged, whilst a reading of 12.2 to 12.4 volts indicates a partially discharged condition.

4 If the battery is to be charged, remove it from the vehicle (Section 4) and charge it as described later in this Section.

Charging

Note: *The following is intended as a guide only. Always refer to the manufacturer's recommendations (often printed on a label attached to the battery) before charging a battery.*

5 It's recommended that a 'smart' or 'intelligent' type charger is used. Once connected to the battery, the recharge, recovering and maintenance of the battery is automatically carried out and monitored by the charger.

6 If the battery is to be charged from a fully discharged state (condition reading less than 12.2 volts), have it recharged by your Hyundai dealer or local automotive electrician, as the charge rate is higher and constant supervision during charging is necessary.

Caution: Do not charge AGM batteries above 14.8 volts, or the battery may be damaged.

4 Battery and battery tray – disconnection, removal and refitting

Battery

Disconnection

1 Open the bonnet, slacken the nut, then with a twisting motion, pull the negative lead clamp from the battery terminal **(see illustration)**.

2 Pull up the plastic cover over the battery positive terminal.

3 Slacken the clamp and pull the positive lead clamp from the battery terminal **(see illustration)**.

Removal

4 Disconnect the battery as described previously in this Section.

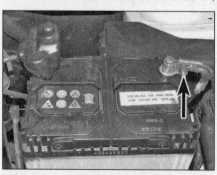
4.1 Slacken the nut and disconnect the negative lead clamp

4.3 Pull the positive lead clamp from the terminal

4.5 Battery retaining clamp bolt

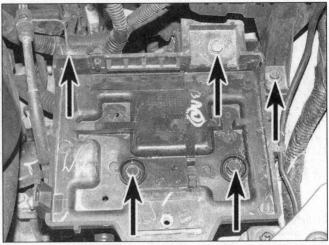

4.8 Battery tray retaining bolts

5 Unscrew the nut or bolt (as applicable), remove the battery retaining clamp, then lift the battery out of the engine compartment **(see illustration)**.

Refitting

⚠️ *Warning: Models equipped with the ISG (Idle stop & go) system equipped vehicle always use the AGM battery only. If the wrong battery is installed, this can potentially lead to engine electrical trouble or ISG system error.*

6 Refitting is a reversal of removal, but smear petroleum jelly on the terminals after reconnecting the leads, and always reconnect the positive lead first, and the negative lead last.

Battery tray

Removal

7 Remove the battery as described previously in this Section.
8 Unclip the wiring looms then undo the 5 bolts and remove the battery tray **(see illustration)**.

Refitting

9 Refitting is a reversal of removal

5 Charging system – testing

Note: *Refer to the warnings given in 'Safety first!' and in Section 1 of this Chapter before starting work.*
1 If the ignition warning light fails to illuminate when the ignition is switched on, first check the alternator wiring connections for security. If satisfactory, check that the warning light bulb has not blown, and that the bulbholder is secure in its location in the instrument panel. If the light still fails to illuminate, check the continuity of the warning light feed wire from the alternator to the bulbholder. If all

is satisfactory, the alternator is at fault and should be renewed or taken to an auto-electrician for testing and repair.
2 If the ignition warning light illuminates when the engine is running, stop the engine and check that the drivebelt is correctly tensioned (see Chapter 1 Section 5) and that the alternator connections are secure. If all is so far satisfactory, have the alternator checked by an auto-electrician.
3 If the alternator output is suspect even though the warning light functions correctly, the regulated voltage may be checked as follows.
4 Connect a voltmeter across the battery terminals and start the engine.
5 Increase the engine speed until the voltmeter reading remains steady; the reading should be approximately 12 to 13 volts, and no more than 14 volts.
6 Switch on as many electrical accessories (eg, the headlights, heated rear window and heater blower) as possible, and check that the alternator maintains the regulated voltage at around 13 to 14 volts.
7 If the regulated voltage is not as stated, the fault may be due to worn brushes, weak brush springs, a faulty voltage regulator, a faulty diode, a severed phase winding or worn or damaged slip-rings. The alternator should

be renewed or taken to an auto-electrician for testing and repair.

6 Alternator – testing, removal and refitting

Testing

1 If the alternator is thought to be faulty, it should be removed from the vehicle and taken to an auto-electrician for testing. However, check the cost of repairs before proceeding, as it may prove more economical to obtain a new or exchange alternator.

Removal

2 Disconnect the battery negative lead as described in Section 4.
3 Remove the auxiliary drivebelt as described in Chapter 1 Section 5.
4 Remove the windscreen washer fluid reservoir as described in Chapter 12 Section 16.
5 Disconnect the alternator wiring plug **(see illustration)**.
6 Undo the retaining nut and remove the main cable from the alternator terminal **(see illustration)**.

6.5 Disconnect the alternator wiring plug

6.6 Pull away the rubber boot to expose the terminal nut

6.7 Remove the alternator top mounting bracket

6.8 Remove the lower mounting bolt

7 Undo the 3 bolts and remove the alternator top mounting bracket from place **(see illustration)**.

8 Undo the lower mounting bolt and manoeuvre the alternator from place through the right-hand headlight aperture **(see illustration)**.

Refitting

9 Refitting is a reversal of removal, noting the following points:

a) During removal, the lower mounting bolt retaining sleeve can move. If it does, and the alternator will not fit back into its mounting, push back the retaining sleeve into the housing.

b) Refit the auxiliary drivebelt as described in Chapter 1 Section 5.

c) Tighten all fasteners to their specified torque where given.

---

7 Starting system – testing

Note: *Refer to the precautions given in Safety first! and in Section 1 of this Chapter before starting work.*

1 If the starter motor fails to operate when the ignition key is turned to the appropriate position, the following possible causes may be responsible.

a) The battery is faulty.

b) The electrical connections between the switch, solenoid, battery and starter motor are somewhere failing to pass the necessary current from the battery through the starter to earth.

c) The solenoid is faulty.

d) The starter motor is mechanically or electrically defective.

2 To check the battery, switch on the headlights. If they dim after a few seconds, this indicates that the battery is discharged – recharge (see Section 3) or renew the battery. If the headlights glow brightly, operate the ignition switch and observe the lights. If they dim, then this indicates that current is reaching the starter motor; therefore the fault must lie in the starter motor. If the lights continue to glow

brightly (and no clicking sound can be heard from the starter motor solenoid), this indicates that there is a fault in the circuit or solenoid – see following paragraphs. If the starter motor turns slowly when operated, but the battery is in good condition, then this indicates that either the starter motor is faulty, or there is considerable resistance somewhere in the circuit.

3 If a fault in the circuit is suspected, disconnect the battery leads (including the earth connection to the body), the starter/solenoid wiring and the engine/transmission earth strap. Thoroughly clean the connections, and reconnect the leads and wiring, then use a voltmeter or test lamp to check that full battery voltage is available at the battery positive lead connection to the solenoid, and that the earth is sound. Smear petroleum jelly around the battery terminals to prevent corrosion – corroded connections are amongst the most frequent causes of electrical system faults.

4 If the battery and all connections are in good condition, check the circuit by disconnecting the trigger wire from the solenoid terminal. Connect a voltmeter or test lamp between the wire end and a good earth (such as the battery negative terminal), and check that the wire is live when the ignition switch is turned to the 'start' position. If it is, then the circuit is sound – if not the circuit wiring can be checked as described in Chapter 12 Section 2.

5 The solenoid contacts can be checked by

connecting a voltmeter or test lamp between the battery positive feed connection on the starter side of the solenoid and earth. When the ignition switch is turned to the 'start' position, there should be a reading or lighted bulb, as applicable. If there is no reading or lighted bulb, the solenoid is faulty and should be renewed.

6 If the circuit and solenoid are proved sound, the fault must lie in the starter motor. Begin checking the starter motor by removing it and having the brushes checked. If the fault does not lie in the brushes, the motor windings must be faulty. In this event, it may be possible to have the starter motor overhauled by a specialist, but check on the availability and cost of spares before proceeding, as it may prove more economical to obtain a new or exchange motor.

---

8 Starter motor – removal and refitting

Removal

Caution: There are two kinds of starter, ISG type starter and the other. When replacing the starter, confirm that the part number and connector shape. ISG (Idle stop & go) system-equipped models always use the ISG-type starter only. If the other starter has installed, this can potentially lead to engine electrical trouble or ISG system error.

1 Raise the front of the vehicle and support it securely on axle stands, as described in *'Vehicle jacking and support'*.

2 Disconnect the battery negative lead as described in Section 4.

3 Disconnect the wiring plug from the S terminal, and undo the nut and remove the cable from the B terminal **(see illustration)**.

4 Unscrew and remove the starter motor mounting bolts **(see illustration)**.

Refitting

5 Refitting is a reversal of removal, tightening the starter motor retaining bolts to the specified torque.

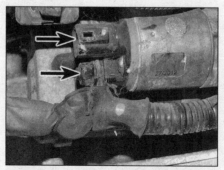

8.3 Disconnect the wiring plug, undo the nut and disconnect the cable (engine removed for clarity)

8.4 Undo the mounting bolts and remove the starter

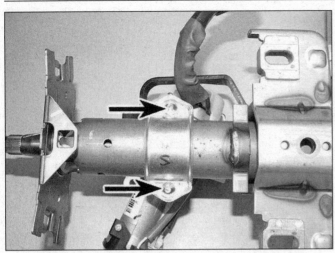

10.2 The switch/lock assembly is secured by shear bolts

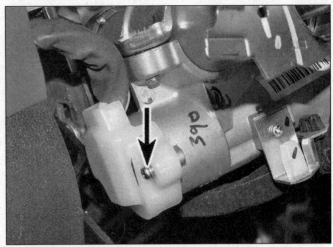

10.8 Ignition switch retaining screw

9 Starter motor – testing and overhaul

1 If the starter motor is thought to be suspect, it should be removed from the vehicle and taken to an auto-electrician for testing. Most auto-electricians will be able to supply and fit brushes at a reasonable cost. However, check on the cost of repairs before proceeding as it may prove more economical to obtain a new or exchange motor.

10.13 With the key turned to 'ON', depress the retaining pin and remove the ignition barrel

10 Ignition switch and lock barrel – removal and refitting

Ignition switch/steering lock assembly

Removal

1 Remove the steering column assembly as described in Chapter 10 Section 13.
Caution: The steering column shafts must not be rotated during this procedure.
2 The ignition switch/steering column lock assembly is secured to the steering column using 'shear' bolts. Drill-out the shear bolts, or unscrew them using a sharp chisel and hammer (see illustration). Obtain replacement shear bolts.
3 Remove the collar, followed by the ignition switch/steering lock assembly.

Refitting

4 Position the ignition switch/steering lock assembly, insert the new shear bolts, and tighten them until their heads shear off.
5 The remainder of refitting is a reversal of removal.

Ignition switch contact assembly

Removal

6 Disconnect the battery negative lead as described in Section 4.
7 Remove the steering column lower shroud as described in Chapter 11 Section 26.
8 Undo the retaining screw, disconnect the wiring plug and remove the ignition switch (see illustration).

Refitting

9 Refitting is a reversal of removal.

Ignition key lock barrel

Removal

10 Disconnect the battery negative lead as described in Section 4.
11 Remove the steering column lower shroud as described earlier in Chapter 11 Section 26.
12 Insert the ignition key into the barrel, and turn it to position 'On'.
13 Using a small screwdriver, depress the retaining pin, and withdraw the barrel assembly from the housing (see illustration).

Refitting

14 Refitting is a reversal of removal, but check the operation of the barrel/lock before refitting the steering column shrouds.

Chapter 5 Part B
Ignition system

Contents

Degrees of difficulty

Easy, suitable for novice with little experience	**Fairly easy,** suitable for beginner with some experience	**Fairly difficult,** suitable for competent DIY mechanic	**Difficult,** suitable for experienced DIY mechanic	**Very difficult,** suitable for expert DIY or professional

Specifications

System type
All models. . . . . Digital (distributorless) ignition system controlled by the engine management ECU.

Firing order. 1-3-4-2
Spark plugs . . . . See Chapter 1 specifications
Ignition timing. . . . . Controlled by the engine management ECU
Ignition coil:
   Primary resistance (at 23°C). . . . . 0.82 ohms ± 10%
   Secondary resistance (at 23°C) . . . . 15.5 kilo-ohms ± 15%

Torque wrench setting	Nm	lbf ft
Knock sensor retaining bolt	21	16

1 General information

1 The ignition system is integrated with the fuel injection system to form a combined engine management system under the control of one ECU (see Chapter 4A for further information).

2 The ignition side of the system is of the digital (distributorless) type, consisting of a coil 'pack' attached to the spark plugs by high-tension leads. The engine management ECU uses the inputs from the various sensors to calculate the required ignition advance setting and coil charging time depending on engine temperature, load and speed.

3 A knock sensor is also incorporated into the ignition system. Mounted onto the cylinder block, the sensor detects the high-frequency vibrations caused when the engine starts to pre-ignite, or 'pink'. Under these conditions, the knock sensor sends an electrical signal to the ECU which in turn retards the ignition advance setting in small steps until the 'pinking' ceases.

3.3 Disconnect spark plug leads

3.5a Undo 1 mounting bolt from the front of the coil pack ...

3.5b ... and 2 around the back of the coil pack

2 Ignition system – testing

⚠️ *Warning: Due to the high voltages produced by the electronic ignition system, extreme care must be taken when working on the system with the ignition switched on. Persons with surgically implanted cardiac pacemaker devices should keep well clear of the ignition circuits, components and test equipment.*

1 If a fault appears in the engine management (fuel injection/ignition) system first ensure that the fault is not due to a poor electrical connection or poor maintenance; ie, check that the air cleaner filter element is clean, the spark plugs are in good condition, that the engine breather hoses are clear and undamaged, referring to Chapter for further information. If the engine is running very roughly, check the compression pressures as described in Chapter 2A Section 2.

2 If these checks fail to reveal the cause of the problem, the vehicle should be taken to a Hyundai dealer or suitably equipped repairer for testing. A diagnostic connector is incorporated in the engine management wiring circuit into which a special electronic diagnostic tester can be plugged (Chapter 4A Section 9). The tester will locate the fault quickly and simply alleviating the need to test all the system components individually which is a time-consuming operation that carries a high risk of damaging the ECU.

3 The only ignition system checks which can be carried out by the home mechanic are those described in Chapter 1 Section 15, relating to the spark plugs, and the ignition coil test described in this Section 3. If necessary, the system wiring and wiring connectors can be checked as described in Chapter 12 Section 2, ensuring that the ECU wiring connectors have first been disconnected.

3 Ignition coil – removal, testing and refitting

Removal

1 Remove the air cleaner assembly as described in Chapter 4A Section 2.
2 Disconnect the battery negative lead as described in Chapter 5A Section 4.
3 Pull the HT lead caps from the spark plugs **(see illustration)**.
Caution: Pull only on the HT caps, not the leads.
4 Disconnect 3 wiring plugs and remove 2 of them from the coil pack mounting bracket.
5 Undo the bolts and remove the coil pack from place **(see illustrations)**.

Testing

6 Testing of the coil consists of using a multimeter set to its resistance function, to check the primary and secondary windings for continuity and resistance. Compare the results obtained to those given in the Specifications at the start of this Chapter. Note the resistance of the coil windings varies slightly according to the coil temperature and the figures in the Specifications are values for the coil at 23°C.
7 Check that there is no continuity between the HT lead terminals and the coil body/mounting bracket.
8 If faulty, the coil should be renewed.

Refitting

9 Refitting is a reversal of removal, taking care to tighten the bolts to the correct torque setting, and ensuring the HT leads are correctly reconnected.

4 Ignition timing – checking and adjustment

1 The ignition timing is constantly being monitored and adjusted by the engine management ECU, and nominal values cannot be given. Therefore, it is not possible for the home mechanic to check the ignition timing.
2 The only way in which the timing can be checked is using special electronic test equipment, connected to the engine management system diagnostic connector (refer to Chapter 4A Section 9 for further information).

5 Knock sensor – removal and refitting

Removal

1 The knock sensor is located on the front face of the cylinder block.
2 Raise the front of the vehicle and support it securely on axle stands, as described in *'Vehicle jacking and support'*.
3 Trace the wiring back from the sensor to its wiring plug, and disconnect it from the main harness.
4 Undo the sensor retaining bolt and manoeuvre it from position **(see illustration)**.

Refitting

5 Refitting is a reversal of removal, tightening the retaining bolt to the specified torque.

5.4 Undo the retaining bolt and remove the sensor

Chapter 6
Clutch

Contents

Degrees of difficulty

Easy, suitable for novice with little experience		Fairly easy, suitable for beginner with some experience		Fairly difficult, suitable for competent DIY mechanic		Difficult, suitable for experienced DIY mechanic		Very difficult, suitable for expert DIY or professional	

Specifications

Type . . . .   Single dry plate with diaphragm spring, hydraulically operated

Friction plate diameter . . . .   190 mm

Torque wrench settings	Nm	lbf ft
Master cylinder retaining bolts.	25	18
Pressure plate retaining bolts.	15	10
Slave cylinder mounting bolts	20	15

1 General information

1 The clutch assembly consists of a friction plate, a pressure plate, a release bearing and release fork; all of these components are contained in the large cast-aluminium alloy bellhousing, sandwiched between the engine and the transmission. The release mechanism is operated by cable.

2 The friction plate is fitted between the engine flywheel and the clutch pressure plate, and is allowed to slide on the transmission input shaft splines.

3 The pressure plate assembly is bolted to the engine flywheel. When the engine is running, drive is transmitted from the crankshaft, via the flywheel, to the friction plate (these components being clamped securely together by the pressure plate assembly) and from the friction plate to the transmission input shaft.

4 To interrupt the drive, the spring pressure must be relaxed. This is done by means of the clutch release bearing, fitted concentrically around the transmission input shaft. The bearing is pushed onto the pressure plate assembly by means of the release fork actuated by the clutch cable.

5 The clutch pedal is connected to a cable, which acts on the release arm at the front of the transmission casing. The release fork pivots on its mountings, and the other end of the fork then presses the release bearing against the pressure plate spring fingers. This causes the springs to deform and releases the clamping force on the pressure plate.

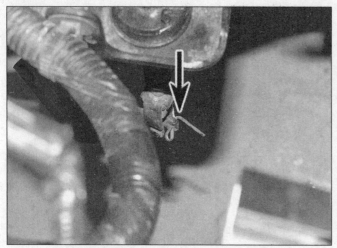

2.1 Remove the split pin from the end of the cable

2.2 Pull the cable from the bracket

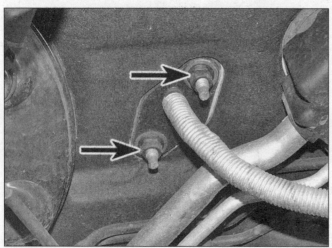

2.3 Cable/pedal bracket retaining nuts

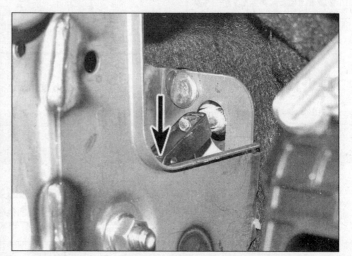

2.5 Detach the end of the cable from the clutch pedal

2 Clutch cable – removal, refitting and adjustment

Removal

1 Remove the split pin securing the end of the clutch cable to the lever at the front of the gearbox (see illustration).
2 Pull the clutch cable from the bracket on the gearbox (see illustration).
3 Working in the engine bay, undo the 2 nuts holding the clutch cable/pedal bracket to the bulkhead (see illustration).
4 Remove the driver's side lower facia panel as described in Chapter 11 Section 26.
5 Detach the clutch cable from the rear of the clutch pedal (see illustration).
6 Pull the cable through from the engine bay.

Refitting

7 Refitting is a reversal of removal

Adjustment

8 After refitting, rotate the cable adjuster nut to obtain a distance of 3 – 4 mm between the nut and the cable damper (see illustration).

3 Clutch assembly – removal, inspection and refitting

⚠️ **Warning: Dust created by clutch wear and deposited on the clutch components may contain asbestos, which is a health hazard. DO NOT blow it out with compressed air, or inhale any of it. DO NOT use petrol or petroleum-based solvents to clean off the dust. Brake system cleaner or**

methylated spirit should be used to flush the dust into a suitable receptacle. After the clutch components are wiped clean with rags, dispose of the contaminated rags and cleaner in a sealed, marked container.

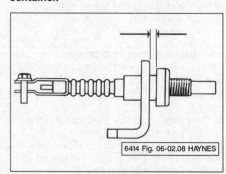

6414 Fig. 06-02.08 HAYNES

2.8 The clearance between the nut and damper should be 3 – 4 mm

3.3 Pressure plate retaining bolts

3.13 The spring hub must face away from the flywheel

Removal

1 Unless the complete engine/transmission is to be removed from the car and separated for major overhaul (see Chapter 2B Section 4), the clutch can be reached by removing the transmission as described in Chapter 7A Section 5.

2 Before disturbing the clutch, use chalk or a marker pen to mark the relationship of the pressure plate assembly to the flywheel.

3 Working in a diagonal sequence, slacken the pressure plate bolts by half a turn at a time, until spring pressure is released and the bolts can be unscrewed by hand (see illustration).

4 Prise the pressure plate assembly off its locating dowels, and collect the friction plate, noting which way round the friction plate is fitted.

Inspection

Note: *Due to the amount of work necessary to remove and refit clutch components, it is usually considered good practice to renew the clutch friction plate, pressure plate assembly and release bearing as a matched set, even if only one of these is actually worn enough to require renewal. It is also worth considering the renewal of the clutch components on a preventative basis if the engine and/or transmission have been removed for some other reason.*

5 When cleaning clutch components, read first the warning at the beginning of this Section; remove dust using a clean, dry cloth, and working in a well-ventilated atmosphere.

Note: *Although some friction materials may no longer contain asbestos, it is safest to assume that they DO, and to take precautions accordingly.*

6 Check the friction plate facings for signs of wear, damage or oil contamination. If the friction material is cracked, burnt, scored or damaged, or if it is contaminated with oil or grease (shown by shiny black patches), the friction plate must be renewed.

7 If the friction material is still serviceable, check that the centre boss splines are unworn, that the torsion springs are in good condition and securely fastened, and that all the rivets are tight. If any wear or damage is found, the friction plate must be renewed.

8 If the friction material is fouled with oil, this must be due to an oil leak from the crankshaft left-hand oil seal, from the sump-to-cylinder block joint, or from the transmission input shaft. Renew the seal or repair the joint, as appropriate, before installing the new friction plate.

9 Check the pressure plate assembly for obvious signs of wear or damage; shake it to check for loose rivets or worn or damaged fulcrum rings, and check that the drive straps securing the pressure plate to the cover do not show signs (such as a deep yellow or blue discoloration) of overheating. If the diaphragm spring is worn or damaged, or if its pressure is in any way suspect, the pressure plate assembly should be renewed.

10 Examine the machined bearing surfaces of the pressure plate and of the flywheel; they should be clean, completely flat, and free from scratches or scoring. If either is discoloured from excessive heat, or shows signs of cracks, it should be renewed – although minor damage of this nature can sometimes be polished away using emery paper.

11 Check that the release bearing contact surface rotates smoothly and easily, with no sign of noise or roughness. Also check that the surface itself is smooth and unworn, with no signs of cracks, pitting or scoring. If there is any doubt about its condition, the bearing must be renewed.

Refitting

12 On reassembly, ensure that the bearing surfaces of the flywheel and pressure plate are completely clean, smooth, and free from oil or grease. Use solvent to remove any protective grease from new components.

13 Fit the friction plate so that its spring hub assembly faces away from the flywheel; there may also be a marking showing which way round the plate is to be refitted (see illustration).

14 Refit the pressure plate assembly, aligning the marks made on dismantling (if the original pressure plate is re-used), and locating the pressure plate on its locating dowels. Fit the new pressure plate bolts, but tighten them only finger-tight, so that the friction plate can still be moved.

15 The friction plate must now be centralised, so that when the transmission is refitted, its input shaft will pass through the splines at the centre of the friction plate.

16 Centralisation can be achieved by passing a screwdriver or other long bar through the friction plate and into the hole in the crankshaft; the friction plate can then be moved around until it is centred on the crankshaft hole. Alternatively, a clutch-aligning tool can be used to eliminate the guesswork; these can be obtained from most accessory shops (see illustration). A home-made aligning tool can be fabricated from a length of

3.16 Use a clutch aligning tool to centralise the plate and cover

4.2 Derail the spring from its mounting

4.3 Undo and remove the bolt from the release fork

4.4 Remove the thrust bearing

4.5 Remove the clutch release shaft and spring

metal rod or wooden dowel which fits closely inside the crankshaft hole, and has insulating tape wound around it to match the diameter of the friction plate splined hole.

17 When the friction plate is centralised, tighten the pressure plate bolts evenly and in a diagonal sequence to the specified torque setting.

18 Refit the transmission as described in Chapter 7A Section 5.

4 Clutch release mechanism – removal, inspection and refitting

Removal

1 Remove the gearbox assembly as described in Section 7A Section 5.

2 Derail the return spiring from its mounting **(see illustration)**.

3 Remove the retaining bolt from the clutch release fork **(see illustration)**.

4 Slide forward the thrust bearing so it disengages from the fork **(see illustration)**.

5 Remove the clutch release shaft and return spring **(see illustration)**.

Inspection

6 Check the release mechanism, renewing any worn or damaged parts. Carefully check all bearing surfaces and points of contact.

7 When checking the release bearing itself, note that it is often considered worthwhile to renew it as a matter of course. Check that the contact surface rotates smoothly and easily, with no sign of roughness, and that the surface itself is smooth and unworn, with no signs of cracks, pitting or scoring. If there is any doubt about its condition, the bearing must be renewed.

Refitting

8 Apply a smear of molybdenum disulphide grease to the shaft pivot bushes and the contact surfaces of the release fork.

Note: *When installing the clutch, apply grease to each part, but be careful not to apply excessive grease; it can cause clutch slippage and judder.*

9 Apply multipurpose grease onto the back of the release bearing.

10 Install the release bearing to the release fork.

11 Install the return spring to the release fork, ensuring it is also located in the groove in the gearbox casing.

12 Refit the shaft and securely tighten the reamer bolt.

13 Refit the transmission as described in Chapter 7A Section 5.

Chapter 7 Part A
Manual gearbox

Contents

Degrees of difficulty

Easy, suitable for novice with little experience	**Fairly easy,** suitable for beginner with some experience 🔧	**Fairly difficult,** suitable for competent DIY mechanic 🔧	**Difficult,** suitable for experienced DIY mechanic 🔧	**Very difficult,** suitable for expert DIY or professional

Specifications

General

Type	Transversely mounted, front-wheel-drive layout with integral differential/final drive. 5 forward speeds, 1 reverse speed
Code	M5EF2 (5-speed)

Lubrication

Recommended oil	See 'Lubricants and fluids'
Capacity	1.9 litres

Torque wrench settings

	Nm	lb ft
Support bracket mounting bolts	56	42
Upper and lower mounting bolts	48	35
Rear link rod-to-gearbox bracket	56	42
Shift lever assembly bolts	11	8
Starter motor installation bolt	30	22

1 General information

1 The transmission is contained in a cast-aluminium alloy casing bolted to the engine's left-hand end, and consists of the gearbox and final drive differential.

2 Drive is transmitted from the crankshaft via the clutch to the input shaft, which has a splined extension to accept the clutch friction plate and rotates in roller bearings at its right-hand end and ball-bearings at its left-hand end. From the input shaft, drive is transmitted to the output shaft which rotates in roller bearings at its right-hand end and ball-bearings at its left-hand end. From the output shaft, the drive is transmitted to the differential crownwheel which rotates with the differential case and gears in taper roller bearings, thus driving the sun gears and driveshafts. The rotation of the differential gears on their shaft allows the inner roadwheel to rotate at a slower speed than the outer roadwheel when the car is cornering.

3 The input and output shafts are arranged side-by-side, parallel to the crankshaft and driveshafts, so that their gear pinion teeth are in constant mesh. In the neutral position, the relevant input shaft and output shaft gear pinions rotate freely, so that drive cannot be transmitted to the output shaft and crownwheel.

4 Gear selection is via a dashboard-mounted lever and twin selector cable mechanism. The selector cables cause the appropriate selector fork to move its respective synchro-sleeve along the shaft, to lock the gear to the synchro-hub. Since the synchro-hubs are splined to the input and output shafts, this locks the gear to the shaft so that drive can be transmitted. To ensure that gearchanging can be made quickly and quietly, a synchromesh system is fitted to all forward gears.

2.2 Wipe the area around the plugs

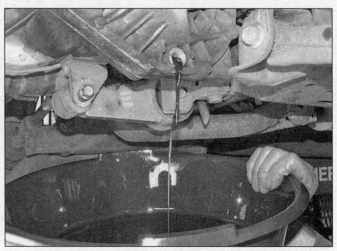
2.4 Remove the drain plug and allow oil to drain

2 Gearbox oil – draining and refilling

1 Park the vehicle on a level surface, if possible over an inspection pit or on a ramp as the filler/level and drain plugs are accessed from under the engine compartment. If necessary jack up the vehicle and support on axle stands, as described in 'Vehicle jacking and support'.
2 Wipe clean the area around the filler/level and drain plugs **(see illustration)**.
3 Undo the filler/level plug and clean it.
4 Position a suitable container beneath the transmission, then undo the drain plug. Allow the oil to completely drain **(see illustration)**.
5 Wipe clean the drain plug then refit with a new gasket and tighten it.
6 Fill the transmission with the correct grade and quantity of oil, referring to Chapter 1

Section 22 when checking the level. Refit and tighten the filler/level plug.
7 Where applicable, lower the vehicle to the ground.

3 Gearchange selector cables – removal and refitting

Removal

Note: *Both gearshift cables come as a complete unit and cannot be changed individually.*
1 Remove the battery and battery tray as described in Chapter 5A Section 4.
2 Remove the centre console assembly as described in Chapter 11 Section 24.
3 Using a trim removal tool, prise out the driver's and passenger's lower vent panels **(see illustrations)**.

4 Using a trim removal tool, remove the gear lever upper and lower surround trims as described in Chapter 11 Section 26.
5 Prise apart the retaining clip and remove the select cable assembly **(see illustration)**.
6 Remove the second shift cable assembly

3.3a Remove driver's lower vent panel ...

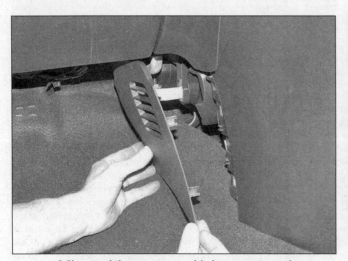
3.3b ... and the passenger-side lower vent panel

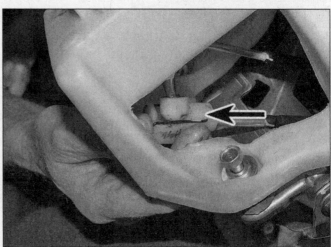
3.5 Prise apart wire clip and detach the shift cable

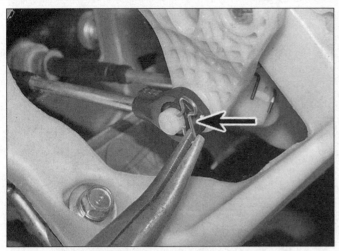

3.6 Remove the pin and detach the second cable

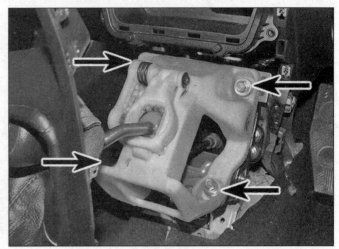

3.7 Undo the bolts and remove the lever assembly

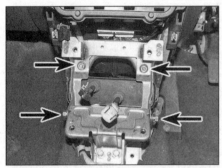

3.8 Remove the gear lever mounting bracket

3.9 Then undo the bolts and remove the gearshift cable bracket

3.10 Undo the 2 nuts and remove the retainer

by moving the pin and detaching the cable **(see illustration)**.

7 Remove the gear lever assembly by removing the 4 bolts **(see illustration)**.

8 Undo the 4 bolts and remove the gear lever mounting framework **(see illustration)**.

9 Then undo the 3 bolts and remove the gearshift cable mounting bracket **(see illustration)**.

10 Underneath the facia, undo the 2 nuts and withdraw the retainer **(see illustration)**.

11 Under the bonnet, remove the shift cable and selector cable at the gear linkage **(see illustrations)**.

Refitting

12 Refitting is a reversal of removal.

13 Check the operation of the gearlever, then refit the battery tray and battery as described in Chapter 5A Section 4.

3.11a Remove the pin and detach the first cable from the gear linkage by the gearbox ...

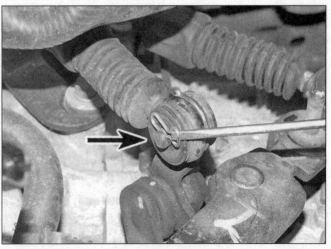

3.11b ... then remove the pin and on the second cable and detach from the linkage

5.6 Reversing light switch

5.7 Vehicle speed sensor plug

4 Gearchange lever assembly – removal and refitting

Removal

1 Remove the centre console as described in Chapter 11 Section 26.

2 Remove the gear lever surround and lower gear lever surround panel as described in Chapter 11 Section 26.

3 Release the retaining clip and detach the select cable assembly as described in Section 3.

4 Remove the gearchange lever assembly from place by removing the 4 bolts as described in Section 3.

Refitting

5 Refitting is a reversal of removal.

5 Gearbox – removal and refitting

Removal

1 Slacken both front roadwheel bolts, then raise the front of the vehicle and support it securely on axle stands, as described in *'Vehicle jacking and support'*. Remove both front roadwheels.

2 Remove the battery and battery tray as described in Chapter 5A Section 4.

3 Remove both driveshafts as described in Chapter 8 Section 2.

4 Remove the wiper motor as described in Chapter 12 Section 15 and unbolt the panel below as described in Chapter 2B Section 4.

5 Remove the clutch cable from its mounting bracket s described in Chapter 6 Section 2.

6 Disconnect the reversing light switch wiring plug **(see illustration)** …

7 … and the vehicle speed sensor wiring plug **(see illustration)**.

8 Remove the gearchange cables as described in Section 3.

9 Remove the shift cable bracket **(see illustration)**.

10 Undo the bolt and remove the earth cable **(see illustration)**.

11 Position a trolley jack under the the engine and gearbox. Use a block of wood on the jack head to prevent damage.

12 Undo and remove the gearbox upper mounting bolts.

13 Remove the starter motor as described in Chapter 5A Section 8.

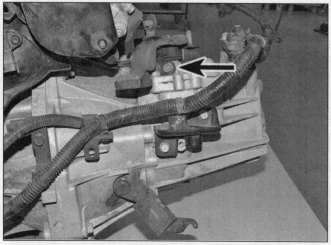

5.9 Undo the bolt and remove the shift cable bracket

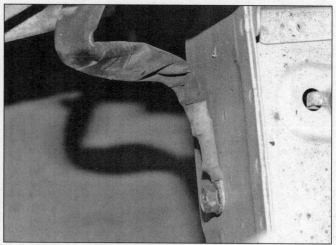

5.10 Unbolt the earth strap

5.14 Undo the gearbox mounting support bracket bolts

7.1 Disconnect the reversing light switch wiring plug

14 Remove the gearbox mounting support bracket bolts **(see illustration)**.

15 Undo the through-bolts and remove the rear engine mounting link rod as described in Chapter 2A Section 13.

16 Place a jack under the gearbox to support it.

17 Undo and remove the gearbox mounting bolts from the engine side.

18 Undo and remove the lower mounting bolts.

19 Check that all pipes, hoses and wiring are moved clear then carefully pull the transmission away from the engine. Lower the trolley jack and with the help of an assistant, remove the transmission from under the car.

Caution: Support the transmission to ensure that it remains steady on the jack head. Keep the transmission level until the input shaft is fully withdrawn from the clutch friction plate.

 Warning: Take care, the transmission is heavy!

Refitting

20 Refitting is a reversal of removal, noting the following points:

a) *Ensure the gearbox input shaft splines are clean and dry – do not apply any lubricant.*

b) *Tighten all fasteners to their specified torque, where given.*

c) *Refill the gearbox with new oil as described in Section 2.*

6 Gearbox overhaul – general information

1 Overhauling a manual gearbox unit is a difficult and involved job for the DIY home mechanic. In addition to dismantling and reassembling many small parts, clearances must be precisely measured and, if necessary, changed by selecting shims and spacers. Internal gearbox components are also often difficult to obtain, and in many instances, extremely expensive. Because of this, if the gearbox develops a fault or becomes noisy, the best course of action is to have the unit overhauled by a specialist repairer, or to obtain an exchange reconditioned unit.

2 Nevertheless, it is not impossible for the more experienced mechanic to overhaul the gearbox, provided the special tools are available, and the job is done in a deliberate step-by-step manner, so that nothing is overlooked.

3 The tools necessary for an overhaul include internal and external circlip pliers, bearing pullers, a slide hammer, a set of pin punches, a dial test indicator, and possibly a hydraulic press. In addition, a large, sturdy workbench and a vice will be required.

4 During dismantling of the gearbox, make careful notes of how each component is fitted, to make reassembly easier and more accurate.

5 Before dismantling the gearbox, it will help if you have some idea what area is malfunctioning. Certain problems can be closely related to specific areas in the gearbox, which can make component examination and replacement easier. Refer to the 'Fault finding 13 Section 9 ' Section of this manual for more information.

7 Reversing light switch – testing, removal and refitting

Testing

1 The reversing light circuit is controlled by a plunger-type switch screwed into the top of the transmission casing **(see illustration)**. If a fault develops, first ensure that the circuit fuse has not blown.

2 To test the switch, disconnect the wiring connector, and use a multimeter (set to the resistance function) or a battery-and-bulb test circuit to check that there is continuity between the switch terminals only when reverse gear is selected. If this is not the case, and there are no obvious breaks or other damage to the wires, the switch is faulty, and must be renewed.

Removal

3 Working in the engine compartment, disconnect the wiring plug, then unscrew the switch from the casing.

Refitting

4 Refit and securely tighten the switch, then reconnect the wiring plug.

Notes

Chapter 7 Part B
Automatic transmission

Contents

Degrees of difficulty

Easy, suitable for novice with little experience	Fairly easy, suitable for beginner with some experience	Fairly difficult, suitable for competent DIY mechanic	Difficult, suitable for experienced DIY mechanic	Very difficult, suitable for expert DIY or professional

Specifications

Torque wrench settings	Nm	Lb ft
Lower mounting bolts	49	35
Upper mounting bolts	49	35
Torque convertor mounting bolts	50	36
Transaxle insulator mounting bracket	50	36
Rear roll stopper mounting bolts	56	42
Starter motor mounting bolts	31	22
Control cable assembly	12	9
Shift lever assembly	12	9

1 General information

1 All information on the automatic transmissions is included here. Information for the manual transmission can be found in Part A of this chapter.

2 Because of the complexity of the automatic transmissions and the specialised equipment necessary to perform most service operations, this chapter contains only those procedures related to general diagnosis, routine maintenance, adjustment and removal and installation.

3 If the transmission requires major repair work, it should be left to a dealer service department or an automotive or transmission repair shop. Once properly diagnosed you can, however, remove and install the transmission yourself and save the expense, even if the repair work is done by a transmission shop.

2 Diagnosis – general

1 Automatic transmission malfunctions may be caused by five general conditions:
● Poor engine performance
● Improper adjustments
● Hydraulic malfunctions
● Mechanical malfunctions
● Malfunctions in the computer or its signal network

2 Diagnosis of these problems should always begin with a check of the easily repaired items: fluid level and condition, shift cable adjustment and shift lever installation. Next, perform a road test to determine if the problem has been corrected or if more diagnosis is necessary. If the problem persists after the preliminary tests and corrections are completed, additional diagnosis should be performed by a dealer service department or other qualified transmission repair shop. On modern electronically controlled automatic transmissions, a scan tool is helpful in retrieving trouble codes relating to the transmission.

3 Fluid level check and renewal

Fluid level check

1 Drive the vehicle to warm the transmission to normal operating temperature.

2 Park the vehicle on a level surface.

3 Move the gear selector lever through all gear positions. This will fill the torque converter with transmission fluid. Set the selector lever to the "N" (Neutral) position. Turn the engine off.

4 Before removing the oil level dipstick, wipe all contaminants from around the dipstick guide tube. Then take out the dipstick and check the level of the fluid.
● Check that the fluid level is in the "HOT" mark on the oil level dipstick. If fluid level is low, add the correct fluid until the level reaches the "HOT" mark.
● If the fluid level is abnormally high, drain off the excess, then check the drained fluid for contamination by coolant. The presence of engine coolant in the automatic transmission fluid indicates that a failure has occurred in the internal radiator oil cooler walls that separate the coolant from the transmission fluid.

● If the fluid is foaming, drain it and refill the transmission, then check for coolant in the fluid, or a high fluid level.

Note: *If the fluid smells as if it is burning, it means that the fluid has been contaminated by fine particles from the bushes and friction materials, a transmission overhaul may be necessary.*

Note: *Low fluid level can cause a variety of abnormal conditions because it allows the pump to take in air along with fluid. Air trapped in the hydraulic system forms bubbles, which are compressible. Therefore, pressures will be erratic, causing delayed shifting, slipping clutches and brakes, etc. Improper filling can also raise fluid level too high. When the transaxle has too much fluid, gears churn up foam and cause the same conditions which occur with low fluid level, resulting in accelerated deterioration of automatic transaxle fluid. In either case, air bubbles can cause overheating, and fluid oxidation, which can interfere with normal valve, clutch, and brake operation. Foaming can also result in fluid escaping from the transaxle vent where it may be mistaken for a leak.*

5 Insert the oil level dipstick securely.

Note: *When new, automatic transmission fluid should be red, The red dye is added so the assembly plant can identify it as transmission fluid and distinguish it from engine oil or antifreeze. The red dye, which is not an indicator of fluid quality, is not permanent. As the vehicle is driven the transmission fluid will begin to look darker. The color may eventually appear light brown.*

Fluid renewal

6 Disconnect the hose that connects the transmission and the oil cooler (inside the radiator), then start the engine and let the fluid drain out.

Caution: *The engine should be stopped within one minute after it is started. If the fluid has all drained out before then, the engine should be stopped at that point.*

7 Remove the drain plug from the bottom of the transmission case to drain the rest of the fluid **(see illustration)**.

8 Re-install the drain plug with a new gasket, and tighten it to the specified torque.

9 Pour the new fluid in through the oil filler tube.

10 Reconnect the oil cooler hose, and firmly replace the oil level dipstick.

11 Top up the last of the transmission fluid.

12 Start the engine and run it at idle for 1-2 minutes.

13 Move the select lever through all positions, and then move it to the "N" or "P" position.

14 Drive the vehicle until the fluid temperature rises to the normal temperature (70-80°C, 158-176°F), and then check the fluid level again. The fluid level must be at the HOT mark.

15 Firmly insert the oil level dipstick into the oil filler tube.

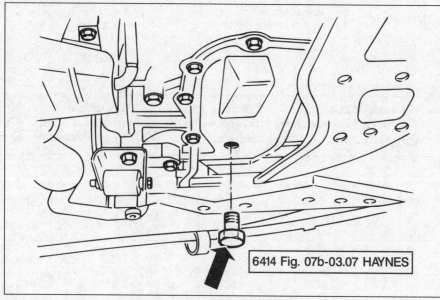

6414 Fig. 07b-03.07 HAYNES

3.7 Automatic transmission fluid drain plug

4 Gearbox –
removal and refitting

Removal

Note: *Mark all hoses and connectors to avoid errors when reconnecting.*

1 Disconnect the battery terminals then remove the battery and battery tray as described in Chapter 5A Section 4.

2 Remove the wiper arms and wiper motor as described in Chapter 12 Section 15 and unbolt the panel below as described in Chapter 2B Section 4.

3 Disconnect the inhibitor switch wiring plug **(see illustration)**.

4 Disconnect the solenoid valve and input speed sensor wiring plugs **(see illustration)**.

5 Disconnect the output speed sensor connector **(see illustration)**.

6 Undo the nut, disconnect the end selector cable, then release the tabs and pull the outer cable from the bracket **(see illustration)**.

7 Remove the oil level dipstick, oil cooler hoses and the earth cable from the transmission.

8 Undo and remove the transmission's upper mounting bolts and the starter motor mounting bolts.

9 Position a trolley jack under the engine. Use a block of wood on the jack head to prevent damage.

10 Remove the gearbox support mounting bracket bolts.

11 Jack up the vehicle and support it on axle stands as described in *'Vehicle jacking and support'*.

12 Drain the gearbox fluid as described in Section 3.

13 Undo the fasteners and remove the engine/transmission undershield (where applicable).

14 Disconnect and remove the driveshafts as described in Chapter 8 Section 2.

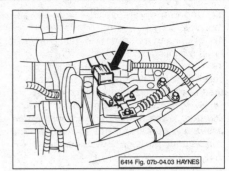

4.3 Inhibitor switch wiring plug

15 Undo the bolts and remove the cover under the flywheel, then undo and remove the torque converter mounting bolts **(see illustration)**.

16 Place a jack beneath the transmission case and use it to support the transmission.

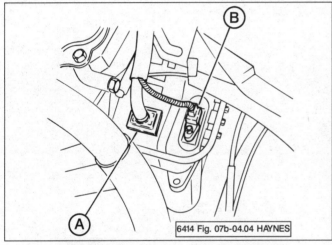

4.4 Solenoid valve (A) and input speed sensor (B)

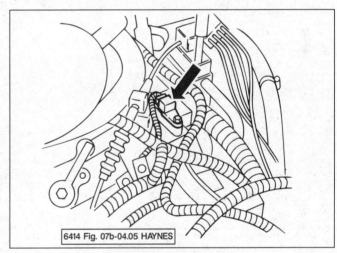

4.5 Output speed sensor

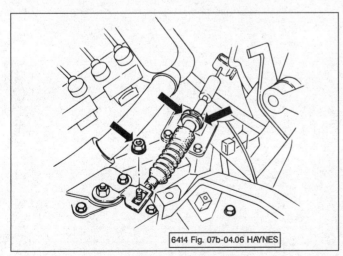

4.6 Undo the cable end fitting nut, then release the tabs and slide the outer cable upwards

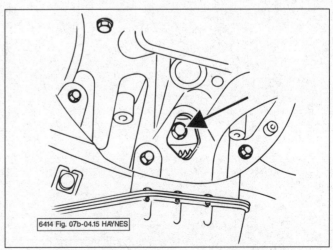

4.15 Access the torque converter mounting bolts through an opening under the engine sump

17 Undo and remove the rear engine mounting bolts.

18 Undo and remove the transmission's lower mounting bolts.

19 Slide the gearbox from the engine, taking care to ensure the torque converter stays in the transmission bell housing. Lower the jack slowly, to remove the transmission.

Caution: When removing the transmission assembly, be careful not to damage any surrounding parts or body components.

Refitting

20 Install the transmission assembly, then install the lower mounting bolts, tightening them to the specified torque.

21 Refit the torque converter mounting bolts, rotating the crankshaft clockwise as necessary to gain access.

22 Tighten the torque converter mounting bolts to the specified torque, then refit the cover.

23 Re-install the driveshafts as described in Chapter 8 Section 2.

24 Install the transmission support mounting bracket bolts, tightening them to the specified torque.

25 Install the gearbox upper mounting bolts and the starter motor mounting bolts, tightening them to the specified torque.

26 The remainder of refitting is a reversal of removal, noting the following points:

● Adjust the shift cables as described earlier in Section 5.

● Refill the transmission fluid as described in Section 3.

● Reconnect the battery negative lead as described in Chapter 5A Section 4.

5 Selector cable – adjustment

Adjustment

1 To improve access, remove the battery and battery tray as described in Chapter 5A Section 4.

2 Slacken the locking nut at the end of the selector cable above the transmission casing **(see illustration 4.6)**.

3 Working inside the cabin, move the selector lever to position 'N'.

4 Gently press the shift lever on the top of the transmission rearwards to eliminate any freeplay, then securely tighten the lock nut.

5 Check the operation of the selector mechanism before venturing out onto the road.

Chapter 8
Driveshafts

Contents

Degrees of difficulty

Easy, suitable for novice with little experience	**Fairly easy,** suitable for beginner with some experience	**Fairly difficult,** suitable for competent DIY mechanic	**Difficult,** suitable for experienced DIY mechanic	**Very difficult,** suitable for expert DIY or professional

Specifications

Type . . . . Unequal-length, solid steel shafts, splined to inner and outer constant velocity joints

Lubrication type. . . . . Outer (wheel side): Bechem HTBJ. Inner (transmission side): One Luber C

Quantity:
  Inner joint 100g
  Outer joint: 70g

Torque wrench settings	Nm	Lb ft
Driveshaft nut*	220	160
Roadwheel bolts	100	74
Shock absorber-to-hub carrier	110	80
Trackrod end-to-hub carrier*	66	48

Do not re-use

1 General information

1 Power is transmitted from the differential to the roadwheels by the driveshafts, via inner and outer constant velocity (CV) joints.
2 The outer ball-and-cage type CV joints allow smooth transmission of drive to the wheels at all steering and suspension angles. Drive is transmitted by means of a number of radially static steel balls that run in grooves between the two halves of the joint.
3 The inner CV joints are of the tripod type. Drive is transmitted across the joint by means of three rollers, mounted on the driveshaft in a tripod arrangement, that are radially static but are free to slide in the grooved joint body.
4 The joints are protected by rubber gaiters, and are packed with grease to provide permanent lubrication. If wear is detected in the joint, it can be detached from the driveshaft and renewed. Normally, the CV joints do not require additional lubrication, unless they have been overhauled or the rubber gaiters have been damaged, allowing the grease to become contaminated. Refer to Chapter 1 Section 8 for guidance in checking the condition of the driveshaft gaiters.
5 Both driveshafts are splined at their outer ends, to accept the wheel hubs, and are threaded so that the hubs can be fastened to the driveshafts by means of a staked nut.

2 Driveshaft – removal and refitting

Note: *A balljoint separator tool will be required for this operation. A new driveshaft retaining nut and inner CV joint clip retaining clip will be required for refitting.*

Removal

1 Slacken the front roadwheel bolts, raise the front of the vehicle and support it securely on axle stands, as described in 'Vehicle jacking and support'. Remove the relevant front roadwheel.
2 Drain the gearbox oil as described in

2.3 Use a chisel to raise the stake holding the retaining nut

A tool to hold the front hub stationary whilst the driveshaft nut is slackened can be fabricated from two lengths of steel strip (one long, one short) and a nut and bolt; then nut and bolt forming a pivot of a forked tool.

2.5 If necessary, tap the driveshaft to separate it from the hub carrier

Chapter 7A Section 2 or Chapter 7B Section 3.

3 Using a hammer and chisel or similar tool, tap up the staking securing the driveshaft retaining nut in position **(see illustration)**.

4 The front wheel hub must be held stationary in order to loosen the driveshaft nut. Ideally, the hub should be held by a suitable tool bolted into place using two of the roadwheel bolts (see **Tool Tip**). Alternatively, have an assistant firmly apply the foot brake to prevent the hub from rotating. Using a socket and extension bar, slacken and remove the driveshaft retaining nut.

 Warning: The nut is extremely tight. Discard the nut – a new one must be used on refitting.

5 Separate the driveshaft from the hub carrier **(see illustration)**. If necessary, tap the driveshaft end from the hub using a soft-faced hammer or similar.

6 Undo the retaining bolt and remove the bracket holding the ABS sensor cable **(see illustration)**.

7 Loosen and remove the bolts mounting the top of the hub carrier to the suspension strut **(see illustration)**.

8 Pull the hub carrier outwards at the top and withdraw the driveshaft outer constant

velocity joint from the hub assembly **(see illustration)**. If necessary, the joint can be tapped out of the hub using a soft-faced mallet. Support the end of the driveshaft – do not allow the end of the driveshaft to hang down as this will strain the joint components and gaiters. Take care not to strain the ABS wheel speed sensor wiring.

9 Insert a lever between the inner joint and the differential casing, and separate the driveshaft from the differential **(see illustration)**.

10 Loosely refit one of the strut lower mounting bolts to support the hub carrier while the driveshaft is removed.

Refitting

11 Refitting is a reversal of removal, taking note of the following points.

● Renew the inner joint circlip.
● Tighten all fasteners to their specified torque (where given).
● Before inserting the driveshaft to the transmission case, apply gear oil on the oil seal contacting surface of the transmission case and driveshaft spline. Set the opening side of the circlip facing downward.
● The driveshaft nuts should be replaced with new ones. After tightening the driveshaft nut, stake it using a chisel and hammer.

12 Refill the gearbox with oil as described in Chapter 7A Section 2.

13 Refit the roadwheel and lower the vehicle to the ground then tighten the retaining bolts to the specified torque.

3 Driveshaft oil seals

Removal

1 Remove the driveshafts as described earlier in Section 2.

2 Using a suitable lever, gently prise away

2.6 ABS sensor cable mounting bracket

2.7 Loosen the bolts holding the hub carrier to the strut

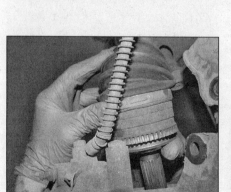

2.8 Withdraw the driveshaft joint from the hub

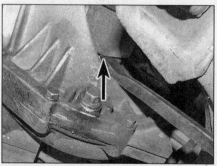

2.9 Lever between the driveshaft joint and the differential casing

3.2 Lever out the oil seal from the gearbox

3.3a Offer up the new seal ...

3.3b ... and use a socket to press the new oil seal into place

the edge of the oil seal and remove it from the gearbox **(see illustration)**.

Refitting

3 Press the new oil seal squarely into the aperture in the gearbox **(see illustrations)**.

---

4   Driveshaft CV boot renewal

Inner CV boot replacement

1 Remove the driveshaft as described in Section 2.
2 Release the rubber gaiter retaining clips by cutting them off with a pair of side-cutters **(see illustration)**.
3 Make orientation marks between the driveshaft tripoidal inner end housing and shaft to aid reassembly **(see illustration)**.
4 Once the tripoidal inner housing has been removed, make orientation marks between the driveshaft spider and shaft to aid reassembly **(see illustration)**.
5 Remove the retaining circlip from the end of the driveshaft **(see illustration)**.
6 Use a copper hammer to gently drift the spider off the end of the driveshaft **(see illustration)**.
7 Slide the old boot off the end of the driveshaft **(see illustration)**.

Refitting

8 Clean away all the old grease and grime.
9 Slide the inner CV boot retaining clip onto the driveshaft **(see illustration)**.

4.2 Cut off the retaining clips

4.3 Make orientation marks for reassembly

4.4 Make an orientation mark on the spider

4.5 Remove the retaining circlip

4.6 Drift the spider off the driveshaft

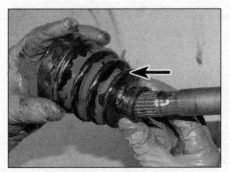

4.7 Slide the boot off the driveshaft

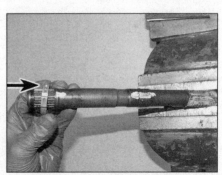

4.9 Slide the new inner clip onto the driveshaft

4.10 Slide the new inner CV boot onto the driveshaft

4.11 Drift the spider back onto the driveshaft

4.12a Attach the retaining circlip to the driveshaft

4.12b Make sure the ends of the circlip do not foul the spider rollers

4.13 Attach the inner CV boot clip

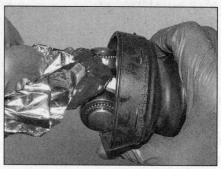

4.14 Pack the inner CV joint with grease

10 Slide new inner CV boot onto the driveshaft **(see illustration)**.

11 Drift spider back on to driveshaft, ensuring that orientation marks line up **(see illustration)**.

12 Attach the retaining circlip to the end of the driveshaft **(see illustration)**.

Note: *Ensure that the tails of the clip sit between the rollers of the spider to avoid any possibility of interference **(see illustration)**.*

13 Attach the clip to the inner end of CV boot **(see illustration)**.

14 Pack the inner cv boot with grease, ensuring that all surfaces of the spider are also covered **(see illustration)**.

15 Refit the driveshaft tripoidal inner end housing, ensuring that the orientation marks made earlier line up correctly, then slide the gaiter over the edge of the housing. Manoeuvre the new retaining clip into place, and secure it **(see illustration)**.

Outer CV boot replacement

16 Remove the driveshaft as described in Section 2.

17 Remove the inner boot as described earlier in this Section.

Note: *If carrying out this procedure on the longer offside driveshaft, the harmonic balancer must be removed to allow the outer*

CV boot to be removed. Cut off the clips and slide it off the end of the driveshaft.

18 Release the CV boot retaining clips by cutting them off with a pair of side-cutters **(see illustration)**.

19 Slide the outer CV boot off the same end as the inner CV boot **(see illustration)**.

20 If any of the constant velocity joint components are found to be worn or damaged, it will be necessary to renew the complete joint assembly as the internal parts are not available separately. If the joint is in satisfactory condition, obtain a new gaiter, circlip, retaining clips, and the correct type of grease. These components are all available

4.15 Refit the tripoidal end housing and fit the clip

4.18 Cut off the rubber gaiter's retaining clips

4.19 Slide the outer boot off the driveshaft

4.21 Slide the new boot onto the driveshaft

4.22a Pack the CV joint with grease …

4.22b … and do the same to the CV boot

individually from Hyundai dealers, but may be supplied as a complete repair kit from other sources.

Refitting

21 Clean away all the old grease and grime, then slide the new boot along the driveshaft **(see illustration)**.

22 Pack the CV joint with the specified grease, then twist the joint to ensure that all the recesses are filled **(see illustrations)**.

23 Slide the new CV boot over the CV joint and attach the outer retaining clip **(see illustration)**.

Note: *Ensure that the outer clip is fitted with tail of fastener behind the direction of forward rotation.*

24 Slide the inner clip along the driveshaft to the inner edge of the CV boot **(see illustration)**.

4.23 Slide the new boot over the joint and attach the outer clip

25 If working on the offside driveshaft, install the dynamic damper. This procedure is a reversal of removal.

4.24 Slide the inner clip along the driveshaft and fit to the boot

26 Refit the driveshaft as described in Section 2.

Chapter 9
Braking system

Contents

Degrees of difficulty

Easy, suitable for novice with little experience	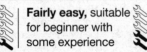	Fairly easy, suitable for beginner with some experience		Fairly difficult, suitable for competent DIY mechanic		Difficult, suitable for experienced DIY mechanic		Very difficult, suitable for expert DIY or professional	

Specifications

Front brakes

Caliper type	Single piston sliding caliper
Disc type	Ventilated
Diameter	241 mm
Thickness:	
New	18 mm
Minimum	16 mm
Pad friction material minimum thickness	1.5 mm

Rear drum brake

Drum inner diameter:	
New	180 mm
Maximum	182 mm
Brake shoe lining thickness	
New	4.5 mm
Minimum	1.0 mm

Torque wrench settings

	Nm	lb ft
Bleed screw	10	7
Front brake caliper bracket-to-hub carrier	88	65
Front caliper guide pin bolts*	27	20
Disc retaining screw	5	4
Lateral acceleration/yaw rate sensor nuts	9	7
Master cylinder nuts	15	11
Rear wheel cylinder bolts	8	6
Roadwheel bolts	100	74
Servo retaining nuts	14	11
Wheel speed sensors:		
Front wheel sensor	9	7
Rear wheel sensor	9	6

*Do not re-use

1 General information

1 The braking system is of the vacuum servo-assisted, dual-circuit hydraulic type. The arrangement of the hydraulic system is such that each circuit operates one front and one rear brake from a tandem master cylinder. Under normal circumstances, both circuits operate in unison. However, in the event of hydraulic failure in one circuit, full braking force will still be available at two diagonally opposite wheels.

2 The front disc brakes are actuated by single-piston sliding type calipers, which ensure that equal pressure is applied to each brake pad.

3 The rear drum brakes incorporate leading and trailing shoes, which are actuated by twin-piston wheel cylinders. A self-adjusting mechanism is incorporated, to automatically compensate for brake shoe wear. As the brake shoe linings wear, the footbrake operation automatically operates the adjuster mechanism to reduce the lining-to-drum clearance. The mechanical handbrake linkage operates the brake shoes via a lever attached to the trailing brake shoe.

Note: *When servicing any part of the system, work carefully and methodically; also observe scrupulous cleanliness when overhauling any part of the hydraulic system. Always renew components (in axle sets, where applicable) if in doubt about their condition, and use only genuine Hyundai replacement parts, or at least those of known good quality. Note the warnings given in 'Safety first!' and at relevant points in this Chapter concerning the dangers of asbestos dust and hydraulic fluid.*

2 Hydraulic system – bleeding

Warning: Hydraulic fluid is poisonous; wash off immediately and thoroughly in the case of skin contact, and seek immediate medical advice if any fluid is swallowed or gets into the eyes. Certain types of hydraulic fluid are flammable, and may ignite when allowed into contact with hot components; when servicing any hydraulic system, it is safest to assume that the fluid is flammable, and to take precautions against the risk of fire as though it is petrol that is being handled. Hydraulic fluid is also an effective paint stripper, and will attack plastics; if any is spilt, it should be washed off immediately, using copious quantities of fresh water. Finally, it is hygroscopic (it absorbs moisture from the air) – old fluid may be contaminated and unfit for further use. When topping-up or renewing the fluid, always use the recommended type, and ensure that it comes from a freshly-opened sealed container.

General

1 The correct operation of any hydraulic system is only possible after removing all air from the components and circuit; and this is achieved by bleeding the system.

2 During the bleeding procedure, add only clean, unused hydraulic fluid of the recommended type; never re-use fluid that has already been bled from the system. Ensure that sufficient fluid is available before starting work.

3 If there is any possibility of incorrect fluid being already in the system, the brake components and circuit must be flushed completely with uncontaminated, correct fluid, and new seals should be fitted throughout the system.

4 If hydraulic fluid has been lost from the system, or air has entered because of a leak, ensure that the fault is cured before proceeding further.

5 Park the car on level ground, switch off the engine and select first or reverse gear, then chock the wheels and release the handbrake.

6 Check that all pipes and hoses are secure, unions tight and bleed screws closed. Remove the dust caps (where applicable), and clean any dirt from around the bleed screws.

7 Unscrew the master cylinder reservoir cap, and top the master cylinder reservoir up to the MAX level line.

Caution: Ensure that the ignition is switched off before starting the bleeding procedure, to avoid any possibility of voltage being applied to the hydraulic modulator before the bleeding procedure is completed. Ideally, the battery should be disconnected. If voltage is applied to the modulator before the bleeding procedure is complete, this will effectively drain the hydraulic fluid in the modulator, rendering the unit unserviceable. Do not, therefore, attempt to 'run' the modulator in order to bleed the brakes.

8 Due to the standard fitment of ABS to all models, a pressure-bleeding kit must be used for bleeding the hydraulic system.

9 These kits are usually operated by the reservoir of pressurised air contained in the spare tyre. However, note that it will probably be necessary to reduce the pressure to a lower level than normal; refer to the instructions supplied with the kit.

Note: *Hyundai specifies a maximum tyre pressure of 1.0 bar.*

10 By connecting a pressurised, fluid-filled container to the master cylinder reservoir, bleeding can be carried out simply by opening each screw in turn (in the specified sequence), and allowing the fluid to flow out until no more air bubbles can be seen in the expelled fluid.

11 This method has the advantage that the large reservoir of fluid provides an additional safeguard against air being drawn into the system during bleeding.

12 If the system has been only partially disconnected, and suitable precautions were taken to minimise fluid loss, it should be necessary only to bleed that part of the system.

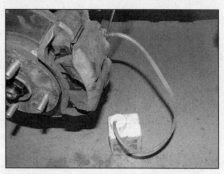

2.14 Open each bleed screw in turn

13 If the complete system is to be bled, then it should be done working in the following sequence:

a) *Right-hand front brake*
b) *Left-hand front brake*
c) *Right-hand rear brake*
d) *Left-hand rear brake*

14 Bleed each brake in turn until clean fluid, free of air bubbles, is seen to emerge **(see illustration)**. Pause between bleeding each brake to ensure that the fluid level in the reservoir is above the MIN level.

15 When bleeding is complete, and firm pedal feel is restored, wash off any spilt fluid, tighten the bleed screws, and refit their dust caps.

16 Check the hydraulic fluid level in the master cylinder reservoir, and top-up if necessary.

17 Discard any fluid that has been bled from the system; it will not be fit for re-use.

18 Check the feel of the brake pedal. If it feels at all spongy, air must still be present in the system, and further bleeding is required.

Warning: Do not operate the vehicle if you are in doubt about the effectiveness of the braking system. If considerable air was present in the system prior to bleeding, it is possible for some of this air to remain trapped in the hydraulic modulator. If the pedal continues to feel spongy after repeated bleedings, or if any of the brake system warning lights remain on, have the vehicle towed to a Hyundai dealer to be bled with the use of Hyundai diagnostic equipment.

3 Hydraulic pipes and hoses – renewal

Note: *Before starting work, refer to the warnings in Section and Section 2.*

1 If any pipe or hose is to be renewed, minimise fluid loss by first removing the master cylinder reservoir cap, then tighten the cap down onto a piece of polythene to obtain an airtight seal. Alternatively, flexible hoses can be sealed, if required, using a proprietary brake hose clamp; metal brake pipe unions can be plugged (if care is taken not to allow dirt into the system) or capped immediately they are disconnected. Place a wad of rag

3.2 Slide out the spring clip after slackening the union nut

under any union that is to be disconnected, to catch any spilt fluid.

2 If a flexible hose is to be disconnected, unscrew the brake pipe union nut before removing the spring clip which secures the hose to its mounting bracket **(see illustration)**.

3 To unscrew the union nuts, it is preferable to obtain a brake pipe spanner of the correct size; these are available from most large motor accessory shops. Failing this, a close-fitting open-ended spanner will be required, although if the nuts are tight or corroded, their flats may be rounded-off if the spanner slips. In such a case, a self-locking wrench is often the only way to unscrew a stubborn union, but it follows that the pipe and the damaged nuts must be renewed on reassembly. Always clean a union and surrounding area before disconnecting it. If disconnecting a component with more than one union, make a careful note of the connections before disturbing any of them.

4 If a brake pipe is to be renewed, it can be obtained, cut to length and with the union nuts and end flares in place, from Hyundai dealers. All that is then necessary is to bend it to shape, following the line of the original, before fitting it to the vehicle. Alternatively, most motor accessory shops can make up brake pipes from kits, but this requires very careful measurement of the original, to ensure that the replacement is of the correct length. The safest answer is usually to take the original to the shop as a pattern.

5 On refitting, do not overtighten the union nuts. It is not necessary to exercise brute force to obtain a sound joint.

6 Ensure that the pipes and hoses are

correctly routed, with no kinks, and that they are secured in the clips or brackets provided. After fitting, remove the polythene from the reservoir, and bleed the hydraulic system as described in Section 2. Wash off any spilt fluid, and check carefully for fluid leaks.

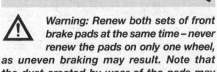

4 Front brake pads – renewal

⚠️ **Warning: Renew both sets of front brake pads at the same time – never renew the pads on only one wheel, as uneven braking may result. Note that the dust created by wear of the pads may contain asbestos, which is a health hazard. Never blow it out with compressed air, and don't inhale any of it. An approved filtering mask should be worn when working on the brakes. DO NOT use petrol or petroleum-**

based solvents to clean brake parts; use brake cleaner or methylated spirit only.

1 Apply the handbrake, then slacken the front roadwheel bolts. Jack up the front of the vehicle and support it on axle stands as described in *'Vehicle jacking and support'*. Remove both front roadwheels.

2 If new pads are to be fitted, reduce the fluid level in the master cylinder reservoir to the minimum level using a syringe (or similar).

3 Follow the relevant accompanying photos for the actual pad replacement procedure **(see illustration 4.3a to 4.3s)**. Be sure to stay in order and read the caption under each illustration.

e) New pads may have an adhesive foil on the backplates. Remove this foil prior to installation.

f) Apply a thin smear of anti-seize grease only to the areas shown.

g) When pushing the caliper piston back to accommodate new pads, keep a close eye on the fluid level in the reservoir.

4.3a Lever the caliper outwards slightly to create clearance between the pads and disc

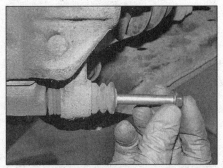

4.3b Unscrew the lower guide pin bolt

4.3c Rotate the caliper upwards from place ...

4.3d ... and suspend it from the strut using wire, to prevent straining the fluid hose

4.3e Remove the inner brake pad ...

4.3f ... and the outer brake pad

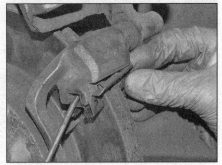

4.3g Unclip the upper ...

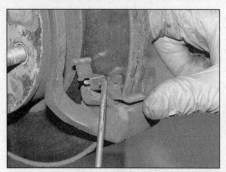

4.3h ... and lower shims

4.3i Clean the mounting bracket with aerosol brake cleaner and a soft brush

4.3j Measure the thickness of the pads friction material – if it's less than 1.5 mm, renew all the front brake pads

4.3k Press the lower ...

4.3l ... and upper shims into place

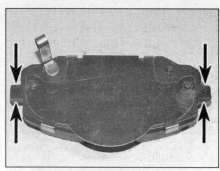

4.3m Apply a thin smear of high-temperature, anti-seize grease to the edges of the pad backplate where it contacts the mounting bracket

4.3n Fit the inner brake pad, with the audible wear indicator (where applicable) ...

4.3o ... and outer pad. Make sure the friction material is against the disc face!

4.3p If new pads have been fitted, push the piston fully into the caliper body using a piston retraction tool. Keep an eye on the brake fluid reservoir level as the piston is pushed back!

4.3q Slide the caliper into place ...

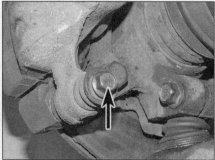

4.3r ... insert the guide pin bolt ...

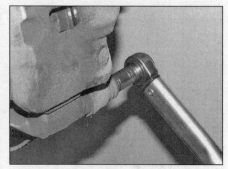

4.3s ... and tighten it to the specified torque

4 Repeat the above procedure on the remaining caliper.

5 Depress the brake pedal repeatedly, until the pads are pressed into firm contact with the brake disc, and normal (non-assisted) pedal pressure is restored.

6 Apply a little anti-seize grease to the hub surface where it contacts the wheel, then refit the roadwheels, lower the vehicle to the ground and tighten the roadwheel bolts to the specified torque.

7 Check the hydraulic fluid level as described in 'Weekly checks'.

Caution: New pads will not give full braking efficiency until they have bedded-in. Be prepared for this, and avoid hard braking as far as possible for the first hundred miles or so after pad renewal.

5 Front brake disc – inspection, removal and refitting

Inspection

Note: *If either disc requires renewal, BOTH should be renewed at the same time, to ensure even and consistent braking. New brake pads should also be fitted.*

1 Apply the handbrake, then jack up the front of the car and support it on axle stands as described in 'Vehicle jacking and support'. Remove the appropriate front roadwheel.

2 Slowly rotate the brake disc so that the full area of both sides can be checked; remove the brake pads if better access is required to the inboard surface. Light scoring is normal in the area swept by the brake pads, but if heavy scoring or cracks are found, the disc must be renewed.

3 It is normal to find a lip of rust and brake dust around the disc's perimeter; this can be scraped off if required. If, however, a lip has formed due to excessive wear of the brake pad swept area, then the disc's thickness must be measured using a micrometer **(see illustration)**. Take measurements at several places around the disc, at the inside and outside of the pad swept area; if the disc has worn at any point to the specified minimum

thickness or less, the disc must be renewed.

4 If the disc is thought to be warped, it can be checked for run-out. Either use a dial gauge mounted on any convenient fixed point, while the disc is slowly rotated, or use feeler blades to measure (at several points all around the disc) the clearance between the disc and a fixed point, such as the caliper mounting bracket. If the measurements obtained are at the specified maximum or beyond, the disc is excessively warped, and must be renewed; however, it is worth checking first that the hub bearing is in good condition (Chapters 1 and/ or 10). If the run-out is excessive, the disc must be renewed.

5 Check the disc for cracks, especially around the wheel stud holes, and any other wear or damage, and renew if necessary.

Removal

6 Mark the relationship between the disc and the hub with chalk or a marker pen, to allow correct refitting.

7 Remove the brake pads as described in Section 4, then remove the remaining upper guide pin bolt.

8 Suspend the caliper from a rigid point on the suspension, using wire or a cable tie. Do not allow it to hang unsupported as this will strain the brake hose.

9 Undo the 2 retaining bolts and remove the caliper mounting bracket **(see illustration)**.

10 Undo the retaining screw(s) and remove the disc from the hub **(see illustration)**. If necessary, liberally apply releasing fluid to the area between the disc and hub, and use a large hammer to force the disc from the hub.

Refitting

11 If a new disc is being fitted, remove the protective coating from the surface using an appropriate cleaner.

12 Locate the disc on the hub so that the roadwheel bolt and retaining screw holes are all correctly lined up; use the alignment marks made during removal.

13 Refit the disc retaining screw(s) and tighten them to the specified torque.

14 Refit the caliper mounting bracket, then apply a little thread-locking compound and tighten the bolts to the specified torque.

15 Refit the brake pads as described in Section 4.

6 Front brake caliper – removal, overhaul and refitting

Caution: Before starting work, refer to the warnings at the beginning of Section 2 and Section 4 concerning the dangers of hydraulic fluid and asbestos dust.

Removal

1 Remove the front brake pads as described in Section 4.

2 To minimise fluid loss during the following operations, remove the master cylinder reservoir filler cap, then tighten it down onto a piece of polythene, to obtain an airtight seal. Alternatively, use a brake hose clamp to seal off the flexible hydraulic hose running to the caliper.

Caution: Do not use an ordinary G-clamp or mole grips for this purpose, as these can easily damage the hydraulic hose internally, possibly leading to failure.

3 Clean the area surrounding the brake hose union, then slacken the union half a turn.

4 Hold the brake hose and rotate the caliper to unscrew the hose union from the caliper body. Cover the open ends of the union and the caliper fluid inlet, to prevent dirt ingress. Alternatively, the flexible brake hose may be separated from the rigid brake pipe at the bracket mounted on the inner wheel arch.

Overhaul

5 At the time of writing, no replacement parts appear to be available for the front calipers. If they are defective, replacement calipers must be fitted.

Refitting

6 Hold the brake hose and rotate the caliper to screw the hose union back into the caliper body.

7 Refit the brake pads as described in Section 4, then tighten the brake hose securely.

8 Bleed the brake hydraulic system as described in Section 2.

5.3 Measure the disc thickness using a micrometer

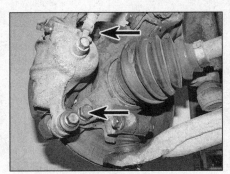

5.9 Caliper mounting bracket retaining bolts

5.10 Undo the screws and remove the disc

7.3 Use two M8 bolts to force the drum from the hub

7 Rear brake drum – removal, inspection and refitting

Warning: Before starting work, refer to the warning at the beginning of Section 4 concerning the dangers of asbestos dust.

Removal

1 Chock the front wheels, slacken the rear wheel bolts, raise the rear of the vehicle and support it securely on axle stands, as described in 'Vehicle jacking and support'. Fully release the handbrake, and remove the rear roadwheels.

2 If the original drum is to be refitted, mark the relationship between the drum and the hub. Slacken and remove the two retaining bolts and pull the drum from the hub.

3 If the drum is binding on the brake shoes, screw two M8 bolts into the threaded holes in the drum and progressively tighten them against the hub flange to push the drum from the hub **(see illustration)**.

Inspection

Note: *If either drum requires renewal, BOTH should be renewed at the same time, to ensure even and consistent braking. New brake shoes should also be fitted.*

4 Working carefully, remove all traces of brake dust from the drum, but avoid inhaling the dust, as it is a health hazard.

5 Clean the outside of the drum, and check it for obvious signs of wear or damage, such as cracks around the roadwheel stud holes; renew the drum if necessary.

6 Carefully examine the inside of the drum. Light scoring of the friction surface is normal, but if heavy scoring is found, the drum must be renewed.

7 It is usual to find a lip on the drum's inboard edge which consists of a mixture of rust and brake dust; this should be carefully scraped away, to leave a smooth surface which can be polished with fine (120- to 150-grade) emery paper. If, however, the lip is due to the friction surface being recessed by excessive wear, then the drum must be renewed.

8 If the drum is thought to be excessively worn, or oval, its internal diameter must be measured at several points using an internal micrometer. Take measurements in pairs, the second at right-angles to the first, and compare the two, to check for signs of ovality. Provided that it does not enlarge the drum to beyond the specified maximum diameter, it may be possible to have the drum refinished by skimming or grinding; if this is not possible, the drums on both sides must be renewed. Note that if the drum is to be skimmed, BOTH drums must be refinished, to maintain a consistent internal diameter on both sides.

Refitting

9 If a new brake drum is to be installed, use a suitable solvent to remove any preservative coating that may have been applied to its internal friction surfaces. Note that it may also be necessary to shorten the adjuster strut length, by rotating the serrated strut wheel, to allow the drum to pass over the brake shoes – see Section 8 for details.

10 If the original drum is being refitted, align the marks made on the drum and hub before removal, then fit the drum over the hub. Refit the retaining screws and tighten them securely.

11 Depress the footbrake repeatedly to expand the brake shoes against the drum, and ensure that normal pedal pressure is restored.

12 Check and if necessary adjust the handbrake as described in Section 13.

13 Refit the roadwheels, and lower the vehicle to the ground. Tighten the retaining bolts to the specified torque.

8 Rear brake shoes – renewal

Warning: Renew BOTH sets of rear brake shoes at the same time – NEVER renew the shoes on only one wheel, as uneven braking may result.

Warning: Before starting work, refer to the warning given at the beginning of Section 4, concerning the dangers of asbestos dust.

1 Remove the rear brake drums as described in Section 7.

2 Working carefully, and taking the necessary precautions, remove all traces of brake dust from the brake drum, backplate and shoes.

3 Measure the thickness of the friction material of each brake shoe at several points; if either shoe is worn at any point to the specified minimum thickness or less, all four shoes must be renewed as a set. The shoes should also be renewed if any are fouled with hydraulic fluid, oil or grease; there is no satisfactory way to degrease friction material once contaminated.

4 If any of the brake shoes are worn unevenly, or contaminated, trace and rectify the cause before reassembly.

5 Note the position of each shoe, and the location of the return springs and self-adjuster mechanism to aid refitting later **(see illustration)**.

6 Remove the brake shoe hold-down pins from the backplate by depressing the clips and turning them **(see illustration)**.

7 Pull out the shoe a little, detach the upper

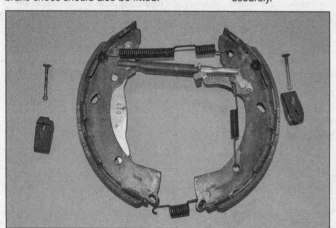

8.5 Note the positions of the brake components

8.6 Depress the hold-down pin clips, then rotate them 90° to release them

8.7a Detach the upper return spring

8.7b Pull out the brake shoes and remove the lower return spring

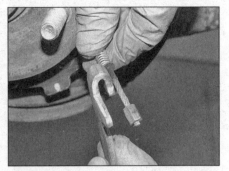

8.8 Detach the handbrake cable from the lever

return spring, then pull out the brake shoe assembly and remove the lower return spring. Make sure not to damage the dust cover on the wheel cylinder. (see illustrations).
8 Disconnect the handbrake cable (see illustration). Remove the brake shoes.
9 Retain the wheel cylinder pistons in the wheel cylinder using a cable tie or a strong elastic band. Do not depress the brake pedal until the brakes are reassembled.
10 Carefully examine the self-adjuster mechanism for signs of wear or damage. Pay particular attention to the threads and the toothed adjuster wheel, and renew if necessary.
11 Check the condition of all return springs and renew any that show signs of distortion or other damage.
12 Peel back the rubber protective caps, and check the wheel cylinder for fluid leaks or other damage; check that both cylinder

pistons are free to move easily. Refer to Section 9, if necessary, for information on wheel cylinder renewal.
13 Prior to installation, clean the backplate, and apply a thin smear of high-temperature brake grease or anti-seize compound to all those surfaces of the backplate which bear on the shoes, particularly the wheel cylinder pistons and lower pivot point. Do not allow the lubricant to foul the friction material (see illustration).
14 Connect the handbrake cable to the lever on the trailing brake shoe.
15 Fit upper brake shoe return spring, and the self-adjuster mechanism into the recess in the trailing brake shoe, then engage the leading shoe with the other end of the adjuster mechanism (see illustrations).
16 Fit the lower brake shoe return spring, engaging it with the slots in the shoes.

Remove the elastic band or cable tie from the wheel cylinder.
17 Manoeuvre the leading shoe into position and secure it with the hold-down pin and spring clip.
18 Turn the serrated wheel at the end of the self-adjuster mechanism, to retract the brake shoes – this will give additional clearance to allow the drum to pass over the shoes during refitting.
19 Insert the ratchet lever and spring (see illustrations).
20 Refit the brake drum as described in Section 7.
21 Repeat the above procedure on the remaining rear brake.
22 Apply the brake pedal and handbrake lever several times to settle the self-adjusting mechanism. With both rear roadwheels refitted and the rear of the car still raised,

8.13 Add grease to the backplate surfaces the brake shoes touch

8.15a Engage the self-adjusting mechanism with the trailing shoe ...

8.15b ... and fit the upper return spring

8.15c Engage the leading shoe with the adjustment mechanism

8.19a Insert the ratchet lever ...

8.19b ... and spring

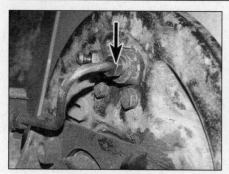

9.2 Unscrew the union nut

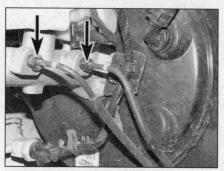

10.3 Disconnect the rigid brake pipes from the master cylinder

turn the wheels by hand to check that the brake shoes are not binding. Check, and if necessary adjust, the operation of the handbrake, as described in Section 13.

23 On completion, check the brake hydraulic fluid level in the master cylinder reservoir as described in *'Weekly checks'*.

Caution: New shoes will not give full braking efficiency until they have bedded-in. Be prepared for this, and avoid hard braking as far as possible for the first hundred miles or so after shoe renewal.

9 Rear wheel cylinder – removal, overhaul and refitting

⚠️ *Warning: Before starting work, refer to the warnings at the beginning of Section 2 and Section 4 concerning the dangers of hydraulic fluid and asbestos dust.*

Removal

1 To minimise fluid loss during the following operations, remove the master cylinder reservoir filler cap, then tighten it down onto a piece of polythene, to obtain an airtight seal.

2 Clean the brake backplate around the wheel cylinder mounting bolts and the hydraulic pipe union, then unscrew the union nut and disconnect the hydraulic pipe **(see illustration)**. Cover the open ends of the pipe and the wheel cylinder to prevent dirt ingress.

3 Remove the two securing bolts, then withdraw the wheel cylinder from the backplate.

Overhaul

4 At the time of writing, it would appear that no replacement parts are available for the rear wheel cylinders. If defective, the complete cylinders must be replaced.

Refitting

5 Refitting is a reversal of removal, noting the following points:

a) Tighten the mounting bolts to the specified torque.

b) Before refitting the roadwheel and lowering the car to the ground, remove the polythene from the fluid reservoir, and bleed the hydraulic system as described in Section 2. Note that if no other part of the system has been disturbed, it should only be necessary to bleed the relevant rear circuit.

10 Master cylinder – removal, overhaul and refitting

Note: *Before starting work, refer to the warning at the beginning of Section 2 concerning the dangers of hydraulic fluid.*

Removal

1 Remove the air cleaner assembly as described in Chapter 4A Section 2.

2 Disconnect the brake fluid level switch wiring plug then remove the master cylinder fluid reservoir filler cap, and syphon the hydraulic fluid from the reservoir. Do not syphon the fluid by mouth, as it is poisonous; use a syringe or an old poultry baster. Alternatively, open any convenient bleed screw in the system, and gently pump the brake pedal to expel the fluid through a tube connected to the screw (see Section 2).

3 Mark their positions, then undo the union nuts and disconnect the rigid brake pipes from the master cylinder **(see illustration)**.

4 Undo the retaining nuts and detach the master cylinder from the servo unit.

Refitting

5 Remove all traces of dirt from the master cylinder and servo unit mating surfaces and, where applicable, fit a new seal between the master cylinder body and the servo.

6 Fit the master cylinder to the servo unit, ensuring that the servo unit pushrod enters the master cylinder bore centrally. Refit the master cylinder mounting nuts, and tighten them to the specified torque.

7 Wipe clean the brake pipe unions, then refit them to the correct master cylinder ports, as noted before removal, and tighten the union nuts securely.

8 Reconnect the brake fluid supply hose(s) to the master cylinder.

9 Refill the master cylinder reservoir with fresh hydraulic fluid of the specified type (see 'Lubricants and fluids'), and bleed the complete hydraulic system as described in Section 2. Note that it may also be necessary to bleed the clutch hydraulic system as described in Section.

10 On completion, thoroughly check the operation of the brake and clutch systems.

11 Stop-light switch – removal and refitting

Removal

1 Remove the lower driver's side facia cover as described in Chapter 11 Section 26.

2 Working under the facia, depress the brake pedal and brace it against the facia mounting bracket using a suitable tool.

3 Disconnect the stop lamp switch wiring plug **(see illustration)**.

4 Undo the stop lamp switch lock nut from the top of the brake pedal assembly and manoeuvre the switch from place **(see illustration)**.

Refitting

5 Insert the stop-light switch into position.

6 Tighten the lock nut while pushing the brake pedal, then reconnect the wiring plug.

7 Adjust the stop lamp switch clearance and

11.3 Stop lamp switch wiring plug

11.4 Undo the lock nut and remove the switch

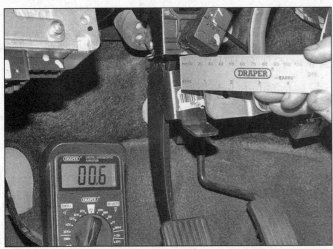

11.7 Adjust the brake light switch so it has around 3 mm of play

12.3a Remove the spring clip ...

brake pedal free play **(see illustration)**. The stop light switch should be adjusted so that the brake pedal moves approximately 3 mm before the brake lights illuminate.

8 Refit the lower facia panel.

12 Brake pedal –
removal and refitting

1 Remove the driver's side lower facia panel as described in Chapter 11 Section 26.
2 Remove the stop light light switch as described earlier in Section 11.
3 Working under the dashboard, remove the split pin and mounting clip for the brake pedal hinge pin **(see illustrations)**.
4 Withdraw the hinge pin from place and disengage the brake pedal return spring **(see illustration)**.
5 Manoeuvre the brake pedal from place.

Refitting

6 Refitting is a reversal of removal.

13 Handbrake –
checking and adjustment

Checking

1 The handbrake should be capable of holding the parked vehicle stationary, even on steep slopes, when applied with moderate force. The mechanism should be firm and positive in feel, with no trace of stiffness or sponginess from the cables, and the mechanism should release immediately the handbrake lever is released. If the mechanism does not operate satisfactorily, it should be checked immediately.
2 To check the operation of the handbrake, chock the front wheels, raise the rear of the vehicle and support it securely on axle stands, as described in *'Vehicle jacking and support'*. Release the handbrake lever.

12.3b ... then the hinge pin mounting clip

3 Depress the brake pedal several times to establish the correct shoe-to-drum clearance.
4 With the pedal released, check that the rear roadwheels can be rotated – slight dragging is acceptable, but it should be possible to turn each wheel easily.
5 Apply the handbrake lever and check that the rear roadwheels start to drag after one click of the ratchet mechanism, and are fully locked within 7 clicks of the ratchet.
6 Fully release the handbrake, and check that the rear roadwheels can again be rotated by hand.
7 If the handbrake does not operate as

13.8 Lift out the rubber mat

12.4 Withdraw the pin and disengage the return spring

described, carry out the adjustment procedure as follows.

Adjustment

8 Lift out the rubber mat in the rear section of the centre console **(see illustration)**. If better access is required, remove the centre console as described in Chapter 11 Section 24.
9 Using a spanner or suitable socket, turn the adjuster nut clockwise to apply tension to the cables, or anti-clockwise to release the tension on the cables, as necessary **(see illustration)**. Check the operation of the

13.9 Handbrake adjuster nut

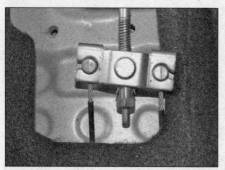

14.4 Slacken the nut and detach the cables

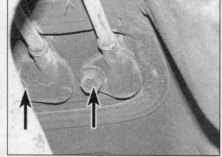

14.5 Undo the bolts and pull the outer cables from the floorpan

14.7 Prise out the cable retaining clip

handbrake as described previously and repeat the adjustment procedure as required.
10 On completion, refit the trim panel, and lower the vehicle to the ground.

14 Handbrake cables – removal and refitting

Removal

1 There are two rear handbrake cables, one on each side of the car. To renew either rear cable, proceed as follows.
2 Remove the brake shoes as described in Section 8.
3 Carefully remove centre console as described in Chapter 11 Section 24.
4 At the base of the handbrake lever, fully slacken the handbrake adjuster nut, to remove all tension from the cable draw bar, then disconnect the relevant handbrake inner cable from the draw bar **(see illustration)**.
5 Undo the bolts and release the outer cables from the floorpan **(see illustration)**.
6 Working along the length of the relevant cable, release the retaining clips/brackets.
7 Prise out the retaining clip and pull the handbrake cable from the brake backplate **(see illustration)**.
8 Manoeuvre the cable(s) from under the vehicle.

Refitting

9 Refitting is a reversal of removal. On

completion, adjust the handbrake as described in Section 13.

15 Handbrake lever – removal and refitting

Removal

1 Detach both handbrake cables from the lever draw bar, as described in Section 14.
2 Disconnect the warning switch wiring plug.
3 Undo the retaining bolts, and manoeuvre the handbrake lever assembly from place.

Refitting

4 Refitting is a reversal of removal. On completion, adjust the handbrake as described in Section 13.

16 Handbrake 'on' warning light switch – removal and refitting

Removal

1 Remove the centre console as described in Chapter 11 Section 24.
2 Disconnect the switch wiring plug **(see illustration)**.
3 Release the retaining clip and remove the switch from its location.

Refitting

4 Refitting is a reversal of removal.

17 Vacuum servo unit check valve – removal, testing and refitting

Removal

1 Disconnect the vacuum pipe at the quick-release connector between the check valve and the servo.
2 Disconnect the vacuum hose from the throttle body or manifold as applicable **(see illustration)**.
3 The valve is integral with the hose. If the valve is faulty, the complete hose assembly must be renewed.

Testing

4 Examine the vacuum hose, check the valve for signs of damage, and renew if necessary.
5 The valve may be tested by blowing through the hose in both directions; air should glow through the valve in one direction only – when blown through the from the servo unit end of the hose. Renew the hose assembly is this not the case.

Refitting

6 Refitting is a reversal of removal.
7 On completion, start the engine and check the valve to servo unit connection for signs of air leaks. Test the operation of the braking system before venturing out onto the road.

18 Anti-lock braking system (ABS) – general information

General information

1 ABS is fitted as standard equipment on all models covered by this manual. The purpose of the system is to prevent the wheels locking during heavy braking. This is achieved by automatic release of the brake on the relevant wheel, followed by modulated re-application of the brake. The system comprises an electronic control unit, a hydraulic modulator, hydraulic solenoid valves (located in the modulator unit), an electrically-driven fluid return pump, and four wheel speed sensors.

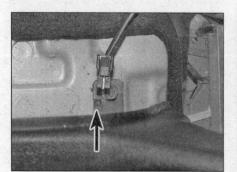

16.2 Disconnect the wiring plug from the switch terminal

17.2 Release the clamp and disconnect the vacuum hose

2 The solenoids (which control the fluid pressure to the calipers/wheel cylinders) are controlled by the electronic control unit, which itself receives signals from the wheel speed sensors. The wheel speed sensors monitor the speed of rotation of each wheel. By comparing the speed signals from the four wheels, the control unit can determine when a wheel is decelerating at an abnormal rate, compared to the speed of the of the other wheels. Using this information, the control unit can predict when a wheel is about to lock, and is able to reduce the fluid pressure to the brake on the relevant wheel to prevent it locking. Once the rotational speed of the monitored wheel returns to approximately that of the other wheels, the hydraulic fluid pressure is increased in stages, to enable braking to continue.

3 During normal operation, the system functions in the same way as a conventional non-ABS braking system.

19 Anti-lock braking system (ABS) components – removal and refitting

ABS hydraulic and electronic control unit

Removal

1 Remove the battery and battery tray as described in Chapter 5A Section 4.

2 Release the locking clip and disconnect the ECU wiring harness plug.

3 Wipe clean the area around the brake pipe unions on the side of the unit, and place absorbent rags beneath the pipe unions to catch any surplus fluid. Make a note of the correct fitted positions of the unions,

then unscrew the union nuts and carefully withdraw the pipes. Plug or tape over the pipe ends and unit orifices to minimise the loss of fluid, and to prevent the entry of dirt into the system.

4 Undo the retaining nuts/bolts, and remove the unit from the engine compartment.

Refitting

5 If a new control unit assembly is being fitted, it will be supplied prefilled with hydraulic fluid, and sealed with blanking plugs. Leave the plugs in position until just before connecting the brake pipes.

6 Locate the control unit in position and refit the retaining nuts/bolts.

7 Reconnect the brake pipes to their correct locations as noted during removal and tighten the union nuts securely.

8 Reconnect the ECU wiring plug.

9 Refit the battery tray and battery as described in Chapter 5A Section 4.

10 Bleed the complete brake hydraulic system as described in Section 2.

Front wheel speed sensor

Removal

11 Slacken the front roadwheel bolts, raise the front of the vehicle and support it securely on axle stands, as described in 'Vehicle jacking and support'. Remove the relevant front wheel.

12 Disconnect the battery negative lead as described in Chapter 5A Section 4.

13 The sensor is located on the top of the front wheel hub carrier. Trace the wiring back from the sensor, and separate the two halves of the wiring connector. Note the routing of the wiring to aid correct refitting.

14 Unscrew the retaining bolt and withdraw the sensor from the hub carrier.

Refitting

15 Refitting is a reversal of removal, noting the following points:

a) Ensure that the mating faces of the sensor and the hub carrier are clean, and apply a smear of high melting-point brake grease to the sensor location in the swivel hub before refitting.

b) Ensure that the end face of the sensor is clean.

c) Route the wiring as noted before removal.

Rear wheel sensor

16 The rear wheel sensor is integral with the rear hub. Removal of the hub is described in Chapter 10 Section 10.

Lateral acceleration/yaw rate sensor

Removal

17 Disconnect the battery negative lead as described in Chapter 5A Section 4.

18 The sensor is located under the driver's side carpet. Remove the driver's seat as described in Chapter 11 Section 21.

19 Disconnect the wiring plug, undo the retaining nuts and manoeuvre the sensor from place.

Refitting

20 Refitting is a reversal of removal, noting the following points:

a) Tighten the sensor retaining nuts to the specified torque.

b) Ensure the arrow on the sensor points forwards.

c) If a new sensor has been fitted, it must be calibrated using Hyundai diagnostic equipment (Witech/Examiner or equivalent). Entrust this task to a Hyundai dealer or suitably equipped repairer.

Chapter 10
Suspension and steering

Contents

Degrees of difficulty

| **Easy,** suitable for novice with little experience | | **Fairly easy,** suitable for beginner with some experience | **Fairly difficult,** suitable for competent DIY mechanic | **Difficult,** suitable for experienced DIY mechanic | **Very difficult,** suitable for expert DIY or professional | |

Specifications

Front suspension
Type . . . .   Independent, with MacPherson struts and transverse lower suspension arms. Anti-roll bar fitted to all models.

Rear suspension
Type . . . .   Semi-independent torsion beam axle, with coil springs and telescopic shock absorbers

Steering system
Type . . . .   Rack-and-pinion with electrically-operated power assistance

Front wheel alignment and steering angles
Toe-in . . . . $0° \pm 0.2°$ (0 mm $\pm$ 0.5 mm)

Rear wheel alignment angles
Toe-in . . . . $0°4' \pm 0°2$ (1.0 mm $\pm$ 0.5 mm)

Tyre pressures . . . .   see end of 'Weekly checks'

Torque wrench settings

	Nm	lbf ft
Front suspension:		
Anti-roll bar clamp bolts.	22	16
Anti-roll bar link rod nut	40	29
Lower arm-to-hub carrier	66	48
Lower arm-to-subframe*	113	82
Driveshaft nut*	220	160
Hub carrier-to-strut.	110	80
Subframe bolts	150	109
Suspension strut upper mounting cup-to-piston nut.	48	35
Roadwheel bolts.	100	73
Rear suspension		
Drum brake backplate bolts (M8)	25	18
Shock absorber lower mounting bolts	110	80
Shock absorber upper mounting bolts.	110	80
Stub axle bolts	80	58
Hub nut.	100	73
Steering		
Column mounting bolts/nuts	16	11
Column universal joint pinch bolt	32	24
Steering rack mounting bolts	70	51
Steering wheel bolt.	45	33
Track rod end-to-hub carrier	25	19

Do not re-use

1 General information

Front suspension

1 The front suspension is independent, comprising transverse lower wishbones, coil spring-over-damper MacPherson strut units and an anti-roll bar. The hub carriers are bolted to the base of the strut units and are linked to the lower arms by means of balljoints. The entire front suspension assembly is mounted on a subframe, which is in turn bolted to the vehicle body.

Rear suspension

2 The rear suspension incorporates a torsion

TOOL TiP

A tool to hold the front hub stationary whilst the driveshaft nut is slackened can be fabricated from two lengths of steel strip (one long, one short) and a nut and bolt; the nut and bolt forming the pivot of a forked tool.

beam axle with trailing arms, coil springs and separate double-acting telescopic shock absorbers. The components form a discrete sub-assembly which can be unbolted from the underside of the vehicle separately or as a complete unit. No anti-roll bar is fitted.

Steering

3 The two-piece steering shaft runs in a tubular column assembly, which is bolted to a bracket mounted on the vehicle bulkhead. The upper shaft is attached to the intermediate shaft by means of a universal joint and the intermediate shaft is similarly connected to the steering gear pinion by a second universal joint.

4 The rack-and-pinion steering gear is mounted on the front subframe, and is connected by means of track rods to the steering arms projecting rearwards from the swivel hubs. The track rods are fitted with balljoints at their inner and outer ends, to allow for suspension movement, and are threaded to facilitate adjustment.

5 Electrically operated power steering is fitted to all models. The power assistance is

2.5 Remove the bolts securing the strut to the hub carrier

provided by an electric motor and gearbox assembly which is integral with the steering column. The system is controlled by an electronic control unit.

2 Front hub carrier assembly – removal and refitting

Note: *A balljoint separator tool will be required for this operation and a new driveshaft retaining nut will be required for refitting.*

Removal

1 Slacken the front roadwheel bolts, raise the front of the vehicle and support it securely on axle stands, as described in *'Vehicle jacking and support'*. Remove the roadwheels.

2 Using a hammer and chisel or similar tool, tap up the staking securing the driveshaft retaining nut in position.

3 The front wheel hub must be held stationary in order to loosen the driveshaft nut. Ideally, the hub should be held by a suitable tool bolted into place using two of the roadwheel bolts (see **Tool Tip**). Alternatively, have an assistant firmly apply the foot brake to prevent the hub from rotating. Using a socket and extension bar, slacken and remove the driveshaft retaining nut.

Caution: The nut is extremely tight. Discard the nut – a new one must be fitted.

4 Remove the wheels speed sensor as described in Chapter 9 Section 19.

5 Undo the bolts and nuts and disconnect the front strut assembly from the hub carrier **(see illustration)**.

6 Unscrew the nut securing the track rod end to the hub carrier. Release the track rod end tapered shank using a balljoint separator tool as described in Section 17.

2.9a Lower arm-to-hub carrier bolt

2.9b Lever the lower arm balljoint shank down from the hub carrier

3.4 Remove the bearing retaining circlip

7 Remove the front brake disc as described in Chapter 9 Section 5.

8 Undo the retaining bolts and remove the brake disc shield (where fitted).

9 Liberally apply releasing fluid, then loosen the bolt and separate the hub carrier assembly from the lower arm **(see illustrations)**.

Refitting

10 Refitting is a reversal of removal.

---

3 Front hub bearings – renewal

Note: *Various special tools, including a hydraulic press will be required for this operation (see text). If the necessary tools are not available, the hub carrier assembly should be removed as described in Section 2 and taken to a suitably equipped engineering works for renewal of the bearing.*

1 Remove the hub carrier assembly as described in Section 2.

2 Press the wheel hub flange from the bearing and extract the hub, together with the bearing inner race.

3 The bearing inner race must now be removed from the wheel hub using a suitable puller. To provide sufficient clearance for the puller legs, force the inner race away from the hub flange using a hammer and small chisel inserted between the inner race and the hub flange. When sufficient clearance exists, engage the puller legs behind the inner race and draw the race off the wheel hub.

4 Extract the circlip from the hub carrier **(see illustration)**.

5 Press the bearing out of the hub. Note that a flange on the outboard side of the hub carrier means that the bearing can only be removed in one direction.

6 Before installing the new bearing, thoroughly clean the bearing location in the hub carrier.

7 Fit the new bearing from the inboard side the hub carrier and press it fully into position, applying pressure only to the bearing outer race.

8 Fit the bearing retaining circlip to its groove in the hub carrier so that the circlip's gap is

aligned with the aperture for the ABS wheel speed sensor (otherwise the sensor will not function correctly and the ABS failure warning lamp will illuminate).

9 Suitably support the bearing inner race on the press bed and press the wheel hub into the bearing.

10 On completion, check that the wheel hub rotates freely in the bearing without resistance or roughness.

11 Refit the hub carrier assembly as described in Section 2.

---

4 Front suspension strut – removal and refitting

Removal

1 Slacken the front wheel bolts, raise the front

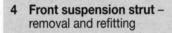

4.2 Remove the ABS sensor wiring bracket

of the vehicle and support it securely on axle stands, as described in *'Vehicle jacking and support'*. Remove the roadwheels.

2 Loosen the mounting bolt and remove the ABS sensor wiring bracket from the front strut assembly **(see illustration)**.

3 Undo the nut and disconnect the anti-roll bar link rod from the front strut. Insert an Allen key into the link rod shank to prevent rotation **(see illustration)**.

4 Undo the mounting bolts connecting the front strut to the hub carrier **(see illustration)**.

5 Remove the wiper motor as described in Chapter 12 Section 15.

6 Undo the fasteners and remove the panel beneath the wiper motor location **(see illustration)**. Feed the wiring loom and grommet through the panel as it's withdrawn.

7 Undo the strut mounting cap nut **(see**

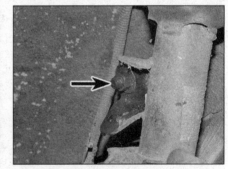

4.3 Insert an Allen key into the shank to prevent rotation

4.4 Remove the hub carrier-to-strut bolts/ nuts

4.6 Undo the fasteners and lift out the panel (right-hand fasteners arrowed)

4.7 Undo the nut at the top of the strut

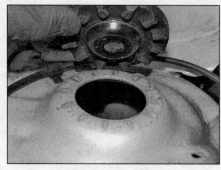

4.8 Recover the top cap

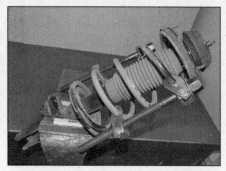

5.2 Fit compressors to the coil spring

illustration). Support the strut to prevent it falling once the nut is removed.

8 Manoeuvre the strut from place, and recover the top cap (see illustration).

Refitting

9 Refitting is a reversal of removal, ensuring that all nuts and bolts are tightened to the correct torque, where specified.

5 Front suspension strut – overhaul

Note: *Suitable compressor tools will be required for this operation.*

1 Remove the front suspension strut as described in Section 4.

2 Fit suitable spring compressors to the coil spring, and compress the spring sufficiently to enable the upper mounting to be turned by hand (see illustration).

⚠️ *Warning: Ensure that the coil spring is compressed sufficiently to remove all the tension from the upper mounting, before attempting to remove the piston rod nut.*

3 Unscrew the nut securing the strut piston rod to the upper mounting, while counterholding the piston with a suitable tool (see illustration).

4 Withdraw the upper mounting, spacer, spring seat, then withdraw the bump stop and gaiter (see illustrations).

5 Carefully remove the spring, complete with compressors.

6 With the strut assembly now dismantled, examine all the components for wear, damage or deformation. Renew any components as necessary (see illustration).

7 Examine the strut body for signs of fluid leakage or damage and the piston rod for signs of pitting or scoring. While holding it in an upright position, test the operation of the strut by moving the piston rod through a full stroke, and then through short strokes of 50 to 100 mm. In both cases, the resistance felt should be smooth and continuous. If the resistance is jerky, or uneven, or if there is any visible sign of wear or damage to the strut, renewal is necessary.

8 If any doubt exists about the condition of the coil spring, carefully remove the spring compressors, and check the spring for distortion and signs of cracking. Renew the spring if it is damaged or distorted, or if there is any doubt about its condition.

Caution: Coil springs are classified by their height when under load – this is indicated by a coloured paint marking on the side

5.3 Undo the piston rod nut

5.4a Withdraw the upper mounting …

5.4b … spacer …

5.4c … spring seat …

5.4d … bump stop and gaiter

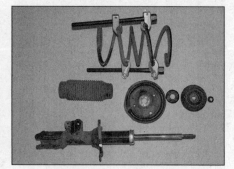

5.6 Examine the strut components

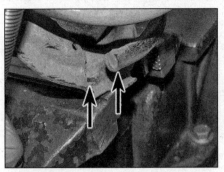
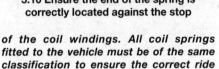

5.10 Ensure the end of the spring is correctly located against the stop

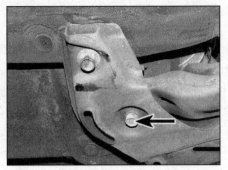

6.2a Lower arm rear …

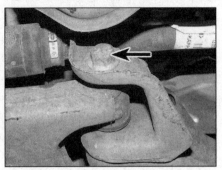

6.2b … and front mounting bolts

of the coil windings. All coil springs fitted to the vehicle must be of the same classification to ensure the correct ride height.

9 Begin reassembly by refitting the dust cover and bump rubber.

10 Ensure that the coil spring is compressed sufficiently to enable the upper mounting components to be fitted, then fit the spring over the piston rod, ensuring that the spring is the right way up and the lower end of the spring is correctly located in the recess on the lower spring seat **(see illustration)**.

11 Locate the upper spring seat/mounting over the piston rod.

12 Fit the piston rod top nut, then tighten the nut to the specified torque, counterholding the piston rod in a manner similar to that used during dismantling.

13 Remove the spring compressors and refit the strut to the car as described in Section 4.

6 Front suspension lower arm – removal and refitting

Removal

1 Slacken the front wheel bolts, raise the front of the vehicle and support it securely on axle stands, as described in 'Vehicle jacking and support'. Remove the front roadwheels.

2 Unscrew the lower arm front and rear mounting bolts **(see illustrations)**.

3 Detach the lower arm from the base of the hub carrier as described in Section 2.

4 With the lower arm removed, examine the arm itself, and the mounting bushes, for wear, cracks or damage.

5 Check the balljoint for wear, excessive play, or stiffness. Also check the balljoint dust boot for cracks or damage.

6 The mounting bushes and balljoint assembly are integral with the suspension lower arm, and cannot be renewed independently. If either the bushes or the balljoint are worn or damaged, the complete suspension lower arm assembly must be renewed.

Refitting

7 Refitting is a reversal of removal, noting the following points:

a) Refit the roadwheel, and lower the car to the ground.

b) Make sure that the car is parked on level ground, then release the handbrake. Roll the vehicle backwards and forwards, and bounce the front of the vehicle to settle the suspension components.

c) Chock the wheels, then tighten all the suspension arm mounting nuts and bolts to the specified torque.

d) On completion, have the front wheel toe setting checked at the earliest opportunity.

Caution: Final tightening of the suspension lower arm and anti-roll bar attachments must be carried out with the car resting on its roadwheels, or damage to the rubber bushes will result.

7 Front suspension lower arm balljoint – renewal

1 The balljoint is integral with the suspension lower arm. If the balljoint is worn or damaged, the complete lower arm must be renewed, as described in Section 6.

8 Front anti-roll bar – removal and refitting

Removal

1 Slacken the front wheel bolts, raise the front of the vehicle and support it securely on axle stands, as described in 'Vehicle jacking and support'. Remove the front roadwheels.

2 Remove the front subframe as described in Section 9.

3 Undo the mounting bolts securing the anti-roll bar to the subframe and separate.

4 Remove the bracket and mounting bush from the anti-roll bar.

5 Paint alignment marks between the subframe and vehicle body to aid refitting.

6 Inspect the rubber bushes for cracks or deterioration.

7 Check the anti-roll bar for signs of damage, wear or serious corrosion.

Refitting

8 Refitting is a reversal of removal, bearing in mind the following points:

a) Moderately tighten the anti-roll bar mountings initially, then tighten them all to the specified torque after the car has been lowered to the ground and is resting on its roadwheels.

b) Tighten all fasteners to their specified torque where given.

c) Align the previously made marks prior to tightening the subframe mounting bolts.

9 Front subframe – removal and refitting

Removal

1 Slacken the front wheel bolts, raise the front of the vehicle and support it securely on axle stands, as described in 'Vehicle jacking and support'. Remove the front roadwheels.

2 Working in the driver's footwell, remove the bolt and then disconnect the universal joint assembly from the pinion of the steering rack **(see illustration 13.6)**.

3 Detach the trackrod end from the hub carrier as described in Section 17.

4 Remove the lower mounting bolt/nut and then disconnect the lower arm from the hub carrier **(see illustrations 2.9a and 2.9b)**.

5 Remove the centre exhaust pipe as described in Chapter 4A Section 13.

6 Undo the bolts and remove the rear, lower engine mounting link rod **(see illustration)**.

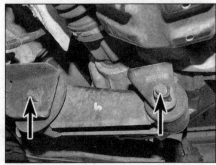

9.6 Rear engine mounting link rod bolts

9.8 Subframe rear, right-hand mounting bolt

10.3 Disconnect the speed sensor wiring plug

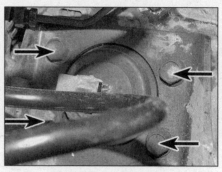

10.4 Hub mounting bolts

7 Paint alignment marks between the subframe and the vehicle body to aid refitting.
8 Position a workshop/trolley jack under the subframe, then undo the retaining bolts and lower the subframe from place **(see illustration)**.

Refitting

9 Raise the subframe into position, align the previously made marks, then tighten the retaining bolts to the specified torque.
10 The remainder of refitting is a reversal of removal, noting the following points:
a) *Tighten all fasteners to their specified torque where given.*
b) *Moderately tighten the anti-roll bar mountings initially, then tighten them all to the specified torque after the car has been lowered to the ground and is resting on its roadwheels.*
c) *Have the front wheel alignment checked at the earliest opportunity.*

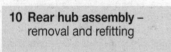

10 Rear hub assembly – removal and refitting

Note: *A new rear hub retaining nut must be used on refitting.*

Removal

1 The rear hub bearings are integral with the hubs themselves, and cannot be renewed separately. If the bearings require renewal, the complete hub assembly must be renewed.
2 Remove the brake shoes as described in Chapter 9 Section 8.
3 Disconnect the wheel speed sensor connector **(see illustration)**.
4 Undo the 4 mounting bolts, then remove the rear hub assembly **(see illustration)**.

Refitting

5 Refitting is a reversal of removal.
6 Tighten the hub retaining bolts to the specified torque.
7 Refit the brake shoes as described in Chapter 9 Section 8.
8 Refit the roadwheel and lower the vehicle to the ground.

11 Rear suspension components – removal and refitting

1 Chock the front wheels, slacken the rear roadwheel bolts, raise the rear of the vehicle and support it securely on axle stands, as

described in *'Vehicle jacking and support'*. Remove the rear roadwheels.

Shock absorber

Removal

2 Using a trolley jack positioned under the rear axle trailing arm, raise the trailing arm to take the strain from the shock absorber.
3 Slacken and withdraw the shock absorber upper retaining bolt **(see illustration)**.
4 Undo the bolt and nut, then remove the rear shock absorber from the axle **(see illustration)**.
5 Examine the shock absorber for signs of fluid leakage or damage. While holding it in an upright position, test the operation of the shock absorber by moving the piston through a full stroke, and then through short strokes of 50 to 100 mm. In both cases, the resistance felt should be smooth and continuous. If the resistance is jerky, or uneven, or if there is any visible sign of wear or damage, renewal is necessary.

Refitting

6 Refitting is a reversal of removal. The shock absorber mountings are offset, so it is impossible to fit the shock absorber the wrong way round. Tighten the upper and lower retaining bolts to the specified

11.3 Shock absorber upper retaining bolt/nut

11.4 Rear shock absorber lower mounting bolt

torque, but delay this operation until the full weight of the car is resting on its roadwheels.

Coil spring

Removal

7 Using a trolley jack positioned under the rear axle trailing arm, raise the trailing arm to take the strain from the shock absorbers.

8 Slacken and withdraw the shock absorber lower retaining bolts on both sides as described earlier in this Section.

9 Lower the trailing arm gradually using a trolley jack, until the coil spring is released from its lower seat on the trailing arm and its upper seat on the underbody. Make a note of the orientation of the coil spring, to aid correct refitting later.

Note: *While the spring is out of the car, check the condition of the rear bump stop. If it is worn or damaged, lift out and replace before refitting the spring.*

Refitting

10 Refitting is a reversal of removal. Ensure that the spring is correctly seated in the mounting collar **(see illustration)**. Tighten the shock absorber retaining bolts to the specified torque, but delay this operation until the full weight of the car is resting on its roadwheels.

11 Refit the shock absorber lower mounting bolt, and tighten it as described earlier in this Section.

Rear axle assembly

Removal

12 Remove the rear brake shoes on both sides as described in Chapter 9 Section 8.

13 Using brake hose clamps, clamp the brake flexible hydraulic hoses located adjacent to each rear axle mounting.

14 Clean the area around the brake pipe-to-flexible hose union nuts, and unscrew the pipe unions on each side. Extract the retaining clips and detach the flexible hoses from the brackets on the rear axle. Cover the open ends of the pipes and hoses to prevent dirt ingress.

15 Slacken and remove the bolts securing the rear wheel speed sensors to the rear of the stub axles and withdraw the sensors from their location. Suspend the sensors away from the working area, to avoid the possibility of damage.

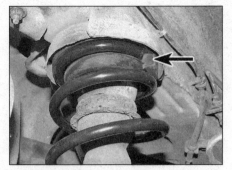
11.10 Ensure that the spring is correctly mounted in the collar

16 Release the handbrake cables, and the rear wheel speed sensor cables from their clips on the rear axle.

17 Remove both rear coil springs as described previously in this Section.

18 Suitably support the rear axle assembly on a trolley jack and engage the help of an assistant.

19 Undo the bolts securing the rear axle mounting brackets to the underbody on both sides. Slowly lower the jack and guide the axle assembly down and out from under the car.

Refitting

20 Guide the axle assembly into position, refit the mounting bracket retaining bolts and tighten them to the specified torque.

21 Refit the rear coil springs as described previously in this Section.

22 Ensure that the mating faces of the wheel speed sensors and the stub axles are clean, and apply a smear of high melting-point brake grease to the sensor locations in the stub axles. Clean the end face of the sensors, locate them place and secure with the retaining bolts.

23 Refit the flexible brake hydraulic hoses to their mounting brackets and secure with the retaining clips. Reconnect the brake pipe union to each hose and tighten the union nut securely. Remove the brake hose clamps from the hoses.

24 Secure the handbrake cables, and rear wheel speed sensor cables in their clips on the rear axle.

25 Refer to Chapter 9 and refit the rear brake

shoes then bleed the brake hydraulic system. Note that if no other part of the system has been disturbed, it should only be necessary to bleed the rear circuits.

26 Have the wheel alignment checked at the earliest opportunity.

12 Steering wheel – removal and refitting

Removal

1 Remove the airbag unit from the steering wheel as described in Chapter 12 Section 21.

2 Ensure the steering wheel is in its centre position, and the roadwheels are pointing straight-ahead.

3 Slacken and remove the steering wheel retaining nut **(see illustration)**. Counterhold the steering wheel to prevent rotation as the bolt is released.

4 If no marks are visible, make alignment marks between the steering wheel and the end of the steering column shaft, to aid correct refitting later **(see illustration)**.

5 Disconnect the steering wheel switches wiring plug, and lift the steering wheel off the column splines. If it is tight, twist it from side-to-side, whilst pulling upwards to release it from the shaft splines. Once the wheel is released, feed the airbag and horn switch wiring through the aperture in the steering wheel and remove the wheel from the car.

6 With the steering wheel removed, the clock spring assembly should be locked in place. It is advisable to secure the moving and fixed portions of the clock spring together using tape to prevent rotation with the steering wheel removed.

Refitting

7 Check that the airbag clock spring is still centred correctly as previously described. Remove the tape used to secure the clock spring moving and fixed portions together.

8 Feed the airbag and horn switch wiring through the steering wheel and locate the wheel on the column splines. Ensure that the marks made on the steering wheel and column shaft are aligned.

9 Fit the steering wheel retaining bolt, and tighten it to the specified torque.

10 Reconnect the horn wiring plug.

11 Refit the airbag unit as described in Chapter 12 Section 21.

13 Steering column – removal, inspection and refitting

Removal

1 Remove the steering wheel as described in Section 12.

2 Remove the steering column shrouds as described in Chapter 11 Section 26.

12.3 Undo the steering wheel nut

12.4 Make alignment marks between the column shaft and wheel

13.6 Undo the universal joint pinch bolt

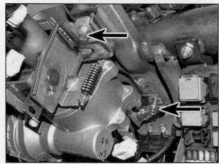

13.8 The column is secured by 2 bolts each side (right-hand bolts arrowed)

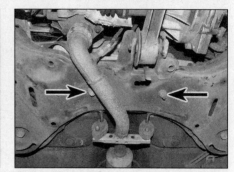

15.7 Steering rack mounting bolts

3 Remove the rotary contact unit as described in Chapter 12 Section 21.
4 Remove the indicator and wipers levers from the steering column shaft as described in Chapter 12 Section 5.
5 Remove the drivers side lower facia panel as described in Chapter 11 Section 26.
6 Working under the facia, slacken and remove the steering column lower universal joint pinch bolt **(see illustration)**. Make a reference mark on the joint and rack pinion, so they can aligned in the correct position during reassembly. Discard the bolt – a new one must be fitted.
7 Note their fitted positions, then disconnect all wiring plugs from the steering column and power steering unit.
8 Undo the 4 mounting bolts then remove the steering column and power steering assembly **(see illustration)**.
Caution: If the column is to be refitted to the vehicle, do not release the column adjustment lever, otherwise the column may be irreparably damaged.

Inspection

9 The steering column incorporates a telescopic safety feature. In the event of a front-end crash, the lower section of the shaft collapses and prevents the steering wheel injuring the driver. Before refitting the steering column, examine the column and mountings for signs of damage and deformation, and renew as necessary.
10 Check the steering shaft for signs of free play in the column bushes. If any damage or wear is found on the steering column bushes, it may be possible to have the column overhauled. Consult a Hyundai dealer or specialist.

Refitting

11 Refitting is a reversal of removal, noting the following points:
a) *Ensure that the front wheels are in the straight-ahead position then engage the universal joint with the steering gear pinion, aligning the marks made on removal.*
b) *Tighten all retaining nuts and bolts to the specified torque.*
c) *Refit the steering column combination*

switch assembly as described in Chapter 12 Section 5.
d) *Refit the steering wheel as described in Section 12.*
e) *If a new column has been fitted, it may need to be calibrated using Hyundai diagnostic equipment. Entrust this task to a Hyundai dealer or suitably equipped repairer.*

14 Power steering electric motor – removal and refitting

1 It would appear at the time of writing, that no separate parts are available for the steering column (except for the steering lock/ignition switch assembly – see Chapter 5A Section 10). Consequently, if faulty, the complete steering column assembly must be renewed. Consult a Hyundai parts specialist.

15 Steering rack – removal, overhaul and refitting

Removal

1 Turn the steering wheel to its centre position, so that the wheels are pointing straight ahead.
2 Slacken the front wheel bolts, raise the front of the vehicle and support it securely on axle stands, as described in 'Vehicle jacking and support'.
3 Working in the driver's footwell, unscrew the clamp bolt securing the intermediate shaft lower universal joint **(see illustration 13.6)**. Make suitable alignment marks on the steering gear pinion and universal joint to ensure correct orientation when refitting. Discard the bolt – a new one must be fitted.
4 Unscrew the nut and then disconnect the anti-roll bar link from the front strut **(see illustration 4.3)**.
5 Unscrew the nut securing the track rod end to the hub carrier. Release the track rod end tapered shank using a balljoint separator tool as described in Section 17.
6 Undo the bolts securing the front strut to the lower arm as described in Section 6.

7 Undo the nuts securing the steering rack to the subframe **(see illustration)**.
8 Undo the nuts securing the front exhaust pipe to the catalytic converter, remove the bolt securing the pipe support bracket to the transmission bell housing, then release the rubber mounting and move the exhaust pipe to one side. Recover the gasket.
9 Undo the bolts and remove the front subframe as described in Section 9.
10 Detach the steering rack from the front subframe.

Overhaul

11 Examine the steering rack assembly for signs of wear, leakage or damage. If overhaul of the steering rack assembly is necessary, the task must be entrusted to a Hyundai dealer or specialist.

Refitting

12 Refitting is a reversal of removal, bearing in mind the following points:
a) *Centralise the steering rack by turning the pinion so that the rack moves to full left lock. Now move the rack to full right lock, counting the number of turns of the pinion. Turn the pinion back by half the number of turns counted.*
b) *Ensure that the wheels are in the straight-ahead position then engage steering gear pinion with the universal joint, aligning the marks made on removal.*
c) *Tighten all retaining nuts and bolts to the specified torque.*
d) *Have the front wheel toe setting checked at the earliest opportunity.*

16 Steering rack rubber gaiters – renewal

1 Remove the relevant track rod end as described in Section 17.
2 Make an alignment mark between the track rod end locknut and the track rod, to allow the locknut to be accurately positioned when refitting. Unscrew the locknut from the end of the track rod.
3 Mark the correct fitted position of the gaiter on the track rod, then release the gaiter

securing clips **(see illustration)**. Slide the gaiter from the steering rack, and off the end of the track rod.

4 Thoroughly clean the track rod and the steering rack housing, using fine abrasive paper to polish off any corrosion, burrs or sharp edges which might damage the new gaiter sealing lips on installation. Scrape off all the grease from the old gaiter, and apply it to the track rod inner balljoint. (This assumes that grease has not been lost or contaminated as a result of damage to the old gaiter. Use fresh grease if in doubt.)

5 Carefully slide the new gaiter onto the track rod, and locate it on the steering gear housing. Align the outer edge of the gaiter with the mark made on the track rod prior to removal, then secure it in position with new retaining clips.

6 Screw the track rod end locknut onto the end of the track rod and position it accurately in accordance with the mark made on removal.

7 Refit the track rod end as described in Section 17.

17 Track rod end –
removal and refitting

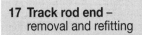

Removal

1 Slacken the front wheel bolts, raise the front of the vehicle and support it securely on axle stands, as described in 'Vehicle jacking and support'.

2 Hold the track rod, and unscrew the track rod end locknut by a quarter of a turn **(see illustration)**. Do not move the locknut from this position, as it will serve as a handy reference mark on refitting.

3 Pull out the split pin, and partially unscrew the nut securing the track rod end to the hub carrier **(see illustration)**.

4 Using a balljoint separator tool, separate the track rod end from the hub carrier **(see illustration)**. Remove the nut and lift the track rod end from the hub carrier.

5 Counting the exact number of turns

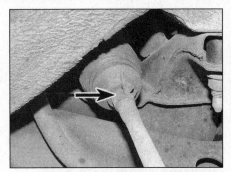

16.3 Gaiter outer securing clip

necessary to do so, unscrew the track rod end from the track rod.

Refitting

6 Carefully clean the track rod end and the track rod threads.

7 Renew the track rod end if the rubber dust cover is cracked, split or perished, or if the movement of the balljoint is either sloppy or too stiff. Also check for other signs of damage such as worn threads.

8 Screw the track rod end onto the track rod by the number of turns noted during removal. This should bring it to within a quarter of a turn from the locknut. Hold the track rod and securely tighten the locknut.

9 Ensure that the balljoint taper is clean, then engage the taper with the hub carrier.

10 Refit the track rod end retaining nut, and tighten the nut to the specified torque.

11 Refit the wheel, and lower the car to the ground.

12 Have the front wheel toe setting checked at the earliest opportunity.

18 Wheel alignment and
steering angles –
general information

Definitions

1 A car's steering and suspension geometry is defined in four basic settings **(see illustration)** – all angles are usually expressed

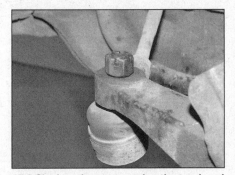

17.3 Slacken the nut securing the track rod end balljoint

17.4 Use a balljoint separator tool to separate the track rod end from the hub carrier

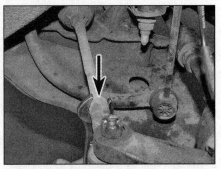

17.2 Slacken the trackrod end locknut a quarter of a turn

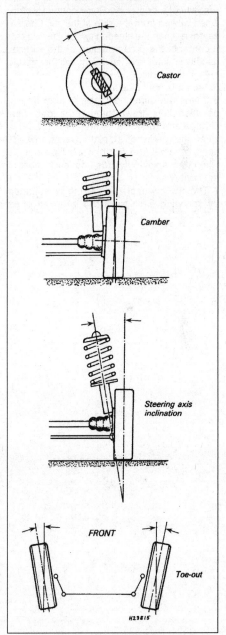

18.1 Steering/suspension geometry details

in degrees (toe settings are also expressed as a measurement); the steering axis is defined as an imaginary line drawn through the axis of the suspension strut, extended where necessary to contact the ground.

2 Camber is the angle between each roadwheel and a vertical line drawn through its centre and tyre contact patch, when viewed from the front or rear of the car. Positive camber is when the roadwheels are tilted outwards from the vertical at the top; negative camber is when they are tilted inwards.

3 The front camber angle is not adjustable.

4 Castor is the angle between the steering axis and a vertical line drawn through each roadwheel's centre and tyre contact patch, when viewed from the side of the car. Positive castor is when the steering axis is tilted so that it contacts the ground ahead of the vertical; negative castor is when it contacts the ground behind the vertical.

5 Castor is not adjustable.

6 Toe is the difference, viewed from above, between lines drawn through the roadwheel centres and the car's centre-line. "Toe-in" is when the roadwheels point inwards, towards each other at the front, while "toe-out" is when they splay outwards from each other at the front.

7 The front wheel toe setting is adjusted by screwing each track rod in or out of its balljoint, to alter the effective length of the track rod assembly.

8 Rear wheel toe setting is not adjustable.

Checking and adjustment

Front wheel toe setting

9 Due to the special measuring equipment necessary to check the wheel alignment, and the skill required to use it properly, the checking and adjustment of these settings is best left to a Hyundai dealer or similar expert. Note that most tyre-fitting shops now possess sophisticated checking equipment.

10 To check the toe setting, a tracking gauge must first be obtained. Two types of gauge are available, and can be obtained from motor accessory shops. The first type measures the distance between the front and rear inside edges of the roadwheels, as previously described, with the car stationary. The second type, known as a "scuff plate", measures the actual position of the contact surface of the tyre, in relation to the road surface, with the car in motion. This is achieved by pushing or driving the front tyre over a plate, which then moves slightly according to the scuff of the tyre, and shows this movement on a scale. Both types have their advantages and disadvantages, but either can give satisfactory results if used correctly and carefully.

11 Make sure that the steering is in the straight-ahead position when making measurements.

12 If adjustment is necessary, apply the handbrake then jack up the front of the car and support it securely on axle stands.

13 First clean the track rod threads; if they are corroded, apply penetrating fluid before starting adjustment. Release the rubber gaiter outer clips, peel back the gaiters and apply a smear of grease so that both are free and will not be twisted or strained as their respective track rods are rotated.

14 Retain the track rod with a suitable spanner and slacken the locknut. Alter the length of the track rod, by screwing them into or out of the balljoints by rotating the track rod using an open-ended spanner fitted to the track rod flats provided; shortening the track rods (screwing them onto their balljoints) will reduce toe-in/increase toe-out.

15 When the setting is correct, hold the track rod and tighten the locknut to the specified torque setting.

16 Check that the toe setting has been correctly adjusted by lowering the car to the ground and re-checking the toe setting; re-adjust if necessary. Ensure that the rubber gaiters are seated correctly and are not twisted or strained, and secure them in position with the retaining clips; where necessary fit a new retaining clip.

Chapter 11
Bodywork and fittings

Contents

Degrees of difficulty

Easy, suitable for novice with little experience	**Fairly easy,** suitable for beginner with some experience	**Fairly difficult,** suitable for competent DIY mechanic	**Difficult,** suitable for experienced DIY mechanic	**Very difficult,** suitable for expert DIY or professional

Specifications

Torque wrench settings	Nm	lbf ft
Seat belt anchorage	47	34
Seat belt inertia reel	47	34
Seat belt stalks	47	34

1 General information

1 The bodyshell is composed of pressed-steel sections which are welded together, although some use of structural adhesives is made. In addition, the front wings are bolted on.

2 The bonnet, door and some other panels vulnerable to corrosion are fabricated from zinc-coated metal. Almost 90% (by weight) of the vehicle body is galvanised to resist corrosion. A coating of anti-chip primer, applied prior to paint spraying provides further protection.

3 Extensive use is made of plastic materials, mainly in the interior, but also in exterior components. The outer sections of the front and rear bumpers are injection-moulded from a synthetic material which is very strong, and yet light. Plastic components such as wheel arch liners are fitted to the underside of the vehicle, to improve the body's resistance to corrosion.

2 Maintenance – bodywork and underframe

1 The general condition of a vehicle's bodywork is the one thing that significantly affects its value. Maintenance is easy but needs to be regular. Neglect, particularly after minor damage, can lead quickly to further deterioration and costly repair bills. It is important also to keep watch on those parts of the vehicle not immediately visible, for instance the underside, inside all the wheel arches and the lower pan of the engine compartment.

2 The basic maintenance routine for the bodywork is washing – preferably with a lot of water, from a hose. This will remove all the loose solids, which may have stuck to the vehicle. It is important to flush these off in such a way as to prevent grit from scratching the finish. The wheel arches and underframe need washing in the same way to remove any accumulated mud, which will retain moisture and tend to encourage rust. Paradoxically, the best time to clean the underframe and wheel arches is in wet weather when the mud is thoroughly wet and soft. In very wet weather the underframe is usually cleaned of large accumulations automatically and this is a good time for inspection.

3 Periodically, except on vehicles with a wax-based underbody protective coating, it is a good idea to have the whole of the underframe of the vehicle steam cleaned, engine compartment included, so that a thorough inspection can be carried out to see what minor repairs and renovations are necessary. Steam cleaning is available at many

garages and is necessary for removal of the accumulation of oily grime, which sometimes is allowed to become thick in certain areas. If steam-cleaning facilities are not available, there are some excellent grease solvents available which can be brush applied. The dirt can then be simply hosed off. Note that these methods should not be used on vehicles with wax-based underbody protective coating or the coating will be removed. Such vehicles should be inspected annually, preferably just prior to winter, when the underbody should be washed down and any damage to the wax coating repaired. Ideally, a completely fresh coat should be applied. It would also be worth considering the use of such wax-based protection for injection into door panels, sills, box sections, etc, as an additional safeguard against rust damage where such protection is not provided by the vehicle manufacturer.

4 After washing paintwork, wipe off with a chamois leather to give an unspotted clear finish. A coat of clear protective wax polish will give added protection against chemical pollutants in the air. If the paintwork sheen has dulled or oxidised, use a cleaner/polisher combination to restore the brilliance of the shine. This requires a little effort, but such dulling is usually caused because regular washing has been neglected. Care needs to be taken with metallic paintwork, as special non-abrasive cleaner/polisher is required to avoid damage to the finish. Always check that the door and ventilator opening drain holes and pipes are completely clear so that water can be drained out. Bright work should be treated in the same way as paintwork. Windscreens and windows can be kept clear of the smeary film that often appears by the use of a proprietary glass cleaner. Never use any form of wax or other body or chromium polish on glass.

3 Maintenance – upholstery and carpets

1 Mats and carpets should be brushed or vacuum cleaned regularly to keep them free of grit. If they are badly stained remove them from the vehicle for scrubbing or sponging and make quite sure they are dry before refitting. Seats and interior trim panels can be kept clean by wiping with a damp cloth. If they do become stained (which can be more apparent on light coloured upholstery) use a little liquid detergent and a soft nail brush to scour the grime out of the grain of the material. Do not forget to keep the headlining clean in the same way as the upholstery. When using liquid cleaners inside the vehicle do not over-wet the surfaces being cleaned. Excessive damp could get into the seams and padded interior causing stains, offensive odours or even rot. If the inside of the vehicle gets wet accidentally it is worthwhile taking some trouble to dry it out properly, particularly where carpets are involved. Do not leave oil or electric heaters inside the vehicle for this purpose.

4 Minor body damage – repair

Minor scratches

1 If the scratch is very superficial, and does not penetrate to the metal of the bodywork, repair is very simple. Lightly rub the area of the scratch with a paintwork renovator, or a very fine cutting paste, to remove loose paint from the scratch and to clear the surrounding bodywork of wax polish. Rinse the area with clean water.

2 In the case of metallic paint, the most commonly found scratches are not in the paint, but in the lacquer top coat, and appear white. If care is taken, these can sometimes be rendered less obvious by very careful use of paintwork renovator (which would otherwise not be used on metallic paintwork); otherwise, repair of these scratches can be achieved by applying lacquer with a fine brush.

3 Apply touch-up paint to the scratch using a fine paintbrush; continue to apply fine layers of paint until the surface of the paint in the scratch is level with the surrounding paintwork. Allow the new paint at least two weeks to harden, and then blend it into the surrounding paintwork by rubbing the scratch area with a paintwork renovator or a very fine cutting paste. Finally, apply wax polish.

4 Where the scratch has penetrated right through to the metal of the bodywork, causing the metal to rust, a different repair technique is required. Remove any loose rust from the bottom of the scratch with a penknife, and then apply rust-inhibiting paint to prevent the formation of rust in the future. Using a rubber or nylon applicator, fill the scratch with bodystopper paste. If required, this paste can be mixed with cellulose thinners to provide a very thin paste, which is ideal for filling narrow scratches. Before the stopper-paste in the scratch hardens, wrap a piece of smooth cotton rag around the top of a finger. Dip the finger in cellulose thinners, and then quickly sweep it across the surface of the stopper-paste in the scratch; this will ensure that the surface of the stopper-paste is slightly hollowed. The scratch can now be painted over as described earlier in this Section.

Dents

5 When deep denting of the vehicle's bodywork has taken place, the first task is to pull the dent out, until the affected bodywork almost attains its original shape. There is little point in trying to restore the original shape completely, as the metal in the damaged area will have stretched on impact and cannot be reshaped fully to its original contour. It is better to bring the level of the dent up to a point which is about 3 mm below the level of the surrounding bodywork. In cases where the dent is very shallow anyway, it is not worth trying to pull it out at all. If the underside of

the dent is accessible, it can be hammered out gently from behind, using a mallet with a wooden or plastic head. Whilst doing this, hold a suitable block of wood firmly against the outside of the panel to absorb the impact from the hammer blows and thus prevent a large area of the bodywork from being 'belled-out'.

6 Should the dent be in a section of the bodywork, which has a double skin or some other factor making it inaccessible from behind, a different technique is called for. Drill several small holes through the metal inside the area – particularly in the deeper section. Then screw long self-tapping screws into the holes just sufficiently for them to gain a good purchase in the metal. Now the dent can be pulled out by pulling on the protruding heads of the screws with a pair of pliers.

7 The next stage of the repair is the removal of the paint from the damaged area, and from an inch or so of the surrounding 'sound' bodywork. This is accomplished most easily by using a wire brush or abrasive pad on a power drill, although it can be done just as effectively by hand using sheets of abrasive paper. To complete the preparation for filling, score the surface of the bare metal with a screwdriver or the tang of a file, or alternatively, drill small holes in the affected area. This will provide a really good 'key' for the filler paste.

8 To complete the repair see the Section on filling and re-spraying.

Rust holes or gashes

9 Remove all paint from the affected area and from an inch or so of the surrounding 'sound' bodywork, using an abrasive pad or a wire brush on a power drill. If these are not available a few sheets of abrasive paper will do the job just as effectively. With the paint removed you will be able to gauge the severity of the corrosion and therefore decide whether to renew the whole panel (if this is possible) or to repair the affected area. New body panels are not as expensive as most people think and it is often quicker and more satisfactory to fit a new panel than to attempt to repair large areas of corrosion.

10 Remove all fittings from the affected area except those, which will act as a guide to the original shape of the damaged bodywork. Then, using tin snips or a hacksaw blade, remove all loose metal and any other metal badly affected by corrosion. Hammer the edges of the hole inwards in order to create a slight depression for the filler paste.

11 Wire-brush the affected area to remove the powdery rust from the surface of the remaining metal. Paint the affected area with rust-inhibiting paint – if the back of the rusted area is accessible, treat this also.

12 Before filling can take place it will be necessary to block the hole in some way. This can be achieved by the use of aluminium or plastic mesh, or aluminium tape.

13 Aluminium or plastic mesh is probably

the best material to use for a large hole. Cut a piece to the approximate size and shape of the hole to be filled, then position it in the hole so that its edges are below the level of the surrounding bodywork. It can be retained in position by several blobs of filler paste around its periphery.

14 Aluminium tape should be used for small or very narrow holes. Pull a piece off the roll and trim it to the approximate size and shape required, then pull off the backing paper (if used) and stick the tape over the hole; it can be overlapped if the thickness of one piece is insufficient. Burnish down the edges of the tape with the handle of a screwdriver or similar, to ensure that the tape is securely attached to the metal underneath.

Filling and re-spraying

15 Before using this Section, see the Sections on dent, deep scratch, rust holes and gash repairs.

16 Many types of bodyfiller are available, but generally speaking those proprietary kits which contain a tin of filler paste and a tube of resin hardener are best for this type of repair. A wide, flexible plastic or nylon applicator will be found invaluable for imparting a smooth and well-contoured finish to the surface of the filler.

17 Mix up a little filler on a clean piece of card or board – measure the hardener carefully (follow the maker's instructions on the pack) otherwise the filler will set too rapidly or too slowly. Using the applicator, apply the filler paste to the prepared area; draw the applicator across the surface of the filler to achieve the correct contour and to level the filler surface. As soon as a contour that approximates to the correct one is achieved, stop working the paste – if you carry on too long, the paste will become sticky and begin to 'pick up' on the applicator. Continue to add thin layers of filler paste at twenty-minute intervals until the level of the filler is just proud of the surrounding bodywork.

18 Once the filler has hardened, excess can be removed using a metal plane or file. From then on, progressively finer grades of abrasive paper should be used, starting with a 40-grade production paper and finishing with 400-grade (or higher) wet-and-dry paper. Always wrap the abrasive paper around a flat rubber, cork, or wooden block – otherwise the surface of the filler will not be completely flat. During the smoothing of the filler surface, the wet-and-dry paper should be periodically rinsed in water. This will ensure that a very smooth finish is imparted to the filler at the final stage.

19 At this stage the 'dent' should be surrounded by a ring of bare metal, which in turn should be encircled by the finely 'feathered' edge of the good paintwork. Rinse the repair area with clean water, until all of the dust produced by the rubbing-down operation has gone.

20 Spray the whole repair area with a light coat of primer – this will show up any imperfections in the surface of the filler. Repair these imperfections with fresh filler paste or bodystopper, and once more smooth the surface with abrasive paper. If bodystopper is used, it can be mixed with cellulose thinners to form a really thin paste, which is ideal for filling small holes. Repeat this spray-and-repair procedure until you are satisfied that the surface of the filler, and the feathered edge of the paintwork are perfect. Clean the repair area with clean water, and allow to dry fully.

21 The repair area is now ready for final spraying. Paint spraying must be carried out in a warm, dry, windless and dust-free atmosphere. This condition can be created artificially if you have access to a large indoor working area, but if you are forced to work in the open, you will have to pick your day very carefully. If you are working indoors, dousing the floor in the work area with water will help to settle the dust that would otherwise be in the atmosphere. If the repair area is confined to one body panel, mask off the surrounding panels; this will help to minimise the effects of a slight mis-match in paint colours. Bodywork fittings (e.g. rubbing strips, door handles, etc) will also need to be masked off. Use genuine masking tape and several thicknesses of newspaper for the masking operations.

22 Before commencing to spray, agitate the aerosol can thoroughly, and then spray a test area (an old tin, or similar) until the technique is mastered. Cover the repair area with a thick coat of primer; the thickness should be built up using several thin layers of paint rather than one thick one. Using 400-grade (or higher) wet-and-dry paper, rub down the surface of the primer until it is really smooth. While doing this, the work area should be thoroughly doused with water, and the wet-and-dry paper periodically rinsed in water. Allow to dry before spraying on more paint.

23 Spray on the top coat, again building up the thickness by using several thin layers of paint. Start spraying at the top of the repair area and then, using a side-to-side motion, work downwards until the whole repair area and about 2 inches of the surrounding original paintwork is covered. Remove all masking material 10 to 15 minutes after spraying on the final coat of paint.

24 Allow the new paint at least two weeks to harden, then, using a paintwork renovator or a very fine cutting paste, blend the edges of the paint into the existing paintwork. Finally, apply wax polish.

Plastic components

25 With the use of more and more plastic body components by the vehicle manufacturers (e.g. bumpers, spoilers, and in some cases major body panels), rectification of more serious damage to such items has become a matter of either entrusting repair work to a specialist in this field, or renewing complete components. Repair of such damage by the DIY owner is not really feasible, owing to the cost of the equipment and materials required for effecting such repairs. The basic technique involves making a groove along the line of the crack in the plastic using a rotary burr in a power drill. The damaged part is then welded back together by using a hot-air gun to heat up and fuse a plastic filler rod into the groove. Any excess plastic is then removed and the area rubbed down to a smooth finish. It is important that a filler rod of the correct plastic is used, as body components can be made of a variety of different types (e.g. polycarbonate, ABS, polypropylene).

26 Damage of a less serious nature (abrasions, minor cracks etc) can be repaired by the DIY owner using a two-part epoxy filler repair material. Once mixed in equal proportions, this is used in similar fashion to the bodywork filler used on metal panels. The filler is usually cured in twenty to thirty minutes, ready for sanding and painting.

27 If the owner is renewing a complete component himself, or if he has repaired it with epoxy filler, he will be left with the problem of finding a suitable paint for finishing which is compatible with the type of plastic used. At one time the use of a universal paint was not possible, owing to the complex range of plastics encountered in body component applications. Standard paints, generally speaking, will not bond to plastic or rubber satisfactorily. However, it is now possible to obtain a plastic body parts finishing kit, which consists of a pre-primer treatment, a primer and coloured top coat. Full instructions are normally supplied with a kit, but basically the method of use is to first apply the pre-primer to the component concerned and allow it to dry for up to 30 minutes. Then the primer is applied and left to dry for about an hour before finally applying the special coloured top coat. The result is a correctly coloured component where the paint will flex with the plastic or rubber, a property that standard paint does not normally possess.

5 Major body damage – repair

1 Where serious damage has occurred, or large areas need renewal due to neglect, it means that complete new panels will need welding in, and this is best left to professionals. If the damage is due to impact, it will also be necessary to completely check the alignment of the bodyshell, and this can only be carried out accurately by a Hyundai dealer using special jigs. If the body is left misaligned, it is primarily dangerous as the car will not handle properly, and secondly, uneven stresses will be imposed on the steering, suspension and possibly transmission, causing abnormal wear, or complete failure, particularly to such items as the tyres.

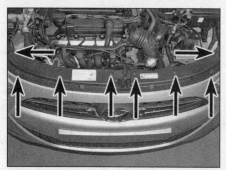

6.2 Undo the upper cover's bolts and clips

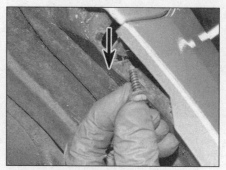

6.3 Undo the side mounting bolt in each wheelarch

6.4 Release the 6 mounting clips beneath the bumper (one shown)

6 Bumpers –
removal and refitting

Front bumper

Removal

1 For improved access, firmly apply the handbrake, then jack up the front of the car and support it securely on axle stands, as described in *'Vehicle jacking and support'*.

2 Undo the radiator upper cover 2 mounting bolts and 6 clips **(see illustration)**.

3 Undo the side mounting bolt in each wheelarch **(see illustration)**.

4 Remove the 6 mounting clips underneath the bumper **(see illustration)**.

5 Disconnect the wiring plugs for the front fog lamps as described in Chapter 12 Section 6.

6 Prise open the clips holding each end of the bumper to each front wing **(see illustration)**.

7 With the help of an assistant, carefully manoeuvre the front bumper from place.

Refitting

8 Refitting is a reversal of removal.

Rear bumper

Removal

9 Chock the front wheels, slacken the rear wheel bolts, raise the rear of the vehicle and support it securely on axle stands, as described in *'Vehicle jacking and support'*.

10 Remove the tail light cluster as described in Chapter 12 Section 9. Tape the rear light bulbs up and out of the way to avoid breakages.

11 Undo the 3 screws in the bottom of each rear light aperture **(see illustration)**.

12 Undo the 2 screws in the centre of the upper edge of the bumper **(see illustration)**.

13 Undo the screws and remove the rear mudflaps (where fitted).

14 Remove the number plate light assembly as described in Chapter 12 Section 6.

15 Undo the 3 screws securing the bumper to the wheelarch liner and rear wing **(see illustration)**.

16 Remove the screw each side securing the bumper to the rear wing **(see illustration)**.

17 Remove the rear exhaust pipe and silencer as described in Chapter 4A Section 13.

18 Undo the bolts and remove the rear heat shield **(see illustration)**. A spray of releasing fluid may help to loosen the bolts.

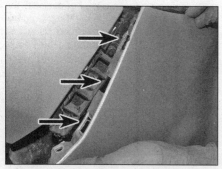

6.6 Prise open the clips at each end of the bumper

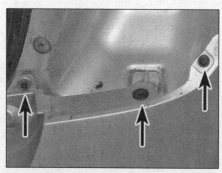

6.11 Undo the screws in each light opening

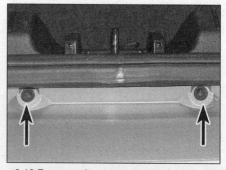

6.12 Remove the screws in the centre of the bumper's upper edge

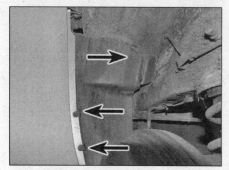

6.15 Remove the screws in the rear wheelarch

6.16 Remove the screws below the bumper (right hand screw arrowed)

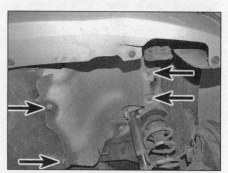

6.18 Remove the rear heat shield

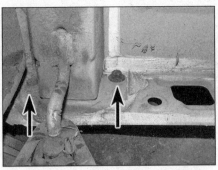

6.19 Undo the crash bar mounting bolts

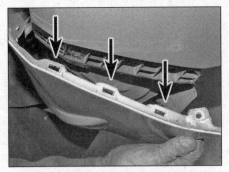

6.20 Disengage the clips and remove the bumper

6.21 Disconnect the numberplate lights

19 Working underneath, undo the 2 mounting bolts at each end of the rear crash bar **(see illustration)**.

20 Pull out the front edge of the bumper to disengage the clips, and with the help of an assistant, manoeuvre the bumper rearwards from place **(see illustration)**.

21 Prise out the number plate lights and disconnect **(see illustration)**.

Refitting

22 Refitting is a reversal of removal.

7 Tailgate – removal, refitting and adjustment

Removal

1 Open the tailgate, and remove the parcel shelf.

2 Remove the tailgate inner trim panel as described in Section 23.

3 Remove the high-level brake light as described in Chapter 12 Section 9.

4 Disconnect the wiring connectors for the tailgate lock and tailgate wiper motor and unbolt the earth leads. Check for any other wiring connectors which must be disconnected to facilitate tailgate removal. Carefully label each wiring harness connector to aid correct refitting.

5 Tie a length of cord to the wiring harness, then bind the loose ends of the cabling

together using PVC tape. Prise the wiring harness grommet from the upper edge of the tailgate, then feed the wiring through the aperture in the tailgate. Untie the cord from the harness, but leave it in place in the tailgate, to aid refitting later.

6 Disconnect the fluid hose from the tailgate washer nozzle, then tie a length of cord to the hose and draw it out of the tailgate, using the same procedure carried out on the wiring harness.

7 Have an assistant support the tailgate in the open position.

8 Detach the upper ends of the support struts from the tailgate as described in Section 8.

9 Make alignment marks between the tailgate hinges and the vehicle body, then slacken and unscrew the bolts securing the hinges to the tailgate, and lift the tailgate from the vehicle **(see illustration)**.

Refitting

10 Refitting is a reversal of removal, bearing in mind the following points:

a) Tie the cord to the wiring harness and use it to pull the harness through the aperture and into the tailgate. Repeat the procedure on the washer fluid hose.

b) Do not fully tighten the hinge bolts until the tailgate adjustment has been checked, as described in the following paragraphs.

Adjustment

11 Close the tailgate carefully, in case the alignment is incorrect, which may cause

scratching on the tailgate or the body as the tailgate is closed, and check for alignment with the adjacent panels. If necessary, slacken the bolts that secure the hinges to the bodywork and re-align the tailgate to suit. Once the tailgate is correctly aligned, tighten the hinge bolts securely.

12 Check that the tailgate fastens and releases in a satisfactory manner. If adjustment is necessary, slacken the striker plate retaining bolts, and adjust the position of the striker to suit. Once the lock is operating correctly, securely tighten the striker plate retaining bolts.

13 If necessary, adjust the protrusion of the rubber buffers at the lower edge of the tailgate by screwing them in or out, as appropriate.

8 Tailgate strut – removal and refitting

Removal

1 Open the tailgate and support it using suitable wooden props.

2 At the upper end of each strut, lever out the balljoint spring clip a little, then compress the strut slightly by hand and then prise the strut balljoint from the stud on the tailgate **(see illustration)**.

Warning: The strut may still be under tension and could extend suddenly once detached from its mountings.

3 Release the lower end of each strut in the same way.

Refitting

4 Refitting is a reversal of removal.

9 Tailgate lock components – removal and refitting

Tailgate lock

Removal

1 Remove the tailgate inner trim panel as described in Section 23.

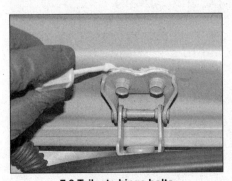

7.9 Tailgate hinge bolts

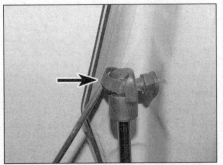

8.2 Lever out the balljoint spring slightly

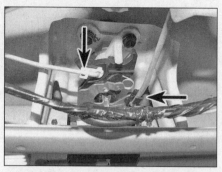

9.2 Rotate the latch rod clips and disconnect

9.3 Undo the lock bolts and remove it from the tailgate

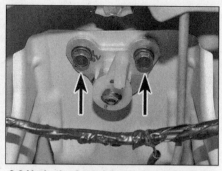

9.6 Undo the 2 retaining bolts and remove the lock cylinder

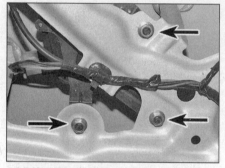

9.7 Undo the 3 bolts and disconnect the wiring plug, then manoeuvre from place

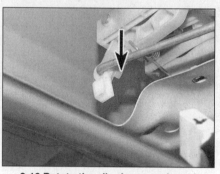

9.10 Rotate the clip downwards and remove the rod from the handle

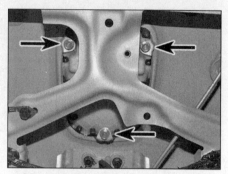

9.11 Undo the 3 bolts and remove the handle

2 Rotate the clips for the tailgate handle rod and latch rod and disconnect **(see illustration)**. Disconnect the wiring plug.
3 Undo the lock retaining bolts, manoeuvre the lock from place **(see illustration)**.

Refitting

4 Refitting is a reversal of removal. Ensure the lock operates correctly prior to closing the tailgate.

Tailgate lock cylinder

5 Remove the tailgate lock mechanism as described earlier in this Section.
6 Undo the two retaining bolts and manoeuvre the lock cylinder from place **(see illustration)**.

Tailgate lock actuator

7 Rotate the clip and disconnect the rod

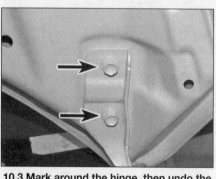

10.3 Mark around the hinge, then undo the bolts and remove the bonnet

(hidden), then undo the 3 retaining bolts and disconnect the wiring plug **(see illustration)**. Manoeuvre the actuator from place.

Tailgate release control

Removal

8 Remove the tailgate inner trim panel as described in Section 23.
9 Remove the wiper motor as described in Chapter 12 Section 16.
10 Rotate the clip on the end of the rod downwards and disconnect the rod from the exterior handle **(see illustration)**.
11 Undo the 3 mounting bolts, then remove the outside handle **(see illustration)**.

Refitting

12 Refitting is a reversal of removal.

Striker plate

Removal

13 Mark the position of the striker plate in relation to the bodywork using a pencil or marker pen, to aid accurate refitting.
14 Slacken and unscrew the bolts securing the striker plate to the body.

Refitting

15 Refitting is a reversal of removal. Use the markings made during removal to give the correct alignment.
16 Check that the tailgate fastens and releases in a satisfactory manner. If adjustment is necessary, slacken the striker plate retaining bolts, and adjust the position

of the plate to suit. Once the lock is operating correctly, securely tighten the striker plate retaining bolts.

10 Bonnet – removal and refitting

Removal

1 Open the bonnet and prop it up with a stout pole.
2 Disconnect the washer jet hose at the bonnet connector.
3 Mark the relationship between the hinges and the edge of the bonnet using a soft pencil or marker pen. Slacken and unscrew the bolts; have an assistant support the bonnet as the last bolts are removed **(see illustration)**.
4 With the help of an assistant, lift off the bonnet and set it down on its edge, using a dust sheet to protect the paintwork.

Refitting

5 Refit the bonnet and retaining bolts, using the markings made during removal to achieve the correct alignment. Note that the bolt mounting holes are slotted to allow adjustment if required. On completion, tighten the bolts to the specified torque.
6 Reconnect the washer hose, then check that the bonnet fastens and releases in a satisfactory manner. If necessary, adjust the bonnet lock assembly, as described in Section 11.

11.2 Undo the 4 bolts to remove the lock (2 left-side bolts obscured)

12.3 Disconnect the cable from the rear of the release lever

12.4 Detach the cable from the facia panel

11 Bonnet lock assembly – removal and refitting

Removal

1 Open the bonnet and mark the relationship between the lock assembly and the front body panel using a soft pencil or marker pen.
2 Slacken and unscrew the 4 nuts/bolts and withdraw the lock assembly from its location **(see illustration)**.
3 Disconnect the release cable and remove the lock assembly.

Refitting

4 Refitting is a reversal of removal. Use the alignment markings made during removal to aid accurate refitting. Check that the bonnet fastens and releases in a satisfactory manner, noting that the mounting holes are slotted to allow adjustment of the lock, if required. On completion, tighten the bolts securely.
5 If necessary, adjust the protrusion of the rubber buffers on the front body panel (located above each headlamp unit) by screwing them in or out, as appropriate. When the rubber buffers are correctly adjusted, there should be just enough free movement to allow the bonnet to be closed and locked easily, without using excessive force, but not enough to allow the bonnet to rattle when secured in the locked position.

12 Bonnet release cable – removal and refitting

Removal

1 Disconnect the release cable from the bonnet lock assembly as described in Section 11.
2 Remove the driver's side lower facia panel as described in Section 26.
3 Disconnect the cable from the rear of the bonnet release lever **(see illustration)**.

4 Detach the release cable from the rear of the driver's side lower facia panel **(see illustration)**.
5 Working around the engine bay, extract the release cable from its securing clips.
6 Tie a length of string to the end of the cable in the engine compartment, then carefully pull the cable through the bulkhead grommet into the passenger's compartment. Untie the string from the cable, but leave it in place in the bulkhead, to aid refitting.

Refitting

7 Refitting is a reversal of removal, using the string to draw the cable through the bulkhead into the engine compartment. Reconnect the cable to the bonnet lock and adjust the lock position as described in Section 11.

13.1 Inner mirror cover can be prised from place

13 Door inner trim panel – removal and refitting

Front door
Removal

1 Prise off the door mirror inner cover **(see illustration)**.
2 Prise out the cap, undo the screw in the interior release handle panel, then remove the panel **(see illustration)**.
3 Remove the screw from the interior door pull **(see illustration)**.
4 Prise off caps and remove 2 screws from the door panel edge **(see illustration)**.

13.2 Prise out the cap and remove the screw

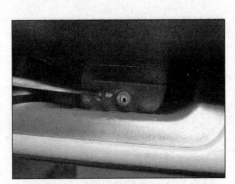

13.3 Remove the screw from the interior door pull

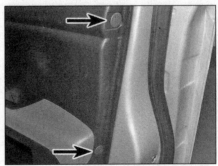

13.4 Remove the screws

13.6 Prise the door trim panel away from the door

13.10 Undo the mounting screw

13.11 Remove the screw in the door pull

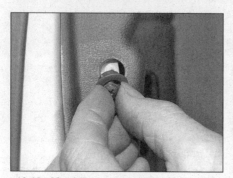

13.12a Mounting screw on the front edge of the door trim

13.12b Mounting screw on the rear edge of the door trim

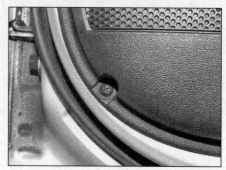

13.12c Screw at the bottom front corner of the trim

5 Undo the remaining screws around the door trim panel edge.

6 Using a trim removal tool, prise the door trim panel away from the door (see illustration).

7 Gently lift the door inner trim panel from place. Disconnect any wiring plugs as they become accessible.

If work is to be carried out on the door internal components, it will be necessary to remove the plastic sealing sheet from the inside of the door. Remove the door speaker (Chapter 12 Section 18), then start at one corner of the sheet and carefully peel it away, using a sharp blade to split the sealant bead, if necessary.

8 Store the detached sealing sheet such that it cannot become contaminated with dust; this will allow it to be re-used later.

Refitting

9 Refitting is a reversal of removal, bearing in mind the following points:

a) *Ensure that the sealing sheet is correctly refitted, press it on firmly to ensure that it is adequately sealed around its edges. It should be possible to use the original sealant, but if necessary, new sealant can be obtained from a Hyundai dealer.*

b) *Make sure that the weather strip engages securely with the edge of the door as the panel is refitted.*

Rear door

Removal

10 Prise off the cap, then undo the mounting screw and remove the interior door release handle (see illustration).

11 Remove the cap from the mounting screw in the door pull handle and remove (see illustration).

12 Remove the caps from the 3 screws around the edge of the door trim and undo (see illustrations).

13 Using a trim removal tool, gently prise the door trim away from the door to release the mounting clips (see illustration) then lift the door trim upwards to remove.

14 Disconnect the wiring plug inside the door trim (see illustration).

Refitting

15 Refitting is a reversal of removal, bearing in mind the following points:

a) *Ensure that the sealing sheet is correctly refitted, press it on firmly to ensure that it is adequately sealed around its edges. It should be possible to use the original sealant, but if necessary, new sealant can be obtained from a Hyundai dealer.*

b) *Make sure that the weather strip engages securely with the edge of the door as the panel is refitted.*

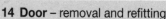
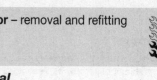

14 Door – removal and refitting

Removal

1 Disconnect the battery negative lead as described in Chapter 5A Section 4.

2 Remove the interior door trim panel as described in Section 13.

13.13 Prise the trim away from the door

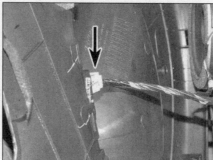

13.14 Disconnect the wiring plug

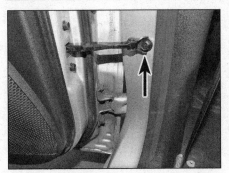

14.5 Undo the check strap securing bolt

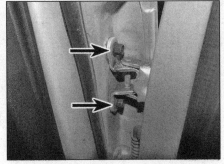

14.6 Undo the door hinge bolts

15.3 Rotate the retaining clip upwards to release the link rod

3 Remove the door window glass as described in Section 17.
4 Prise out the rubber gaiter from the pillar, then disconnect the door wiring plug.
5 Undo the bolt securing the check strap to the pillar **(see illustration)**.
6 Have an assistant support the door, then undo the hinge bolts, and lift the door from place **(see illustration)**.

Refitting

7 Refitting is a reversal of removal.

---

15 Door handle and lock components – removal and refitting

Front door exterior handle

Removal

1 Fully raise the window glass.
2 Remove the door inner trim panel and plastic sealing sheet, as described in Section 13.
3 Rotate the clip and disconnect the the exterior handle-to-lock link rod from the lock **(see illustration)**.
4 Remove the front door lock cylinder as described next in this Section.
5 Undo the retaining bolt, then lift and manoeuvre the handle assembly from the outside of the door **(see illustration)**.

Refitting

6 Locate the handle in position and connect the link rod to the door lock mechanism.

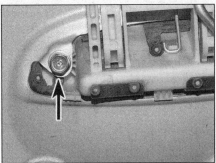

15.5 Undo the retaining bolt and manoeuvre the handle from the door

7 Refit the handle and tighten the lock cylinder and handle retaining bolts.
8 Refit the sealing sheet and door inner trim panel as described in Section 13.

Front door lock cylinder

Removal

9 Fully raise the window.
10 Remove the inner door panel and sealing sheet as described in Section 13.
11 Undo the 2 retaining bolts and manoeuvre the window channel from the door **(see illustration)**.
12 Rotate the clips and detach the lock and door release rods **(see illustration)**.
13 Undo the retaining bolt and manoeuvre the lock cylinder from place **(see illustration)**.

Refitting

14 Refitting is reversal of removal

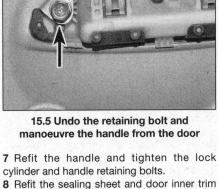

15.11 Undo 2 bolts and remove the window channel from the door

Front door interior handle

Removal

15 Remove the door inner trim panel as described in Section 13.
16 Undo the screw and slide the door interior handle rearwards to release it **(see illustration)**, thendisconnect the lock cable (upper, grey) and the door latch cable (lower, black).

Refitting

17 Refitting is a reversal of removal.

Front door lock mechanism

Removal

18 Fully raise the window glass.
19 Remove the front door inner trim panel and sealing sheet as described in Section 13. Note that it's only necessary to remove the sealing sheet in the area of the door lock.

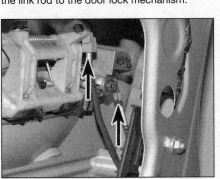

15.12 Rotate the clips and remove the rods

15.13 Undo the bolt and remove the lock cylinder

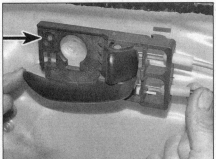

15.16 Slide the handle backwards then detach the cables

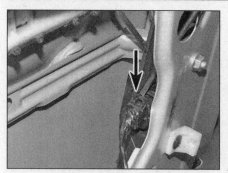

15.20 Disconnect the wiring plug

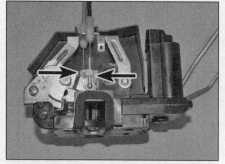

15.21 Unclip the lock operating rods (lock removed for clarity)

15.23a Front door lock retaining bolts

20 Disconnect the wiring plug from the door lock. If it proves reluctant to release by hand, press the release tab with the end of a screwdriver **(see illustration)**.
21 Rotate the clips and disconnect the operating link rods from the door lock **(see illustration)**.
22 Undo the 2 retaining bolts and manoeuvre the window channel from the door as described earlier in this Section.
23 Undo the 3 retaining bolts and manoeuvre the lock assembly, complete with the cables from the door frame **(see illustrations)**.

Refitting

24 Refitting is a reversal of removal.

Front door lock cable removal

25 Remove the door lock as described earlier in this Section.

26 The cable removal procedure is exactly the same as that described for the rear door lock cable later in this Section.

Rear door exterior handle

Removal

27 Remove the rear door inner trim panel and sealing sheet as described in Section 13. Note that it's only necessary to remove the sealing sheet in the area of the door lock.
28 Rotate the clip and disconnect the lock rod **(see illustration)**.
29 Undo the mounting bolts (press out the curcular grommet from behind to access the second bolt) securing the lock mechanism to the door, and manoeuvre the handle from place **(see illustrations)**.

Refitting

30 Refitting is a reversal of removal.

Rear door interior handle

31 The rear door interior handle removal and refitting procedure is identical to that for the front door, as described previously in this Section.

Rear door lock mechanism

Removal

32 Fully raise the window, then remove the door inner trim panel as described in Section 13.
33 Remove the interior door release handle as described earlier in this Section. Gently remove the sealing sheet. Note that it's only necessary to remove the sealing sheet in the area of the door lock.
34 Unclip the lock and door release cables **(see illustration)**.

15.23b Manoeuvre the lock from the door

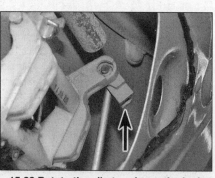

15.28 Rotate the clip to release the lock rod

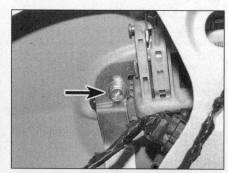

15.29a Undo the first bolt ...

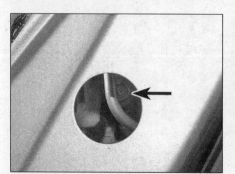

15.29b ... then press out the grommet and remove the second bolt ...

15.29c ... and finally manoeuvre the handle from place

15.34 Unclip the lock and release cables

15.35 Disconnect the lock wiring plug

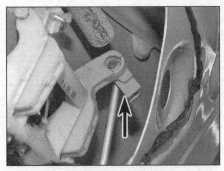

15.36 Rotate the clip and push the latch rod from place

15.37 Door lock retaining bolts

15.38 Swivel the lock so the child lock clears the door

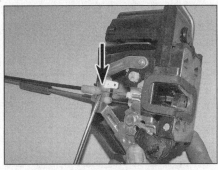

15.41 Prise out the cable locator

15.42 Rotate the clip and remove the cable

35 Disconnect the lock wiring plug **(see illustration)**.
36 Rotate the clip and manoeuvre the locking rod from place **(see illustration)**.
37 Undo the 3 retaining bolts securing the

lock mechanism to the door frame **(see illustration)**.
38 Manoeuvre the door lock from place, taking care to swivel the lock so that the child lock release clears the door **(see illustration)**.

Refitting

39 Refitting is a reversal of removal.

Rear door lock cable removal

40 Remove the door lock as described earlier in this Section.

Door release cable

41 Prise out the cable locator from the door lock mounting **(see illustration)**.
42 Rotate the retaining clip and remove the cable from place **(see illustration)**.

Door locking cable

43 Using a flat-bladed screwdriver, gently prise away the lock shield **(see illustration)**.
44 Prise the lock cable locator from the lock mounting **(see illustration)**.
45 Release the lock cable from the lock mechanism **(see illustration)**.

Refitting

46 Refitting is reversal of removal.

15.43 Prise away the lock shield

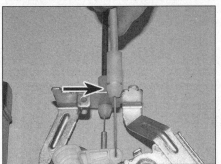

15.44 Prise the cable locator from its housing

16 Exterior mirror components
– removal and refitting

Mirror assembly

Removal

1 Remove the door trim panel as described in Section 13.
2 Disconnect the mirror wiring plug then undo the 3 retaining bolts **(see illustration)**.

15.45 Lift the locking cable from the mechanism

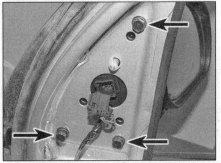

16.2 Exterior mirror retaining bolts

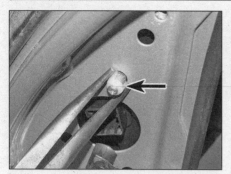

16.3 Compress the clip and manoeuvre the mirror out

16.6 Carefully release the mirror glass clips

Mirror motor assembly

12 Remove the mirror glass as described earlier in this Section.
13 Undo the 3 screws and manoeuvre the mirror motor from place (see illustration) then disconnect the wiring plug.
14 Refitting is a reversal of removal.

17 Door window glass and regulator – removal and refitting

Front window glass

Removal

1 Lower the window two thirds of the way down.
2 Disconnect the battery negative lead as described in Chapter 5A Section 4.
3 Remove the door inner trim panel, sealing sheet and door panel mounting bracket as described in Section 13.
4 Pull up the inner weather strip (see illustration).
5 Undo the glass retaining bolts from the regulator (see illustration).
6 Lift the glass, rotating it a few degrees anticlockwise and carefully pull it out through the inside of the window slot (see illustration), taking care as you manoeuvre the clips out past the exterior weather strip.

Refitting

7 Locate the glass in the door, engage the regulator mechanism at the base of the glass and tighten the 2 retaining bolts.
8 Refit the inner weather strip to the door.
9 Refit the door sealing sheet and inner trim panel as described in Section 13.

Front window regulator

Removal

10 Detach the window glass from the regulator as described previously in this Section, then slide the glass to the top of the door frame, and secure it there with adhesive tape.

16.10 Undo the 3 screws and remove the mirror shroud

16.13 Undo 3 screws and remove the mirror motor

3 Using a pair of long-nosed pliers, compress the retaining clip and manoeuvre the mirror unit from place (see illustration).

Refitting

4 Refitting is a reversal of removal.

Mirror glass

Removal

5 Push the lower edge of the glass inwards to create an opening between the upper edge of the glass and the mirror body.
6 Insert a small trim removal tool between the mirror glass and the mirror body, and carefully release the mirror glass securing clips (see illustration).

 Warning: Protect your hands and eyes from glass splinters.

7 Where applicable, disconnect the heater element wiring from the rear of the glass, and withdraw the glass from the mirror assembly.

Refitting

8 Where applicable, reconnect the wires to the rear of the mirror glass, then push the glass into position to engage the securing clips.

Mirror shroud

9 Remove the mirror glass as described earlier in this Section.
10 Undo the 3 screws and manoeuvre the mirror shroud from place (see illustration).
11 Refitting is a reversal of removal.

17.4 Pull up the inner weather strip

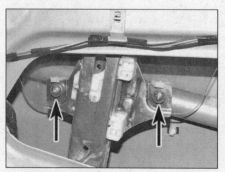

17.5 Undo the glass retaining bolts in the regulator

17.6 Rotate the glass and pull it out

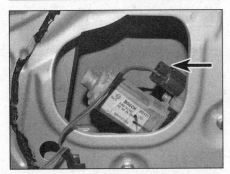

17.11 Disconnect the window motor wiring plug

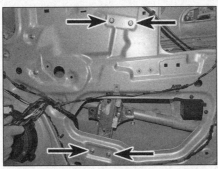

17.12 Front window regulator retaining nuts

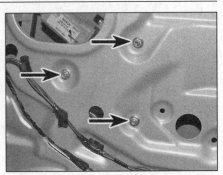

17.13a Undo 3 retaining bolts ...

17.13b ... and manoeuvre the assembly from the door

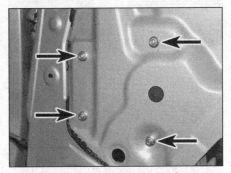

17.17 Undo the regulator mounting nuts

17.18 Disconnect the regulator wiring plug

11 Disconnect the wiring plug from the motor **(see illustration)**.

12 Undo the 4 retaining nuts on the window carriage, and disengage it from the door **(see illustration)**.

13 Undo the 3 retaining bolts and manoeuvre the regulator and window carriage assembly from the door **(see illustrations)**.

Refitting

14 Refitting is a reversal of removal, noting the following points:
a) Attach the window glass to the regulator as described previously, before tightening the regulator retaining nuts.
b) Check the operation of the window mechanism before refitting the door inner

trim panel, and if necessary apply grease to the joints.
c) Refit the door sealing sheet and inner trim panel as described in Section 13.

Rear window regulator

Removal

15 Lower the window approximately 8 cm, then disconnect the battery negative lead as described in Chapter 5A Section 4.

16 Remove the door inner trim panel and sealing sheet as described in Section 13.

17 Undo the 4 nuts securing the regulator to the door **(see illustration)**.

18 Disconnect the regulator wiring plug **(see illustration)**.

19 Secure the window glass to the door frame using adhesive tape **(see illustration)**.

20 Disengage the regulator arm from the window support and manoeuvre the assembly from the door **(see illustration)**.

Refitting

21 Refitting is a reversal of removal, noting the following points:
a) Attach the window to the regulator before tightening the retaining nuts.
b) Check the operation of the regulator before refitting the sealing sheet and door inner trim panel.

Rear window glass

22 Remove the door trim, sealing shield and regulator as described earlier in this section.

23 Gently lower the window glass to the bottom of the door **(see illustration)**.

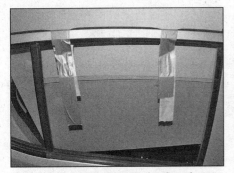

17.19 Secure the glass to the door frame

17.20 Disengage the regulator arm and remove it from the door

17.23 Lower the window glass to the bottom of the door

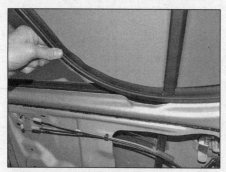

17.24 Lift up and remove the inner weather strip

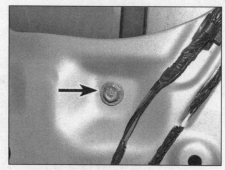

17.25 Undo the bolt for the window channel support

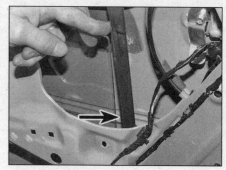

17.26 Disengage the channel from the glass

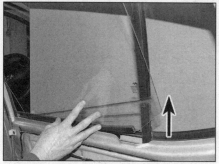

17.27 Manoeuvre the glass from the door

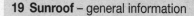

17.29 Undo the screw at the top of the window channel

24 Gently lift and remove the inner window weather strip (see illustration).
25 Undo the retaining bolt for the window channel support (see illustration).
26 Disengage the window channel from the glass by sliding it towards the rear of the door (see illustration).
27 Slide the glass rearward to disengage it from the forward channel and manoeuvre it from the inside of the door (see illustration).

Rear quarterlight glass

28 Remove the door trim, regulator and window glass as described earlier in this Section.
29 Lift up the door surround rubber and undo the retaining screw at the top of the window channel (see illustration).
30 Press out the retaining clip and prise away

the window weather strip at the rear edge of the door (see illustration).
31 Disengage the internal window rubbers and pull forward the window channel to disengage it from the quarterlight surround (see illustration).
32 Gently manoeuvre the quarterlight window from place (see illustration).

Refitting

33 Refitting is a reversal of removal

18 Windscreen and fixed window glass – general information

1 Due to the methods of attachment, and the special equipment required to complete

the task successfully, removal and refitting of the windscreen and tailgate window should be entrusted to a Hyundai dealer or an automotive glass specialist.

19 Sunroof – general information

1 Due to the complexity of the sunroof mechanism, considerable expertise is needed to repair, renew or adjust the sunroof components successfully. Removal of the roof first requires the headlining to be removed, which is a complex and tedious operation, and not a task to be undertaken lightly. Therefore, any problems with the sunroof should be referred to a Hyundai dealer.
2 If the sunroof motor fails to operate, first check the relevant fuse. If the fault cannot be traced and rectified, the sunroof can be opened and closed manually, using the special crank handle supplied in the vehicle toolkit to turn the motor spindle.
3 To gain access to the motor spindle, ensure that the ignition key is in the 'off' position, then carefully prise the overhead console from its location. Engage the crank handle with the spindle, and turn the handle to open or close the sunroof.
4 Once the roof is closed, remove the crank handle, and clip the overhead console back into place.

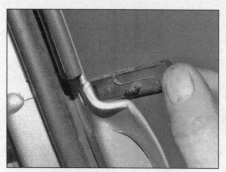

17.30 Press out the weather strip

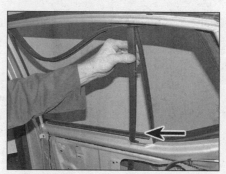

17.31 Pull forward the window channel

17.32 Manoeuvre the quarterlight from place

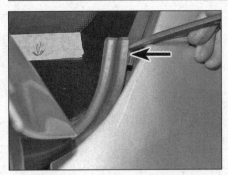

20.2 Use a trim removal tool to prise up the trim

20.3a Plastic expansion rivets (right-hand side arrowed)

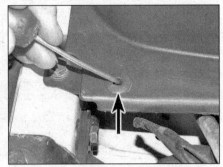

20.3b Press down the centre pins of the plastic rivets

20 Body exterior fittings – removal and refitting

Windscreen scuttle panel

1 Remove the wiper arms as described in Chapter 12 Section 14.

2 Using a trim removal tool, carefully release the trim at each end of the scuttle panel **(see illustration)**.

3 Push down the centre pins, prise out the plastic expansion rivets at the edge of the scuttle panel **(see illustrations)**.

4 Disconnect the washer hose from the right-hand end of the scuttle trim **(see illustration)**.

5 Carefully pull the windscreen scuttle panel downwards and forwards to release the clips at the base of the windscreen, and remove it along with the rubber sealing strip **(see illustration)**.

6 Refitting is a reversal of removal.

Wheel arch liners

7 The wheel arch liners are secured by a combination of plastic nuts, push-in clips and screws – removal is self-evident and straightforward. Multiple liner panels are used which overlap each other at their edges. In some instances it may be necessary to move aside adjoining panels for access to a specific panel.

Body trim strips and badges

8 The various body trim strips and badges

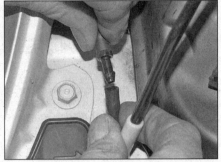

20.4 Disconnect the washer hose

are held in position with a special adhesive tape. Removal requires the trim/badge to be heated, to soften the adhesive, and then cut away from the surface. Due to the high risk of damage to the vehicle paintwork during this operation, it is recommended that this task should be entrusted to a Hyundai dealer or specialist.

21 Seats – removal and refitting

Front seats

Removal

1 Disconnect the battery negative cable as described in Chapter 5A Section 4, and

20.5 Pull up the scuttle panel along with the rubber sealing strip

wait for at least 3 minutes before beginning work.

2 Slide the seat towards the front of the car to gain access to the two bolts at the rear, then slacken and remove them **(see illustration)**.

3 Slide the seat fully rearwards, the disconnect the seat wiring plugs **(see illustration)**.

4 Undo the bolts at the front of the seat rails, then manoeuvre the seat from the vehicle **(see illustration)**.

Caution: The seats are heavy!

Refitting

5 Refitting is a reversal of removal.

Rear seat

Rear seat cushion

6 Undo the 4 retaining bolts along the front edge of the cushion, then move the cushion

21.2 Undo the bolts at the rear of the seat rails

21.3 Disconnect the seat wiring plugs

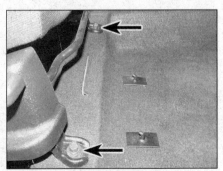

21.4 Remove the front bolts then take out the seat

forwards, and manoeuvre it from place **(see illustration)**.

7 Refitting is a reversal of removal.

Rear seat backrest

8 Remove the rear seat cushion as described previously in this Section, then undo the bolt and remove the rear centre seat belt buckle **(see illustration)**.

9 Fold the rear seat backrest forwards, undo the 4 bolts securing the backrests to the mounting brackets, then manoeuvre the backrests from place **(see illustration)**.

10 Refitting is a reversal of removal. Tighten the seat belt anchorage bolt to the specified torque.

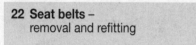

22 Seat belts –
removal and refitting

Note: *Record the positions of the washers and spacers on the seat belt anchors, and ensure they are refitted in their original positions.*

Front seat belt

Removal

⚠️ *Warning: The front seat belt inertia reels are equipped with a pyrotechnic pretensioner mechanism. Refer to the airbag system precautions contained in Chapter 12 Section 20 which apply equally to the seat belt pretensioners. Do not tamper with the inertia reel pretensioner unit in*

21.9 Undo the bolts and remove the backrest (right-hand seat shown)

22.8 Undo the bolt and detach the upper seat belt anchor

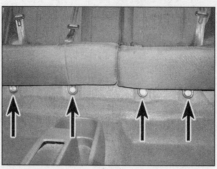

21.6 Undo the 4 bolts along the front of the front lower edge of the cushion

any way, and do not attempt to test the unit.

1 De-activate the airbag system (which will also de-activate the pyrotechnic pretensioner mechanism, where fitted), as described in Chapter 12 Section 20, before attempting to remove the seatbelt.

2 Disconnect the battery negative cable as described in Chapter 5A Section 4, and wait for at least three minutes before beginning work.

3 Remove the front seat as described in Section 21.

4 Remove the door sill trim as described in Section 23.

5 Undo the mounting bolt and detach the seatbelt from the lower anchorage point **(see illustration)**.

6 Remove the B-pillar trim panel as described in Section 23.

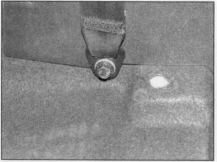

22.5 Undo mounting bolt and remove lower anchorage point

22.9 Undo the reel mounting bolts

21.8 Remove the centre seat belt buckle bolt

7 Use a trim removal tool to prise off the upper anchor cover **(see illustration)**.

8 Undo the seat belt upper anchorage bolt **(see illustration)**.

9 Undo the mounting bolts, then manoeuvre the inertia reel from place **(see illustration)**.

10 Raise the tab using a flat-bladed screwdriver, then disconnect the wiring plug **(see illustration)**.

Refitting

11 Refitting is a reversal of removal. Tighten the seat belt bolts to their specified torque.

Rear seat belts

Removal

Outer seat belts

12 Remove the rear seat as described in Section 21.

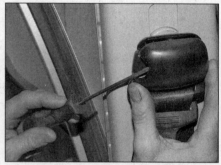

22.7 Prise away the upper anchor cover

22.10 Raise the tab, then disconnect the wiring plug

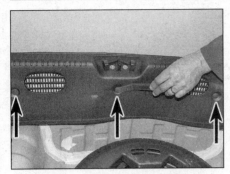

22.14 Remove the tailgate sill trim clips

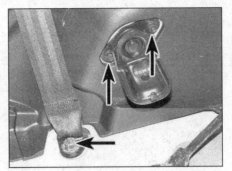

22.15 Undo the seat belt mount and the seat mounting bracket

22.18 Upper seat belt mount

13 Remove the rear door sill panel as described in Section 23.

14 Using a trim removal tool, prise out the clips then remove the tailgate sill trim **(see illustration)**.

15 Undo the retaining bolt and manoeuvre the seat belt lower anchor from position, then undo the seat mounting bracket bolts **(see illustration)**.

16 Remove the luggage compartment side trim panel, and C-pillar trim panel as described in Section 23.

17 Disconnect the rear lamp wiring plug.

18 Undo the bolt and manoeuvre the upper seat belt mount from place **(see illustration)**.

19 Undo the retaining bolt and manoeuvre the seat belt inertia reel from position **(see illustration)**.

Centre seat belt

20 Removal of the centre inertia reel involves removal of the seat backrest cover. This is a procedure that we recommend is entrusted to a Hyundai dealer or upholstery specialist.

Refitting

21 Refitting is a reversal of removal. Tighten the seat belt fasteners to their specified torque.

Seat belt stalks

Front seat belt stalks

22 Remove the relevant front seat as described in Section 21.

23 Undo the retaining bolt and detach the stalk from the seat frame.

24 Refitting is a reversal of removal, tightening the stalk retaining bolt to the specified torque.

Rear seat stalks

25 Remove the rear seat cushion as described in Section 21.

26 Undo the retaining bolt and remove the stalk.

27 Refitting is a reversal of removal, tightening the seat belt stalk retaining bolt to the specified torque.

23 Interior trim – removal and refitting

Interior trim panels – general

1 The interior trim panels are secured using either screws or various types of trim fasteners, usually studs or clips.

2 Check that there are no other panels overlapping the one to be removed; usually there is a sequence that has to be followed that will become obvious on close inspection.

3 Remove all obvious fasteners, such as screws. If the panel will not come free, it is held by hidden clips or fasteners. These are usually situated around the edge of the panel and can be prised up to release them; note, however

that they can break quite easily so new ones should be available. The best way of releasing such clips, without the correct type of tool, is to use a large flat-bladed screwdriver. Note that some panels are secured by plastic expanding rivets, where the centre pin must be prised up before the rivet can be removed. Note in many cases that the adjacent sealing strip must be prised back to release a panel.

4 When removing a panel, never use excessive force or the panel may be damaged; always check carefully that all fasteners have been removed or released before attempting to withdraw a panel.

5 Refitting is the reverse of the removal procedure; secure the fasteners by pressing them firmly into place and ensure that all disturbed components are correctly secured to prevent rattles.

Door sill trim panels

Rear doors

6 Undo the retaining screws in the panel by the rear seat, then using a trim removal tool, prise out the retaining clip and manoeuvre the trim panel from place **(see illustration)**.

Front doors

7 Using a trim removal tool, prise out the mounting clips then manoeuvre the sill trim from place **(see illustration)**.

Kick panel

8 Using a trim removal tool, gently prise the

22.19 Undo the bolt and remove the inertia reel assembly

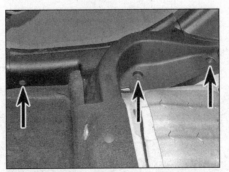

23.6 Undo the screws by the rear seat and remove the clip at the front end of the sill trim

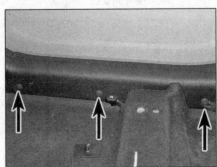

23.7 Prise out the mounting clips

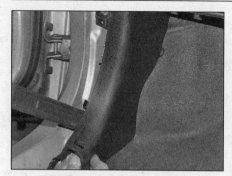

23.8 Prise away the kick panel

23.9 Prise the lower vent panels from place

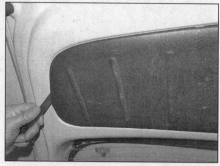

23.10 Use a trim tool to prise away the tailgate inner panel

kick panel away from the side of the car **(see illustration)**.

Lower vent panels

9 Using a trim removal tool, gently prise the lower vent panels from place **(see illustration)**.

Tailgate inner trim panel

10 Using a flat-bladed trim removal tool or similar, gently work your way around the edge, prise the panel from the tailgate to release the clips **(see illustration)**. Some clips may break as they are removed, so replace these before refitting trim.
11 To refit the panel, locate it in position and work your way around the edge to press it back into place.

A-pillar trim panel

12 Remove the door weather strip from the

area of the A-pillar.
13 Using a flat-bladed trim removal tool, gently prise away the top of the panel from the A-pillar, then lift it up to remove it from place **(see illustration)**.
14 Refitting is a reversal of removal; secure the fasteners by pressing them firmly into place and ensure that all disturbed components are correctly secured to prevent rattles.

B-pillar trim panel

15 If improved access is required, remove the relevant front seat as described in Section 21.
16 Pull away the rubber weather strips from the door aperture in the area around the B-pillar.
17 Remove the sill trims from the front and rear door openings as described earlier in this Section.

18 Using a trim removal tool, remove the front seat belt upper anchor cover as described in Section 22.
19 Undo the seat belt upper anchorage bolt.
20 Using a trim removal tool, gently prise away the lower trim from the B-pillar, then prise the upper panel from place **(see illustrations)**.
21 Refitting is a reversal of removal.

Headlining

22 The rigid headlining is clipped to the roof, and can only be withdrawn once all fittings such as the grab handles, sunvisors, interior light, and related trim panels have been removed, and the door, tailgate and sunroof aperture sealing strips have been prised clear.
23 As with carpet removal, taking out the headlining is not especially difficult, just time-consuming.

C-pillar/Luggage compartment side trim panels

24 Remove the parcel shelf, and lift out the luggage compartment floor covering.
25 Pull away the rubber weather strip along the bottom of the tailgate aperture, then remove the tailgate sill trim as described in Section 23.
26 If working on the right-hand side, remove the luggage compartment storage box by prising up the two caps and undoing the 2 bolts beneath, then manoeuvre it from place **(see illustration)**.
27 Remove the weather strip from around the rear door aperture **(see illustration)**.

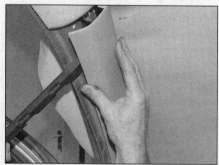

23.13 Prise away the top of the trim, then lift it upwards to remove

23.20a Prise away the lower trim panel

23.20b Then prise away the upper trim panel

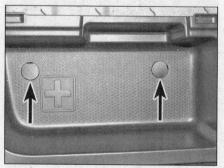

23.26 Remove the caps, undo the bolts and remove the storage box

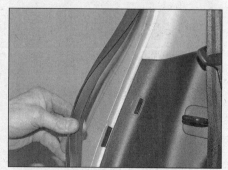

23.27 Remove the rear door weather strip

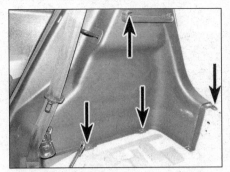

23.28 Undo the side panel retaining screws

23.29 Prise the panels inwards to release the clips

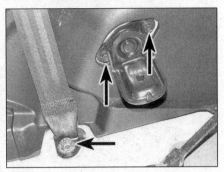

23.30 Undo the bolts for the seat belt and seat backrest

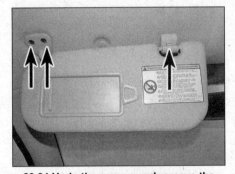

23.34 Undo the screws and remove the sunvisor mountings

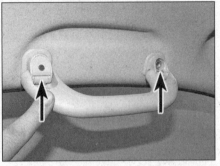

23.36 Flip open the covers, undo the bolts and remove the handle

Carpet

38 The passenger compartment floor carpet is in one piece (with a separate piece used in the luggage area), and is secured at its edges by screws or clips, usually the same fasteners used to secure the various adjoining trim panels.

39 Carpet removal and refitting is reasonably straightforward, but very time-consuming, due to the fact that all adjoining trim panels must be removed first, as must components such as the seats, the centre console and seat belt lower anchorages.

28 Undo the 4 retaining screws securing the luggage compartment side panel (see illustration).

29 Using a trim removal tool or similar, prise both the luggage compartment side panel and the C-pillar panel inwards at the same time to release the clips (see illustration).

30 Undo the lower seatbelt mounting bolt and undo the seat backrest mount bolts (see illustration).

31 Thread the seatbelt through the aperture in the C-pillar panel and remove both the C-pillar panel and luggage compartment panel from place.

32 Working around the tailgate edge and using a trim removal tool or similar, prise the C-pillar panel and luggage compartment side panel inwards, taking care not to break the clips. Manoeuvre the panels forward from place.

33 Refitting is a reversal of removal.

Sunvisors

34 The sunvisors are secured by 1 screw at the inner end, and 2 screws at the outer (see illustration). Undo the screws and remove the sunvisor.

35 Refitting is a reversal of removal.

Grab handles

36 Fold open the covers, undo the bolts and remove the grab handle (see illustration).

37 Refitting is a reversal of removal.

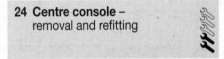

24 Centre console – removal and refitting

Removal

1 Remove the front seats as described in Section 21.

2 Remove the pads from the bottom of each storage recess, including the cupholders (see illustration).

3 Undo the screw in the base of the cupholder and in the rearmost storage recess ... (see illustrations).

4 ... then remove the centre console from

24.2 Hook out the rubber pads in the storage recesses

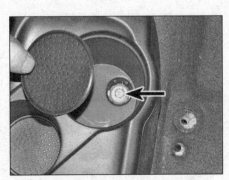

24.3a Undo the screw in the cupholder ...

24.3b ... and the screw in the rear storage recess

24.4 Remove the centre console from place

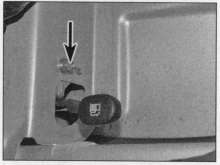

25.4 Undo the release lever retaining bolt

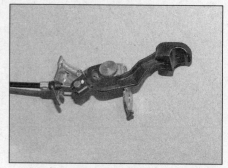

25.5 Disconnect the cable from the lever and bracket assembly

place **(see illustration)**. Disconnect any wiring plugs as they become accessible

Refitting

5 Refitting is a reversal of removal.

25 Fuel filler flap release cable – removal and refitting

Removal

1 Remove the driver's front seat as described in Section 21.
2 Remove the driver's door sill trim panel as described in Section 23.
3 Remove the drivers side kick panel as described in Section 23.

25.6 Carefully prise the actuator from the vehicle body in the filler flap aperture

4 Lift the carpet and undo the retaining bolt for the release lever **(see illustration)**.
5 Using a trim removal tool, lift the bottom edge of the B-pillar trim, then pull the cable and lever rearward through the chassis rail to remove it. Prise out the outer cable from the mounting bracket and release the cable end fitting from the lever **(see illustration)**.
6 Then tie a long length of string to the front end of the cable, then working in the fuel filler flap area, carefully prise the end actuator from place and pull the cable through, leaving the string in place **(see illustration)**. Simply tie the string to the new cable and pull it back through from the driver's seat area.

Refitting

7 Refitting is a reversal of removal

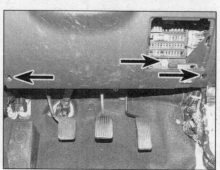

26.1 Rotate the stops then remove the glovebox

26 Facia panels – removal and refitting

> **Warning: All models are equipped with an airbag system. The driver's airbag is mounted in the steering wheel centre pad and, where fitted, the passenger's airbag is mounted in the passenger's side of the facia. Make sure that the safety precautions given in Chapter 12 Section 20 are followed, to prevent personal injury.**

Glovebox

Removal

1 Open the glovebox, then rotate the 'stops' anti-clockwise and remove them from either side **(see illustration)**.
2 Manoeuvre the glovebox from the facia.

Refitting

3 Refitting is a reversal of removal.

Driver's side lower facia panel

Removal

4 Remove the fusebox cover trim **(see illustration)**.
5 Undo the 2 mounting screws and one bolt, then lower the panel from place **(see illustration)**.
6 Disconnect the wiring plug for the onboard diagnostic socket **(see illustration)**.

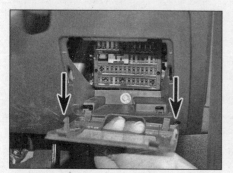

26.4 Pull away the fusebox cover

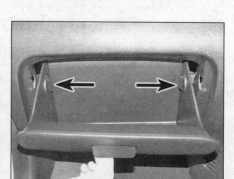

26.5 Undo the 2 screws and 1 bolt (arrowed)

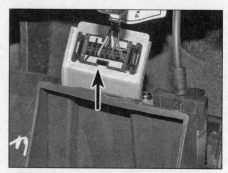

26.6 Disconnect the diagnostic socket

26.7 Disconnect the bonnet release cable

26.10 Prise the side panel from place

26.14a Steering column lower shroud front retaining screws

7 Detach the bonnet release cable by removing the locator from place and disconnecting the cable from the back of the lever **(see illustration)**.
8 Remove the lower facia panel.

Refitting

9 Refitting is a reversal of removal.

Facia side panels

10 Using a trim removal tool around the curved edge of the panel, prise the side facia panel from place **(see illustration)**. Disconnect any wiring plugs as the panel is withdrawn.

Refitting

11 First locate the panel's forward edge into place, then press the rest of the panel back into place.

Steering column shrouds

Removal

12 Fully lower and extend the steering column.
13 Remove the steering wheel as described in Chapter 10 Section 12.
14 The lower shroud is retained by 3 screws. Undo the screws and remove the lower shroud **(see illustrations)**.
15 The upper shroud clips into the lower shroud and to the top of the steering column, so can just be lifted away **(see illustration)**.

Refitting

16 Refitting is a reversal of removal.

Instrument panel surround

Removal

17 Fully lower and extend the steering column.
18 Using a flat-bladed screwdriver or similar, prise off the driver's side airvent **(see illustration)**.
19 Undo the retaining screw each side, and remove the instrument panel surround by pulling it directly rearwards **(see illustrations)**.

Refitting

20 Refitting is a reversal of removal.

Central air vent panel

Removal

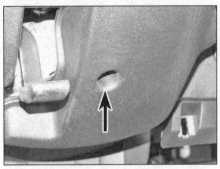

26.14b Steering column lower shroud bottom retaining screw

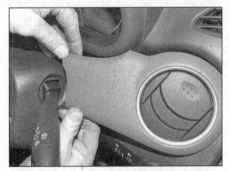

26.18 Use a trim removal tool to prise off the driver's-side vent

21 Using a trim removal tool, gently prise out the centre air vent panel from place **(see illustration)**.
Note: *To improve access and reduce the*

26.19b Pull the surround rearwards to remove

26.15 Prise away the upper shroud from the top of the steering column

26.19a Undo the mounting screw each side

possibility of damage, remove the glovebox as described earlier in this Section and press the panel from behind to ease the insertion of the trim removal tool.

26.21 Gently lever out the centre panel

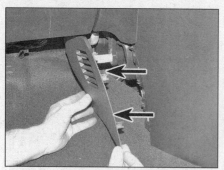

26.23 Prise the lower vent panels from place

26.24 Prise up the gear lever surround

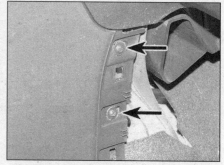

26.25 Undo the 4 screws (right hand-side screws arrowed) and remove the panel

Refitting

22 Refitting is a reversal of removal.

Lower vent panels

23 Using a trim removal tool, gently prise the lower vent panels from place (**see illustration**).

Lower gear lever surround panel

24 Using a trim removal tool, gently prise up the gear lever surround trim (**see illustration**).
25 Undo the 4 screws at the forward bottom edge of the lower gear lever surround panel and manoeuvre from place (**see illustration**).

Complete facia assembly

Removal

26 Remove the front seats as described in Section 21.
27 Disconnect the battery negative lead as described in Chapter 5A Section 4.
28 Remove the audio unit support frame as described is Section 12 Section 17.
29 Remove the heater/air conditioning control panel as described in Chapter 3 Section 8.
30 Remove the instrument cluster as described in Chapter 12 Section 11.
31 Remove the driver's side lower facia panel as described previously in this Section.

26.33 Prise off the passenger-side vent

32 Remove the glovebox as described previously in this Section.
33 Using a flat-bladed trim removal tool, prise off the passenger-side dashboard air vent from the facia (**see illustration**).
34 Working underneath the dashboard, disconnect the passenger's-side airbag wiring plug (**see illustration**).
35 Remove both A-pillar trim panels as described in Section 23.
36 Remove both door sill trims as described in Section 23.
37 Remove both kick panels as described earlier in this Section.
38 The facia is now secured by a total

26.34 Disconnect the passenger airbag wiring plug

of 16 nuts, including 2 hidden behind the passenger air vent assembly. Undo the nuts, disconnect all wiring plugs as they become available and unclip the aerial lead from the A-pillar (**see illustration**). Check that nothing remains connected between the facia and the bulkhead, and with the help of an assistant, manoeuvre the facia rearwards, and out from the cabin (**see illustration**).

Refitting

39 Refitting is a reversal of removal, noting the following points:

a) *Reinstate all electrical connections according to the labels made during removal and ensure that cables are secured in their clips, using the original routing.*
b) *Refer to the Chapters/Sections indicated and refit all components disturbed during the removal process.*
c) *On completion, reconnect the battery negative terminal and check the operation of all controls, gauges and instruments disturbed during the removal process, including the heating/air conditioning system.*

Refitting

40 Refitting is a reversal of removal

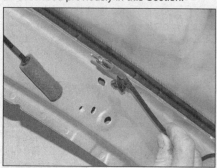

26.38a Disconnect and unclip the aerial lead from the A-pillar

26.38b Manoeuvre the facia from place

Chapter 12
Body electrical systems

Contents

Degrees of difficulty

Easy, suitable for novice with little experience	Fairly easy, suitable for beginner with some experience	Fairly difficult, suitable for competent DIY mechanic	Difficult, suitable for experienced DIY mechanic	Very difficult, suitable for expert DIY or professional

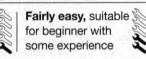

Specifications

Bulbs

	Wattage
Exterior lights:	
Direction indicators	21 PY
Direction indicator side repeater	5 capless
Front foglight	27
Front sidelight	5 capless
Headlight	55/60 H4
High level stop light	5 capless
Number plate light	5 capless
Rear fog light	21
Reverse	16 capless
Stop/tail light	21/5
Interior lights:	
Front courtesy lights	10
Luggage compartment lights	5

Torque wrench settings

	Nm	lbf ft
Airbag control unit bolts	4	3
Impact sensor bolts	9	7
Passenger airbag nuts	14	11

1 General information and precautions

1 The electrical system is of 12 volt negative earth type. Power for the lights and all electrical accessories is supplied by a lead-acid type battery, which is charged by the alternator.

2 This Chapter covers repair and service procedures for the various electrical components not associated with the engine. Information on the battery, alternator and starter motor can be found in Chapter 5A.

3 It should be noted that, prior to working on any component in the electrical system, the battery negative terminal should first be disconnected, to prevent the possibility of electrical short-circuits and/or fires (refer to Chapter 5A Section 4).

⚠ *Warning: Before carrying out any work on the electrical system, read through the precautions given in 'Safety first!' at the beginning of this manual, and in Chapter 5A.*

⚠ *Warning: All models are equipped with an airbag system and may also have pyrotechnic seat belt pretensioners. When working on the electrical system, refer to the precautions given in Section 20, to avoid the possibility of personal injury.*

2 Electrical fault finding – general information

General

1 A typical electrical circuit consists of an electrical component; any switches, relays, motors, fuses, fusible links or circuit breakers related to that component, and the wiring and connectors which link the component to both the battery and the chassis. To help to pin-point a problem in an electrical circuit, wiring diagrams are included at the end of this Chapter.

2 Before attempting to diagnose an electrical fault, first study the appropriate wiring diagram to obtain a complete understanding of the components included in the particular circuit concerned. The possible sources of a fault can be narrowed down by noting if other components related to the circuit are operating properly. If several components or circuits fail at one time, the problem is likely to be related to a shared fuse or earth connection.

3 Electrical problems usually stem from simple causes, such as loose or corroded connections, a faulty earth connection, a blown fuse, a melted fusible link, or a faulty relay (refer to Section 3 for details of testing relays). Visually inspect the condition of all fuses, wires and connections in a problem circuit before testing the components. Use the wiring diagrams to determine which terminal connections will need to be checked in order to pin-point the trouble spot.

4 The basic tools required for electrical fault finding include a circuit tester or voltmeter (a 12 volt bulb with a set of test leads can also be used for certain tests); a self-powered test light (sometimes known as a continuity tester); an ohmmeter (to measure resistance); a battery and set of test leads; and a jumper wire, preferably with a circuit breaker or fuse incorporated, which can be used to bypass suspect wires or electrical components. Before attempting to locate a problem with test instruments, use the wiring diagram to determine where to make the connections.

⚠ *Warning: Under no circumstances may live measuring instruments such as ohmmeters, voltmeters or a bulb and test leads be used to test any of the airbag circuitry. Any testing of these components must be left to a Hyundai dealer or specialist, as there is a danger of activating the system if the correct procedures are not followed.*

5 To find the source of an intermittent wiring fault (usually due to a poor or dirty connection, or damaged wiring insulation), a 'wiggle' test can be performed on the wiring. This involves wiggling the wiring by hand to see if the fault occurs as the wiring is moved. It should be possible to narrow down the source of the fault to a particular section of wiring. This method of testing can be used in conjunction with any of the tests described in the following sub-Sections.

6 Apart from problems due to poor connections, two basic types of fault can occur in an electrical circuit – open-circuit, or short-circuit.

7 Open-circuit faults are caused by a break somewhere in the circuit, which prevents current from flowing. An open-circuit fault will prevent a component from working, but will not cause the relevant circuit fuse to blow.

8 Short-circuit faults are caused by a 'short' somewhere in the circuit, which allows the current flowing in the circuit to 'escape' along an alternative route, usually to earth. Short-circuit faults are normally caused by a breakdown in wiring insulation, which allows a feed wire to touch either another wire, or an earthed component such as the bodyshell. A short-circuit fault will normally cause the relevant circuit fuse to blow.

Finding an open-circuit

9 To check for an open-circuit, connect one lead of a circuit tester or voltmeter to either the negative battery terminal or a known good earth.

10 Connect the other lead to a connector in the circuit being tested, preferably nearest to the battery or fuse.

11 Switch on the circuit, bearing in mind that some circuits are live only when the ignition switch is moved to a particular position.

12 If voltage is present (indicated either by the tester bulb lighting or a voltmeter reading, as applicable), this means that the section of the circuit between the relevant connector and the battery is problem-free.

13 Continue to check the remainder of the circuit in the same fashion.

14 When a point is reached at which no voltage is present, the problem must lie between that point and the previous test point with voltage. Most problems can be traced to a broken, corroded or loose connection.

Finding a short-circuit

15 To check for a short-circuit, first disconnect the load(s) from the circuit (loads are the components which draw current from a circuit, such as bulbs, motors, heating elements, etc).

16 Remove the relevant fuse from the circuit, and connect a circuit tester or voltmeter to the fuse connections.

17 Switch on the circuit, bearing in mind that some circuits are live only when the ignition switch is moved to a particular position.

18 If voltage is present (indicated either by the tester bulb lighting or a voltmeter reading, as applicable), this means that there is a short-circuit.

19 If no voltage is present, but the fuse still blows with the load(s) connected, this indicates an internal fault in the load(s).

Finding an earth fault

20 The battery negative terminal is connected to 'earth' – the metal of the engine/transmission and the car body – and most systems are wired so that they only receive a positive feed, the current returning through the metal of the car body (see illustrations). This means that the component mounting and the body form part of that circuit. Loose or corroded mountings can therefore cause a range of electrical faults, ranging from total failure of a circuit, to a puzzling partial fault. In particular, lights may shine dimly (especially when another circuit sharing the same earth point is in operation), motors (eg, wiper motors or the heater fan motor) may run slowly, and the operation of one circuit may have an apparently unrelated effect on another.

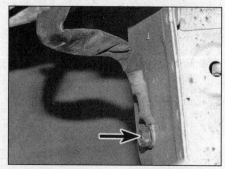

2.20a Main earth connection between the engine/transmission and the vehicle body – left-hand front chassis member

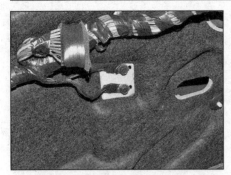

2.20b Other earth connections may be on the passengers compartment front bulkhead …

2.20c … tailgate frame …

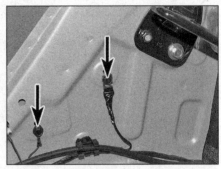

2.20d … and the right-hand side quarter panel

21 Note that on many vehicles, earth straps are used between certain components, such as the engine/transmission and the body, usually where there is no metal-to-metal contact between components due to flexible rubber mountings, etc.

22 To check whether a component is properly earthed, disconnect the battery and connect one lead of an ohmmeter to a known good earth point. Connect the other lead to the wire or earth connection being tested. The resistance reading should be zero; if not, check the connection as follows.

23 If an earth connection is thought to be faulty, dismantle the connection and clean back to bare metal both the bodyshell and the wire terminal or the component earth connection mating surface. Be careful to remove all traces of dirt and corrosion, and then use a knife to trim away any paint, so that a clean metal-to-metal joint is made.

24 On reassembly, tighten the joint fasteners securely; if a wire terminal is being refitted, use serrated washers between the terminal and the bodyshell to ensure a clean and secure connection. When the connection is remade, prevent the onset of corrosion in the future by applying a coat of petroleum jelly or silicone-based grease or by spraying on (at regular intervals) a proprietary ignition sealer or a water-dispersant lubricant.

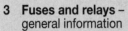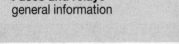

3 Fuses and relays –
general information

Fuses

1 Fuses are designed to break a circuit when a predetermined current is reached, in order to protect the components and wiring which could be damaged by excessive current flow. Any excessive current flow will be due to a fault in the circuit, usually a short-circuit (see Section 2).

2 The main fuses are located in the fusebox in the engine compartment, whilst other are located under the driver side of the facia (see illustrations). The fuse allocations are given on the underside of each fusebox cover. A

plastic tool to remove fuses is attached to the underside of the fusebox lid in the engine compartment.

3 To gain access to the facia fuses, prise off the cover to the lower right side of the steering column.

4 To access the fuses and circuit breakers that are located in the fuse/relay box in the engine compartment; release the clip and lift off the cover to gain access (see illustration).

5 A blown fuse can be recognised from its melted or broken wire (see illustration).

6 To remove a fuse, first ensure that the relevant circuit is switched off.

7 Using the plastic tool clipped to the main fusebox, pull the fuse from its location.

8 Spare fuses are provided in the main fusebox.

9 Before renewing a blown fuse, trace and rectify the cause, and always use a fuse of

the correct rating (fuse ratings are specified on the inside of the fusebox cover panel). Never substitute a fuse of a higher rating, or make temporary repairs using wire or metal foil; more serious damage, or even fire, could result.

10 Note that the fuses are colour-coded as follows. Refer to the wiring diagrams for details of the fuse ratings used and the circuits protected.

Colour	Rating
Orange	5A
Red	10A
Blue	15A
Yellow	20A
Clear or White	25A
Green	30A

3.2a Engine compartment fusebox

3.2b Fusebox under the driver's side of the facia

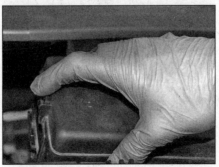

3.4 Squeeze the clip and open the engine compartment fusebox cover

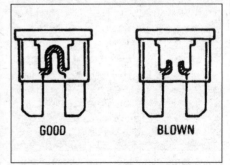

3.5 A blown fuse is recognised from its melted or broken wire

Relays

11 A relay is an electrically-operated switch, which is used for the following reasons:

a) *A relay can switch a heavy current remotely from the circuit in which the current is flowing, therefore allowing the use of lighter-gauge wiring and switch contacts.*

b) *A relay can receive more than one control input, unlike a mechanical switch.*

c) *A relay can have a timer function – for example, the intermittent wiper relay.*

12 The main and optional equipment relays are primarily located in the engine compartment fuse/relay box (see Fuses). Additional relays may be fitted, depending on model and specification and these are generally mounted adjacent to the component being controlled.

13 If a circuit or system controlled by a relay develops a fault, and the relay is suspect, operate the system. If the relay is functioning, it should be possible to hear it click as it is energised. If this is the case, the fault lies with the components or wiring of the system. If the relay is not being energised, then either the relay is not receiving a main supply or a switching voltage, or the relay itself is faulty. Testing is by the substitution of a known good unit, but be careful – while some relays are identical in appearance and in operation, others look similar but perform different functions.

14 To remove a relay, first ensure that the relevant circuit is switched off. The relay can then simply be pulled out from the socket, and pushed back into position.

4 Electrical connectors – general information

1 Most electrical connections on these vehicles are made with multiwire plastic connectors. The mating halves of many connectors are secured with locking clips molded into the plastic connector shells. The mating halves of some large connectors, such as some of those under the instrument panel, are held together by a bolt through the center of the connector.

2 To separate a connector with locking clips, use a small screwdriver to pry the clips apart carefully, then separate the connector halves. Pull only on the shell, never pull on the wiring harness, as you may damage the individual wires and terminals inside the connectors. Look at the connector closely before trying to separate the halves. Often the locking clips are engaged in a way that is not immediately clear. Additionally, many connectors have more than one set of clips.

3 Each pair of connector terminals has a male half and a female half. When you look at the end view of a connector in a diagram, be sure to understand whether the view shows the harness side or the component side of the connector. Connector halves are mirror images of each other, and a terminal shown on the right side end-view of one half will be on the left side end-view of the other half.

4 It is often necessary to take circuit voltage measurements with a connector connected. Whenever possible, carefully insert a small straight pin (not your meter probe) into the rear of the connector shell to contact the terminal inside, then clip your meter lead to the pin. This kind of connection is called "backprobing." When inserting a test probe into a terminal, be careful not to distort the terminal opening. Doing so can lead to a poor connection and corrosion at that terminal later. Using the small straight pin instead of a meter probe results in less chance of deforming the terminal connector. "T" pins are a good choice as temporary meter connections. They allow for a larger surface area to attach the meter leads too.

Electrical connectors

5 Typical electrical connectors:

4.5a Most electrical connectors have a single release tab that you depress to release the connector

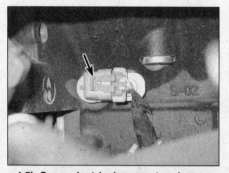
4.5b Some electrical connectors have a retaining tab which must be pried up to free the connector

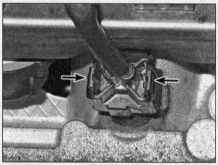
4.5c Some connectors have two release tabs that you must squeeze to release the connector

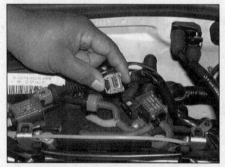
4.5d Some connectors use wire retainers that you squeeze to release the connector

4.5e Critical connectors often employ a sliding lock (1) that you must pull out before you can depress the release tab (2)

4.5f Here's another sliding-lock style connector, with the lock (1) and the release tab (2) on the side of the connector

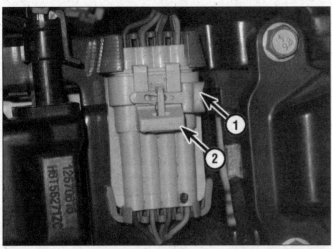

4.5g On some connectors the lock (1) must be pulled out to the side and removed before you can lift the release tab (2)

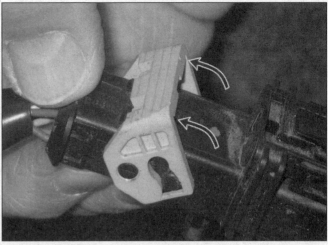

4.5h Some critical connectors, like the multi-pin connectors at the Electronic Control Module employ pivoting locks that must be flipped open

5 Switches – removal and refitting

Steering column combination switch assembly

Removal

1 Remove the steering column shrouds as described in Chapter 11 Section 26.
2 Disconnect the wiring plugs for the multifunction switches (see illustration).
3 Disconnect the switches by pushing the lock pins next to each switch (see illustration).

Refitting

4 Refitting is a reversal of removal.

Central switch panel

5 Refer to Chapter 11 Section 26.

Stop-light switch

6 Refer to Chapter 9 Section 11.

Horn switch

7 The horn switch is integral with the driver's airbag assembly. If a faulty, the complete assembly must be replaced.

Handbrake-on warning light switch

8 Refer to Chapter 9 Section 16.

Reversing light switch

9 Refer to Chapter 7A Section 7.

Interior light door switch

10 To remove the rear door switch, remove the luggage compartment side trim and C-pillar trim as described in Chapter 11

Section 23. To remove the front door switch, remove the B-pillar trim panel as described in Chapter 11 Section 23.
11 Disconnect the wiring plug then undo the retaining screw and gently pull the switch through (see illustration).

Ignition switch

12 Remove the steering column shrouds as described in Chapter 11 Section 26.

5.2 Disconnect the wiring plugs

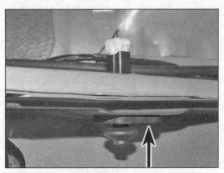

5.11 Door switch retaining screw

13 Disconnect the wiring plug, undo the screw and remove the ignition switch (see illustration).
14 Refitting is the reversal of removal.

Foglights/headlamp levelling/panel brightness switch panel

15 Remove the facia side panel and driver's side lower facia panel as described in Chapter 11 Section 26.

5.3 Press-in the locking pin and slide the switch outwards

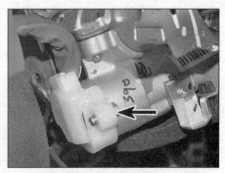

5.13 Ignition switch retaining screw

5.16a Squeeze the tabs and push the switch from the dash

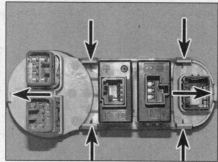

5.16b Switch retaining tabs

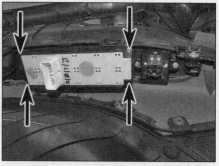

5.19 Undo the 4 screws and remove the window switch

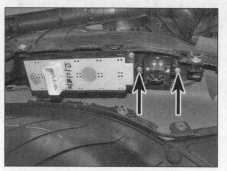

5.20 Undo the 2 screws and manoeuvre the switch from place

5.21 Switch mounting screws

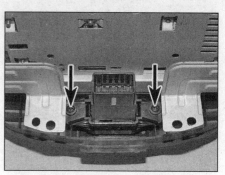

5.24 Undo the screws and remove the hazard switch

16 Reaching behind the facia, squeeze the 6 plastic tabs and push the switch rearwards to release it from the facia **(see illustrations)**. Disconnect the wiring plugs as the switch assembly is withdrawn.

17 Disconnect the wiring plugs

Electric window/mirror switches

18 Remove the door trim panel as described in Chapter 11 Section 13 and unplug the connector.

19 In the front doors, unscrew the 4 mounting screws and manoeuvre the switch from place **(see illustration)**.

20 For the door mirror switch, undo the 2 retaining screws and remove the switch from place **(see illustration)**.

21 In the rear doors, unscrew the 2 mounting screws and manoeuvre the switch from place **(see illustration)**.

22 Refitting is a reversal of removal.

Hazard light switch

23 Remove the audio unit as described in Section 17.

24 Undo the 2 retaining screws and remove the hazard light switch **(see illustration)**.

6 Bulbs (exterior lights) – renewal

General

1 Whenever a bulb is renewed, note the following points:

a) Disconnect the battery negative lead as described in Chapter 5A Section 4 before starting work.

b) Remember that if the light has just been in use, the bulb may be extremely hot.

c) Always check the bulb contacts and holder, ensuring that there is clean metal-to metal contact between the bulb and the socket contacts. Clean off any corrosion or dirt before fitting a new bulb.

d) Wherever bayonet-type bulbs are fitted, ensure that the live contact(s) bear firmly against the bulb contact.

e) Always ensure that the new bulb is of the correct rating and that it is completely clean before fitting it; this applies particularly to headlight/foglight bulbs (see below).

f) With quartz halogen bulbs (headlights and similar applications), use a tissue or clean cloth when handling the bulb; do not touch the bulb glass with the fingers. Even small quantities of grease from the fingers will cause blackening and premature failure. If a bulb is accidentally touched, clean it with methylated spirit and a clean rag.

Headlight

2 Remove the front bumper as described in Chapter 11 Section 6.

3 Undo the 2 top headlamp mounting bolts **(see illustration)**.

4 Undo the mounting bolt by the washer reservoir neck **(see illustration)**.

5 Pull the headlight unit forward to release

6.3 Headlight upper mounting bolts

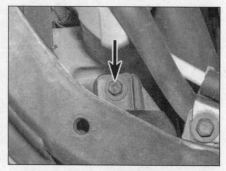

6.4 Undo the mounting bolt by washer reservoir neck

6.6 Rotate the cap anti-clockwise

6.7 Pull the wiring plug from the bulb

6.8 Move the retaining clip to one side and fold it down

it, then disconnect the wiring plug and manouevre the headlight from place.

6 Rotate the rubber cap anti-clockwise at the rear of the headlight bulb anti-clockwise and remove it **(see illustration)**.

7 Pull the wiring plug from the rear of the bulb **(see illustration)**.

8 Release the retaining spring clip and remove the bulb from the headlight unit **(see illustration)**.

9 When handling the new bulb, use a tissue or clean cloth to avoid touching the glass with the fingers; moisture and grease from the skin can cause blackening and rapid failure of this type of bulb. If the glass is accidentally touched, wipe it clean using methylated spirit. Avoid knocking or shaking the bulb as this may weaken the filament.

10 Install the new bulb, using a reversal of the removal procedure. Ensure that its locating tabs are correctly located in the light

unit cut-outs and secure the bulb in position with the retaining clip **(see illustration)**.

Front side lights

11 Remove the headlight unit as described earlier in this Section.

12 Turn the rubber cap at the rear of the headlamp bulb anti-clockwise and remove as described earlier in this Section.

13 Pull the sidelight bulbholder from place **(see illustration)**.

14 Pull the capless bulb from the holder **(see illustration)**.

15 Install the new bulb using a reversal of the removal procedure.

Front directional indicator

16 The front-left indicator can be removed with the headlight unit in situ. Simply rotate the bulbholder anti-clockwise and remove. If renewing the right-hand side light, proceed as follows:

17 Remove the front bumper as described in Chapter 11 Section 6.

18 Remove the headlight unit as described earlier in this Section.

19 Rotate the rubber cap at the rear of the indicator bulb anti-clockwise and remove it **(see illustration)**.

20 Press-in and rotate the bayonet bulb anti-clockwise a little to remove it from the bulbholder **(see illustration)**.

21 Install a new bulb using a reversal of the removal procedure. Note that the bulbs bayonet pins are offset – the bulb will only fit correctly in one position.

Side repeater

22 Using a flat-bladed screwdriver or similar, gently push the side repeater forwards, and prise the rear edge from the wing panel **(see illustration)**.

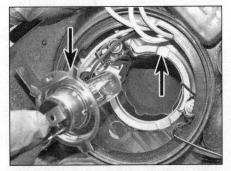

6.10 Ensure the lugs align with the cut-outs

6.13 Pull out the bulbholder

6.14 Pull out the capless bulb

6.19 Turn cap at rear of bulb and remove

6.20 Press-in the bulb, rotate it anti-clockwise and pull it from the holder

6.22 Push the side repeater forwards, and pull out the rear edge

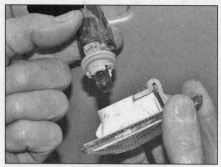

6.23 Rotate the bulbholder anti-clockwise

6.28 Rotate the bulb/holder anti-clockwise

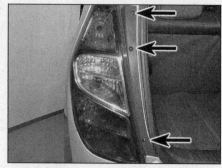

6.31 Rear light retaining screws

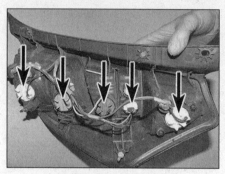

6.32 Rear light bulbholders

6.33a Depress the bayonet bulb, rotate it anti-clockwise and pull it from the holder

6.33b Capless bulbs simply pull from the holder

23 Rotate the bulbholder anti-clockwise a little, and pull it from the lens (see illustration).
24 Pull the bulb from the holder.
25 Install a new bulb using a reversal of the removal procedure.

Front foglight

26 Remove the front wheelarch liner as described in Chapter 11 Section 20.
27 Disconnect the fog light wiring plug
28 Rotate the bulb anti-clockwise and remove it (see illustration). Note that the bulb is integral with the holder
29 When handling the new bulb, use a tissue or clean cloth to avoid touching the glass with the fingers; moisture and grease from the skin can cause blackening and rapid failure of this type of bulb. If the glass is accidentally touched, wipe it clean using methylated spirit.

Avoid knocking or shaking the bulb as this may weaken the filament.
30 Install a new bulb using a reversal of the removal procedure.

Rear light assembly

31 Undo the 3 screws and manoeuvre the light assembly from place (see illustration).
32 Rotate each bulbholder anti-clockwise and gently pull them from the light assembly (see illustration).
33 Depress the relevant bulb, rotate it anti-clockwise slightly and pull it from the bulbholder (see illustrations). Note that some bulbs are 'capless' and simply pull from the bulbholder.
34 The bulbs contained are:
● Brake light
● Reversing light (capless)

● Rear indicator
● Tail light
● Rear foglight
35 Refitting is a reversal of removal. Note that some bayonet bulbs have offset pins – they will only fit correctly in one position.
36 When refitting the light unit, ensure the locating pins engage correctly with the corresponding holes in the vehicle body (see illustration).

High level stop light

37 Remove the high level brake light as described in Section 9.
38 Release the clips and detach the bulbholder assembly from the lens (see illustration).
39 Pull the relevant bulb from the holder (see illustration).

6.36 Ensure the pins align with the corresponding holes

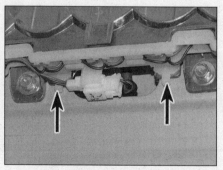

6.38 Release the clips and pull out the bulbholder

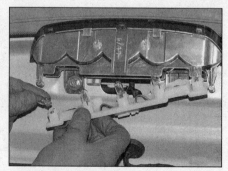

6.39 The capless bulbs pull out from the holder

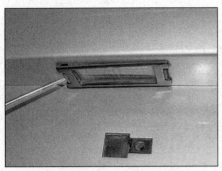

6.41 Compress the clip and prise the number plate light from place

7.3 Pull the bulb from the contacts

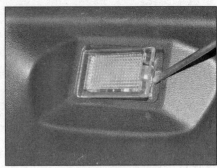

7.5 Prise out the lens

40 Install a new bulb, using a reversal of the removal procedure.

Number plate light

41 Using a flat-bladed screwdriver or similar, gently prise the number plate light lens from place **(see illustration)**.
42 Twist the bulbholder anti-clockwise, the pull out the bulb.
43 Install a new bulb, using a reversal of the removal procedure.

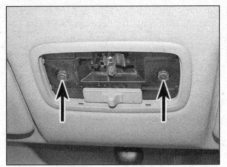

8.2a Undo the 2 bolts …

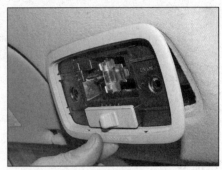

8.2b … and prise down the front edge

7 Bulbs (interior lights) – removal and refitting

1 Disconnect the battery negative lead as described in Chapter 5A Section 4.

Front courtesy lights

2 Using a trim removal tool, gently prise the lens cover from place.
3 Pull the festoon type bulb from the contacts **(see illustration)**.
4 Install a new bulb and press the light lens back into place.

Luggage compartment light

5 Using a flat-bladed screwdriver or similar, gently prise the lens from place **(see illustration)**.
6 Pull the capless bulb from the holder.
7 Install a new bulb using a reversal of the removal procedure.

8 Interior light unit – removal and refitting

1 Using a trim removal tool, prise away the interior light lens as described in Section 7.
2 Undo the 2 bolts and prise down the front edge of the light unit then manoeuvre it from place **(see illustrations)**.
3 Disconnect the wiring plug.
4 Refitting is a reversal of removal.

9 Exterior light units – removal and refitting

Headlight

1 The headlight is removed during the bulb replacement procedure. Refer to Section 6.
2 Refitting is a reversal of removal. On completion, it is advisable to have the headlight beam alignment checked with reference to Section 10.

Side repeater light

3 The side repeater light is removed during the bulb replacement procedure. Refer to Section 6.

Rear light cluster

4 The rear light cluster is removed during the

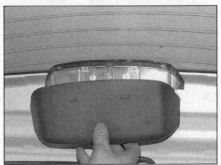

9.7 Slide the cover downwards

bulb replacement procedure. Refer to Section 6.
5 Refitting is a reversal of removal.

High-level brake light

6 Undo the 2 nuts and remove the rear spoiler (where fitted) as described in Chapter 11 Section 20.
7 Where there is no spoiler, slide the high-level brake light cover downwards from place **(see illustration)**.
8 Undo the retaining bolts and remove the high-level brake light from place **(see illustration)**. Disconnect the wiring plug as the light is withdrawn.
9 Refitting is a reversal of removal.

Front fog light

10 Undo the fasteners and partially release the front section of the wheelarch liner.
11 Disconnect the fog light wiring plug.

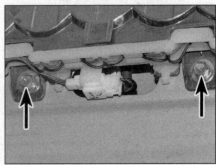

9.8 High-level brake light retaining bolts

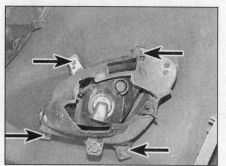
9.12 Fog light mounting screws

10.2 Headlight beam adjustment screws

11.4 Instrument panel retaining screws

12 Undo the mounting screws and manoeuvre the fog light assembly from place **(see illustration)**.
13 Refitting is a reversal of removal.

10 Headlight beam adjustment – general information

1 Accurate adjustment of the headlight beam is only possible using optical beam setting equipment and this work should therefore be carried out by a Hyundai dealer or suitably-equipped workshop.
2 For reference, the headlights can be adjusted by rotating the adjuster screws on the rear of the headlight unit **(see illustration)**.
3 All models have an electrically-operated headlight beam adjustment system which is controlled through the switch in the facia. On these models ensure that the switch is set to the off position before adjusting the headlight

aim. Note that the headlight aim motor cannot be renewed separately from the headlight.

11 Instrument panel – removal and refitting

Removal

1 Disconnect the battery negative lead as described in Chapter 5A Section 4.
2 Fully lower and extend the steering wheel/column.
3 Remove the instrument panel surround as described in Chapter 11 Section 26.
4 Undo the 4 retaining screws **(see illustration)**, and manoeuvre the instrument panel rearwards from position. Disconnect the wiring plugs as they become accessible.
5 No further dismantling of the panel is recommended. The panel is illuminated by non-replaceable LEDs.

Refitting

6 Refitting is a reversal of removal. If a new instrument panel is fitted, the data stored in the body computer may need to be transferred to the new panel using Hyundai diagnostic equipment (Examiner or equivalent). Entrust this task to a Hyundai dealer or suitably equipped repairer.

12 Horn – removal and refitting

Removal

1 Remove the front bumper as described in Chapter 11 Section 6.
2 Disconnect the wiring plug, undo the retaining bolt/nut and remove the horn(s) **(see illustration)**.

Refitting

3 Refitting is a reversal of removal.

13 Alarm siren – removal and refitting

1 Disconnect the battery and remove the battery tray as described in Chapter 5A Section 4.
2 Undo the mounting bolt and disconnect the wiring plug **(see illustration)**.
3 Refitting is a reversal of removal.

14 Wiper arm – removal and refitting

Removal

1 Operate the wiper motor, then switch if off so that the wiper arm returns to the at-rest/parked position.

Windscreen wiper arms

2 Prise off the wiper arm spindle nut cover, then slacken and remove the spindle nut **(see illustrations)**.

12.2 Horn retaining bolt

13.2 Alarm siren mounting bolt

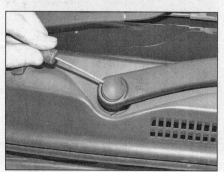
14.2a Prise off the cover ...

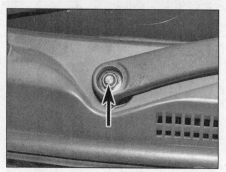
14.2b ... and undo the spindle nut

14.4 If necessary, use a puller to release the arm from the spindle

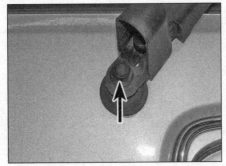

14.5 Lift up the cover to access the spindle nut

14.6 Special wiper arm pullers are available

3 Use masking tape to mark the position of the wipers on the windscreen.

4 Lift the blade off the glass, and pull the wiper arm off its spindle. If necessary, the arm can be carefully removed using a suitable puller **(see illustration)**. If both windscreen wiper arms are removed, note their locations, as different arms are fitted to the driver's and passenger's sides.

Tailgate wiper arm

5 Lift up the spindle cover, then slacken and remove the spindle nut **(see illustration)**.

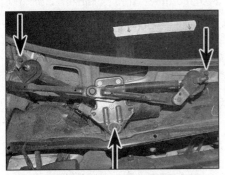

15.3 Undo the bolts and manoeuvre the wiper motor assembly from place

6 Lift the blade from the glass, and pull the wiper arm from the spindle. If necessary, the arm can be removed using a suitable puller **(see illustration)**.

Refitting

7 Refit the wiper arms to the spindles, and tighten the retaining nuts securely.

---

15 Windscreen wiper motor and linkage – removal and refitting

Removal

Windscreen wiper motor assembly

1 Remove the wiper arms as described in Section 14.
2 Remove the windscreen scuttle panel as described in Chapter 11 Section 20.
3 Undo the 3 retaining bolts, and manoeuvre the wiper motor assembly from place **(see illustration)**. Disconnect the linkage and wiring plug as they become accessible.

Rear wiper motor

4 Remove the rear wiper arm as described in Section 14.
5 Remove the tailgate lower trim panel as described in Chapter 11 Section 23.
6 Disconnect the wiper motor wiring plug.
7 Undo the 3 bolts and remove the rear wiper motor **(see illustration)**.

Refitting

8 Refitting is a reversal of removal.

---

16 Windscreen/tailgate washer system components – removal and refitting

Washer motor

Removal

1 Disconnect the battery negative lead as described in Chapter 5A Section 4.
2 Remove the front bumper as described in Chapter 11 Section 6.
3 Disconnect the hoses and the wiring plug from the washer motor **(see illustration)**.
4 Release the top retaining tab and gently

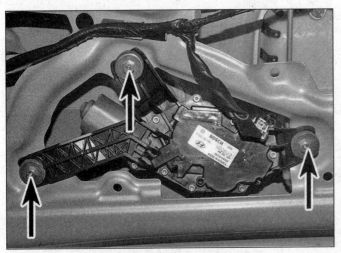

15.7 Rear wiper motor retaining bolts

16.3 The front and rear hose connections are marked 'F' and 'R' on the pump outlets

16.4 Release tab and manoeuvre motor from the reservoir

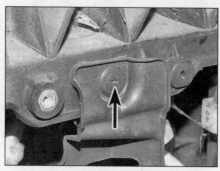

16.7a Remove upper mounting bolt on each side ...

16.7b ... then the mounting bolt at each front wing ...

16.7c ... then the 3 mounting bolts at each end of the front crash bar ...

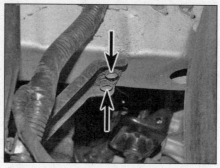

16.7d ... and finally the 2 mounting bolts holding each end of the frame stay bracket at each side

16.9 Pull forward the frame and brace it

16.12 Undo the 3 mounting bolts and remove the reservoir

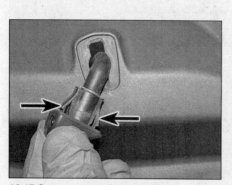

16.17 Squeeze together the clips to release the jet

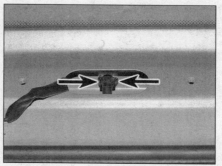

16.19 Squeeze together the clips to release the jet

manoeuvre the motor from the reservoir, taking care not to damage the seal (see illustration).

Washer reservoir

Removal

5 Remove the front bumper as described in Chapter 11 Section 6.

6 Remove both headlights as described in Section 9.

7 Undo the 14 bolts and displace the entire front upper mounting frame (see illustrations).

8 Disconnect the bracket for the high-pressure air conditioning pipe.

9 Pull forward the right-hand end of the upper mounting frame and brace with a suitable wedge (see illustration).

10 Disconnect the hoses and the wiring plug from the washer motor.

11 Unclip the wiring harness from the edge of the reservoir.

12 Undo the 3 reservoir mounting bolts and displace it rearwards (see illustration).

13 Undo the hidden bolt for the wiring harness and move the harness out of the way.

14 Manoeuvre the washer reservoir from place, detaching the wiring harness clips as they become available.

Refitting

15 Refitting is a reversal of removal.

Washer jets

Removal

Windscreen washer jets

16 Remove the windscreen scuttle panel as described in Chapter 11 Section 20.

17 Disconnect the washer hose, squeeze together the retaining clips, and remove the jet(s) from the panel (see illustration).

Tailgate screen jet

18 Remove the high-level brake light as described in Section 9.

19 Squeeze together the clips and push the jet from the tailgate (see illustration). Disconnect the hose as the jet is withdrawn.

Refitting

20 Refitting is a reversal of removal. If necessary, the aim of the jet can be adjusted using a fine needle inserted into the jet orifice.

17 Facia-mounted audio unit – removal and refitting

Facia Radio/Audio unit

Removal

1 Disconnect the battery negative lead as described in Chapter 5A Section 4.
2 Remove the centre switch/air vent panel as described in Chapter 11 Section 26.
3 Undo the 4 retaining screws and remove the unit from place, disconnecting the wiring plugs as they become accessible **(see illustration)**.

Refitting

4 Refitting is a reversal of removal, ensuring that the wiring is correctly routed behind the unit.

Aerial

Note: *This is a complex task requiring patience and dexterity to accomplish without damage to the headlining.*

Removal

5 Remove the headlining as described in Chapter 11 Section 23.
6 Disconnect the aerial wiring plug.
7 Undo the nut, recover the split-washer, and remove the aerial from the vehicle roof.

Refitting

8 Refitting is a reversal of removal.

18 Speakers – removal and refitting

Note: *Applies to front and rear doors.*
1 Remove the door inner trim panel as described in Chapter 11 Section 13.
2 Disconnect the speaker wiring plug.
3 Undo the 4 screws and remove the speaker **(see illustration)**.
4 Refitting is a reversal of removal.

19 Anti-theft system and engine immobiliser – general information

1 All models in the range are equipped as standard with a central locking system incorporating an electronic engine immobiliser function.
2 The electronic engine immobiliser is operated by a transponder fitted to the ignition key, in conjunction with an analogue module fitted around the ignition switch.
3 When the ignition key is inserted in the switch and turned to the ignition 'on' position, the control module sends a preprogrammed recognition code signal to the module on the ignition switch. If the recognition code signal matches that of the transponder on the ignition

17.3 Undo the 4 screws and remove the audio unit

key, an unlocking request signal is sent to the engine management ECU allowing the engine to be started. If the ignition key signal is not recognised, the engine management system remains immobilised.
4 When the ignition is switched off, a locking signal is sent to the ECU and the engine is immobilised until the unlocking request signal is again received.
5 If a fault develops with the system, have the body control computer interrogated using Hyundai diagnostic equipment.

20 Airbag system – general information, precautions and system de-activation

General information

1 A driver's airbag, passenger airbag, side airbags and side window airbags are fitted as standard on all models. The driver's airbag is located in the steering wheel centre pad and the passenger's airbag is located above the glovebox in the facia. The side airbags are located in the front seat backs and the side window airbags in the headlining.
2 The airbag and seat belt pyrotechnic safety systems are armed only when the ignition is switched on, however, a reserve power source maintains a power supply to the systems in the event of a break in the main electrical system. The airbags are activated by crash sensors, and controlled by an electronic control unit located under the centre of the facia. The side airbags and side window airbags are activated by severe side impact and operate in conjunction with the main system. The pyrotechnic seat belt pretensioners operate independently of the main system.
3 The airbags are inflated by a gas generator, which forces the bag out from its location in the steering wheel, facia, seat back frame or roof headlining.

Precautions

 Warning: The following precautions must be observed when working on vehicles equipped with an airbag system, to prevent the possibility of personal

18.3 Door speakers are secured by 4 screws

injury. Many of the precautions are equally applicable to the pyrotechnic seat belt pretensioners and should be similarly observed.

General

4 The following precautions must be observed when carrying out work on a vehicle equipped with an airbag:
a) *Do not disconnect the battery with the engine running.*
b) *Before carrying out any work in the vicinity of the airbag, removal of any of the airbag components, or any welding work on the vehicle, de-activate the system as described in the following sub-Section.*
c) *Do not attempt to test any of the airbag system circuits using test meters or any other test equipment.*
d) *If the airbag warning light comes on, or any fault in the system is suspected, consult a Hyundai dealer without delay. Do not attempt to carry out fault diagnosis, or any dismantling of the components.*

When handling an airbag

a) *Transport the airbag by itself, bag upward.*
b) *Do not put your arms around the airbag.*
c) *Do not drop the airbag or expose it to impacts.*
d) *Do not attempt to dismantle the airbag unit.*
e) *Do not connect any form of electrical equipment to any part of the airbag circuit.*

When storing an airbag

a) *Store the unit in a cupboard with the airbag upward.*
b) *Do not expose the airbag to temperatures above 80°C.*
c) *Do not expose the airbag to flames.*
d) *Do not attempt to dispose of the airbag – consult a Hyundai dealer.*
e) *Never refit an airbag which is known to be faulty or damaged.*

De-activation

5 The system must be de-activated before carrying out any work on the airbag components or surrounding area:
a) *Switch on the ignition and check the operation of the airbag warning light on the instrument panel. The light should illuminate when the ignition is switched on, then extinguish.*

b) *Switch off the ignition.*
c) *Remove the ignition key.*
d) *Switch off all electrical equipment.*
e) *Disconnect the battery negative lead as described in Chapter 5A Section 4.*
f) *Insulate the battery negative terminal and the end of the battery negative lead to prevent any possibility of contact.*
g) *Wait at least 3 minutes before carrying out any further work.*

Activation

6 To activate the system on completion of any work, proceed as follows:

a) *Ensure that there are no occupants in the vehicle, and that there are no loose objects around the vicinity of the steering wheel/facia.*
b) *Ensure that the ignition is switched off, then reconnect the battery negative lead.*
c) *Open the driver's door and switch on the ignition, without reaching in front of the steering wheel. Check that the airbag warning light illuminates briefly then extinguishes.*
d) *Switch off the ignition.*
e) *If the airbag warning light does not operate correctly, consult a Hyundai dealer before driving the vehicle.*

21 Airbag system components – removal and refitting

Caution: Refer to the warnings in the previous Section before carrying out the following operations.

1 Disconnect the battery negative lead as described in Chapter 5A Section 4 and wait at least 3 minutes before starting work.

Steering wheel airbag

Removal

2 Ensure the front wheels are in the straight-ahead position.
3 Undo the airbag module mounting Torx bolt on each side of the steering wheel and manoeuvre from place **(see illustration)**.
4 Prise up the yellow locking clip, disconnect the wiring plug, then disconnect the earth plug **(see illustration)**.

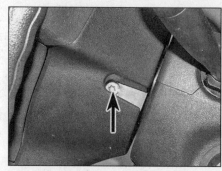
21.3 Airbag mounting Torx bolt

5 If the airbag unit is to be stored for any length of time, refer to the storage precautions given in Section 20.

Refitting

6 Refitting is a reversal of removal, noting the following points:

a) *Do not strike the airbag unit, or expose it to impacts during refitting.*
b) *On completion of refitting, activate the airbag system as described in Section 20.*

7 Reconnect the wiring plugs, and install the airbag module into the steering wheel.
8 Secure the driver's airbag with the new mounting bolts.
9 Connect the battery negative cable.
10 After installing the airbag, confirm proper system operation by turning on the ignition switch: the SRS indicator light should be turned on for about six seconds and then go off. Make sure the horn button works.

Passenger's airbag

Removal

11 Disconnect the battery negative lead as described in Chapter 5A Section 4 and wait at least 3 minutes before starting work.
12 Remove the glovebox as described in Chapter 11 Section 26.
13 Remove the passenger facia end panel as described in Chapter 11 Section 26.
14 Disconnect the airbag switch wiring plug from the facia end panel **(see illustration)**.
15 Disconnect the passenger airbag wiring and remove the 2 bolts holding the airbag mounting to the crossbeam behind the facia

21.4 Disconnect the wiring plugs

(see illustration).
16 Undo the 4 mounting nuts attaching the airbag to the back of the facia **(see illustration)**.
17 Squeeze the 9 tabs holding the airbag panel into the facia and manoeuvre the unit from place.
18 If the airbag unit is to be stored for any length of time, refer to the storage precautions given in Section 20.

Refitting

19 Refitting is a reversal of removal, noting the following points:

a) *Do not strike the airbag unit, or expose it to impacts during refitting.*
b) *Tighten the airbag retaining nuts to the specified torque.*
c) *On completion, activate the airbag system as described in Section 20.*

Front seat airbags

20 Removal of the seat airbags requires the seat upholstery to be removed. This is a complex task, requiring patience and experience. Consequently, we recommend this is entrusted to a Hyundai dealer or specialist.

Airbag control unit

Removal

21 Disconnect the battery negative terminal as described in Chapter 5A Section 4 and wait at least 3 minutes before starting work.
22 Remove the centre console as described in Chapter 11 Section 24.

21.14 Disconnect airbag switch wiring plug

21.15 Undo the passenger airbag mounting bolts

21.16 Passenger airbag retaining nuts (facia removed for clarity)

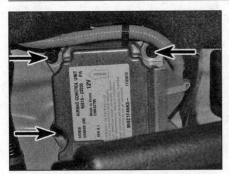

21.23 Airbag control unit bolts

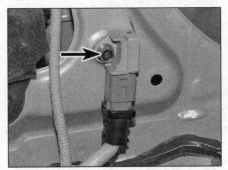

21.32 Side impact sensor retaining bolt

21.35a Release the clip at the top of the contact unit

23 Disconnect the wiring plugs, undo the 3 retaining bolts, and remove the control unit **(see illustration)**.

Refitting

24 Refitting is a reversal of removal, tightening the retaining bolts to their specified torque.

Impact sensors

Front sensors

Caution: Before disconnecting the front impact sensor connector, disconnect the front airbag connector.
Caution: Do not turn the ignition switch on and do not connect the battery cable while replacing the front impact sensor.

25 Disconnect the battery negative terminal as described in Chapter 5A Section 4 and wait at least 3 minutes before starting work.
26 Remove the front headlamp as described in Section 9.
27 Disconnect the impact sensor wiring plug.
28 Undo the retaining bolt and remove the sensor.
29 Refitting is a reversal of removal, tightening the sensor retaining bolt to the specified torque.

Side sensors

Caution: Before disconnecting the side impact sensor connector, disconnect the side airbag connector.
Caution: Do not turn the ignition switch on and do not connect the battery cable while replacing the side impact sensor.

30 Disconnect the battery negative terminal as described in Chapter 5A Section 4 and wait at least 3 minutes before starting work.

21.35b Depress the clip and disconnect the white wiring plug

31 Remove the lower B-pillar trim panel as described in Chapter 11 Section 23.
32 Undo the retaining bolt, and remove the sensor **(see illustration)**. Disconnect the wiring plug as the sensor is withdrawn.
33 Refitting is a reversal of removal, tightening the sensor retaining bolt to the specified torque.

Rotary contact unit (clockspring)

34 Remove the steering column shrouds as described in Chapter 11 Section 26.
35 With a sharp pull, release the retaining clip and pull the contact unit from the column **(see illustrations)**. Disconnect the wiring plugs as the contact unit is withdrawn.
36 Refitting is a reversal of removal, but if there is any doubt as to the correct position of the clock spring, it must be centralised as follows:
a) *Rotate the clockspring unit rotor clockwise until resistance is felt.*
b) *Rotate the clockspring unit rotor fully*

21.35c Lift the shield and disconnect the yellow wiring plug

anti-clockwise, counting the number of rotations.
c) *Half the number of rotations, and turn the rotor clockwise to the central position.*

22 Body computer – removal and refitting

Removal

1 Remove the centre console as described in Chapter 11 Section 24.
2 Remove the heater control unit as described in Chapter 3 Section 8.
3 Undo the 2 retaining bolts, and manoeuvre the body computer from place. Disconnect the wiring plugs from the unit as they become accessible.

Refitting

4 Refitting is a reversal of removal.

FROM 2008 TO 2010

I/P JUNCTION BOX

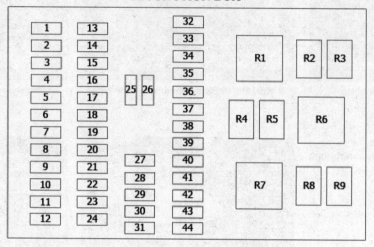

FUSE/RELAY	VALUE	DESCRIPTION	OEM NAME
1	10 A	DRL control module	DRL
2	10 A	Rear defogger relay, Power window relay, Headlamp LH/RH, Headlamp leveling switch, Intake switch, ETACM, SRS control module, Blower relay, Blower switch	IG 2
3	10 A	Headlamp LH, Instrument cluster	H/LP LH
4	10 A	Headlamp RH	H/LP RH
5	25 A	Multifunction switch (Wiper), Rear wiper motor, Sunroof motor	FRT WIPER
6	10 A	Rear fog lamp relay, Rear fog lamp switch	RR FOG LP
7	15 A	Driver / Passenger seat heater warmer switch	SEAT HTD
8	15 A	Multifunction switch (Wiper), Rear wiper motor, Sunroof motor	RR WIPER
9	20 A	Door lock relay, Door unlock relay, ETACM, TACM, Driver door lock actuator	D/LOCK AND S/ROOF
10	25 A	Rear defogger relay, Rear defogger (+)	HTD GLASS
11	-	Not used	-
12	10 A	Start relay, Burglar alarm relay	START
13	-	Not used	-
14	10 A	ABS / ESP control module, Multipurpose check connector, ESP switch	ABS
15	10 A	Hazard switch	T/SIG LP
16	15 A	Vehicle speed sensor, Air flow sensor, Ignition coil, ECM/PCM, Pulse generator, Fuel filter warning switch, Fuel heater relay	IG COIL
17	10 A	Back-up lamp switch, ATM shift lever, Transaxle range switch, Pulse generator	B/UP LP
18	10 A	Instrument cluster	A/BAG IND
19	10 A	SRS control module	A/BAG IND

Fuses and relays

20	10 A	Instrument cluster, ETACM, TACM, Generator, EPS control module	CLUSTER
21	15 A	Cigarette lighter	CIGAR LIGHTER
22	10 A	Digital clock, Audio, Power outside mirror switch	AUDIO ACC
23	10 A	A/C switch	A/CON SW
24	10 A	ECM, PCM rear defogger switch	HTD IND
25	10 A	SRS control module, Room lamp switch, Instrument cluster, PTC heater control module, Rear fog lamp switch, Digital clock, Door warning switch, Luggage lamp, Overhead console lamp	ROOM LP
26	15 A	Audio	AUDIO B+
27	10 A	Stop lamp switch	STOP LP
28	10 A	Hazard switch, Hazard relay	HAZARD
29	10 A	Horn relay, Horn, Dual horn	HORN
30	10 A	Front fog lamp relay, Front fog lamp switch, Front fog lamp LH/RH	F/FOG LP
31	-	Not used	-
32	10 A	Spare fuse	-
33	15 A	Spare fuse	-
34	20 A	Spare fuse	-
35	25 A	Spare fuse	-
36	20 A	Power window main switch	P/WDW LH
37	20 A	Power window main switch, Passenger power window switch	P/WDW RH
38	10 A	Rear combination lamp LH, DRL control module, Headlamp LH, License lamp	TAIL LP LH
39	10 A	Rear combination lamp RH, Head lamp RH	TAIL LP RH
40	-	Diode	-
41	-	Diode	-
42	-	Diode	-
43	-	Diode	-
44	-	Diode	-
R1	-	Power window relay	-
R2	-	Horn relay	-
R3	-	Front fog lamp relay	-
R4	-	Not used	-
R5	-	Tail lamp relay	-
R6	-	Flasher unit	-
R7	-	Blower relay	-
R8	-	Rear defogger relay	-
R9	-	Rear fog lamp relay	-

Fuses and relays (continued)

E/R FUSE AND RELAY BOX

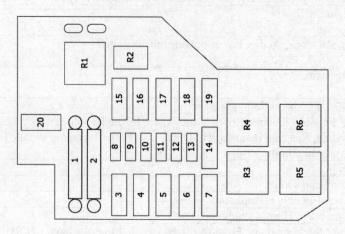

FUSE/RELAY	VALUE	DESCRIPTION	OEM NAME
1	80 A	ESP control unit	MDPS
2	100 A	Generator	MAIN
3	50 A	Heated window 25 A, Door lock and sunroof 20 A, Hazard warning system 10 A, Horn 10 A, Front fog lamp 10 A, Stop lamp 10 A	BATT 2
4	30 A	Power window relay	P/WDW
5	40 A	ABS/ESP control module, Multipurpose check connector	ABS 2
6	40 A	ABS/ESP control module, Multipurpose check connector	ABS 1
7	30 A	Blower relay	BLWR
8	10 A	ECM, PCM	ECU 2
9	15 A	Radiator fan 1 relay, Radiator fan 2 relay, Fuel pump relay, Idle speed actuator, Camshaft position sensor, Immobiliser control module, Injectors, ECM / PCM	INJ
10	10 A	PCM, Purge control solenoid valve, Crankshaft position sensor, Oxygen sensors, Camshaft position sensor, Immobiliser control module, Stop lamp switch, Lambda sensor	SNSR
11	-	Not used	-
12	20 A	Fuel pump relay, Fuel pump check connector, Fuel sender and Fuel pump motor	F PUMP
13	10 A	A/C relay, A/C compressor	A/CON
14	-	Not used	-
15	50 A	Ignition switch, Starter relay	IGN 2
16	30 A	Ignition switch	IGN 1
17	30 A	Tail lamp relay, Power connector (Room lamp 10 A, Audio 15 A), Air conditioning 10 A	BATT 1
18	30 A	Main relay, Fuel pump relay, ECM/PCM	ECU
19	30 A	Radiator fan 1 relay, Radiator fan 2 relay	R/FAN
20	-	Fuse puller	-
R1	-	Main relay	-
R2	-	Fuel pump relay	-
R3	-	Start relay	-
R4	-	A/C relay	-
R5	-	Radiator fan relay 2	-
R6	-	Radiator fan relay 1	-

Fuses and relays (continued)

FROM 2011 TO 2013

I/P FUSE AND RELAY BOX

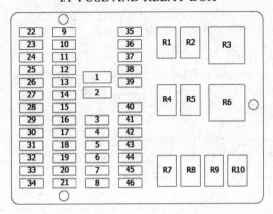

FUSE/RELAY	VALUE	DESCRIPTION	OEM NAME
1	15 A	Audio, DC-DC converter	F1
2	10 A	TACM, ETACM, Door warning switch, Data link connector, Luggage lamp, Room lamp switch, Rear fog lamp switch, Heater control module, Digital clock, Instrument cluster, Overhead console lamp	F2
3	25 A	Rear power window switch LH, Power window main switch, Passenger power window switch	F3
4	25 A	Rear power window switch RH, Power window main switch, Passenger power window switch	F4
5	10 A	Headlamp LH, DRL control module, License lamp, Rear combination lamp LH	F5
6	10 A	Headlamp RH, License lamp, Rear combination lamp RH, Hazard switch, Rheostat, Instrument cluster, Intake switch, Rear fog lamp switch, DRL control module, Blower switch, Heater control module, Headlamp leveling device switch, Audio, Power window main switch, Front fog lamp switch, A/C switch, Digital clock, Rear defogger switch, ISG switch, ATM shift lever, Passenger seat warmer switch, Driver seat warmer switch, Rear fog lamp switch, Buzzer, Rear defogger relay, Diode 1, Diode 2	F6
7	25 A	ICM relay box, Sunroof motor, Driver lock actuator, ETACM	F7
8	30 A	Rear defogger relay	F8
9	10 A	Front wiper motor, Multifunction switch, ECM	F9
10	10 A	Stop lamp switch, ESP switch, EPS control module, ABS control module, Multipurpose check connector	F10
11	10 A	Hazard switch	F11
12	15 A	DC-DC converter, ECM, Vehicle speed sensor, Condenser Ignition coil 1-3, Ignition coil, Pulse generator, Transaxle range switch	F12
13	10 A	Back-up lamp switch, Rear parking assist sensor LH/RH, Rear parking assist sensor center LH/RH	F13
14	10 A	Instrument cluster	F14
15	15 A	SRS control module	F15
16	10 A	Instrument cluster, Heater control module, TACM, ETACM, Seat belt lever, ISG off switch, Rear parking assist buzzer	F16

Fuses and relays (continued)

17	10 A	EPS control module	F17
18	10 A	Digital clock, Audio, DC-DC converter	F18
19	10 A	Front power outlet, Rear power outlet	F19
20	15 A	Cigarette lighter	F20
21	10 A	ICM relay box, Start relay, ECM, Transaxle range switch	F21
22	10 A	Instrument cluster, E/R fuse and relay box	F22
23	10 A	DRL control module	F23
24	10 A	Headlamp LH/RH, Headlamp leveling device switch, Intake switch, TACM, ETACM, Heater control module, Dual pressure switch, Rear defogger relay, Power window switch, E/R fuse and relay box, Diode 5	F24
25	25 A	Front wiper motor, Multifunction switch	F25
26	10 A	Rear fog lamp relay	F26
27	15 A	Driver / passenger seat warmer switch	F27
28	15 A	Rear wiper motor, Sunroof motor, Multifunction switch	F28
29	10 A	Stop lamp switch, Stop lamp relay	F29
30	10 A	Hazard switch, ICM relay box	F30
31	10 A	Horn relay, ICM relay box	F31
32	10 A	Front fog lamp relay	F32
33	10 A	Rear defogger switch, Heater control module, ECM, Driver/passenger power outside mirror	F33
34	10 A	Transaxle range switch, Instrument cluster, Rear combination lamp LH/RH, Back-up lamp switch, ETACM, PCM	F34
35	-	Not used	-
36	-	Not used	-
37	-	Not used	-
38	-	Not used	-
39	-	Not used	-
40	-	Not used	-
41	-	Not used	-
42	-	Not used	-
43	-	Not used	-
44	-	Not used	-
45	-	Not used	-
46	-	Not used	-
R1	-	Driver seat warmer relay	-
R2	-	Power window relay	-
R3	-	Stop lamp relay	-
R4	-	Horn relay	-
R5	-	Front fog lamp relay	-
R6	-	Flasher unit	-
R7	-	Passenger seat warmer relay	-
R8	-	Tail lamp relay	-
R9	-	Rear defogger relay	-
R10	-	Rear fog lamp relay	-

Fuses and relays (continued)

E/R FUSE AND RELAY BOX

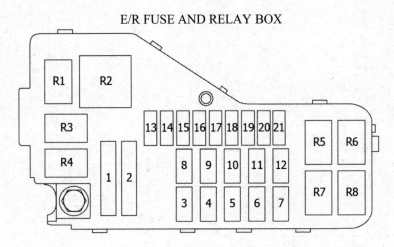

FUSE/RELAY	VALUE	DESCRIPTION	OEM NAME
1	80 A	EPS control module	F1
2	100 A	Alternator	F2
3	50 A	I/P fuse and relay box	F3
4	40 A	I/P fuse and relay box	F4
5	40 A	ABS control module, ESP control module, Multipurpose check connector	F5
6	40 A	ABS control module, ESP control module	F6
7	40 A	Blower relay	F7
8	50 A	Ignition switch	F8
9	40 A	Ignition switch	F9
10	40 A	E/R fuse and relay box (F18, R7), I/P fuse and relay box(F1, F2, F29-F32)	F10
11	30 A	E/R fuse and relay box (F15, R1)	F11
12	40 A	E/R fuse and relay box (R8)	F12
13	15 A	E/R fuse and relay box (R2)	F13
14	10 A	Heater control module, A/C switch	F14
15	10 A	PCM	F15
16	15 A	E/R fuse and relay box (R2, R8), ECM, PCM, Oil control valve 1 and 2,Idle speed actuator, Injector 1-4, Canister purge control solenoid valve	F16
17	10 A	E/R fuse and relay box, ECM, PCM, Camshaft position sensor 1 and 2, Immobiliser control module, Oxygen sensor	F17
18	10 A	E/R fuse and relay box (R5)	F18
19	10 A	Headlamp LH	F19
20	10 A	Headlamp RH	F20
21	30 A	E/R fuse and relay box	F21
R1	-	Main relay	-
R2	-	Fuel pump relay	-
R3	-	Headlamp low relay	-
R4	-	Headlamp high relay	-
R5	-	A/C relay	-
R6	-	Radiator fan relay	-
R7	-	Start relay	-
R8	-	Blower relay	-

Fuses and relays (continued)

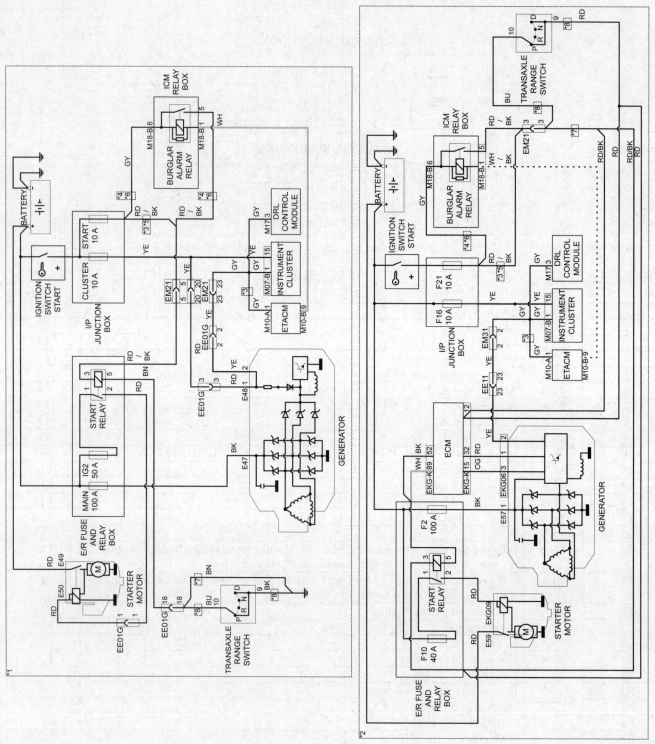

Starting and charging

*1 From 2008 to 2010
*2 From 2011 to 2013
*3 With IMMO
*4 Without IMMO
*5 With security system
*6 Without security system
*7 Manual transmission
*8 Automatic transmission

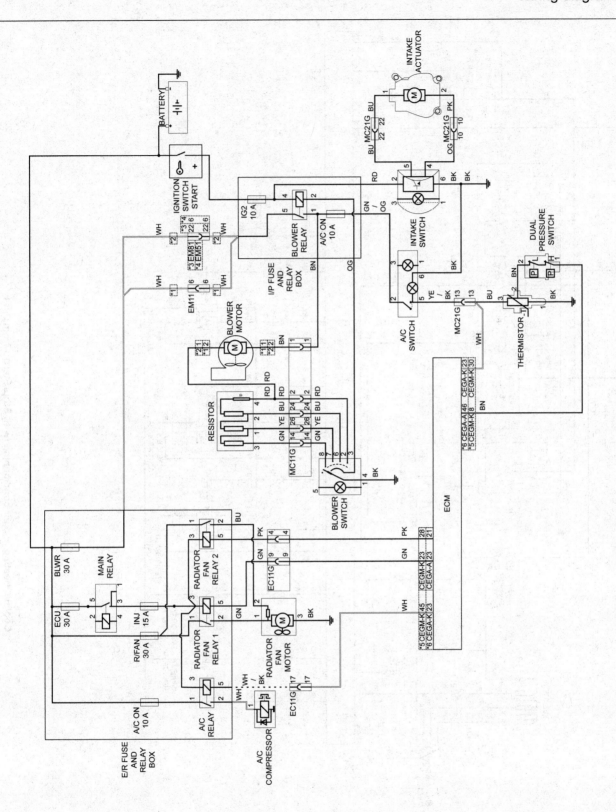

Cooling, heating and air conditioning – up to 2010

*1 LHD models
*2 RHD models
*3 With ESP
*4 Without ESP
*5 Manual transmission
*6 Automatic transmission

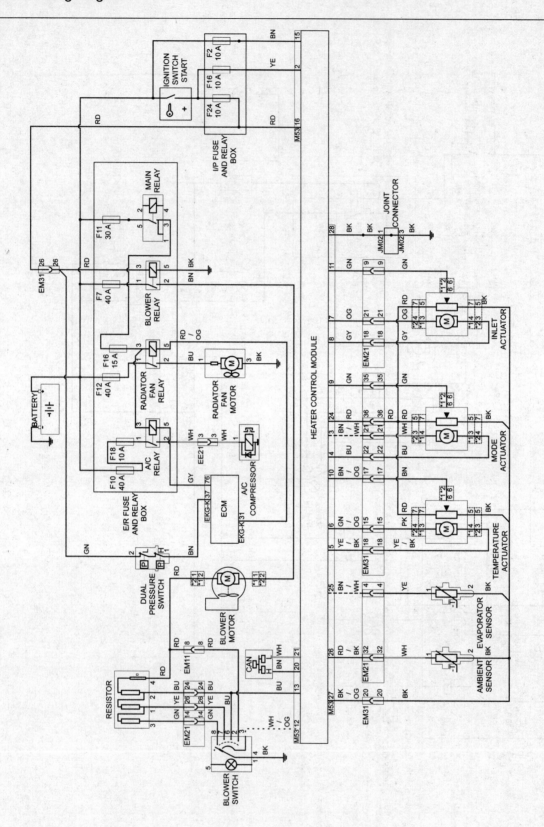

Cooling, heating and air conditioning (with Stop/Start) – from 2011

*1 LHD models
*2 RHD models

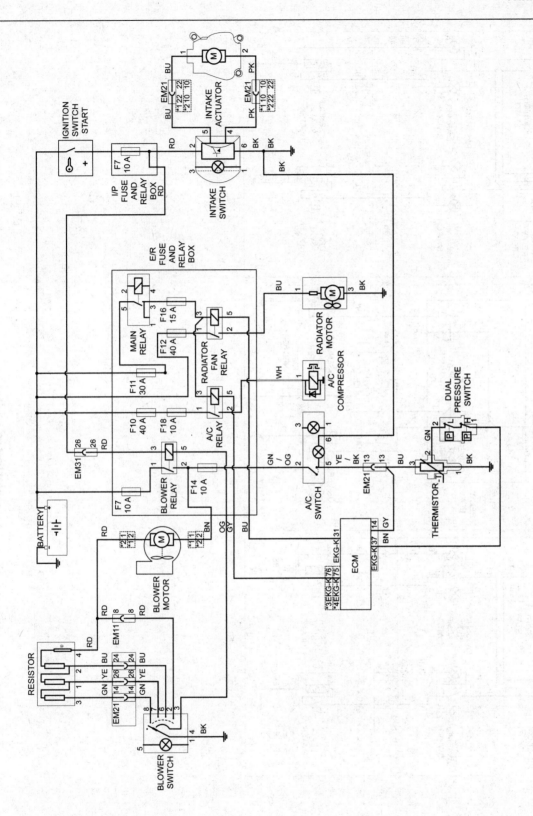

Cooling, heating and air conditioning (without Stop/Start) – from 2011

*1 LHD models
*2 RHD models
*3 With IMMO
*4 Without IMMO

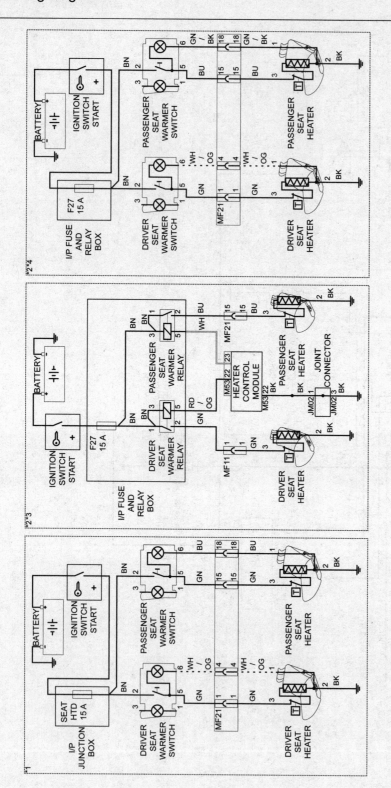

Seat heating

*1 From 2008 to 2010
*2 From 2011 to 2013
*3 With start stop
*4 Without start stop

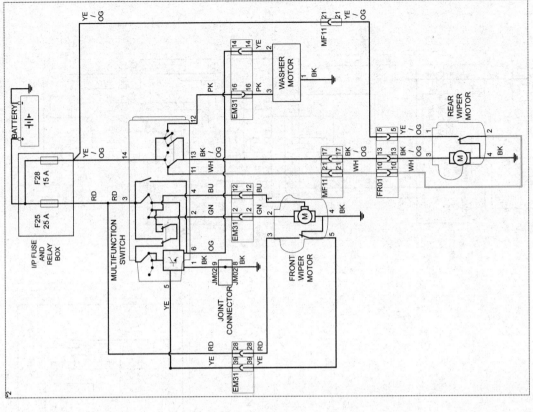

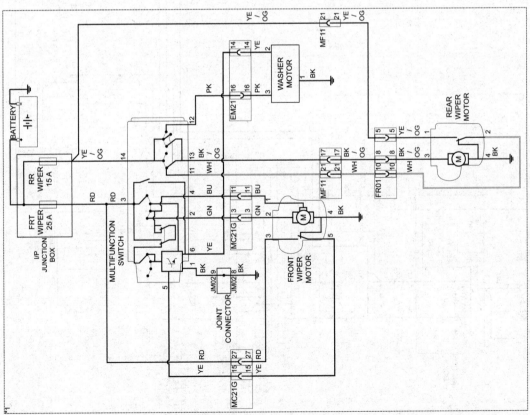

*1 From 2008 to 2010
*2 From 2011 to 2013

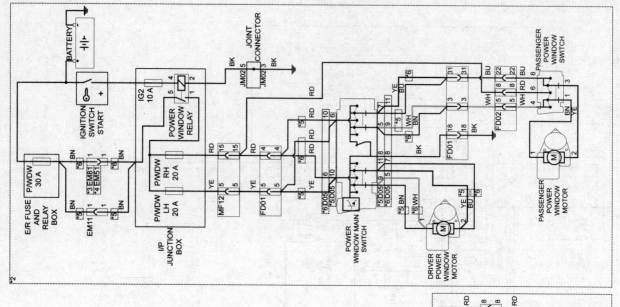

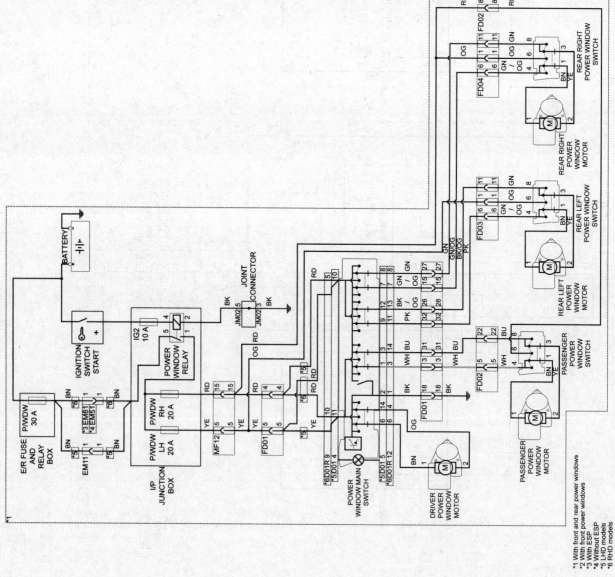

Electric windows – up to 2010

*1 With front and rear power windows
*2 With front power windows
*3 With ESP
*4 Without ESP
*5 LHD models
*6 RHD models

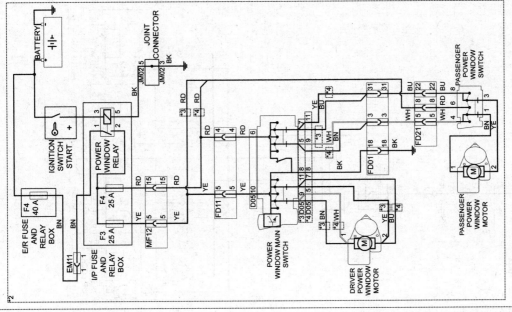

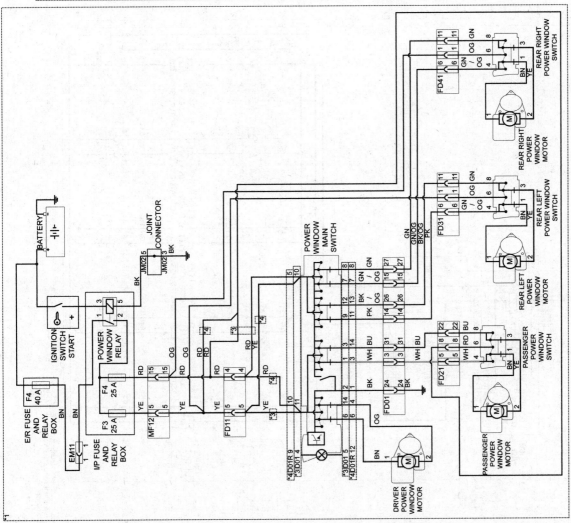

Electric windows – from 2011

*1 With front and rear power windows
*2 With front power windows
*3 LHD models
*4 RHD models

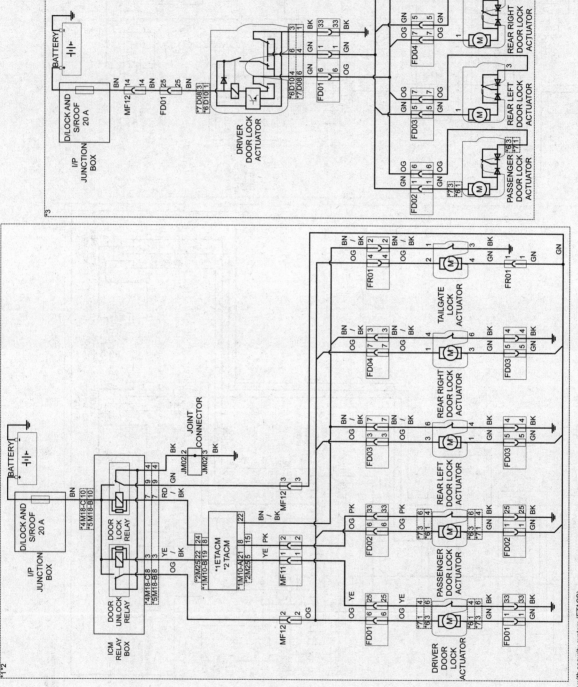

Central locking – up to 2010

*1 With body control unit with security system (ETACS)
*2 With body control unit without security system (TACS)
*3 Without body control unit
*4 With IMMO
*5 Without IMMO
*6 LHD models
*7 RHD models

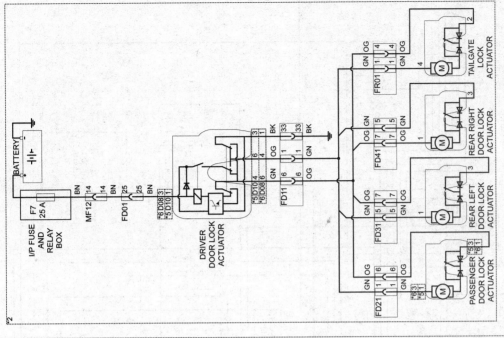

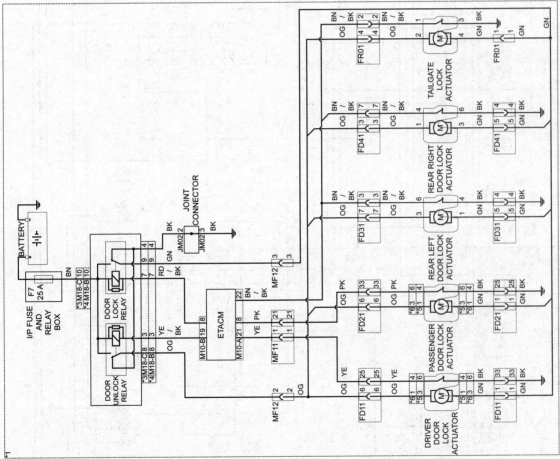

Central locking – from 2011

*1 With body control unit
*2 Without body control unit
*3 With IMMO
*4 Without IMMO
*5 LHD models
*6 RHD models

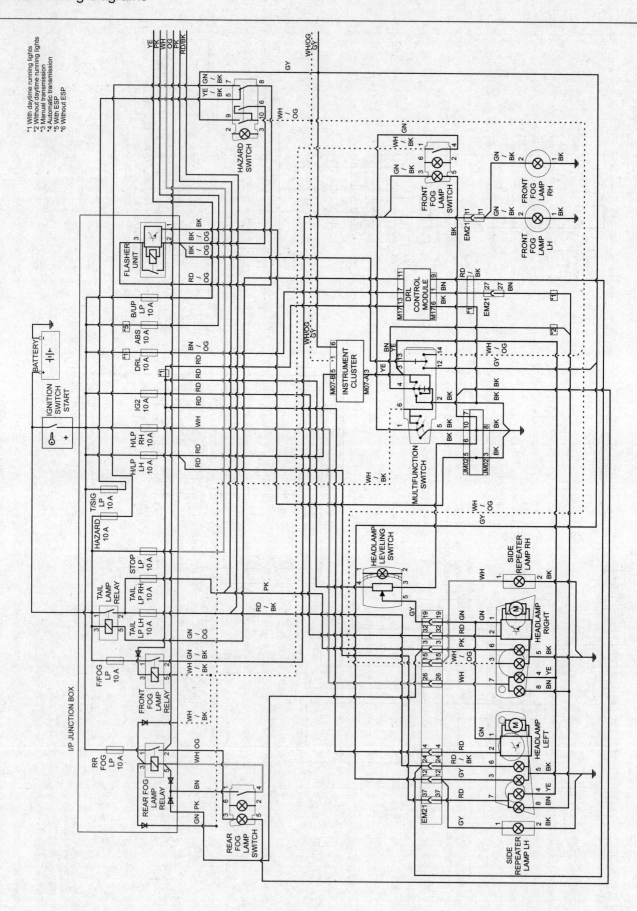

Exterior lighting – up to 2010 Part 1

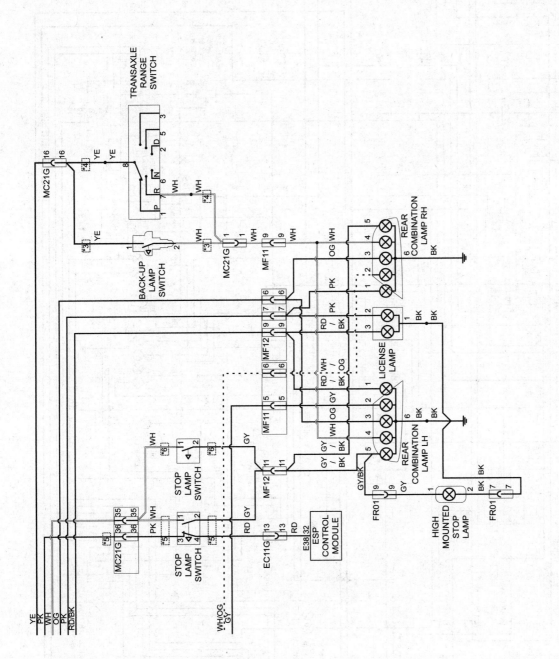

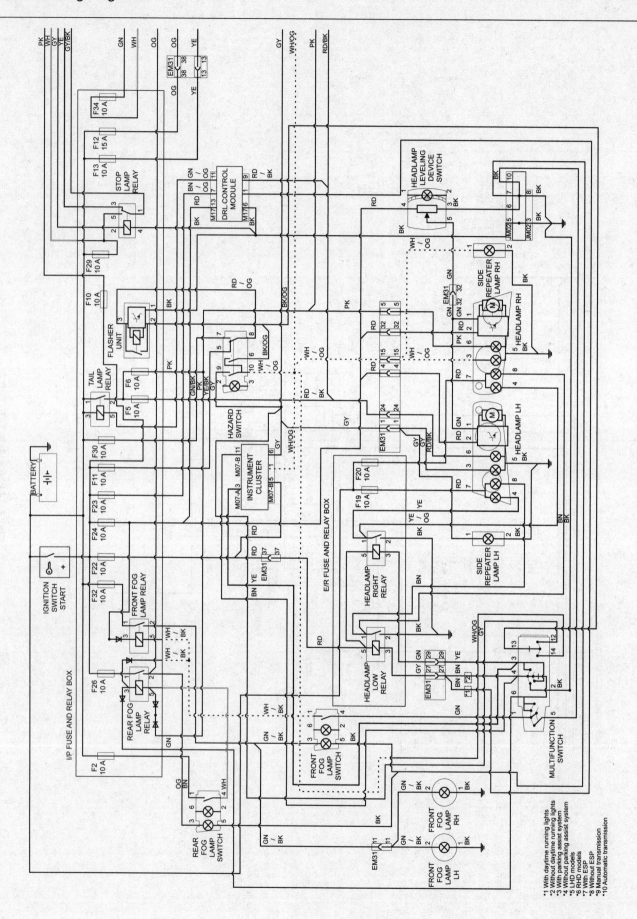

Exterior lighting – from 2011 Part 1

*1 With daytime running lights
*2 Without daytime running lights
*3 With parking assist system
*4 Without parking assist system
*5 LHD models
*6 RHD models
*7 With ESP
*8 Without ESP
*9 Manual transmission
*10 Automatic transmission

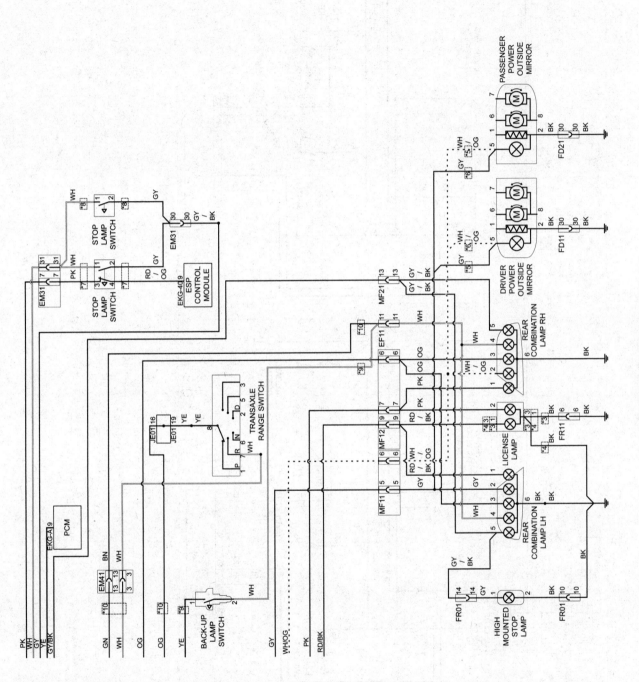

Exterior lighting – from 2011 Part 2

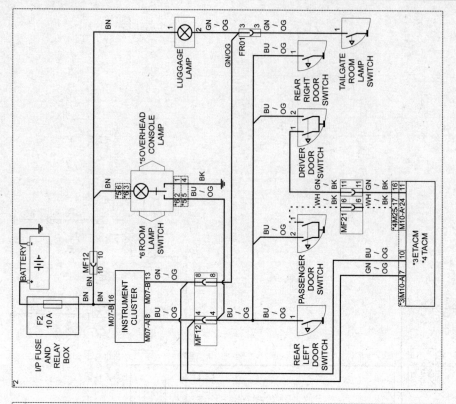

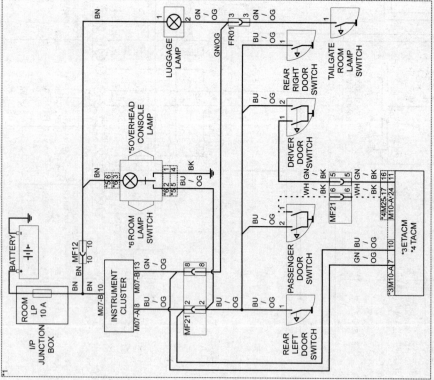

Interior lighting

*1 From 2008 to 2010
*2 From 2011 to 2013
*3 With body control unit with security system (ETACS)
*4 With body control unit without security system (TACS)
*5 With sunroof
*6 Without sunroof

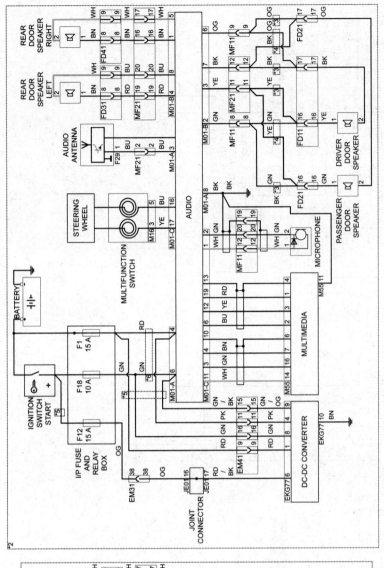

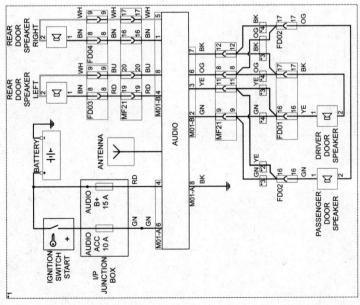

Audio systems

*1 From 2008 to 2010
*2 From 2011 to 2013
*3 LHD models
*4 RHD models
*5 With start stop
*6 Without start stop

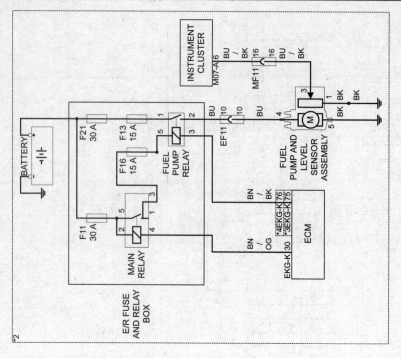

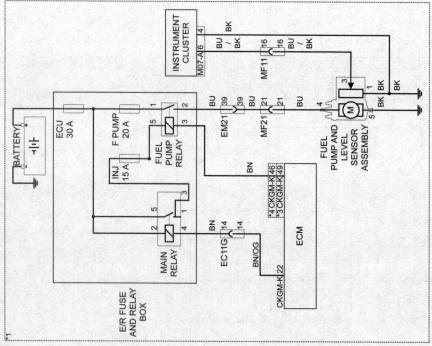

Fuel pump/level sensor

Dimensions and weights

Note: *All figures are approximate, and may vary according to model. Refer to the manufacturer's data for exact figures.*

Dimensions

Overall length:	3565 mm
Overall width (including mirrors).	1902 mm
Overall height	1550 mm
Wheelbase	2380 mm

Weights

Unladen (fuel tank 90% full).	1010 kg
Gross vehicle weight	1410 kg
Maximum load on roof:	50 kg

Fuel economy

Although depreciation is still the biggest part of the cost of motoring for most car owners, the cost of fuel is more immediately noticeable. These pages give some tips on how to get the best fuel economy.

Working it out

Manufacturer's figures

Car manufacturers are required by law to provide fuel consumption information on all new vehicles sold. These 'official' figures are obtained by simulating various driving conditions on a rolling road or a test track. Real life conditions are different, so the fuel consumption actually achieved may not bear much resemblance to the quoted figures.

How to calculate it

Many cars now have trip computers which will

display fuel consumption, both instantaneous and average. Refer to the owner's handbook for details of how to use these.

To calculate consumption yourself (and maybe to check that the trip computer is accurate), proceed as follows.

1. Fill up with fuel and note the mileage, or zero the trip recorder.
2. Drive as usual until you need to fill up again.
3. Note the amount of fuel required to refill the tank, and the mileage covered since the previous fill-up.
4. Divide the mileage by the amount of fuel used to obtain the consumption figure.

For example:

Mileage at first fill-up (a) = 27,903
Mileage at second fill-up (b) = 28,346
Mileage covered (b - a) = 443
Fuel required at second fill-up = 48.6 litres

The half-completed changeover to metric units in the UK means that we buy our fuel in litres, measure distances in miles and talk about fuel consumption in miles per gallon. There are two ways round this: the first is to convert the litres to gallons before doing the calculation (by dividing by 4.546, or see Table 1). So in the example:

48.6 litres ÷ 4.546 = 10.69 gallons
443 miles ÷ 10.69 gallons = 41.4 mpg

The second way is to calculate the consumption in miles per litre, then multiply that figure by 4.546 (or see Table 2).

So in the example, fuel consumption is:

443 miles ÷ 48.6 litres = 9.1 mpl
9.1 mpl x 4.546 = 41.4 mpg

The rest of Europe expresses fuel consumption in litres of fuel required to travel 100 km (l/100 km). For interest, the conversions are given in Table 3. In practice it doesn't matter what units you use, provided you know what your normal consumption is and can spot if it's getting better or worse.

Table 1: conversion of litres to Imperial gallons

litres	1	2	3	4	5	10	20	30	40	50	60	70
gallons	0.22	0.44	0.66	0.88	1.10	2.24	4.49	6.73	8.98	11.22	13.47	15.71

Table 2: conversion of miles per litre to miles per gallon

miles per litre	5	6	7	8	9	10	11	12	13	14
miles per gallon	23	27	32	36	41	46	50	55	59	64

Table 3: conversion of litres per 100 km to miles per gallon

litres per 100 km	4	4.5	5	5.5	6	6.5	7	8	9	10
miles per gallon	71	63	56	51	47	43	40	35	31	28

Maintenance

A well-maintained car uses less fuel and creates less pollution. In particular:

Filters

Change air and fuel filters at the specified intervals.

Oil

Use a good quality oil of the lowest viscosity specified by the vehicle manufacturer (see *Lubricants and fluids*). Check the level often and be careful not to overfill.

Spark plugs

When applicable, renew at the specified intervals.

Tyres

Check tyre pressures regularly. Under-inflated tyres have an increased rolling resistance. It is generally safe to use the higher pressures specified for full load conditions even when not fully laden, but keep an eye on the centre band of tread for signs of wear due to over-inflation.

When buying new tyres, consider the 'fuel saving' models which most manufacturers include in their ranges.

Driving style

Acceleration

Acceleration uses more fuel than driving at a steady speed. The best technique with modern cars is to accelerate reasonably briskly to the desired speed, changing up through the gears as soon as possible without making the engine labour.

Air conditioning

Air conditioning absorbs quite a bit of energy from the engine – typically 3 kW (4 hp) or so. The effect on fuel consumption is at its worst in slow traffic. Switch it off when not required.

Anticipation

Drive smoothly and try to read the traffic flow so as to avoid unnecessary acceleration and braking.

Automatic transmission

When accelerating in an automatic, avoid depressing the throttle so far as to make the transmission hold onto lower gears at higher speeds. Don't use the 'Sport' setting, if applicable.

When stationary with the engine running, select 'N' or 'P'. When moving, keep your left foot away from the brake.

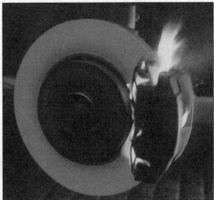

Braking

Braking converts the car's energy of motion into heat – essentially, it is wasted. Obviously some braking is always going to be necessary, but with good anticipation it is surprising how much can be avoided, especially on routes that you know well.

Carshare

Consider sharing lifts to work or to the shops. Even once a week will make a difference.

Electrical loads

Electricity is 'fuel' too; the alternator which charges the battery does so by converting some of the engine's energy of motion into electrical energy. The more electrical accessories are in use, the greater the load on the alternator. Switch off big consumers like the heated rear window when not required.

Freewheeling

Freewheeling (coasting) in neutral with the engine switched off is dangerous. The effort required to operate power-assisted brakes and steering increases when the engine is not running, with a potential lack of control in emergency situations.

In any case, modern fuel injection systems automatically cut off the engine's fuel supply on the overrun (moving and in gear, but with the accelerator pedal released).

Gadgets

Bolt-on devices claiming to save fuel have been around for nearly as long as the motor car itself. Those which worked were rapidly adopted as standard equipment by the vehicle manufacturers. Others worked only in certain situations, or saved fuel only at the expense of unacceptable effects on performance, driveability or the life of engine components.

The most effective fuel saving gadget is the driver's right foot.

Journey planning

Combine (eg) a trip to the supermarket with a visit to the recycling centre and the DIY store, rather than making separate journeys.

When possible choose a travelling time outside rush hours.

Load

The more heavily a car is laden, the greater the energy required to accelerate it to a given speed. Remove heavy items which you don't need to carry.

One load which is often overlooked is the contents of the fuel tank. A tankful of fuel (55 litres / 12 gallons) weighs 45 kg (100 lb) or so. Just half filling it may be worthwhile.

Lost?

At the risk of stating the obvious, if you're going somewhere new, have details of the route to hand. There's not much point in achieving record mpg if you also go miles out of your way.

Parking

If possible, carry out any reversing or turning manoeuvres when you arrive at a parking space so that you can drive straight out when you leave. Manoeuvering when the engine is cold uses a lot more fuel.

Driving around looking for free on-street parking may cost more in fuel than buying a car park ticket.

Premium fuel

Most major oil companies (and some supermarkets) have premium grades of fuel which are several pence a litre dearer than the standard grades. Reports vary, but the consensus seems to be that if these fuels improve economy at all, they do not do so by enough to justify their extra cost.

Roof rack

When loading a roof rack, try to produce a wedge shape with the narrow end at the front. Any cover should be securely fastened – if it flaps it's creating turbulence and absorbing energy.

Remove roof racks and boxes when not in use – they increase air resistance and can create a surprising amount of noise.

Short journeys

The engine is at its least efficient, and wear is highest, during the first few miles after a cold start. Consider walking, cycling or using public transport.

Speed

The engine is at its most efficient when running at a steady speed and load at the rpm where it develops maximum torque. (You can find this figure in the car's handbook.) For most cars this corresponds to between 55 and 65 mph in top gear.

Above the optimum cruising speed, fuel consumption starts to rise quite sharply. A car travelling at 80 mph will typically be using 30% more fuel than at 60 mph.

Supermarket fuel

It may be cheap but is it any good? In the UK all supermarket fuel must meet the relevant British Standard. The major oil companies will say that their branded fuels have better additive packages which may stop carbon and other deposits building up. A reasonable compromise might be to use one tank of branded fuel to three or four from the supermarket.

Switch off when stationary

Switch off the engine if you look like being stationary for more than 30 seconds or so. This is good for the environment as well as for your pocket. Be aware though that frequent restarts are hard on the battery and the starter motor.

Windows

Driving with the windows open increases air turbulence around the vehicle. Closing the windows promotes smooth airflow and

reduced resistance. The faster you go, the more significant this is.

And finally . . .

Driving techniques associated with good fuel economy tend to involve moderate acceleration and low top speeds. Be considerate to the needs of other road users who may need to make brisker progress; even if you do not agree with them this is not an excuse to be obstructive.

Safety must always take precedence over economy, whether it is a question of accelerating hard to complete an overtaking manoeuvre, killing your speed when confronted with a potential hazard or switching the lights on when it starts to get dark.

Conversion factors

Length (distance)

Inches (in)	x 25.4	= Millimetres (mm)	x 0.0394	= Inches (in)
Feet (ft)	x 0.305	= Metres (m)	x 3.281	= Feet (ft)
Miles	x 1.609	= Kilometres (km)	x 0.621	= Miles

Volume (capacity)

Cubic inches (cu in; in³)	x 16.387	= Cubic centimetres (cc; cm³)	x 0.061	= Cubic inches (cu in; in³)
Imperial pints (Imp pt)	x 0.568	= Litres (l)	x 1.76	= Imperial pints (Imp pt)
Imperial quarts (Imp qt)	x 1.137	= Litres (l)	x 0.88	= Imperial quarts (Imp qt)
Imperial quarts (Imp qt)	x 1.201	= US quarts (US qt)	x 0.833	= Imperial quarts (Imp qt)
US quarts (US qt)	x 0.946	= Litres (l)	x 1.057	= US quarts (US qt)
Imperial gallons (Imp gal)	x 4.546	= Litres (l)	x 0.22	= Imperial gallons (Imp gal)
Imperial gallons (Imp gal)	x 1.201	= US gallons (US gal)	x 0.833	= Imperial gallons (Imp gal)
US gallons (US gal)	x 3.785	= Litres (l)	x 0.264	= US gallons (US gal)

Mass (weight)

Ounces (oz)	x 28.35	= Grams (g)	x 0.035	= Ounces (oz)
Pounds (lb)	x 0.454	= Kilograms (kg)	x 2.205	= Pounds (lb)

Force

Ounces-force (ozf; oz)	x 0.278	= Newtons (N)	x 3.6	= Ounces-force (ozf; oz)
Pounds-force (lbf; lb)	x 4.448	= Newtons (N)	x 0.225	= Pounds-force (lbf; lb)
Newtons (N)	x 0.1	= Kilograms-force (kgf; kg)	x 9.81	= Newtons (N)

Pressure

Pounds-force per square inch (psi; lbf/in²; lb/in²)	x 0.070	= Kilograms-force per square centimetre (kgf/cm²; kg/cm²)	x 14.223	= Pounds-force per square inch (psi; lbf/in²; lb/in²)
Pounds-force per square inch (psi; lbf/in²; lb/in²)	x 0.068	= Atmospheres (atm)	x 14.696	= Pounds-force per square inch (psi; lbf/in²; lb/in²)
Pounds-force per square inch (psi; lbf/in²; lb/in²)	x 0.069	= Bars	x 14.5	= Pounds-force per square inch (psi; lbf/in²; lb/in²)
Pounds-force per square inch (psi; lbf/in²; lb/in²)	x 6.895	= Kilopascals (kPa)	x 0.145	= Pounds-force per square inch (psi; lbf/in²; lb/in²)
Kilopascals (kPa)	x 0.01	= Kilograms-force per square centimetre (kgf/cm²; kg/cm²)	x 98.1	= Kilopascals (kPa)
Millibar (mbar)	x 100	= Pascals (Pa)	x 0.01	= Millibar (mbar)
Millibar (mbar)	x 0.0145	= Pounds-force per square inch (psi; lbf/in²; lb/in²)	x 68.947	= Millibar (mbar)
Millibar (mbar)	x 0.75	= Millimetres of mercury (mmHg)	x 1.333	= Millibar (mbar)
Millibar (mbar)	x 0.401	= Inches of water (inH₂O)	x 2.491	= Millibar (mbar)
Millimetres of mercury (mmHg)	x 0.535	= Inches of water (inH₂O)	x 1.868	= Millimetres of mercury (mmHg)
Inches of water (inH₂O)	x 0.036	= Pounds-force per square inch (psi; lbf/in²; lb/in²)	x 27.68	= Inches of water (inH₂O)

Torque (moment of force)

Pounds-force inches (lbf in; lb in)	x 1.152	= Kilograms-force centimetre (kgf cm; kg cm)	x 0.868	= Pounds-force inches (lbf in; lb in)
Pounds-force inches (lbf in; lb in)	x 0.113	= Newton metres (Nm)	x 8.85	= Pounds-force inches (lbf in; lb in)
Pounds-force inches (lbf in; lb in)	x 0.083	= Pounds-force feet (lbf ft; lb ft)	x 12	= Pounds-force inches (lbf in; lb in)
Pounds-force feet (lbf ft; lb ft)	x 0.138	= Kilograms-force metres (kgf m; kg m)	x 7.233	= Pounds-force feet (lbf ft; lb ft)
Pounds-force feet (lbf ft; lb ft)	x 1.356	= Newton metres (Nm)	x 0.738	= Pounds-force feet (lbf ft; lb ft)
Newton metres (Nm)	x 0.102	= Kilograms-force metres (kgf m; kg m)	x 9.804	= Newton metres (Nm)

Power

Horsepower (hp)	x 745.7	= Watts (W)	x 0.0013	= Horsepower (hp)

Velocity (speed)

Miles per hour (miles/hr; mph)	x 1.609	= Kilometres per hour (km/hr; kph)	x 0.621	= Miles per hour (miles/hr; mph)

Fuel consumption*

Miles per gallon, Imperial (mpg)	x 0.354	= Kilometres per litre (km/l)	x 2.825	= Miles per gallon, Imperial (mpg)
Miles per gallon, US (mpg)	x 0.425	= Kilometres per litre (km/l)	x 2.352	= Miles per gallon, US (mpg)

Temperature

Degrees Fahrenheit = (°C x 1.8) + 32   Degrees Celsius (Degrees Centigrade; °C) = (°F - 32) x 0.56

It is common practice to convert from miles per gallon (mpg) to litres/100 kilometres (l/100km), where mpg x l/100 km = 282

Spare parts are available from many sources, including maker's appointed garages, accessory shops, and motor factors. To be sure of obtaining the correct parts, it will sometimes be necessary to quote the vehicle identification number. If possible, it can also be useful to take the old parts along for positive identification. Items such as starter motors and alternators may be available under a service exchange scheme – any parts returned should be clean.

Our advice regarding spare parts is as follows.

Officially appointed garages

This is the best source of parts which are peculiar to your car, and which are not otherwise generally available (eg, badges, interior trim, certain body panels, etc). It is also the only place at which you should buy parts if the vehicle is still under warranty.

Accessory shops

These are very good places to buy materials and components needed for the maintenance of your car (oil, air and fuel filters, light bulbs, drivebelts, greases, brake pads, tough-up paint, etc). Components of this nature sold by a reputable shop are of the same standard as those used by the car manufacturer.

5 Besides components, these shops also sell tools and general accessories, usually have convenient opening hours, charge lower prices, and can often be found close to home. Some accessory shops have parts counters where components needed for almost any repair job can be purchased or ordered.

Motor factors

Good factors will stock all the more important components which wear out comparatively quickly, and can sometimes supply individual components needed for the overhaul of a larger assembly (eg, brake seals and hydraulic parts, bearing shells, pistons, valves). They may also handle work such as cylinder block reboring, crankshaft regrinding, etc.

Tyre and exhaust specialists

These outlets may be independent, or members of a local or national chain. They frequently offer competitive prices when compared with a main dealer or local garage, but it will pay to obtain several quotes before making a decision. When researching prices, also ask what 'extras' may be added – for instance fitting a new valve and balancing the wheel are both commonly charged on top of the price of a new tyre.

Other sources

Beware of parts or materials obtained from market stalls, car boot sales, internet auction sites or similar outlets. Such items are not invariably sub-standard, but there is little chance of compensation if they do prove unsatisfactory. In the case of safety-critical components such as brake pads, there is the risk not only of financial loss, but also of an accident causing injury or death

Second-hand components or assemblies obtained from a car breaker can be a good buy in some circumstances, but this sort of purchase is best made by the experienced DIY mechanic.

Vehicle identification numbers

Modifications are a continuing and unpublicised process in vehicle manufacture, quite apart from major model changes. Spare parts manuals and lists are compiled upon a numerical basis, the individual vehicle identification numbers being essential to correct identification of the component concerned.

2 When ordering spare parts, always give as much information as possible. Quote the car model, year of manufacture, body and engine numbers as appropriate.

3 The vehicle identification plate is affixed to the passengers door pillar. It gives the VIN (vehicle identification number), and details of the trim and paint codes. The VIN is repeated on a plate attached to the right-hand front floor panel, adjacent to the front seat, and is visible through the left-hand lower corner of the windscreen (see illustrations).

4 The engine number is stamped on the front of the cylinder block (see illustration).

Vehicle identification plate on the passengers door pillar

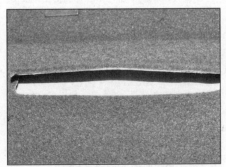

VIN plate on the right-hand front floor panel

The engine number is located at the centre-front of the cylinder block (intake manifold removed for clarity)

Whenever servicing, repair or overhaul work is carried out on the car or its components, observe the following procedures and instructions. This will assist in carrying out the operation efficiently and to a professional standard of workmanship.

Joint mating faces and gaskets

When separating components at their mating faces, never insert screwdrivers or similar implements into the joint between the faces in order to prise them apart. This can cause severe damage which results in oil leaks, coolant leaks, etc upon reassembly. Separation is usually achieved by tapping along the joint with a soft-faced hammer in order to break the seal. However, note that this method may not be suitable where dowels are used for component location.

Where a gasket is used between the mating faces of two components, a new one must be fitted on reassembly; fit it dry unless otherwise stated in the repair procedure. Make sure that the mating faces are clean and dry, with all traces of old gasket removed. When cleaning a joint face, use a tool which is unlikely to score or damage the face, and remove any burrs or nicks with an oilstone or fine file.

Make sure that tapped holes are cleaned with a pipe cleaner, and keep them free of jointing compound, if this is being used, unless specifically instructed otherwise.

Ensure that all orifices, channels or pipes are clear, and blow through them, preferably using compressed air.

Oil seals

Oil seals can be removed by levering them out with a wide flat-bladed screwdriver or similar implement. Alternatively, a number of self-tapping screws may be screwed into the seal, and these used as a purchase for pliers or some similar device in order to pull the seal free.

Whenever an oil seal is removed from its working location, either individually or as part of an assembly, it should be renewed.

The very fine sealing lip of the seal is easily damaged, and will not seal if the surface it contacts is not completely clean and free from scratches, nicks or grooves. If the original sealing surface of the component cannot be restored, and the manufacturer has not made provision for slight relocation of the seal relative to the sealing surface, the component should be renewed.

Protect the lips of the seal from any surface which may damage them in the course of fitting. Use tape or a conical sleeve where possible. Where indicated, lubricate the seal lips with oil before fitting and, on dual-lipped seals, fill the space between the lips with grease.

Unless otherwise stated, oil seals must be fitted with their sealing lips toward the lubricant to be sealed.

Use a tubular drift or block of wood of the appropriate size to install the seal and, if the seal housing is shouldered, drive the seal down to the shoulder. If the seal housing is unshouldered, the seal should be fitted with its face flush with the housing top face (unless otherwise instructed).

Screw threads and fastenings

Seized nuts, bolts and screws are quite a common occurrence where corrosion has set in, and the use of penetrating oil or releasing fluid will often overcome this problem if the offending item is soaked for a while before attempting to release it. The use of an impact driver may also provide a means of releasing such stubborn fastening devices, when used in conjunction with the appropriate screwdriver bit or socket. If none of these methods works, it may be necessary to resort to the careful application of heat, or the use of a hacksaw or nut splitter device. Before resorting to extreme methods, check that you are not dealing with a left-hand thread!

Studs are usually removed by locking two nuts together on the threaded part, and then using a spanner on the lower nut to unscrew the stud. Studs or bolts which have broken off below the surface of the component in which they are mounted can sometimes be removed using a stud extractor.

Always ensure that a blind tapped hole is completely free from oil, grease, water or other fluid before installing the bolt or stud. Failure to do this could cause the housing to crack due to the hydraulic action of the bolt or stud as it is screwed in.

For some screw fastenings, notably cylinder head bolts or nuts, torque wrench settings are no longer specified for the latter stages of tightening, "angle-tightening" being called up instead. Typically, a fairly low torque wrench setting will be applied to the bolts/nuts in the correct sequence, followed by one or more stages of tightening through specified angles.

When checking or retightening a nut or bolt to a specified torque setting, slacken the nut or bolt by a quarter of a turn, and then retighten to the specified setting. However, this should not be attempted where angular tightening has been used.

Locknuts, locktabs and washers

Any fastening which will rotate against a component or housing during tightening should always have a washer between it and the relevant component or housing.

Spring or split washers should always be renewed when they are used to lock a critical component such as a big-end bearing retaining bolt or nut. Locktabs which are folded over to retain a nut or bolt should always be renewed.

Self-locking nuts can be re-used in non-critical areas, providing resistance can be felt when the locking portion passes over the bolt or stud thread. However, it should be noted that self-locking stiffnuts tend to lose their effectiveness after long periods of use, and should then be renewed as a matter of course.

Split pins must always be replaced with new ones of the correct size for the hole.

When thread-locking compound is found on the threads of a fastener which is to be re-used, it should be cleaned off with a wire brush and solvent, and fresh compound applied on reassembly.

Special tools

Some repair procedures in this manual entail the use of special tools such as a press, two or three-legged pullers, spring compressors, etc. Wherever possible, suitable readily-available alternatives to the manufacturer's special tools are described, and are shown in use. In some instances, where no alternative is possible, it has been necessary to resort to the use of a manufacturer's tool, and this has been done for reasons of safety as well as the efficient completion of the repair operation. Unless you are highly-skilled and have a thorough understanding of the procedures described, never attempt to bypass the use of any special tool when the procedure described specifies its use. Not only is there a very great risk of personal injury, but expensive damage could be caused to the components involved.

Environmental considerations

When disposing of used engine oil, brake fluid, antifreeze, etc, give due consideration to any detrimental environmental effects. Do not, for instance, pour any of the above liquids down drains into the general sewage system, or onto the ground to soak away, as this is likely to pollute your local environment. Many local council refuse tips provide a facility for waste oil disposal, as do some garages. You can find your nearest disposal point by calling the Environment Agency on 03708 506 506 or by visiting www.oilbankline.org.uk.

Note: It is illegal and anti-social to dump oil down the drain. To find the location of your local oil recycling bank, call 03708 506 506 or visit www.oilbankline.org.uk.

The jack supplied with the vehicle tool kit should only be used for changing the roadwheels – see "Wheel changing" at the front of this manual. When carrying out any other kind of work, raise the vehicle using a hydraulic trolley jack, and always supplement the jack with axle stands positioned under the vehicle jacking points.

2 When using a trolley jack or axle stands, always position the jack head or axle stand head under, or adjacent to one of the relevant wheel changing jacking points under the sills. Use a block of wood between the jack or axle stand and the sill **(see illustration)**.

3 Do not attempt to jack the vehicle under the sump, final drive unit, or any of the suspension components.

4 Never work under, around, or near a raised vehicle, unless it is adequately supported in at least two places.

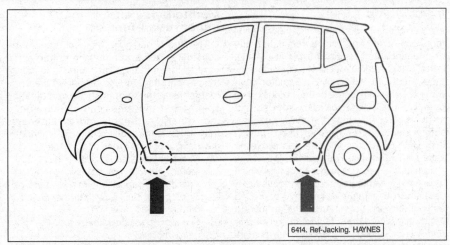

6414. Ref-Jacking. HAYNES

5.2 Reinforced jacking points are located at the front and rear of the sills each side of the car

Introduction

A selection of good tools is a fundamental requirement for anyone contemplating the maintenance and repair of a motor vehicle. For the owner who does not possess any, their purchase will prove a considerable expense, offsetting some of the savings made by doing-it-yourself. However, provided that the tools purchased meet the relevant national safety standards and are of good quality, they will last for many years and prove an extremely worthwhile investment.

To help the average owner to decide which tools are needed to carry out the various tasks detailed in this manual, we have compiled three lists of tools under the following headings: *Maintenance and minor repair, Repair and overhaul*, and *Special*. Newcomers to practical mechanics should start off with the *Maintenance and minor repair* tool kit, and confine themselves to the simpler jobs around the vehicle. Then, as confidence and experience grow, more difficult tasks can be undertaken, with extra tools being purchased as, and when, they are needed. In this way, a *Maintenance and minor repair* tool kit can be built up into a *Repair and overhaul* tool kit over a considerable period of time, without any major cash outlays. The experienced do-it-yourselfer will have a tool kit good enough for most repair and overhaul procedures, and will add tools from the *Special* category when it is felt that the expense is justified by the amount of use to which these tools will be put.

Maintenance and minor repair tool kit

The tools given in this list should be considered as a minimum requirement if routine maintenance, servicing and minor repair operations are to be undertaken. We recommend the purchase of combination spanners (ring one end, open-ended the other); although more expensive than open-ended ones, they do give the advantages of both types of spanner.

☐ *Combination spanners:*
Metric - 8 to 19 mm inclusive
☐ *Adjustable spanner - 35 mm jaw (approx.)*
☐ *Spark plug spanner (with rubber insert) - petrol models*
☐ *Spark plug gap adjustment tool - petrol models*
☐ *Set of feeler gauges*
☐ *Brake bleed nipple spanner*
☐ *Screwdrivers:*
Flat blade - 100 mm long x 6 mm dia
Cross blade - 100 mm long x 6 mm dia
Torx - various sizes (not all vehicles)
☐ *Combination pliers*
☐ *Hacksaw (junior)*
☐ *Tyre pump*
☐ *Tyre pressure gauge*
☐ *Oil can*
☐ *Oil filter removal tool (if applicable)*
☐ *Fine emery cloth*
☐ *Wire brush (small)*
☐ *Funnel (medium size)*
☐ *Sump drain plug key (not all vehicles)*

Repair and overhaul tool kit

These tools are virtually essential for anyone undertaking any major repairs to a motor vehicle, and are additional to those given in the *Maintenance and minor repair* list. Included in this list is a comprehensive set of sockets. Although these are expensive, they will be found invaluable as they are so versatile - particularly if various drives are included in the set. We recommend the half-inch square-drive type, as this can be used with most proprietary torque wrenches.

The tools in this list will sometimes need to be supplemented by tools from the *Special* list:

☐ *Sockets to cover range in previous list (including Torx sockets)*
☐ *Reversible ratchet drive (for use with sockets)*
☐ *Extension piece, 250 mm (for use with sockets)*
☐ *Universal joint (for use with sockets)*
☐ *Flexible handle or sliding T "breaker bar" (for use with sockets)*
☐ *Torque wrench (for use with sockets)*
☐ *Self-locking grips*
☐ *Ball pein hammer*
☐ *Soft-faced mallet (plastic or rubber)*
☐ *Screwdrivers:*
Flat blade - long & sturdy, short (chubby), and narrow (electrician's) types
Cross blade – long & sturdy, and short (chubby) types
☐ *Pliers:*
Long-nosed
Side cutters (electrician's)
Circlip (internal and external)
☐ *Cold chisel - 25 mm*
☐ *Scriber*
☐ *Scraper*
☐ *Centre-punch*
☐ *Pin punch*
☐ *Hacksaw*
☐ *Brake hose clamp*
☐ *Brake/clutch bleeding kit*
☐ *Selection of twist drills*
☐ *Steel rule/straight-edge*
☐ *Allen keys (inc. splined/Torx type)*
☐ *Selection of files*
☐ *Wire brush*
☐ *Axle stands*
☐ *Jack (strong trolley or hydraulic type)*
☐ *Light with extension lead*
☐ *Universal electrical multi-meter*

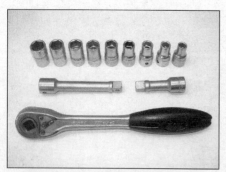
Sockets and reversible ratchet drive

Brake bleeding kit

Torx key, socket and bit

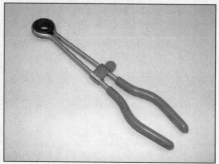
Hose clamp

Angular-tightening gauge

Special tools

The tools in this list are those which are not used regularly, are expensive to buy, or which need to be used in accordance with their manufacturers' instructions. Unless relatively difficult mechanical jobs are undertaken frequently, it will not be economic to buy many of these tools. Where this is the case, you could consider clubbing together with friends (or joining a motorists' club) to make a joint purchase, or borrowing the tools against a deposit from a local garage or tool hire specialist.

The following list contains only those tools and instruments freely available to the public, and not those special tools produced by the vehicle manufacturer specifically for its dealer network. You will find occasional references to these manufacturers' special tools in the text of this manual. Generally, an alternative method of doing the job without the vehicle manufacturers' special tool is given. However, sometimes there is no alternative to using them. Where this is the case and the relevant tool cannot be bought or borrowed, you will have to entrust the work to a dealer.

- [ ] Angular-tightening gauge
- [ ] Valve spring compressor
- [ ] Valve grinding tool
- [ ] Piston ring compressor
- [ ] Piston ring removal/installation tool
- [ ] Cylinder bore hone
- [ ] Balljoint separator
- [ ] Coil spring compressors (where applicable)
- [ ] Two/three-legged hub and bearing puller
- [ ] Impact screwdriver
- [ ] Micrometer and/or vernier calipers
- [ ] Dial gauge
- [ ] Tachometer
- [ ] Fault code reader
- [ ] Cylinder compression gauge
- [ ] Hand-operated vacuum pump and gauge
- [ ] Clutch plate alignment set
- [ ] Brake shoe steady spring cup removal tool
- [ ] Bush and bearing removal/installation set
- [ ] Stud extractors
- [ ] Tap and die set
- [ ] Lifting tackle

Buying tools

Reputable motor accessory shops and superstores often offer excellent quality tools at discount prices, so it pays to shop around.

Remember, you don't have to buy the most expensive items on the shelf, but it is always advisable to steer clear of the very cheap tools. Beware of 'bargains' offered on market stalls, on-line or at car boot sales. There are plenty of good tools around at reasonable prices, but always aim to purchase items which meet the relevant national safety standards. If in doubt, ask the proprietor or manager of the shop for advice before making a purchase.

Care and maintenance of tools

Having purchased a reasonable tool kit, it is necessary to keep the tools in a clean and serviceable condition. After use, always wipe off any dirt, grease and metal particles using a clean, dry cloth, before putting the tools away. Never leave them lying around after they have been used. A simple tool rack on the garage or workshop wall for items such as screwdrivers and pliers is a good idea. Store all normal spanners and sockets in a metal box. Any measuring instruments, gauges, meters, etc, must be carefully stored where they cannot be damaged or become rusty.

Take a little care when tools are used. Hammer heads inevitably become marked, and screwdrivers lose the keen edge on their blades from time to time. A little timely attention with emery cloth or a file will soon restore items like this to a good finish.

Working facilities

Not to be forgotten when discussing tools is the workshop itself. If anything more than routine maintenance is to be carried out, a suitable working area becomes essential.

It is appreciated that many an owner-mechanic is forced by circumstances to remove an engine or similar item without the benefit of a garage or workshop. Having done this, any repairs should always be done under the cover of a roof.

Wherever possible, any dismantling should be done on a clean, flat workbench or table at a suitable working height.

Any workbench needs a vice; one with a jaw opening of 100 mm is suitable for most jobs. As mentioned previously, some clean dry storage space is also required for tools, as well as for any lubricants, cleaning fluids, touch-up paints etc, which become necessary.

Another item which may be required, and which has a much more general usage, is an electric drill with a chuck capacity of at least 8 mm. This, together with a good range of twist drills, is virtually essential for fitting accessories.

Last, but not least, always keep a supply of old newspapers and clean, lint-free rags available, and try to keep any working area as clean as possible.

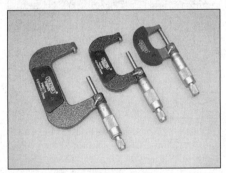

Micrometers

Dial test indicator ("dial gauge")

Oil filter removal tool (strap wrench type)

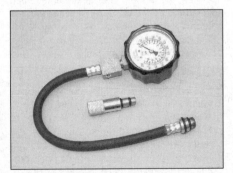

Compression tester

Bearing puller

This is a guide to getting your vehicle through the MOT test. Obviously it will not be possible to examine the vehicle to the same standard as the professional MOT tester. However, working through the following checks will enable you to identify any problem areas before submitting the vehicle for the test.

It has only been possible to summarise the test requirements here, based on the regulations in force at the time of printing. Test standards are becoming increasingly stringent, although there are some exemptions for older vehicles.

An assistant will be needed to help carry out some of these checks.

The checks have been sub-divided into four categories, as follows:

1 Checks carried out **FROM THE DRIVER'S SEAT**

2 Checks carried out **WITH THE VEHICLE ON THE GROUND**

3 Checks carried out **WITH THE VEHICLE RAISED AND THE WHEELS FREE TO TURN**

4 Checks carried out on **YOUR VEHICLE'S EXHAUST EMISSION SYSTEM**

---

1 Checks carried out **FROM THE DRIVER'S SEAT**

Handbrake (parking brake)

☐ Test the operation of the handbrake. Excessive travel (too many clicks) indicates incorrect brake or cable adjustment.
☐ Check that the handbrake cannot be released by tapping the lever sideways. Check the security of the lever mountings.

☐ If the parking brake is foot-operated, check that the pedal is secure and without excessive travel, and that the release mechanism operates correctly.
☐ Where applicable, test the operation of the electronic handbrake. The brake should engage and disengage without excessive delay. If the warning light does not extinguish when the brake is disengaged, this could indicate a fault which will need further investigation.

Footbrake

☐ Depress the brake pedal and check that it does not creep down to the floor, indicating a master cylinder fault. Release the pedal,

wait a few seconds, then depress it again. If the pedal travels nearly to the floor before firm resistance is felt, brake adjustment or repair is necessary. If the pedal feels spongy, there is air in the hydraulic system which must be removed by bleeding.

☐ Check that the brake pedal is secure and in good condition. Check also for signs of fluid leaks on the pedal, floor or carpets, which would indicate failed seals in the brake master cylinder.
☐ Check the servo unit (when applicable) by operating the brake pedal several times, then keeping the pedal depressed and starting the engine. As the engine starts, the pedal will move down slightly. If not, the vacuum hose or the servo itself may be faulty.

Steering wheel and column

☐ Examine the steering wheel for fractures or looseness of the hub, spokes or rim.
☐ Move the steering wheel from side to side and then up and down. Check that the steering wheel is not loose on the column, indicating wear or a loose retaining nut. Continue moving the steering wheel as before, but also turn it slightly from left to right.

☐ Check that the steering wheel is not loose on the column, and that there is no abnormal movement of the steering wheel, indicating wear in the column support bearings or couplings.
☐ Check that the ignition lock (where fitted) engages and disengages correctly.
☐ Steering column adjustment mechanisms (where fitted) must be able to lock the column securely in place with no play evident.

Windscreen, mirrors and sunvisor

☐ The windscreen must be free of cracks or other significant damage within the driver's field of view. (Small stone chips are acceptable.) Rear view mirrors must be secure, intact, and capable of being adjusted.

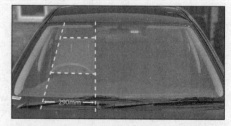

☐ The driver's sunvisor must be capable of being stored in the "up" position.

Seat belts and seats

Note: *The following checks are applicable to all seat belts, front and rear.*

☐ Examine the webbing of all the belts (including rear belts if fitted) for cuts, serious fraying or deterioration. Fasten and unfasten each belt to check the buckles. If applicable, check the retracting mechanism. Check the security of all seat belt mountings accessible from inside the vehicle, ensuring any height adjustable mountings lock securely in place.

☐ Seat belts with pre-tensioners, once activated, have a "flag" or similar showing on the seat belt stalk. This, in itself, is not a reason for test failure.

☐ The front seats themselves must be securely attached and the backrests must lock in the upright position.

Doors

☐ Both front doors must be able to be opened and closed from outside and inside, and must latch securely when closed.

Bonnet and boot/tailgate

☐ The bonnet and boot/tailgate must latch securely when closed.

2 Checks carried out WITH THE VEHICLE ON THE GROUND

Vehicle identification

☐ Number plates must be in good condition, secure and legible, with letters and numbers correctly spaced – spacing at (A) should be 33 mm and at (B) 11 mm. At the front, digits must be black on a white background and at the rear black on a yellow background. Other background designs (such as honeycomb) are not permitted.

☐ The VIN plate and/or homologation plate must be permanently displayed and legible.

Electrical equipment

☐ Switch on the ignition and check the operation of the horn.

☐ Check the windscreen washers and wipers, examining the wiper blades; renew damaged or perished blades. Also check the operation of the stop-lights.

☐ Check the operation of the sidelights and number plate lights. The lenses and reflectors must be secure, clean and undamaged.

☐ Check the operation and alignment of the headlights. The headlight reflectors must not be tarnished and the lenses must be undamaged.

☐ Switch on the ignition and check the operation of the direction indicators (including the instrument panel tell-tale) and the hazard warning lights. Operation of the sidelights and stop-lights must not affect the indicators - if it does, the cause is usually a bad earth at the rear light cluster. Indicators should flash at a rate of between 60 and 120 times per minute – faster or slower than this could indicate a fault with the flasher unit or a bad earth at one of the light units.

☐ Check the operation of the rear foglight(s), including the warning light on the instrument panel or in the switch.

☐ The warning lights must illuminate in accordance with the manufacturer's design. For most vehicles, the ABS and other warning lights should illuminate when the ignition is switched on, and (if the system is operating properly) extinguish after a few seconds. Refer to the owner's handbook.

Footbrake

☐ Examine the master cylinder, brake pipes and servo unit for leaks, loose mountings, corrosion or other damage. If ABS is fitted, this unit should also be examined for signs of leaks or corrosion.

☐ The fluid reservoir must be secure and the fluid level must be between the upper (A) and lower (B) markings.

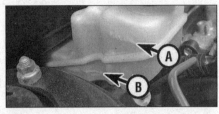

☐ Inspect both front brake flexible hoses for cracks or deterioration of the rubber. Turn the steering from lock to lock, and ensure that the hoses do not contact the wheel, tyre, or any part of the steering or suspension mechanism. With the brake pedal firmly depressed, check the hoses for bulges or leaks under pressure.

Steering and suspension

☐ Have your assistant turn the steering wheel from side to side slightly, up to the point where the steering gear just begins to transmit this movement to the roadwheels. Check for excessive free play between the steering wheel and the steering gear, indicating wear or insecurity of the steering column joints, the column-to-steering gear coupling, or the steering gear itself.

☐ Have your assistant turn the steering wheel more vigorously in each direction, so that the roadwheels just begin to turn. As this is done, examine all the steering joints, linkages, fittings and attachments. Renew any component that shows signs of wear or damage. On vehicles with power steering, check the security and condition of the steering pump, drivebelt and hoses.

☐ Check that the vehicle is standing level, and at approximately the correct ride height.

Shock absorbers

☐ Depress each corner of the vehicle in turn, then release it. The vehicle should rise and then settle in its normal position. If the vehicle continues to rise and fall, the shock absorber is defective. A shock absorber which has seized will also cause the vehicle to fail.

Exhaust system

☐ Start the engine. With your assistant holding a rag over the tailpipe, check the entire system for leaks. Repair or renew leaking sections.

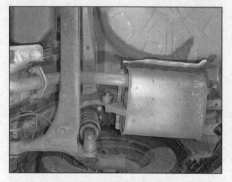

3 Checks carried out **WITH THE VEHICLE RAISED AND THE WHEELS FREE TO TURN**

Jack up the front and rear of the vehicle, and securely support it on axle stands. Position the stands clear of the suspension assemblies. Ensure that the wheels are clear of the ground and that the steering can be turned from lock to lock.

Steering mechanism

☐ Have your assistant turn the steering from lock to lock. Check that the steering turns smoothly, and that no part of the steering mechanism, including a wheel or tyre, fouls any brake hose or pipe or any part of the body structure.

☐ Examine the steering rack rubber gaiters for damage or insecurity of the retaining clips. If power steering is fitted, check for signs of damage or leakage of the fluid hoses, pipes or connections. Also check for excessive stiffness or binding of the steering, a missing split pin or locking device, or severe corrosion of the body structure within 30 cm of any steering component attachment point.

Front and rear suspension and wheel bearings

☐ Starting at the front right-hand side, grasp the roadwheel at the 3 o'clock and 9 o'clock positions and rock gently but firmly. Check for free play or insecurity at the wheel bearings, suspension balljoints, or suspension mount-ings, pivots and attachments.

☐ Now grasp the wheel at the 12 o'clock and 6 o'clock positions and repeat the previous inspection. Spin the wheel, and check for roughness or tightness of the front wheel bearing.

☐ If excess free play is suspected at a component pivot point, this can be confirmed by using a large screwdriver or similar tool and levering between the mounting and the component attachment. This will confirm whether the wear is in the pivot bush, its retaining bolt, or in the mounting itself (the bolt holes can often become elongated).

☐ Carry out all the above checks at the other front wheel, and then at both rear wheels.

Springs and shock absorbers

☐ Examine the suspension struts (when applicable) for serious fluid leakage, corrosion, or damage to the casing. Also check the security of the mounting points.

☐ If coil springs are fitted, check that the spring ends locate in their seats, and that the spring is not corroded, cracked or broken.

☐ If leaf springs are fitted, check that all leaves are intact, that the axle is securely attached to each spring, and that there is no deterioration of the spring eye mountings, bushes, and shackles.

☐ The same general checks apply to vehicles fitted with other suspension types, such as torsion bars, hydraulic displacer units, etc. Ensure that all mountings and attachments are secure, that there are no signs of excessive wear, corrosion or damage, and (on hydraulic types) that there are no fluid leaks or damaged pipes.

☐ Inspect the shock absorbers for signs of serious fluid leakage. Check for wear of the mounting bushes or attachments, or damage to the body of the unit.

Driveshafts (fwd vehicles only)

☐ Rotate each front wheel in turn and inspect the constant velocity joint gaiters for splits or damage. Also check that each driveshaft is straight and undamaged.

Braking system

☐ If possible without dismantling, check brake pad wear and disc condition. Ensure that the friction lining material has not worn excessively, (A) and that the discs are not fractured, pitted, scored or badly worn (B).

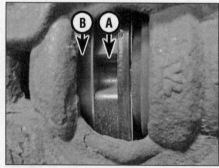

☐ Examine all the rigid brake pipes underneath the vehicle, and the flexible hose(s) at the rear. Look for corrosion, chafing or insecurity of the pipes, and for signs of bulging under pressure, chafing, splits or deterioration of the flexible hoses.

☐ Look for signs of fluid leaks at the brake calipers or on the brake backplates. Repair or renew leaking components.

☐ Slowly spin each wheel, while your assistant depresses and releases the footbrake. Ensure that each brake is operating and does not bind when the pedal is released.

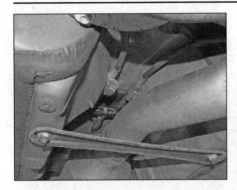

black smoke means unburnt fuel (dirty air cleaner element, or other fuel system fault).

☐ An exhaust gas analyser for measuring carbon monoxide (CO) and hydrocarbons (HC) is now needed. If one cannot be hired or borrowed, have a local garage perform the check.

CO emissions (mixture)

☐ The MOT tester has access to the CO limits for all vehicles. The CO level is measured at idle speed, and at 'fast idle' (2500 to 3000 rpm). The following limits are given as a general guide:

At idle speed – Less than 0.5% CO
At 'fast idle' – Less than 0.3% CO
Lambda reading – 0.97 to 1.03

☐ If the CO level is too high, this may point to poor maintenance, a fuel injection system problem, faulty lambda (oxygen) sensor or catalytic converter. Try an injector cleaning treatment, and check the vehicle's ECU for fault codes.

HC emissions

☐ The MOT tester has access to HC limits for all vehicles. The HC level is measured at 'fast idle' (2500 to 3000 rpm). The following limits are given as a general guide:

At 'fast idle' – Less then 200 ppm

☐ Excessive HC emissions are typically caused by oil being burnt (worn engine), or by a blocked crankcase ventilation system ('breather'). If the engine oil is old and thin, an oil change may help. If the engine is running badly, check the vehicle's ECU for fault codes.

Diesel models

☐ The only emission test for diesel engines is measuring exhaust smoke density, using a calibrated smoke meter. The test involves accelerating the engine at least 3 times to its maximum unloaded speed.

Note: *On engines with a timing belt, it is VITAL that the belt is in good condition before the test is carried out.*

☐ With the engine warmed up, it is first purged by running at around 2500 rpm for 20 seconds. A governor check is then carried out, by slowly accelerating the engine to its maximum speed. After this, the smoke meter is connected, and the engine is accelerated quickly to maximum speed three times. If the smoke density is less than the limits given below, the vehicle will pass:

Non-turbo vehicles: 2.5m-1
Turbocharged vehicles: 3.0m-1

☐ If excess smoke is produced, try fitting a new air cleaner element, or using an injector cleaning treatment. If the engine is running badly, where applicable, check the vehicle's ECU for fault codes. Also check the vehicle's EGR system, where applicable. At high mileages, the injectors may require professional attention.

☐ Examine the handbrake mechanism, checking for frayed or broken cables, excessive corrosion, or wear or insecurity of the linkage. Check that the mechanism works on each relevant wheel, and releases fully, without binding.

☐ It is not possible to test brake efficiency without special equipment, but a road test can be carried out later to check that the vehicle pulls up in a straight line.

Fuel and exhaust systems

☐ Inspect the fuel tank (including the filler cap), fuel pipes, hoses and unions. All components must be secure and free from leaks. Locking fuel caps must lock securely and the key must be provided for the MOT test.

☐ Examine the exhaust system over its entire length, checking for any damaged, broken or missing mountings, security of the retaining clamps and rust or corrosion.

Wheels and tyres

☐ Examine the sidewalls and tread area of each tyre in turn. Check for cuts, tears, lumps, bulges, separation of the tread, and exposure of the ply or cord due to wear or damage. Check that the tyre bead is correctly seated on the wheel rim, that the valve is sound and properly seated, and that the wheel is not distorted or damaged.

☐ Check that the tyres are of the correct size for the vehicle, that they are of the same size and type on each axle, and that the pressures are correct.

☐ Check the tyre tread depth. The legal minimum at the time of writing is 1.6 mm over the central three-quarters of the tread width. Abnormal tread wear may indicate incorrect front wheel alignment or wear in steering or suspension components.

☐ If the spare wheel is fitted externally or in a separate carrier beneath the vehicle, check that mountings are secure and free of excessive corrosion.

Body corrosion

☐ Check the condition of the entire vehicle structure for signs of corrosion in load-bearing areas. (These include chassis box sections, side sills, cross-members, pillars, and all suspension, steering, braking system and seat belt mountings and anchorages.) Any corrosion which has seriously reduced the thickness of a load-bearing area (or is within 30 cm of safety-related components such as steering or suspension) is likely to cause the vehicle to fail. In this case professional repairs are likely to be needed.

☐ Damage or corrosion which causes sharp or otherwise dangerous edges to be exposed will also cause the vehicle to fail.

Towbars

☐ Check the condition of mounting points (both beneath the vehicle and within boot/hatchback areas) for signs of corrosion, ensuring that all fixings are secure and not worn or damaged. There must be no excessive play in detachable tow ball arms or quick-release mechanisms.

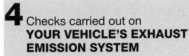

4 Checks carried out on YOUR VEHICLE'S EXHAUST EMISSION SYSTEM

Petrol models

☐ The engine should be warmed up, and running well (ignition system in good order, air filter element clean, etc).

☐ Before testing, run the engine at around 2500 rpm for 20 seconds. Let the engine drop to idle, and watch for smoke from the exhaust. If the idle speed is too high, or if dense blue or black smoke emerges for more than 5 seconds, the vehicle will fail. Typically, blue smoke signifies oil burning (engine wear);

Engine

- ☐ Engine fails to rotate when attempting to start
- ☐ Engine rotates, but will not start
- ☐ Engine difficult to start when cold
- ☐ Engine difficult to start when hot
- ☐ Starter motor noisy or excessively rough in engagement
- ☐ Engine starts, but stops immediately
- ☐ Engine idles erratically
- ☐ Engine misfires at idle speed
- ☐ Engine misfires throughout the driving speed range
- ☐ Engine lacks power
- ☐ Engine backfires
- ☐ Oil pressure warning light illuminated with engine running
- ☐ Engine runs-on after switching off
- ☐ Tapping or rattling noises
- ☐ Knocking or thumping noises
- ☐ Pre-ignition (pinking) or knocking during acceleration or under load
- ☐ Whistling or wheezing noises

Cooling system

- ☐ Overheating
- ☐ Overcooling
- ☐ External coolant leakage
- ☐ Internal coolant leakage
- ☐ Corrosion

Fuel and exhaust systems

- ☐ Excessive fuel consumption
- ☐ Fuel leakage and/or fuel odour
- ☐ Excessive noise or fumes from the exhaust system

Clutch

- ☐ Pedal travels to the floor – no pressure or very little resistance
- ☐ Clutch fails to disengage (unable to select gears)
- ☐ Clutch slips (engine speed increases, with no increase in vehicle speed)
- ☐ Judder as clutch is engaged
- ☐ Noise when depressing or releasing clutch pedal

Manual transmission

- ☐ Noisy in neutral with the engine running
- ☐ Noisy in one particular gear
- ☐ Difficulty in engaging gears
- ☐ Jumps out of gear
- ☐ Vibration
- ☐ Lubricant leaks

Driveshafts

- ☐ Vibration when accelerating or decelerating
- ☐ Clicking or knocking noise on turns (at slow speed on full-lock)

Braking system

- ☐ Vehicle pulls to one side under braking
- ☐ Noise (grinding or high-pitched squeal) when brakes applied
- ☐ Excessive brake pedal travel
- ☐ Brake pedal feels spongy when depressed
- ☐ Excessive brake pedal effort required to stop vehicle
- ☐ Judder felt through brake pedal or steering wheel when braking
- ☐ Pedal pulsates when braking hard
- ☐ Brakes binding

Steering and suspension

- ☐ Vehicle pulls to one side
- ☐ Wheel wobble and vibration
- ☐ Excessive pitching and/or rolling around corners, or during braking
- ☐ Wandering or general instablity
- ☐ Excessively stiff steering
- ☐ Excessive play in steering
- ☐ Lack of power assistance
- ☐ Tyre wear excessive

Electrical system

- ☐ Battery will not hold charge for more than a few days
- ☐ Ignition/no-charge warning light remains illuminated with the engine running
- ☐ Lights inoperative
- ☐ Fuel or temperature gauge inaccurate
- ☐ Horn operates continuously
- ☐ Horn inoperative
- ☐ Wipers fail to operate, or operate very slowly
- ☐ Wiper blades sweep over too large, or too small an area of glass
- ☐ Wiper blades fail to clean the glass effectively
- ☐ Screen or headlight washers inoperative, or unsatisfactory in operation
- ☐ Window glass moves only in one direction
- ☐ Window glass slow to move
- ☐ Window glass fails to move
- ☐ Central locking system inoperative, or unsatisfactory in operation.

Introduction

The vehicle owner who does his or her own maintenance according to the recommended service schedules should not have to use this section of the manual very often. Modern component reliability is such that, provided those items subject to wear or deterioration are inspected or renewed at the specified intervals, sudden failure is comparatively rare. Faults do not usually just happen as a result of sudden failure, but develop over a period of time. Major mechanical failures in particular are usually preceded by characteristic symptoms over hundreds or even thousands of miles. Those components which do occasionally fail without warning are often small and easily carried in the vehicle.

With any fault-finding, the first step is to decide where to begin investigations. Sometimes this is obvious, but on other occasions, a little detective work will be necessary. The owner who makes half a dozen haphazard adjustments or replacements may be successful in curing a fault (or its symptoms), but will be none the wiser if the fault recurs, and ultimately may have spent more time and money than was necessary.

A calm and logical approach will be found to be more satisfactory in the long run. Always take into account any warning signs or abnormalities that may have been noticed in the period preceding the fault – power loss, high or low gauge readings, unusual smells, etc – and remember that failure of components such as fuses or spark plugs may only be pointers to some underlying fault.

The pages which follow provide an easy-reference guide to the more common problems which may occur during the operation of the vehicle. These problems and their possible causes are grouped under headings denoting various components or systems, such as Engine, Cooling system, etc. The Chapter and/or Section which deals with the problem is also shown in brackets. Whatever the fault, certain basic principles apply. These are as follows:

Verify the fault. This is simply a matter of being sure that you know what the symptoms are before starting work. This is particularly important if you are investigating a fault for someone else, who may not have described it very accurately.

Don't overlook the obvious. For example, if the vehicle won't start, is there fuel in the tank? (Don't take anyone else's word on this particular point, and don't trust the fuel gauge either!) If an electrical fault is indicated, look for loose or broken wires before digging out the test gear.

Cure the disease, not the symptom. Substituting a flat battery with a fully-charged one will get you off the hard shoulder, but if the underlying cause is not attended to, the new battery will go the same way. Similarly, changing oil-fouled spark plugs for a new set will get you moving again, but remember that the reason for the fouling (if it wasn't simply an incorrect grade of plug) will have to be established and corrected.

Don't take anything for granted. Particularly, don't forget that a 'new' component may itself be defective (especially if it's been rattling around in the boot for months), and don't leave components out of a fault diagnosis sequence just because they are new or recently-fitted. When you do finally diagnose a difficult fault, you'll probably realise that all the evidence was there from the start.

Engine

Engine fails to rotate when attempting to start

- ☐ Battery terminal connections loose or corroded (Chapter 5A Section 4).
- ☐ Battery discharged or faulty (Chapter 5A Section 3).
- ☐ Broken, loose or disconnected wiring in the starting circuit (Chapter 12 Section 2).
- ☐ Defective starter solenoid or switch (Chapter 5A Section 2).
- ☐ Defective starter motor (Chapter 5A Section 8).
- ☐ Starter pinion or flywheel ring gear teeth loose or broken (Chapter 2A Section 12 or Chapter 5A Section 8).
- ☐ Engine earth strap broken or disconnected (Chapter 12 Section 2).

Engine rotates, but will not start

- ☐ Fuel tank empty.
- ☐ Battery discharged (engine rotates slowly) (Chapter 5A Section 3).
- ☐ Battery terminals loose or corroded (*Weekly checks*).
- ☐ Ignition components damp or damaged (Chapter 0 Section 4 and Chapter 5B Section 2).
- ☐ Fuel injection system faulty (Chapter 4A Section 9).
- ☐ Worn or faulty spark plugs (Chapter 1 Section 15).
- ☐ Major mechanical failure (Chapter 2A).

Engine difficult to start when cold

- ☐ Battery discharged (Chapter 5A Section 3).
- ☐ Battery terminal connections loose or corroded (*Weekly checks*).
- ☐ Worn or faulty spark plugs (Chapter 1 Section 15).
- ☐ Other ignition system fault (Chapter 5B Section 2 or Chapter 1 Section 16).
- ☐ Fuel injection system faulty (Chapter 4A Section 9).
- ☐ Low cylinder compressions (Chapter 2A Section 2).

Engine difficult to start when hot

- ☐ Air filter element dirty or clogged (Chapter 1 Section 21).
- ☐ Fuel injection system faulty (Chapter 4A Section 9).
- ☐ Low cylinder compressions (Chapter 2A Section 2).

Starter motor noisy or excessively rough in engagement

- ☐ Starter pinion or flywheel ring gear teeth loose or broken (Chapter 5A Section 7 or Chapter 2A Section 12).
- ☐ Starter motor mounting bolts loose or missing (Chapter 5A Section 8).
- ☐ Starter motor internal components worn or damaged (Chapter 5A Section 9).

Engine starts, but stops immediately

- ☐ Blocked injector/fuel injection system fault (Chapter 4A).
- ☐ Loose or faulty electrical connections in the ignition circuit (Chapter 1 or Chapter 5B).
- ☐ Vacuum leak at the throttle body or intake manifold (Chapter 4A Section 10 or Chapter 4A Section 11).
- ☐ Immobiliser fault – refer to a Hyundai dealer or specialist.

Engine idles erratically

- ☐ Air filter element clogged (Chapter 1 Section 21).
- ☐ Uneven or low compressions (Chapter 2A Section 2).
- ☐ Vacuum leak at throttle body, intake manifold or associated hoses (Chapter 4A Section 10 or Chapter 4A Section 11).
- ☐ Camshaft lobes worn (Chapter 2A Section 10).
- ☐ Blocked injector/fuel injection system fault (Chapter 4A).
- ☐ Worn or faulty spark plugs (Chapter 1 Section 15).
- ☐ Timing chain incorrectly fitted (Chapter 2A Section 5).

Engine (continued)

Engine misfires at idle speed

- [ ] Faulty injectors/fuel injection system fault (Chapter 4A).
- [ ] Worn or faulty spark plugs (Chapter 1 Section 15).
- [ ] Vacuum leaks at the throttle body, intake manifold or associated hoses (Chapter 4A Section 10 or Chapter 4A Section 11).
- [ ] Uneven or low compressions (Chapter 2A Section 2).
- [ ] Disconnected, leaking or perished crankcase ventilation hoses (Chapter 4B).

Engine misfires throughout the driving speed range

- [ ] Fuel pump faulty, or delivery pressure low (Chapter 4A Section 7).
- [ ] Fuel tank vent blocked, or fuel pipes restricted (Chapter 4A Section 8).
- [ ] Vacuum leak at the throttle body, intake manifold or associated hoses (Chapter 4A Section 10 or Chapter 4A Section 11).
- [ ] Worn or faulty spark plugs (Chapter 1 Section 15).
- [ ] Faulty ignition coil (Chapter 5B Section 3).
- [ ] Fault injector/fuel injection system fault (Chapter 4A).
- [ ] Uneven or low compressions (Chapter 2A Section 2).

Engine lacks power

- [ ] Timing chain incorrectly fitted (Chapter 2A Section 5).
- [ ] Fuel pump faulty (Chapter 4A Section 7).
- [ ] Air filter blocked (Chapter 1 Section 21).
- [ ] Uneven or low compressions (Chapter 2A Section 2).
- [ ] Faulty injectors/injection system fault (Chapter 4A).
- [ ] Brakes binding (Chapter 9).
- [ ] Clutch slipping (Chapter 6).
- [ ] Worn or faulty spark plugs (Chapter 1 Section 15).

Engine backfires

- [ ] Timing chain incorrectly fitted (Chapter 2A Section 5).
- [ ] Vacuum leak at the throttle body, intake manifold or associated hoses (Chapter 4A Section 10 or Chapter 4A Section 11).
- [ ] Blocked injector/fuel injection system fault (Chapter 4A).

Oil pressure warning light illuminated with engine running

- [ ] Low oil level, or incorrect oil grade (*Weekly checks*).

- [ ] Faulty oil pressure sensor (Chapter 2A Section 16).
- [ ] Worn engine bearings and/or oil pump (Chapter 2B).
- [ ] High engine operating temperature (Chapter 3).
- [ ] Oil pressure relief valve defective (Chapter 2A Section 15).
- [ ] Oil pick up strainer clogged (Chapter 2A Section 14).

Engine runs-on after switching off

- [ ] Excessive carbon build-up in engine (Chapter 2B).
- [ ] High engine operating temperature (Chapter 3).
- [ ] Fuel injection system fault (Chapter 4A).
- [ ] Incorrect oil level (*Weekly checks*).

Tapping or rattling noises

- [ ] Worn valve gear or camshaft (Chapter 2A Section 10).
- [ ] Ancillary component fault (coolant pump, alternator etc.) (Chapter 3 and Chapter 5A).

Knocking or thumping noises

- [ ] Worn big-end bearings (regular heavy knocking, perhaps more under load) (Chapter 2B).
- [ ] Worn main bearings (rumbling and knocking, perhaps less under load) (Chapter 2B).
- [ ] Piston slap (most noticeable when cold) (Chapter 2B).
- [ ] Ancillary component fault (coolant pump, alternator, etc.) (Chapter 3 and Chapter 5A).

Pre-ignition (pinking) or knocking during acceleration or under load

- [ ] Ignition timing incorrect/ignition system fault (Chapter 5B Section 2).
- [ ] Incorrect grade of spark plug (Chapter 1 Section 15).
- [ ] Vacuum leak at the throttle body, intake manifold or associated hoses (Chapter 4A Section 10 or Chapter 4A Section 11).
- [ ] Excessive carbon build-up in the cylinder head (Chapter 2B Section 7).

Whistling or wheezing noises

- [ ] Leaking intake manifold or throttle body gasket (Chapter 4A Section 10 or Chapter 4A Section 11).
- [ ] Leaking exhaust manifold or pipe-to-manifold joint (Chapter 4A).
- [ ] Leaking vacuum hose.

Cooling system

Overheating

☐ Insufficient coolant in the system (*Weekly checks*).
☐ Thermostat faulty (Chapter 3 Section 4).
☐ Radiator core blocked, or grille restricted (Chapter 3 Section 3).
☐ Electric cooling fan faulty (Chapter 3 Section 5).
☐ Air lock in cooling system (Chapter 1 Section 25).
☐ Expansion tank pressure cap faulty (Chapter 1 Section 25).
☐ Engine coolant temperature sensor faulty (Chapter 3 Section 6).

Overcooling

☐ Thermostat faulty (Chapter 3 Section 4).
☐ Engine coolant temperature sensor faulty (Chapter 3 Section 6).

External coolant leakage

☐ Deteriorated or damaged hoses or hose clips (Chapter 3 Section 2).
☐ Radiator core or heater matrix leaking (Chapter 3 Section 8).
☐ Pressure cap faulty (Chapter 1 Section 25).
☐ Coolant pump leaking (Chapter 3 Section 7).
☐ Boiling due to overheating.Core plug leaking (Chapter 2B Section 11).

Internal coolant leakage

☐ Leaking cylinder head gasket (Chapter 2A Section 11).
☐ Cracked cylinder head or cylinder block (Chapter 2B).

Corrosion

☐ Infrequent draining and flushing (Chapter 1 Section 25).
☐ Incorrect coolant mixture or inappropriate coolant type (Chapter 1 Section 25)

Fuel and exhaust systems

Excessive fuel consumption

☐ Air filter dirty or clogged (Chapter 1 Section 21).
☐ Faulty injector/fuel injection system fault (Chapter 4A).
☐ Brakes binding (Chapter 9).
☐ Tyres under-inflated (*Weekly checks*).

Fuel leakage and/or fuel odour

☐ Damaged or corroded fuel tank, pipes or connections (Chapter 4A).

Excessive noise or fumes from the exhaust system

☐ Leaking exhaust system or manifold leaks (Chapter 4A).
☐ Leaking or corroded silencers or pipe (Chapter 4A Section 13).
☐ Broken mountings causing body or suspension contact (Chapter 4A Section 13).

Clutch

Pedal travels to the floor – no pressure or very little resistance

- [ ] Broken clutch cable (Chapter 6 Section 2).
- [ ] Broken clutch release bearing (Chapter 6 Section 4).
- [ ] Broken diaphragm spring in clutch pressure plate (Chapter 6 Section 3).

Clutch fails to disengage (unable to select gears)

- [ ] Faulty or seize clutch cable (Chapter 6 Section 2).
- [ ] Clutch disc sticking on the gearbox input shaft splines (Chapter 6 Section 3).
- [ ] Clutch disc sticking on the flywheel or pressure plate (Chapter 6 Section 3).
- [ ] Faulty pressure plate assembly (Chapter 6 Section 3).

Clutch slips (engine speed increases, with no increase in vehicle speed)

- [ ] Clutch disc linings excessively worn (Chapter 6 Section 3).
- [ ] Clutch disc lining contaminated with oil or grease (Chapter 6 Section 3).

- [ ] Faulty pressure plate or weak diaphragm spring (Chapter 6 Section 3).

Judder as clutch is engaged

- [ ] Clutch disc linings contaminated with oil or grease (Chapter 6 Section 3).
- [ ] Clutch disc linings excessively worn (Chapter 6 Section 3).
- [ ] Faulty or distorted pressure plate or diaphragm spring (Chapter 6 Section 3).
- [ ] Worn or loose engine or gearbox mountings (Chapter 2A Section 13).
- [ ] Clutch disc or gearbox input shaft splines worn (Chapter 6 Section 3).

Noise when depressing or releasing clutch pedal

- [ ] Worn clutch release bearing (Chapter 6 Section 4).
- [ ] Worn or dry clutch pedal pivot (Chapter 6 Section 2).
- [ ] Faulty pressure plate assembly (Chapter 6 Section 3).
- [ ] Pressure plate diaphragm spring broken (Chapter 6 Section 3).

Manual transmission

Noisy in neutral with the engine running

- [ ] Input shaft bearings worn (noise apparent with clutch pedal released, but not when depressed) (Chapter 7A Section 6).*
- [ ] Clutch release bearings worn (noise apparent with clutch pedal depressed, possibly less when released (Section).

Noisy in one particular gear

- [ ] Worn, damaged or chipped gear teeth (Chapter 7A Section 6).*

Difficulty in engaging gears

- [ ] Clutch faulty (Chapter 6).
- [ ] Worn synchroniser units (Chapter 7A Section 6).*

Jumps out of gear

- [ ] Worn synchroniser units (Chapter 7A Section 6).*
- [ ] Worn selector forks (Chapter 7A Section 6).*

Vibration

- [ ] Lack of oil (Chapter 7A Section 2).
- [ ] Worn bearings (Chapter 7A Section 6).*

Lubricant leaks

- [ ] Leaking oil seal.Leaking housing joint (Chapter 7A Section 6).*
- [ ] Leaking input shaft oil seal (Chapter 7A).

Note: *Although the corrective action necessary to remedy the symptoms described in beyond the scope of the home mechanic, then above information should be helpful in isolating the cause of the condition, so that the owner can communicate clearly with a professional mechanic.*

Driveshafts

Vibration when accelerating or decelerating

- ☐ Worn constant velocity joint (Chapter 8 Section 2).
- ☐ Bent or distorted driveshaft (Chapter 8 Section 2).

Clicking or knocking noise on turns (at slow speed on full-lock)

- ☐ Lack of constant velocity joint lubricant, possible due to damaged gaiter (Chapter 8 Section 4).
- ☐ Worn constant velocity joint (Chapter 8 Section 4).

Braking system

Vehicle pulls to one side under braking

- ☐ Worn, defective, damaged or contaminated brake pads/shoes on one side (Chapter 9 Section 4 or Chapter 9 Section 8).
- ☐ Seized or partially seized brake caliper/wheel cylinder piston (Chapter 9 Section 6 or Chapter 9 Section 9).
- ☐ A mixture of brake pad/shoe lining materials fitted between sides (Chapter 9 Section 4 or Chapter 9 Section 8).
- ☐ Brake caliper mounting bolts loose (Chapter 9 Section 6).
- ☐ Worn or damaged steering or suspension components (Chapter 10).

Noise (grinding or high-pitched squeal) when brakes applied

- ☐ Brake pad/shoe friction material worn down to metal backing (Chapter 9 Section 4 or Chapter 9 Section 8).
- ☐ Excessive corrosion of brake disc/shoe – may be apparent after the vehicle has been standing for some time (Chapter 9 Section 5 or Chapter 9 Section 7).
- ☐ Foreign object (stone chipping, etc.) trapped between the brake disc and shield.

Excessive brake pedal travel

- ☐ Faulty master cylinder (Chapter 9 Section 10).
- ☐ Air in hydraulic system (Chapter 9 Section 2).
- ☐ Faulty vacuum servo unit (Chapter 9 Section 17).

Brake pedal feels spongy when depressed

- ☐ Air in hydraulic system (Chapter 9 Section 2).
- ☐ Deteriorated flexible rubber brake hoses (Chapter 9 Section 3).
- ☐ Master cylinder mountings loose (Chapter 9 Section 10).
- ☐ Faulty master cylinder (Chapter 9 Section 10).

Excessive brake pedal effort required to stop vehicle

- ☐ Faulty vacuum servo unit.Faulty servo unit check valve (Chapter 9 Section 17).

- ☐ Disconnected, damaged or insecure brake servo vacuum hose (Chapter 9 Section 17).
- ☐ Faulty brake pipe or hose (Chapter 9 Section 3).
- ☐ Seized brake caliper/wheel cylinder (Chapter 9 Section 6 or Chapter 9 Section 9).
- ☐ Brake pads/shoes incorrectly fitted (Chapter 9 Section 4 or Chapter 9 Section 8).
- ☐ Incorrect grade of brake pads/shoes fitted (Chapter 9 Section 4 or Chapter 9 Section 8).
- ☐ Brake pads/shoes contaminated (Chapter 9 Section 4 or Chapter 9 Section 8).

Judder felt through brake pedal or steering wheel when braking

- ☐ Excessive run-out or distortion of brake disc/drum (Chapter 9 Section 5 or Chapter 9 Section 7).
- ☐ Brake pad/shoe linings worn (Chapter 9 Section 4 or Chapter 9 Section 8).
- ☐ Brake caliper mountings loose (Chapter 9 Section 6).
- ☐ Wear in suspension or steering components or mountings (Chapter 10).

Pedal pulsates when braking hard

- ☐ Normal feature of ABS – no fault.

Brakes binding

- ☐ Seized brake caliper/wheel cylinder (Chapter 9 Section 6 or Chapter 9 Section 9).
- ☐ Incorrectly adjusted parking brake (Chapter 9 Section 13).
- ☐ Faulty master cylinder (Chapter 9 Section 10).

Note: *Before assuming that a brake problem exists, make sure that the tyres are in good condition and correctly inflated, that the front wheel alignment is correct, and that the vehicle is not loaded with weight in an unequal manner. Apart from checking the condition of all pipe and hose connections, any faults occurring on the anti-lock braking system should be referred to a Mercedes dealer or specialist for diagnosis.*

Steering and suspension

Vehicle pulls to one side

☐ Defective tyre (*Weekly checks*).
☐ Excessive wear in suspension or steering components (Chapter 1 Section 9).
☐ Incorrect front wheel alignment (Chapter 10 Section 18).
☐ Accident damage to steering or suspension components.

Wheel wobble and vibration

☐ Front roadwheels out of balance (vibration felt mainly through the steering wheel).
☐ Rear roadwheels out of balance (vibration felt mainly throughout the vehicle).
☐ Roadwheels damaged or distorted.
☐ Faulty or damaged tyre (*Weekly checks*).
☐ Worn steering or suspension joints, bushes or components (Chapter 1 Section 9).
☐ Wheel bolts loose.

Excessive pitching and/or rolling around corners, or during braking

☐ Defective shock absorbers (Chapter 1 Section 9).
☐ Broken or weak coil spring and/or suspension components (Chapter 10).
☐ Worn or damaged anti-roll bar or mountings (Chapter 10 Section 8).

Wandering or general instablity

☐ Incorrect wheel alignment (Chapter 10 Section 18).
☐ Worn steering or suspension components (Chapter 1 Section 9).
☐ Roadwheels out of balance.
☐ Faulty or damaged tyre (*Weekly checks*).
☐ Wheel bolts loose.
☐ Defective shock absorbers (Chapter 1 Section 9).

Excessively stiff steering

☐ Seized track rod end balljoint or suspension balljoint (Chapter 10).
☐ Incorrect front wheel alignment (Chapter 10 Section 18).
☐ Steering rack damaged (Chapter 10 Section 15).
☐ Faulty power steering assembly (Chapter 10 Section 13).

Excessive play in steering

☐ Worn steering column universal joints (Chapter 10 Section 13).
☐ Worn steering track rod end balljoints (Chapter 10 Section 17).
☐ Worn steering gear (Chapter 10 Section 15).
☐ Worn steering or suspension joints, bushes or components (Chapter 10).

Lack of power assistance

☐ Faulty electronic power steering motor or control unit (Chapter 10 Section 14).

Tyre wear excessive

☐ Tyres under inflated (wear on both edges) (*Weekly checks*).
☐ Incorrect camber or castor angles (wear on one edge) (Chapter 10 Section 18).
☐ Worn steering or suspension joints, bushes or components (Chapter 1 Section 9).
☐ Accident damage.
☐ Incorrect wheel alignment (feathered edges) (Chapter 10 Section 18).
☐ Tyres over-inflated (worn in centre of tread) (*Weekly checks*).
☐ Worn shock absorbers (Chapter 10 Section 4).
☐ Tyres/wheel out of balance (tyres worn unevenly).
☐ Tyre/wheel damage (*Weekly checks*).

Electrical system

Battery will not hold charge for more than a few days

☐ Battery defective internally (Chapter 5A Section 3).
☐ Battery terminal connections loose or corroded (*Weekly checks*).
☐ Auxiliary drivebelt worn or incorrectly tensioned (Chapter 1 Section 5).
☐ Alternator not charging at correct output (Chapter 5A Section 5).
☐ Short circuit causing continual current drain (Chapter 12 Section 2).

Ignition/no-charge warning light remains illuminated with the engine running

☐ Auxiliary drivebelt broken, worn, or incorrectly adjusted (Chapter 1 Section 5).
☐ Internal fault in alternator or voltage regulator (Chapter 5A Section 6).
☐ Broken, disconnected, or loose wiring in charging circuit (Chapter 12 Section 2).

Lights inoperative

☐ Blown bulb (Chapter 12 Section 6).
☐ Corrosion of bulbholder contacts (Chapter 12 Section 6).
☐ Blown fuse (Chapter 12 Section 3).
☐ Faulty relay (Chapter 12 Section 3).
☐ Broken, loose or disconnected wiring (Chapter 12 Section 2).
☐ Faulty switch (Chapter 12 Section 5).

Fuel or temperature gauge inaccurate

☐ Faulty fuel level sensor (Chapter 4A Section 7).
☐ Faulty engine coolant temperature sensor (Chapter 3 Section 6).
☐ Faulty instrument cluster (Chapter 12 Section 11).

Horn operates continuously

☐ Horn contacts faulty (Chapter 12 Section 5).

Horn inoperative

☐ Horn switch contact faulty (Chapter 12 Section 5).
☐ Horn faulty (Chapter 12 Section 12).
☐ Fuse blown (Chapter 12 Section 3).

Wipers fail to operate, or operate very slowly

☐ Wiper blades stuck to screen, or seized linkage (Chapter 12 Section 15).
☐ Blown fuse (Chapter 12 Section 3).
☐ Faulty relay (Chapter 12 Section 3).
☐ Faulty wiper motor (Chapter 12 Section 15).

Wiper blades sweep over too large, or too small an area of glass

☐ Wiper arms incorrectly positioned on spindles (Chapter 12 Section 14).
☐ Excessive wear of wiper linkage (Chapter 12 Section 15).
☐ Wiper motor or linkage mountings loose (Chapter 12 Section 15).

Wiper blades fail to clean the glass effectively

☐ Wiper blade rubbers worn or perished (*Weekly checks*).
☐ Wiper arms defective (Chapter 12 Section 14).
☐ Insufficient windscreen washer additive to adequately remove road film (*Weekly checks*).

Screen or headlight washers inoperative, or unsatisfactory in operation

☐ Blocked washer jet (Chapter 12 Section 16).
☐ Disconnected, kinked or restricted fluid hose.
☐ Insufficient fluid in washer reservoir (*Weekly checks*).
☐ Blown fuse (Chapter 12 Section 3).
☐ Faulty washer pump (Chapter 12 Section 16).
☐ Faulty switch (Chapter 12 Section 5).

Window glass moves only in one direction

☐ Faulty switch (Chapter 12 Section 5).

Window glass slow to move

☐ Regulator seized or damaged, or in need of lubrication (Chapter 11 Section 17).
☐ Door internal components or trim fouling regulator (Chapter 11 Section 13).
☐ Window guide rubber dirty or in need of lubrication (Silicone spray).
☐ Faulty motor (Chapter 11 Section 17).

Window glass fails to move

☐ Blown fuse (Chapter 12 Section 3).
☐ Broken or disconnected wiring or connections (Chapter 12 Section 2).
☐ Faulty motor (Chapter 11 Section 17).

Central locking system inoperative, or unsatisfactory in operation.

☐ Blown fuse (Chapter 12 Section 2).
☐ Broken or disconnected wiring or connectors (Chapter 12 Section 2).
☐ Faulty door/tailgate lock (Chapter 11 Section 9, 15).
☐ Faulty body control module (Chapter 12 Section 22).
☐ Faulty relay (Chapter 12 Section 3).

A

ABS (Anti-lock brake system) A system, usually electronically controlled, that senses incipient wheel lockup during braking and relieves hydraulic pressure at wheels that are about to skid.

Air bag An inflatable bag hidden in the steering wheel (driver's side) or the dash or glovebox (passenger side). In a head-on collision, the bags inflate, preventing the driver and front passenger from being thrown forward into the steering wheel or windscreen.

Air cleaner A metal or plastic housing, containing a filter element, which removes dust and dirt from the air being drawn into the engine.

Air filter element The actual filter in an air cleaner system, usually manufactured from pleated paper and requiring renewal at regular intervals.

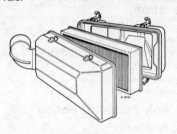
Air filter

Allen key A hexagonal wrench which fits into a recessed hexagonal hole.

Alligator clip A long-nosed spring-loaded metal clip with meshing teeth. Used to make temporary electrical connections.

Alternator A component in the electrical system which converts mechanical energy from a drivebelt into electrical energy to charge the battery and to operate the starting system, ignition system and electrical accessories.

Ampere (amp) A unit of measurement for the flow of electric current. One amp is the amount of current produced by one volt acting through a resistance of one ohm.

Anaerobic sealer A substance used to prevent bolts and screws from loosening. Anaerobic means that it does not require oxygen for activation. The Loctite brand is widely used.

Antifreeze A substance (usually ethylene glycol) mixed with water, and added to a vehicle's cooling system, to prevent freezing of the coolant in winter. Antifreeze also contains chemicals to inhibit corrosion and the formation of rust and other deposits that would tend to clog the radiator and coolant passages and reduce cooling efficiency.

Anti-seize compound A coating that reduces the risk of seizing on fasteners that are subjected to high temperatures, such as exhaust manifold bolts and nuts.

Asbestos A natural fibrous mineral with great heat resistance, commonly used in the composition of brake friction materials.

Asbestos is a health hazard and the dust created by brake systems should never be inhaled or ingested.

Axle A shaft on which a wheel revolves, or which revolves with a wheel. Also, a solid beam that connects the two wheels at one end of the vehicle. An axle which also transmits power to the wheels is known as a live axle.

Axleshaft A single rotating shaft, on either side of the differential, which delivers power from the final drive assembly to the drive wheels. Also called a driveshaft or a halfshaft.

B

Ball bearing An anti-friction bearing consisting of a hardened inner and outer race with hardened steel balls between two races.

Bearing The curved surface on a shaft or in a bore, or the part assembled into either, that permits relative motion between them with minimum wear and friction.

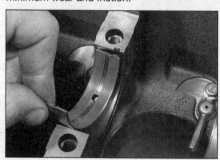
Bearing

Big-end bearing The bearing in the end of the connecting rod that's attached to the crankshaft.

Bleed nipple A valve on a brake wheel cylinder, caliper or other hydraulic component that is opened to purge the hydraulic system of air. Also called a bleed screw.

Brake bleeding Procedure for removing air from lines of a hydraulic brake system.

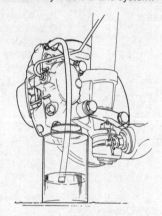
Brake bleeding

Brake disc The component of a disc brake that rotates with the wheels.

Brake drum The component of a drum brake that rotates with the wheels.

Brake linings The friction material which contacts the brake disc or drum to retard the vehicle's speed. The linings are bonded or riveted to the brake pads or shoes.

Brake pads The replaceable friction pads that pinch the brake disc when the brakes are applied. Brake pads consist of a friction material bonded or riveted to a rigid backing plate.

Brake shoe The crescent-shaped carrier to which the brake linings are mounted and which forces the lining against the rotating drum during braking.

Braking systems For more information on braking systems, consult the *Haynes Automotive Brake Manual*.

Breaker bar A long socket wrench handle providing greater leverage.

Bulkhead The insulated partition between the engine and the passenger compartment.

C

Caliper The non-rotating part of a disc-brake assembly that straddles the disc and carries the brake pads. The caliper also contains the hydraulic components that cause the pads to pinch the disc when the brakes are applied. A caliper is also a measuring tool that can be set to measure inside or outside dimensions of an object.

Camshaft A rotating shaft on which a series of cam lobes operate the valve mechanisms. The camshaft may be driven by gears, by sprockets and chain or by sprockets and a belt.

Canister A container in an evaporative emission control system; contains activated charcoal granules to trap vapours from the fuel system.

Canister

Carburettor A device which mixes fuel with air in the proper proportions to provide a desired power output from a spark ignition internal combustion engine.

Castellated Resembling the parapets along the top of a castle wall. For example, a castellated balljoint stud nut.

Castor In wheel alignment, the backward or forward tilt of the steering axis. Castor is positive when the steering axis is inclined rearward at the top.

Catalytic converter A silencer-like device in the exhaust system which converts certain pollutants in the exhaust gases into less harmful substances.

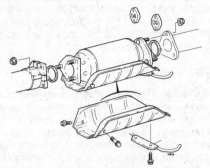

Catalytic converter

Circlip A ring-shaped clip used to prevent endwise movement of cylindrical parts and shafts. An internal circlip is installed in a groove in a housing; an external circlip fits into a groove on the outside of a cylindrical piece such as a shaft.

Clearance The amount of space between two parts. For example, between a piston and a cylinder, between a bearing and a journal, etc.

Coil spring A spiral of elastic steel found in various sizes throughout a vehicle, for example as a springing medium in the suspension and in the valve train.

Compression Reduction in volume, and increase in pressure and temperature, of a gas, caused by squeezing it into a smaller space.

Compression ratio The relationship between cylinder volume when the piston is at top dead centre and cylinder volume when the piston is at bottom dead centre.

Constant velocity (CV) joint A type of universal joint that cancels out vibrations caused by driving power being transmitted through an angle.

Core plug A disc or cup-shaped metal device inserted in a hole in a casting through which core was removed when the casting was formed. Also known as a freeze plug or expansion plug.

Crankcase The lower part of the engine block in which the crankshaft rotates.

Crankshaft The main rotating member, or shaft, running the length of the crankcase, with offset "throws" to which the connecting rods are attached.

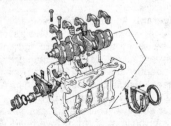

Crankshaft assembly

Crocodile clip See Alligator clip

D

Diagnostic code Code numbers obtained by accessing the diagnostic mode of an engine management computer. This code can be used to determine the area in the system where a malfunction may be located.

Disc brake A brake design incorporating a rotating disc onto which brake pads are squeezed. The resulting friction converts the energy of a moving vehicle into heat.

Double-overhead cam (DOHC) An engine that uses two overhead camshafts, usually one for the intake valves and one for the exhaust valves.

Drivebelt(s) The belt(s) used to drive accessories such as the alternator, water pump, power steering pump, air conditioning compressor, etc. off the crankshaft pulley.

Accessory drivebelts

Driveshaft Any shaft used to transmit motion. Commonly used when referring to the axleshafts on a front wheel drive vehicle.

Drum brake A type of brake using a drum-shaped metal cylinder attached to the inner surface of the wheel. When the brake pedal is pressed, curved brake shoes with friction linings press against the inside of the drum to slow or stop the vehicle.

E

EGR valve A valve used to introduce exhaust gases into the intake air stream.

Electronic control unit (ECU) A computer which controls (for instance) ignition and fuel injection systems, or an anti-lock braking system. For more information refer to the *Haynes Automotive Electrical and Electronic Systems Manual.*

Electronic Fuel Injection (EFI) A computer controlled fuel system that distributes fuel through an injector located in each intake port of the engine.

Emergency brake A braking system, independent of the main hydraulic system, that can be used to slow or stop the vehicle if the primary brakes fail, or to hold the vehicle stationary even though the brake pedal isn't depressed. It usually consists of a hand lever that actuates either front or rear brakes mechanically through a series of cables and linkages. Also known as a handbrake or parking brake.

Endfloat The amount of lengthwise movement between two parts. As applied to a crankshaft, the distance that the crankshaft can move forward and back in the cylinder block.

Engine management system (EMS) A computer controlled system which manages the fuel injection and the ignition systems in an integrated fashion.

Exhaust manifold A part with several passages through which exhaust gases leave the engine combustion chambers and enter the exhaust pipe.

F

Fan clutch A viscous (fluid) drive coupling device which permits variable engine fan speeds in relation to engine speeds.

Feeler blade A thin strip or blade of hardened steel, ground to an exact thickness, used to check or measure clearances between parts.

Feeler blade

Firing order The order in which the engine cylinders fire, or deliver their power strokes, beginning with the number one cylinder.

Flywheel A heavy spinning wheel in which energy is absorbed and stored by means of momentum. On cars, the flywheel is attached to the crankshaft to smooth out firing impulses.

Free play The amount of travel before any action takes place. The "looseness" in a linkage, or an assembly of parts, between the initial application of force and actual movement. For example, the distance the brake pedal moves before the pistons in the master cylinder are actuated.

Fuse An electrical device which protects a circuit against accidental overload. The typical fuse contains a soft piece of metal which is calibrated to melt at a predetermined current flow (expressed as amps) and break the circuit.

Fusible link A circuit protection device consisting of a conductor surrounded by heat-resistant insulation. The conductor is smaller than the wire it protects, so it acts as the weakest link in the circuit. Unlike a blown fuse, a failed fusible link must frequently be cut from the wire for replacement.

G

Gap The distance the spark must travel in jumping from the centre electrode to the side electrode in a spark plug. Also refers to the spacing between the points in a contact breaker assembly in a conventional points-type ignition, or to the distance between the reluctor or rotor and the pickup coil in an electronic ignition.

Adjusting spark plug gap

Gasket Any thin, soft material - usually cork, cardboard, asbestos or soft metal - installed between two metal surfaces to ensure a good seal. For instance, the cylinder head gasket seals the joint between the block and the cylinder head.

Gasket

Gauge An instrument panel display used to monitor engine conditions. A gauge with a movable pointer on a dial or a fixed scale is an analogue gauge. A gauge with a numerical readout is called a digital gauge.

H

Halfshaft A rotating shaft that transmits power from the final drive unit to a drive wheel, usually when referring to a live rear axle.

Harmonic balancer A device designed to reduce torsion or twisting vibration in the crankshaft. May be incorporated in the crankshaft pulley. Also known as a vibration damper.

Hone An abrasive tool for correcting small irregularities or differences in diameter in an engine cylinder, brake cylinder, etc.

Hydraulic tappet A tappet that utilises hydraulic pressure from the engine's lubrication system to maintain zero clearance (constant contact with both camshaft and valve stem). Automatically adjusts to variation in valve stem length. Hydraulic tappets also reduce valve noise.

I

Ignition timing The moment at which the spark plug fires, usually expressed in the number of crankshaft degrees before the piston reaches the top of its stroke.

Inlet manifold A tube or housing with passages through which flows the air-fuel mixture (carburettor vehicles and vehicles with throttle body injection) or air only (port fuel-injected vehicles) to the port openings in the cylinder head.

J

Jump start Starting the engine of a vehicle with a discharged or weak battery by attaching jump leads from the weak battery to a charged or helper battery.

L

Load Sensing Proportioning Valve (LSPV) A brake hydraulic system control valve that works like a proportioning valve, but also takes into consideration the amount of weight carried by the rear axle.

Locknut A nut used to lock an adjustment nut, or other threaded component, in place. For example, a locknut is employed to keep the adjusting nut on the rocker arm in position.

Lockwasher A form of washer designed to prevent an attaching nut from working loose.

M

MacPherson strut A type of front suspension system devised by Earle MacPherson at Ford of England. In its original form, a simple lateral link with the anti-roll bar creates the lower control arm. A long strut - an integral coil spring and shock absorber - is mounted between the body and the steering knuckle. Many modern so-called MacPherson strut systems use a conventional lower A-arm and don't rely on the anti-roll bar for location.

Multimeter An electrical test instrument with the capability to measure voltage, current and resistance.

N

NOx Oxides of Nitrogen. A common toxic pollutant emitted by petrol and diesel engines at higher temperatures.

O

Ohm The unit of electrical resistance. One volt applied to a resistance of one ohm will produce a current of one amp.

Ohmmeter An instrument for measuring electrical resistance.

O-ring A type of sealing ring made of a special rubber-like material; in use, the O-ring is compressed into a groove to provide the sealing action.

Overhead cam (ohc) engine An engine with the camshaft(s) located on top of the cylinder head(s).

Overhead valve (ohv) engine An engine with the valves located in the cylinder head, but with the camshaft located in the engine block.

Oxygen sensor A device installed in the engine exhaust manifold, which senses the oxygen content in the exhaust and converts this information into an electric current. Also called a Lambda sensor.

P

Phillips screw A type of screw head having a cross instead of a slot for a corresponding type of screwdriver.

Plastigage A thin strip of plastic thread, available in different sizes, used for measuring clearances. For example, a strip of Plastigage is laid across a bearing journal. The parts are assembled and dismantled; the width of the crushed strip indicates the clearance between journal and bearing.

Plastigage

Propeller shaft The long hollow tube with universal joints at both ends that carries power from the transmission to the differential on front-engined rear wheel drive vehicles.

Proportioning valve A hydraulic control valve which limits the amount of pressure to the rear brakes during panic stops to prevent wheel lock-up.

R

Rack-and-pinion steering A steering system with a pinion gear on the end of the steering shaft that mates with a rack (think of a geared wheel opened up and laid flat). When the steering wheel is turned, the pinion turns, moving the rack to the left or right. This movement is transmitted through the track rods to the steering arms at the wheels.

Radiator A liquid-to-air heat transfer device designed to reduce the temperature of the coolant in an internal combustion engine cooling system.

Refrigerant Any substance used as a heat transfer agent in an air-conditioning system. R-12 has been the principle refrigerant for many years; recently, however, manufacturers have begun using R-134a, a non-CFC substance that is considered less harmful to the ozone in the upper atmosphere.

Rocker arm A lever arm that rocks on a shaft or pivots on a stud. In an overhead valve engine, the rocker arm converts the upward movement of the pushrod into a downward movement to open a valve.

Rotor In a distributor, the rotating device inside the cap that connects the centre electrode and the outer terminals as it turns, distributing the high voltage from the coil secondary winding to the proper spark plug. Also, that part of an alternator which rotates inside the stator. Also, the rotating assembly of a turbocharger, including the compressor wheel, shaft and turbine wheel.

Runout The amount of wobble (in-and-out movement) of a gear or wheel as it's rotated. The amount a shaft rotates "out-of-true." The out-of-round condition of a rotating part.

S

Sealant A liquid or paste used to prevent leakage at a joint. Sometimes used in conjunction with a gasket.

Sealed beam lamp An older headlight design which integrates the reflector, lens and filaments into a hermetically-sealed one-piece unit. When a filament burns out or the lens cracks, the entire unit is simply replaced.

Serpentine drivebelt A single, long, wide accessory drivebelt that's used on some newer vehicles to drive all the accessories, instead of a series of smaller, shorter belts. Serpentine drivebelts are usually tensioned by an automatic tensioner.

Serpentine drivebelt

Shim Thin spacer, commonly used to adjust the clearance or relative positions between two parts. For example, shims inserted into or under bucket tappets control valve clearances. Clearance is adjusted by changing the thickness of the shim.

Slide hammer A special puller that screws into or hooks onto a component such as a shaft or bearing; a heavy sliding handle on the shaft bottoms against the end of the shaft to knock the component free.

Sprocket A tooth or projection on the periphery of a wheel, shaped to engage with a chain or drivebelt. Commonly used to refer to the sprocket wheel itself.

Starter inhibitor switch On vehicles with an automatic transmission, a switch that prevents starting if the vehicle is not in Neutral or Park.

Strut See MacPherson strut.

T

Tappet A cylindrical component which transmits motion from the cam to the valve stem, either directly or via a pushrod and rocker arm. Also called a cam follower.

Thermostat A heat-controlled valve that regulates the flow of coolant between the cylinder block and the radiator, so maintaining optimum engine operating temperature. A thermostat is also used in some air cleaners in which the temperature is regulated.

Thrust bearing The bearing in the clutch assembly that is moved in to the release levers by clutch pedal action to disengage the clutch. Also referred to as a release bearing.

Timing belt A toothed belt which drives the camshaft. Serious engine damage may result if it breaks in service.

Timing chain A chain which drives the camshaft.

Toe-in The amount the front wheels are closer together at the front than at the rear. On rear wheel drive vehicles, a slight amount of toe-in is usually specified to keep the front wheels running parallel on the road by offsetting other forces that tend to spread the wheels apart.

Toe-out The amount the front wheels are closer together at the rear than at the front. On front wheel drive vehicles, a slight amount of toe-out is usually specified.

Tools For full information on choosing and using tools, refer to the *Haynes Automotive Tools Manual*.

Tracer A stripe of a second colour applied to a wire insulator to distinguish that wire from another one with the same colour insulator.

Tune-up A process of accurate and careful adjustments and parts replacement to obtain the best possible engine performance.

Turbocharger A centrifugal device, driven by exhaust gases, that pressurises the intake air. Normally used to increase the power output from a given engine displacement, but can also be used primarily to reduce exhaust emissions (as on VW's "Umwelt" Diesel engine).

U

Universal joint or U-joint A double-pivoted connection for transmitting power from a driving to a driven shaft through an angle. A U-joint consists of two Y-shaped yokes and a cross-shaped member called the spider.

V

Valve A device through which the flow of liquid, gas, vacuum, or loose material in bulk may be started, stopped, or regulated by a movable part that opens, shuts, or partially obstructs one or more ports or passageways. A valve is also the movable part of such a device.

Valve clearance The clearance between the valve tip (the end of the valve stem) and the rocker arm or tappet. The valve clearance is measured when the valve is closed.

Vernier caliper A precision measuring instrument that measures inside and outside dimensions. Not quite as accurate as a micrometer, but more convenient.

Viscosity The thickness of a liquid or its resistance to flow.

Volt A unit for expressing electrical "pressure" in a circuit. One volt that will produce a current of one ampere through a resistance of one ohm.

W

Welding Various processes used to join metal items by heating the areas to be joined to a molten state and fusing them together. For more information refer to the *Haynes Automotive Welding Manual*.

Wiring diagram A drawing portraying the components and wires in a vehicle's electrical system, using standardised symbols. For more information refer to the *Haynes Automotive Electrical and Electronic Systems Manual*.

Note: *References throughout this index are in the form "***Chapter number***" • "***Page number***". So, for example, 2C•15 refers to page 15 of Chapter 2C.*

Note: *References throughout this index are in the form "Chapter number" • "Page number". So, for example, 2C•15 refers to page 15 of Chapter 2C.*

Preserving Our Motoring Heritage

<
The Model J Duesenberg Derham Tourster. Only eight of these magnificent cars were ever built – this is the only example to be found outside the United States of America

Almost every car you've ever loved, loathed or desired is gathered under one roof at the Haynes Motor Museum. Over 300 immaculately presented cars and motorbikes represent every aspect of our motoring heritage, from elegant reminders of bygone days, such as the superb Model J Duesenberg to curiosities like the bug-eyed BMW Isetta. There are also many old friends and flames. Perhaps you remember the 1959 Ford Popular that you did your courting in? The magnificent 'Red Collection' is a spectacle of classic sports cars including AC, Alfa Romeo, Austin Healey, Ferrari, Lamborghini, Maserati, MG, Riley, Porsche and Triumph.

A Perfect Day Out

Each and every vehicle at the Haynes Motor Museum has played its part in the history and culture of Motoring. Today, they make a wonderful spectacle and a great day out for all the family. Bring the kids, bring Mum and Dad, but above all bring your camera to capture those golden memories for ever. You will also find an impressive array of motoring memorabilia, a comfortable 70 seat video cinema and one of the most extensive transport book shops in Britain. The Pit Stop Cafe serves everything from a cup of tea to wholesome, home-made meals or, if you prefer, you can enjoy the large picnic area nestled in the beautiful rural surroundings of Somerset.

>
John Haynes O.B.E., Founder and Chairman of the museum at the wheel of a Haynes Light 12.

<
Graham Hill's Lola Cosworth Formula 1 car next to a 1934 Riley Sports.

The Museum is situated on the A359 Yeovil to Frome road at Sparkford, just off the A303 in Somerset. It is about 40 miles south of Bristol, and 25 minutes drive from the M5 intersection at Taunton.
Open 9.30am - 5.30pm (10.00am - 4.00pm Winter) 7 days a week, *except Christmas Day, Boxing Day and New Years Day*
Special rates available for schools, coach parties and outings Charitable Trust No. 292048